STRATEGIC
MANAGEMENT

CONCEPTS

2

D1419721

NINTH EDITION

STRATEGIC
MANAGEMENT

CONCEPTS

FRED R. DAVID

Francis Marion University

Prentice
Hall

Pearson Education International

Acquisitions Editor: Michael Ablassmeir
Editor-in-Chief: Jeff Shelstad
Managing Editor (Editorial): Jennifer Glennon
Assistant Editor: Melanie Olsen
Senior Marketing Manager: Shannon Moore
Media Project Manager: Michele Faranda
Managing Editor (Production): Judy Leale
Production Editor: Marcela Maslanczuk
Production Assistant: Joseph Deprospero
Permissions Coordinator: Suzanne Grappi
Associate Director, Manufacturing: Vincent Scelta
Production Manager: Arnold Vila
Design Manager: Maria Lange
Designer: Steven Frim
Interior Design: Steven Frim/Donna Wickes
Cover Design: Steven Frim
Cover Illustration: Roger Allyn Lee/Superstock
Manager, Print Production: Christy Mahon
Composition: Black Dot Group
Cover Printer: Phoenix
Printer/Binder: R.R. Donnelley - Willard

Credits and acknowledgments borrowed from other sources and reproduced, with permission, in this textbook appear on appropriate page within text.

This book may be sold only in those countries to which it is consigned by Pearson Education International. It is not to be re-exported and it is not for sale in the U.S.A., Mexico, or Canada.

Pearson Education LTD.
Pearson Education Australia PTY, Limited
Pearson Education Singapore, Pte. Ltd
Pearson Education North Asia Ltd
Pearson Education, Canada, Ltd
Pearson Educación de Mexico, S.A. de C.V.
Pearson Education-Japan
Pearson Education Malaysia, Pte. Ltd
Pearson Education Upper Saddle River, New Jersey

10 9 8 7 6 5 4 3 2 1
ISBN 0-13-120235-9

To Joy, Forest, Byron, and Meredith—my wife and children—
for their encouragement and love.

BRIEF CONTENTS

CONTENTS

PREFACE

The global recession and war on terrorism has ushered in a radically different and more complex business world than it was just two years ago when the previous edition of this text was published. E-commerce has changed the nature of business to its core. Thousands of strategic alliances and partnerships were formed in 2000–2002. Hundreds of companies declared bankruptcy and interest rates fell to their lowest level in fifty years. Downsizing, rightsizing, reengineering, and countless divestitures, acquisitions, and liquidations permanently altered the corporate landscape. Thousands of firms globalized, and thousands more merged in the last two years. Thousands prospered, and yet thousands more failed. Many manufacturers became e-commerce suppliers, and many rival firms became partners. Long-held competitive advantages eroded, and new ones formed. Both the challenges and opportunities facing organizations of all sizes today are greater than ever.

Changes made in this ninth edition are aimed squarely at illustrating the effect of this new world order on strategic-management theory and practice. Changes in this edition are more substantial than changes made in the last four editions combined! To survive and prosper in the new millennium, organizations must build and sustain competitive advantage. This new edition provides up-to-date, state-of-the-art coverage of strategic-management concepts and techniques for achieving a competitive advantage.

Our mission in preparing the ninth edition of *Strategic Management* was "to create the most current, well-written business policy textbook on the market—a book that is exciting and valuable to both students and professors." To achieve this mission, every page has been revamped, updated, and improved. New strategic-management research and practice are incorporated throughout the chapters, and hundreds of new examples abound. There is a new Cohesion Case on American Airlines—2002.

I believe, along with scores of reviewers, that you will find this edition to be the best ever—and now the best business policy textbook available for communicating both the excitement and value of strategic management. The text is concise and exceptionally well organized. Now published in six different languages—English, Chinese, Spanish, Arabic, Indonesian, and Japanese—this text is perhaps the most widely used strategic-planning book in the world.

 ## SPECIAL NOTE TO PROFESSORS

This textbook meets all AACSB guidelines for the business policy and strategic management course at both the graduate and undergraduate levels. Previous editions of this text have been used at more than five hundred colleges and universities. Prentice Hall maintains a separate web site for this text at **www.prenhall.com/david**. The author maintains the Strategic Management Club Online Web site at **www.strategyclub.com**. Membership is free to both professors and students.

Although the structure of this edition parallels the last, dramatic improvements have been made in readability, currentness, and coverage. In keeping with the mission "to become the most current, well-written business policy textbook on the market," every page has undergone rethinking and rewriting to streamline, update, and improve the caliber of presentation. A net result of this activity is that every chapter is shorter in length. New concepts and practices in strategic management are presented in a style that is clear, focused, and relevant.

 ## TIME-TESTED FEATURES

This edition continues many of the time-tested chapter features and content that have made this text so successful over the last two decades. Trademarks of this text strengthened in this edition are as follows:

Chapters: Time-Tested Features

- The text meets AACSB guidelines which support a practitioner orientation rather than a theory/research approach. This text supports that effort by taking a skills-orientated approach to developing a mission statement, performing an external audit, conducting an internal assessment, and formulating, implementing, and evaluating strategies.
- The global theme permeating all chapters couches strategic-management concepts in a global perspective.
- A simple, integrative strategic-management model appears in all chapters and on the inside front cover of the text.
- A Cohesion Case (American Airlines—2002) appears after Chapter 1 and is revisited at the end of each chapter. This case allows students to apply strategic-management concepts and techniques to a real organization as chapter material is covered. This integrative (cohesive) approach readies students for case analysis.
- End-of-chapter Experiential Exercises effectively apply concepts and techniques in a challenging, meaningful, and enjoyable manner. Eighteen exercises apply text material to the Cohesion Case; ten apply textual material to a college or university; another ten send students into the business world to explore important strategy topics. The exercises are relevant, interesting, and contemporary.
- Excellent pedagogy, including Notable Quotes and Objectives to open each chapter, and Key Terms, Current Readings, Discussion Questions, and Experiential Exercises to close each chapter.
- Excellent coverage of business ethics aimed at more than meeting AACSB standards.
- Excellent coverage of strategy implementation issues such as corporate culture, organizational structure, marketing concepts, and financial tools and techniques.
- A systematic, analytical approach presented in Chapter 6, including matrices such as the TOWS, BCG, IE, GRAND, SPACE, and QSPM.
- The chapter material is again published in four-color.

- The Web site **www.prenhall.com/david** provides chapter and case updates, an online study guide, and support materials.

NEW TO THIS EDITION

In addition to the special time-tested trademarks described above, this edition includes some exciting new chapter features designed to position this text as the clear leader and best choice for teaching business policy and strategic management.

KEY CHAPTER IMPROVEMENTS

- Dramatically improved coverage of global issues and concerns has been woven into every chapter.
- Mostly new E-Commerce Perspective boxed inserts appear in each chapter to portray the increasing reliance upon e-commerce by both large and small firms.
- Mostly new Global Perspective boxed inserts are provided in each chapter to support the expanded global theme.
- Mostly new Natural Environment Perspective boxed inserts appear in each chapter to show strategic relevance of this issue to business.
- All new examples are provided in every chapter.
- New research is integrated into every chapter, with new current readings at the end of each chapter.
- More than one hundred new Web site addresses are provided throughout the chapters in a new Visit the Net feature.

ANCILLARY MATERIALS

- *Instructor's Resource CD-ROM.* Includes improved PowerPoint slides for both cases and concepts, offering professors easy lecture outlines for in-class presentations. Chapter headings and topics are highlighted on up to thirty PowerPoint slides per chapter. The *Instructor's Manual* and *Test Manager Software* are also included.
- *Case Instructor's Manual.* Provides a comprehensive teacher's note for all forty-one cases. The teachers' notes feature detailed analyses, classroom discussion questions with answers, an external and internal assessment, specific recommendations, strategy implementation material, and an epilogue for each case. Each teachers' note is also provided on a PowerPoint slide for convenience to the professor.
- *Instructor's Manual with Test Item File.* Provides lecture notes, teaching tips, answers to all end of chapter Experiential Exercises and Review Questions, additional Experiential Exercises not in the text, sample course syllabi, and a Test Item file with multiple-choice, true/false, and essay questions.
- *Twenty Color Case Video Segments.* To accompany the Cohesion Case, a color video prepared by American Airlines is available to adopters free of charge. Shown near the beginning of the course, the American Airlines video can arouse students'

interest in studying the Cohesion Case and completing Experiential Exercises that apply chapter material to this case. In addition, a collection of nineteen other color case video segments is available free of charge. The segments average fifteen minutes each and were professionally prepared by firms used in cases in this text.

- *The Prentice Hall Companion Website.* **www.prenhall.com/david** features an interactive and exciting online student study guide. Students can access multiple-choice, true/false, and Internet-based essay questions that accompany each chapter in the text. Objective questions are scored online, and incorrect answers are keyed to the text for student review. Supplements are available for faculty download on the password–protected side of the Web site.

- *Standard Web CT—Free to Adoptors.* Standard Web CT, an online course from Prentice Hall, features Companion Website and *Test Manager Software* content in an easy-to-use system. Developed by educators for educators and their students, this online content and tools feature the most advanced educational technology and instructional design available today. The rich set of materials, communication tools, and course management resources can be easily customized either to enhance a traditional course or to create the entire course online.

- *Printed and Computerized Test Bank.* The test bank for this text includes true/false questions, multiple-choice questions, and essay questions for the text chapters. Answers to all objective questions are provided. The test questions given in the *Instructor's Manual* are also available on computerized test software to facilitate preparing and grading tests.

- *Blackboard.* Easy to use, Blackboard's single template and tools make it easy to create, manage, and use online course materials. Instructors can create online courses using the Blackboard tools, which include design, communication, testing, and course management tools. For more information, please visit our Web site located at **http://www.prenhall.com/blackboard**.

- *CourseCompass.* This customizable, interactive online course management tool powered by Blackboard provides the most intuitive teaching and learning environment available. Instructor's can communicate with students, distribute course material, and access student progress online. For further information, please visit our Web site located at **http://www.prenhall.com/coursecompass**.

 ## SPECIAL NOTE TO STUDENTS

Welcome to business policy. This is a challenging and exciting course that will allow you to function as the owner or chief executive officer of different organizations. Your major task in this course will be to make strategic decisions and to justify those decisions through oral and written communication. Strategic decisions determine the future direction and competitive position of an enterprise for a long time. Decisions to expand geographically or to diversify are examples of strategic decisions.

Strategic decision making occurs in all types and sizes of organizations, from General Motors to a small hardware store. Many people's lives and jobs are affected by strategic decisions, so the stakes are very high. An organization's very survival is often at stake. The overall importance of strategic decisions makes this course especially exciting and challenging. You will be called on in business policy to demonstrate how your strategic decisions could be successfully implemented.

In this course, you can look forward to making strategic decisions both as an individual and as a member of a team. No matter how hard employees work, an organization is in real trouble if strategic decisions are not made effectively. Doing the right things (effectiveness) is more important than doing things right (efficiency). For example, Lucent Technologies was prosperous during the 1990s but ineffective strategies in the years 2000–2002 led to massive losses, the ouster of chief executive Richard McGinn, an SEC investigation, a debt-rating one notch above junk, and a battle to raise any turn-around capital. The number of bankruptcies increased 30 percent in 2001, including such well known companies as AMF Bowling, Polaroid cameras, Converse sneakers, Schwinn bicycles, Vlasic pickles, Coleman camping supplies, Chiquita bananas, Sunbeam appliances, Enron, and Burlington Industries. The Houston-based energy firm Enron is the largest U.S. company ever to file for Chapter 11 bankruptcy.

You will have the opportunity in this course to make actual strategic decisions, perhaps for the first time in your academic career. Do not hesitate to take a stand and defend specific strategies that you determine to be the best. The rationale for your strategic decisions will be more important than any actual decision, because no one knows for sure what the best strategy is for a particular organization at a given point in time. This fact accents the subjective, contingency nature of the strategic-management process.

Use the concepts and tools presented in this text, coupled with your own intuition, to recommend strategies that you can defend as being most appropriate for the organizations that you study. You will also need to integrate knowledge acquired in previous business courses. For this reason, business policy is often called a capstone course; you may want to keep this book for your personal library.

This text is practitioner-oriented and applications-oriented. It presents strategic-management concepts that will enable you to formulate, implement, and evaluate strategies in all kinds of profit and nonprofit organizations. The end-of-chapter Experiential Exercises allow you to apply what you've read in each chapter to the American Airlines Cohesion Case and to your own university.

Be sure to visit the Strategic Management Club Online Web site at **www.strategyclub.com**. The templates and links there will save you time in performing analyses and will make your work look professional. Work hard in policy this semester and have fun. Good luck!

 ## ACKNOWLEDGMENTS

Many persons have contributed time, energy, ideas, and suggestions for improving this text over nine editions. The strength of this text is largely attributed to the collective wisdom, work, and experiences of business policy professors, strategic management researchers, students, and practitioners. Names of particular individuals whose published research is referenced in the ninth edition of this text are listed alphabetically in the Name Index. To all individuals involved in making this text so popular and successful, I am indebted and thankful.

Many special persons and reviewers contributed valuable material and suggestions for this edition. I would like to thank my colleagues and friends at Auburn University, Mississippi State University, East Carolina University, and Francis Marion University. These are universities where I have served on the management faculty. Scores of students and professors at these schools shaped development of this text. I would like to thank the following reviewers who contributed valuable suggestions over the years for this text:

Anthony F. Chelte, Western New England College

Leyland M. Lucas, Rutgers University

Joshua D. Martin, Temple University

Bob D. Cutler, Cleveland State University

Cathleen Folker, University of Nebraska–Lincoln

Jeffrey J. Bailey, University of Idaho

David Dawley, Florida State University

J. Michael Geringer, California State University

Evgeny A. Lapshin, Tomsk State Pedagogical University, Russia

Individuals who develop cases for the North American Case Research Association Meeting, the Midwest Society for Case Research Meeting, the Eastern Casewriters Association Meeting, the European Case Research Association Meeting, and Harvard Case Services are vitally important for continued progress in the field of strategic management. From a research perspective, writing business policy cases represents a valuable scholarly activity among faculty. Extensive research is required to structure business policy cases in a way that exposes strategic issues, decisions, and behavior. Pedagogically, business policy cases are essential for students in learning how to apply concepts, evaluate situations, formulate strategies, and resolve implementation problems. Without a continuous stream of updated business policy cases, the strategic management course and discipline would lose much of their energy and excitement.

Scores of Prentice Hall employees and salespersons have worked diligently behind the scenes to make this text a leader in the business policy market. I appreciate the continued hard work of all those persons.

I especially appreciate the wonderful work completed by the ninth edition ancillary authors as follows:

Bruce Barringer, *Instructor's Manual*
    University of Central Florida

Forest David, *Case Instructor's Manual*
    Mississippi State University

Amit Shah, *Test Manager Software and Companion Website Content*
    Frostburg State University

Tony Chelte, *PowerPoint Electronic and Overhead Color Transparencies*
    Western New England College

Forest David, *Case PowerPoints*
    Mississippi State University

I also want to thank you, the reader, for investing the time and effort it took you to read and study this text. As we have entered the new millennium, this book will help you formulate, implement, and evaluate strategies for organizations with which you become associated. I hope you come to share my enthusiasm for the rich subject area of strategic management and for the systematic learning approach taken in this text.

Finally, I want to welcome and invite your suggestions, ideas, thoughts, and comments and questions regarding any part of this text or the ancillary materials. Please call me at 843-661-1431, fax me at 843-661-1432, e-mail me at Fdavid@Fmarion.edu. or write me at the School of Business, Francis Marion University, Florence, South Carolina 29501. I sincerely appreciate and need your input to continually improve this text in future editions. Drawing my attention to specific errors or deficiencies in coverage or exposition will especially be appreciated.

Thank you for using this text.

Fred R. David

INTRODUCTION

HOW TO ANALYZE A BUSINESS POLICY CASE

OUTLINE

- What Is a Business Policy Case?
- Guidelines for Preparing Case Analyses
- Preparing a Case for Class Discussion
- Preparing a Written Case Analysis
- Making an Oral Presentation
- Fifty Tips for Success in Case Analysis

OBJECTIVES

After studying this chapter, you should be able to do the following:

1. Describe the case method for learning strategic-management concepts.
2. Identify the steps in preparing a comprehensive written case analysis.
3. Describe how to give an effective oral case analysis presentation.
4. Discuss fifty tips for doing case analysis.

NOTABLE QUOTES

The essential fact that makes the case method an educational experience of the greatest power is that it makes the student an active rather than a passive participant.

WALLACE B. DONHAM

Two heads are better than one.

UNKNOWN AUTHOR

Good writers do not turn in their first drafts. Ask someone else to read your written case analysis, and read it out loud to yourself. That way, you can find rough areas to clear up.

LAWRENCE JAUCH

One reaction frequently heard is, "I don't have enough information." In reality, strategists never have enough information because some information is not available and some is too costly.

WILLIAM GLUECK

I keep six honest serving men. They taught me all I know. Their names are What, Why, When, How, Where, and Who.

RUDYARD KIPLING

Don't recommend anything you would not be prepared to do yourself if you were in the decision maker's shoes.

A. J. STRICKLAND III

A picture is worth a thousand words.

UNKNOWN AUTHOR

The purpose of this section is to help you analyze business policy cases. Guidelines for preparing written and oral case analyses are given, and suggestions for preparing cases for class discussion are presented. Steps to follow in preparing case analyses are provided. Guidelines for making an oral presentation are described.

WHAT IS A BUSINESS POLICY CASE?

A *business policy case* describes an organization's external and internal condition and raises issues concerning the firm's mission, strategies, objectives, and policies. Most of the information in a business policy case is established fact, but some information may be opinions, judgments, and beliefs. Business policy cases are more comprehensive than those you may have studied in other courses. They generally include a description of related management, marketing, finance/accounting, production/operations, R&D, computer information systems, and natural environment issues. A business policy case puts the reader on the scene of the action by describing a firm's situation at some point in time. Business policy cases are written to give you practice applying strategic-management concepts. The case method for studying strategic management is often called *learning by doing*.

GUIDELINES FOR PREPARING CASE ANALYSES

The Need for Practicality

There is no such thing as a complete case, and no case ever gives you all the information you need to conduct analyses and make recommendations. Likewise, in the business world, strategists never have all the information they need to make decisions: information may be unavailable or too costly to obtain, or it may take too much time to obtain. So in preparing business policy cases, do what strategists do every day—make reasonable assumptions about unknowns, state assumptions clearly, perform appropriate analyses, and make decisions. *Be practical*. For example, in performing a pro forma financial analysis, make reasonable assumptions, state them appropriately, and proceed to show what impact your recommendations are expected to have on the organization's financial position. Avoid saying, "I don't have enough information." You can always supplement the information provided in a case with Internet and library research.

The Need for Justification

The most important part of analyzing cases is not what strategies you recommend, but rather how you support your decisions and how you propose that they be implemented. There is no single best solution or one right answer to a case, so give ample justification for your recommendations. This is important. In the business world, strategists usually do not know if their decisions are right until resources have been allocated and consumed. Then it is often too late to reverse a decision. This cold fact accents the need for careful integration of intuition and analysis in preparing business policy case analyses.

The Need for Realism

Avoid recommending a course of action beyond an organization's means. *Be realistic*. No organization can possibly pursue all the strategies that could potentially benefit the firm. Estimate how much capital will be required to implement what you recommended.

Determine whether debt, stock, or a combination of debt and stock could be used to obtain the capital. Make sure your recommendations are feasible. Do not prepare a case analysis that omits all arguments and information not supportive of your recommendations. Rather, present the major advantages and disadvantages of several feasible alternatives. Try not to exaggerate, stereotype, prejudge, or overdramatize. Strive to demonstrate that your interpretation of the evidence is reasonable and objective.

The Need for Specificity

Do not make broad generalizations such as "The company should pursue a market penetration strategy." *Be specific* by telling *what, why, when, how, where,* and *who*. Failure to use specifics is the single major shortcoming of most oral and written case analyses. For example, in an internal audit say, "The firm's current ratio fell from 2.2 in 2002 to 1.3 in 2003, and this is considered to be a major weakness," instead of, "The firm's financial condition is bad." Rather than concluding from a Strategic Position and Action Evaluation (SPACE) Matrix that a firm should be defensive, be more specific, saying, "The firm should consider closing three plants, laying off 280 employees, and divesting itself of its chemical division, for a net savings of $20.2 million in 2003." Use ratios, percentages, numbers, and dollar estimates. Businesspeople dislike generalities and vagueness.

The Need for Originality

Do not necessarily recommend the course of action that the firm plans to take or actually undertook, even if those actions resulted in improved revenues and earnings. The aim of case analysis is for you to consider all the facts and information relevant to the organization at the time, to generate feasible alternative strategies, to choose among those alternatives, and to defend your recommendations. Put yourself back in time to the point when strategic decisions were being made by the firm's strategists. Based on the information available then, what would you have done? Support your position with charts, graphs, ratios, analyses, and the like—not a revelation from the library. You can become a good strategist by thinking through situations, making management assessments, and proposing plans yourself. *Be original*. Compare and contrast what you recommend versus what the company plans to do or did.

The Need to Contribute

Strategy formulation, implementation, and evaluation decisions are commonly made by a group of individuals rather than by a single person. Therefore, your professor may divide the class into three- or four-person teams and ask you to prepare written or oral case analyses. Members of a strategic-management team, in class or in the business world, differ on their aversion to risk, their concern for short-run versus long-run benefits, their attitudes toward social responsibility, and their views concerning globalization. There are no perfect people, so there are no perfect strategies. Be open-minded to others' views. *Be a good listener and a good contributor*.

PREPARING A CASE FOR CLASS DISCUSSION

Your professor may ask you to prepare a case for class discussion. Preparing a case for class discussion means that you need to read the case before class, make notes regarding the organization's external opportunities/threats and internal strengths/weaknesses, perform appropriate analyses, and come to class prepared to offer and defend some specific recommendations.

The Case Method Versus Lecture Approach

The case method of teaching is radically different from the traditional lecture approach, in which little or no preparation is needed by students before class. The *case method* involves a classroom situation in which students do most of the talking; your professor facilitates discussion by asking questions and encouraging student interaction regarding ideas, analyses, and recommendations. Be prepared for a discussion along the lines of "What would you do, why would you do it, when would you do it, and how would you do it?" Prepare answers to the following types of questions:

- What are the firm's most important external opportunities and threats?
- What are the organization's major strengths and weaknesses?
- How would you describe the organization's financial condition?
- What are the firm's existing strategies and objectives?
- Who are the firm's competitors, and what are their strategies?
- What objectives and strategies do you recommend for this organization? Explain your reasoning. How does what you recommend compare to what the company plans?
- How could the organization best implement what you recommend? What implementation problems do you envision? How could the firm avoid or solve those problems?

The Cross-Examination

Do not hesitate to take a stand on the issues and to support your position with objective analyses and outside research. Strive to apply strategic-management concepts and tools in preparing your case for class discussion. Seek defensible arguments and positions. Support opinions and judgments with facts, reasons, and evidence. Crunch the numbers before class! Be willing to describe your recommendations to the class without fear of disapproval. Respect the ideas of others, but be willing to go against the majority opinion when you can justify a better position.

Business policy case analysis gives you the opportunity to learn more about yourself, your colleagues, strategic management, and the decision-making process in organizations. The rewards of this experience will depend on the effort you put forth, so do a good job. Discussing business policy cases in class is exciting and challenging. Expect views counter to those you present. Different students will place emphasis on different aspects of an organization's situation and submit different recommendations for scrutiny and rebuttal. Cross-examination discussions commonly arise, just as they occur in a real business organization. Avoid being a silent observer.

 ## PREPARING A WRITTEN CASE ANALYSIS

In addition to asking you to prepare a case for class discussion, your professor may ask you to prepare a written case analysis. Preparing a written case analysis is similar to preparing a case for class discussion, except written reports are generally more structured and more detailed. There is no ironclad procedure for preparing a written case analysis because cases differ in focus; the type, size, and complexity of the organizations being analyzed also vary.

When writing a strategic-management report or case analysis, avoid using jargon, vague or redundant words, acronyms, abbreviations, sexist language, and ethnic or racial slurs. And watch your spelling! Use short sentences and paragraphs and simple words

and phrases. Use quite a few subheadings. Arrange issues and ideas from the most important to the least important. Arrange recommendations from the least controversial to the
most controversial. Use the active voice rather than the passive voice for all verbs; for
example, say, "Our team recommends that the company diversify," rather than, "It is recommended by our team to diversify." Use many examples to add specificity and clarity.
Tables, figures, pie charts, bar charts, time lines, and other kinds of exhibits help communicate important points and ideas. Sometimes a picture *is* worth a thousand words.

The Executive Summary

Your professor may ask you to focus the written case analysis on a particular aspect of the
strategic-management process, such as (1) to identify and evaluate the organization's
existing mission, objectives, and strategies; or (2) to propose and defend specific recommendations for the company; or (3) to develop an industry analysis by describing the
competitors, products, selling techniques, and market conditions in a given industry.
These types of written reports are sometimes called *executive summaries*. An executive
summary usually ranges from three to five pages of text in length, plus exhibits.

The Comprehensive Written Analysis

Your professor may ask you to prepare a *comprehensive written analysis*. This assignment
requires you to apply the entire strategic-management process to the particular organization. When preparing a comprehensive written analysis, picture yourself as a consultant who has been asked by a company to conduct a study of its external and internal
environment and to make specific recommendations for its future. Prepare exhibits to
support your recommendations. Highlight exhibits with some discussion in the paper.
Comprehensive written analyses are usually about ten pages in length, plus exhibits.

Steps in Preparing a Comprehensive Written Analysis

In preparing a comprehensive written analysis, you could follow the steps outlined here,
whicn correlate to the stages in the strategic-management process and the chapters in
this text.

Step	*1*	Identify the firm's existing vision, mission, objectives, and strategies.
Step	*2*	Develop vision and mission statements for the organization.
Step	*3*	Identify the organization's external opportunities and threats.
Step	*4*	Construct a Competitive Profile Matrix (CPM).
Step	*5*	Construct an External Factor Evaluation (EFE) Matrix.
Step	*6*	Identify the organization's internal strengths and weaknesses.
Step	*7*	Construct an Internal Factor Evaluation (IFE) Matrix.
Step	*8*	Prepare a Threats-Opportunities-Weaknesses-Strengths (TOWS) Matrix, Strategic Position and Action Evaluation (SPACE) Matrix, Boston Consulting Group (BCG), Matrix Internal-External (IE) Matrix, Grand Strategy Matrix, and Quantitative Strategic Planning Matrix (QSPM) as appropriate. Give advantages and disadvantages of alternative strategies.
Step	*9*	Recommend specific strategies and long-term objectives. Show how much your recommendations will cost. Itemize these costs clearly for each projected year. Compare your recommendations to actual strate-gies planned by the company.
Step	*10*	Specify how your recommendations can be implemented and what results you can expect. Prepare forecasted ratios and pro forma financial statements. Present a timetable or agenda for action.

Step 11   Recommend specific annual objectives and policies.

Step 12   Recommend procedures for strategy review and evaluation.

 ## MAKING AN ORAL PRESENTATION

Your professor may ask you to prepare a business policy case analysis, individually or as a group, and present your analysis to the class. Oral presentations are usually graded on two parts: content and delivery. *Content* refers to the quality, quantity, correctness, and appropriateness of analyses presented, including such dimensions as logical flow through the presentation, coverage of major issues, use of specifics, avoidance of generalities, absence of mistakes, and feasibility of recommendations. *Delivery* includes such dimensions as audience attentiveness, clarity of visual aids, appropriate dress, persuasiveness of arguments, tone of voice, eye contact, and posture. Great ideas are of no value unless others can be convinced of their merit through clear communication. The guidelines presented here can help you make an effective oral presentation.

Organizing the Presentation

Begin your presentation by introducing yourself and giving a clear outline of topics to be covered. If a team is presenting, specify the sequence of speakers and the areas each person will address. At the beginning of an oral presentation, try to capture your audience's interest and attention. You could do this by displaying some products made by the company, telling an interesting short story about the company, or sharing an experience you had that is related to the company, its products, or its services. You could develop or obtain a video to show at the beginning of class; you could visit a local distributor of the firm's products and tape a personal interview with the business owner or manager. A light or humorous introduction can be effective at the beginning of a presentation.

Be sure the setting of your presentation is well organized, with chairs, flip charts, a transparency projector, and whatever else you plan to use. Arrive at least fifteen minutes early at the classroom to organize the setting, and be sure your materials are ready to go. Make sure everyone can see your visual aids well.

Controlling Your Voice

An effective rate of speaking ranges from 100 to 125 words per minute. Practice your presentation out loud to determine if you are going too fast. Individuals commonly speak too fast when nervous. Breathe deeply before and during the presentation to help yourself slow down. Have a cup of water available; pausing to take a drink will wet your throat, give you time to collect your thoughts, control your nervousness, slow you down, and signal to the audience a change in topic.

Avoid a monotone by placing emphasis on different words or sentences. Speak loudly and clearly, but don't shout. Silence can be used effectively to break a monotone voice. Stop at the end of each sentence, rather than running sentences together with *and* or *uh*.

Managing Body Language

Be sure not to fold your arms, lean on the podium, put your hands in your pockets, or put your hands behind you. Keep a straight posture, with one foot slightly in front of the other. Do not turn your back to the audience; doing so is not only rude, but it also prevents your voice from projecting well. Avoid using too many hand gestures. On occasion, leave the podium or table and walk toward your audience, but do not walk around too much. Never block the audience's view of your visual aids.

Maintain good eye contact throughout the presentation. This is the best way to persuade your audience. There is nothing more reassuring to a speaker than to see members of the audience nod in agreement or smile. Try to look everyone in the eye at least once during your presentation, but focus more on individuals who look interested than on those who seem bored. Use humor and smiles as appropriate throughout your presentation to stay in touch with your audience. A presentation should never be dull!

Speaking from Notes

Be sure not to read to your audience, because reading puts people to sleep. Perhaps worse than reading is memorizing. Do not try to memorize anything. Rather, practice using notes unobtrusively. Make sure your notes are written clearly so you will not flounder when trying to read your own writing. Include only main ideas on your note cards. Keep note cards on a podium or table if possible so that you won't drop them or get them out of order; walking with note cards tends to be distracting.

Constructing Visual Aids

Make sure your visual aids are legible to individuals in the back of the room. Use color to highlight special items. Avoid putting complete sentences on visual aids; rather, use short phrases and then elaborate on issues orally as you make your presentation. Generally, there should be no more than four to six lines of text on each visual aid. Use clear headings and subheadings. Be careful about spelling and grammar; use a consistent style of lettering. Use masking tape or an easel for posters—do not hold posters in your hand. Transparencies and handouts are excellent aids; however, be careful not to use too many handouts or your audience may concentrate on them instead of you during the presentation.

Answering Questions

It is best to field questions at the end of your presentation, rather than during the presentation itself. Encourage questions, and take your time to respond to each one. Answering questions can be persuasive because it involves you with the audience. If a team is giving the presentation, the audience should direct questions to a specific person. During the question-and-answer period, be polite, confident, and courteous. Avoid verbose responses. Do not get defensive with your answers, even if a hostile or confrontational question is asked. Staying calm during potentially disruptive situations, such as a cross-examination, reflects self-confidence, maturity, poise, and command of the particular company and its industry. Stand up throughout the question-and-answer period.

FIFTY TIPS FOR SUCCESS IN CASE ANALYSIS

Business policy students who have used this text over eight editions offer you the following fifty tips for success in doing case analysis:

1. View your case analysis and presentation as a product that must have some competitive factor to differentiate it favorably from the case analyses of other students.

2. Prepare your case analysis far enough in advance of the due date to allow time for reflection and practice. Do not procrastinate.

3. Develop a mind-set of *why*, continually questioning your own and others' assumptions and assertions.

4. The best ideas are lost if not communicated to the reader, so as ideas develop, think of their most appropriate presentation.

5. Maintain a positive attitude about the class, working *with* problems rather than against them.

6. Keep in tune with your professor, and understand his or her values and expectations.

7. Since business policy is a capstone course, seek the help of professors in other specialty areas when necessary.

8. Other students will have strengths in functional areas that will complement your weaknesses, so develop a cooperative spirit that moderates competitiveness in group work.

9. Read your case frequently as work progresses so you don't overlook details.

10. When preparing a case analysis as a group, divide into separate teams to work on the external analysis and internal analysis. Each team should write its section as if it were to go into the paper; then give each group member a copy.

11. At the end of each group session, assign each member of the group a task to be completed for the next meeting.

12. Have a good sense of humor.

13. Capitalize on the strengths of each member of the group; volunteer your services in your areas of strength.

14. Set goals for yourself and your team; budget your time to attain them.

15. Become friends with the library.

16. Foster attitudes that encourage group participation and interaction. Do not be hasty to judge group members.

17. Be creative and innovative throughout the case analysis process.

18. Be prepared to work. There will be times when you will have to do more than your share. Accept it, and do what you have to do to move the team forward.

19. Think of your case analysis as if it were really happening; do not reduce case analysis to a mechanical process.

20. To uncover flaws in your analysis and to prepare the group for questions during an oral presentation, assign one person in the group to actively play the devil's advocate.

21. Do not schedule excessively long group meetings; two-hour sessions are about right.

22. A goal of case analysis is to improve your ability to think clearly in ambiguous and confusing situations; do not get frustrated that there is no single best answer.

23. Push your ideas hard enough to get them listened to, but then let up; listen to others and try to follow their lines of thinking; follow the flow of group discussion, recognizing when you need to get back on track; do not repeat yourself or others unless clarity or progress demands repetition.

24. Do not confuse symptoms with causes; do not develop conclusions and solutions prematurely; recognize that information may be misleading, conflicting, or wrong.

25. Work hard to develop the ability to formulate reasonable, consistent, and creative plans; put yourself in the strategist's position.

26. Develop confidence in using quantitative tools for analysis. They are not inherently difficult; it is just practice and familiarity you need.

27. Develop a case-writing style that is direct, assertive, and convincing; be concise, precise, fluent, and correct.

28. Have fun when at all possible. It is frustrating at times, but enjoy it while you can; it may be several years before you are playing CEO again.

29. Acquire a professional typist and proofreader. Do not perform either task alone.

30. Strive for excellence in writing and in the technical preparation of your case. Prepare nice charts, tables, diagrams, and graphs. Use color and unique pictures. No messy exhibits!

31. In group cases, do not allow personality differences to interfere. When they occur, they must be understood for what they are—and then put aside.

32. Do not forget that the objective is to learn; explore areas with which you are not familiar.

33. Pay attention to detail.

34. Think through alternative implications fully and realistically. The consequences of decisions are not always apparent. They often affect many different aspects of a firm's operations.

35. Get things written down (drafts) as soon as possible.

36. Read everything that other group members write, and comment on it in writing. This allows group input into all aspects of case preparation.

37. Provide answers to such fundamental questions as *what, when, where, why, who,* and *how.*

38. Adaptation and flexibility are keys to success; be creative and innovative.

39. Do not merely recite ratios or present figures. Rather, develop ideas and conclusions concerning the possible trends. Show the importance of these figures to the corporation.

40. Support reasoning and judgment with factual data whenever possible.

41. Neatness is a real plus; your case analysis should look professional.

42. Your analysis should be as detailed and specific as possible.

43. A picture speaks a thousand words, and a creative picture gets you an A in many classes.

44. Let someone else read and critique your paper several days before you turn it in.

45. Emphasize the Strategy Selection and Strategy Implementation sections. A common mistake is to spend too much time on the external or internal analysis parts of your paper. Always remember that the meat of the paper or presentation is the strategy selection and implementation sections.

46. Make special efforts to get to know your group members. This leads to more openness in the group and allows for more interchange of ideas. Put in the time and effort necessary to develop these relationships.

47. Be constructively critical of your group members' work. Do not dominate group discussions. Be a good listener and contributor.

48. Learn from past mistakes and deficiencies. Improve upon weak aspects of other case presentations.

49. Learn from the positive approaches and accomplishments of classmates.

50. Use the Strategic Management Club Online at **www.strategyclub.com.**

MASTERING STRATEGY

Mastering Strategy is the first product in the *Mastering Business* series. It offers students an interactive, multimedia experience as they follow the people and issues of Cango, Inc., a small Internet startup. The text, video, and interactive exercises provide students an opportunity to simulate the strategic planning experience and to chart the future activities for Cango.

> Strategy has an impact across an entire organization, and the behaviors involved are often very subtle. Using this material really provides an opportunity to give an experiential approach to strategic concepts as applied in the business world. The videos and exercises demonstrate actual theories, practices and assumptions in daily operations. These are practical applications as faced in the real world, with real language, problems and relevant issues faced by modern companies.
>
> Students are drawn into a living, breathing, dynamic company and immediately get a feeling for strategy in operation, rather than in retrospect. This helps students assimilate their learning in a systemic manner as they move from watching the events unfold for the company to applying their own intuition about the problems and solutions. When they are on the mark, they see the results in the company's performance. If they are off the mark, they learn what they don't know and where they need to go back for a deeper understanding.
>
> —Helen Rothberg, Professor at the Marist College School of Management and co-author of the Strategy series

THE MASTERING STRATEGY ENVIRONMENT

Students will learn strategy concepts within the context of Cango, Inc., a fictitious Internet company that focuses its efforts in the entertainment arena of the e-commerce world. The company began by retailing books on the Internet and has branched out to offer CDs, videos, MP3 files, and customized players. Cango employs mostly recent college graduates who are enthusiastic about working with an online business and its possibilities for expansion. Currently, Cango is experiencing great growth, but little profit.

Thus, Cango employees are always on the lookout for new ventures. The company is considering hosting streaming video, e-books and e-book readers, and partnerships with other firms. One example would be a film studio so that Cango can serve the needs of independent filmmakers and tap into the growing popularity of home video hardware and software.

The company's goals are to get bigger and better, and to someday make a significant profit. In *Mastering Strategy,* the firm transforms from a small, independent company to one listed on the NASDAQ through the Initial Public Offering (IPO) process. The firm's founder and the management team must deal with all the implications of this change, both within the company and in the context of the external world of investors, the board of directors, and potential competitors. Visit **www.prenhall.com/mastering business** to find out more.

STRATEGIC MANAGEMENT

CONCEPTS

1 THE NATURE OF STRATEGIC MANAGEMENT

CHAPTER OUTLINE

CHAPTER OBJECTIVES

After studying this chapter, you should be able to do the following:

1. Describe the strategic-management process.
2. Explain the need for integrating analysis and intuition in strategic management.
3. Define and give examples of key terms in strategic management.
4. Discuss the nature of strategy formulation, implementation, and evaluation activities.
5. Describe the benefits of good strategic management.
6. Explain why good ethics is good business in strategic management.
7. Explain the advantages and disadvantages of entering global markets.
8. Discuss the relevance of Sun Tzu's *The Art of War* to strategic management.

NOTABLE QUOTES

If we know where we are and something about how we got there, we might see where we are trending—and if the outcomes which lie naturally in our course are unacceptable, to make timely change.

ABRAHAM LINCOLN

Without a strategy, an organization is like a ship without a rudder, going around in circles. It's like a tramp; it has no place to go.

JOEL ROSS AND MICHAEL KAMI

Plans are less important than planning.

DALE McCONKEY

The formulation of strategy can develop competitive advantage only to the extent that the process can give meaning to workers in the trenches.

DAVID HURST

Most of us fear change. Even when our minds say change is normal, our stomachs quiver at the prospect. But for strategists and managers today, there is no choice but to change.

ROBERT WATERMAN, JR.

If business is not based on ethical grounds, it is of no benefit to society and will, like all other unethical combinations, pass into oblivion.

C. MAX KILLAN

If a man take no thought about what is distant, he will find sorrow near at hand. He who will not worry about what is far off will soon find something worse than worry.

CONFUCIUS

It is human nature to make decisions based on emotion, rather than on fact. But nothing could be more illogical.

TOSHIBA CORPORATION

No business can do everything. Even if it has the money, it will never have enough good people. It has to set priorities. The worst thing to do is a little bit of everything. This makes sure that nothing is being accomplished. It is better to pick the wrong priority than none at all.

PETER DRUCKER

Executives, consultants, and B-school professors all agree that strategic planning is now the single most important management issue and will remain so for the next five years. Strategy has become a part of the main agenda at lots of organizations today. Strategic planning is back with a vengeance.

JOHN BYRNE

Planners should not plan, but serve as facilitators, catalysts, inquirers, educators, and synthesizers to guide the planning process effectively.

A. HAX AND N. MAJLUF

This chapter provides an overview of strategic management. It introduces a practical, integrative model of the strategic-management process; it defines basic activities and terms in strategic management; and it discusses the importance of business ethics.

This chapter initiates several themes that permeate all the chapters of this text. First, *global considerations impact virtually all strategic decisions!* The boundaries of countries no longer can define the limits of our imaginations. To see and appreciate the world from the perspective of others has become a matter of survival for businesses. The underpinnings of strategic management hinge upon managers' gaining an understanding of competitors, markets, prices, suppliers, distributors, governments, creditors, shareholders, and customers worldwide. The price and quality of a firm's products and services must be competitive on a worldwide basis, not just on a local basis. A "Global Perspective" box is provided in all chapters of this text to emphasize the importance of global factors in strategic management.

A second theme is that *electronic commerce (e-commerce) has become a vital strategic-management tool.* An increasing number of companies are gaining a competitive advantage by using the Internet for direct selling and for communication with suppliers, customers, creditors, partners, shareholders, clients, and competitors who may be dispersed globally. E-commerce allows firms to sell products, advertise, purchase supplies, bypass intermediaries, track inventory, eliminate paperwork, and share information. In total, e-commerce is minimizing the expense and cumbersomeness of time, distance, and space in doing business, thus yielding better customer service, greater efficiency, improved products, and higher profitability.

The Internet and personal computers are changing the way we organize our lives; inhabit our homes; and relate to and interact with family, friends, neighbors, and even ourselves. The Internet promotes endless comparison shopping, which thus enables consumers worldwide to band together to demand discounts. The Internet has transferred power from business to individuals so swiftly that in another decade there may be "regulations" imposed on groups of consumers. Politicians may one day debate the need for "regulation on consumers" rather than "regulation on big business" because of the Internet's empowerment of individuals. Buyers used to face big obstacles when attempting to get the best price and service, such as limited time and data to compare, but now consumers can quickly scan hundreds of vendor offerings. Or they can go to Web sites, such as CompareNet.com, that offer detailed information on more than 100,000 consumer products.

The Internet has changed the very nature and core of buying and selling in nearly all industries. It has fundamentally changed the economics of business in every single industry worldwide. Slogans and companies such as broadband, e-Bay, e-Trade, e-commerce, e-mail, and e-Toys have become an integral part of everyday life worldwide. Business-to-business e-commerce is five times greater than consumer e-commerce. Fully 74 percent of Americans think the Internet will change society more than the telephone and television combined.[1] An "E-commerce Perspective" box is included in each chapter to illustrate how electronic commerce impacts the strategic-management process.

A third theme is that *the natural environment has become an important strategic issue.* Global warming, bioterrorism, and increased pollution suggest that perhaps there is now no greater threat to business and society than the continuous exploitation and decimation of our natural environment. Mark Starik at George Washington University says, "Halting and reversing worldwide ecological destruction and deterioration . . . is a strategic issue that needs immediate and substantive attention by all businesses and managers." A "Natural Environment Perspective" box is provided in all chapters to illustrate how firms are addressing natural environment and bioterrorism concerns.

WHAT IS STRATEGIC MANAGEMENT?

Once there were two company presidents who competed in the same industry. These two presidents decided to go on a camping trip to discuss a possible merger. They hiked deep into the woods. Suddenly, they came upon a grizzly bear that rose up on its hind legs and snarled. Instantly, the first president took off his knapsack and got out a pair of jogging shoes. The second president said, "Hey, you can't outrun that bear." The first president responded, "Maybe I can't outrun that bear, but I surely can outrun you!" This story captures the notion of strategic management, which is to achieve and maintain competitive advantage.

Defining Strategic Management

Strategic management can be defined as the art and science of formulating, implementing, and evaluating cross-functional decisions that enable an organization to achieve its objectives. As this definition implies, strategic management focuses on integrating management, marketing, finance/accounting, production/operations, research and development, and computer information systems to achieve organizational success. The term *strategic management* in this text is used synonymously with the term *strategic planning*. The latter term is more often used in the business world, whereas the former is often used in academia. Sometimes the term *strategic management* is used to refer to strategy formulation, implementation, and evaluation, with *strategic planning* referring only to strategy formulation. The purpose of strategic management is to exploit and create new and different opportunities for tomorrow; *long-range planning,* in contrast, tries to optimize for tomorrow the trends of today.

The term *strategic planning* originated in the 1950s and was very popular between the mid-1960s to mid-1970s. During these years, strategic planning was widely believed to be the answer for all problems. At the time, much of corporate America was "obsessed" with strategic planning. Following that "boom," however, strategic planning was cast aside during the 1980s as various planning models did not yield higher returns. The 1990s, however, brought the revival of strategic planning, and the process is widely practiced today in the business world.

The term *strategic management* is used at many colleges and universities as the subtitle for the capstone course in business administration, Business Policy, which integrates material from all business courses. The Strategic Management Club Online at **www.strategyclub.com** offers many benefits for business policy students.

Stages of Strategic Management

The *strategic-management process* consists of three stages: strategy formulation, strategy implementation, and strategy evaluation. *Strategy formulation* includes developing a vision and mission, identifying an organization's external opportunities and threats, determining internal strengths and weaknesses, establishing long-term objectives, generating alternative strategies, and choosing particular strategies to pursue. Strategy-formulation issues include deciding what new businesses to enter, what businesses to abandon, how to allocate resources, whether to expand operations or diversify, whether to enter international markets, whether to merge or form a joint venture, and how to avoid a hostile takeover.

Because no organization has unlimited resources, strategists must decide which alternative strategies will benefit the firm most. Strategy-formulation decisions commit

VISIT THE NET

Designed by the publisher, Prentice Hall, especially for this textbook, this Web site provides sample tests and extra materials to supplement chapter concepts. www.prenhall.com/david

an organization to specific products, markets, resources, and technologies over an extended period of time. Strategies determine long-term competitive advantages. For better or worse, strategic decisions have major multifunctional consequences and enduring effects on an organization. Top managers have the best perspective to understand fully the ramifications of strategy-formulation decisions; they have the authority to commit the resources necessary for implementation.

Strategy implementation requires a firm to establish annual objectives, devise policies, motivate employees, and allocate resources so that formulated strategies can be executed. Strategy implementation includes developing a strategy-supportive culture, creating an effective organizational structure, redirecting marketing efforts, preparing budgets, developing and utilizing information systems, and linking employee compensation to organizational performance.

Strategy implementation often is called the action stage of strategic management. Implementing strategy means mobilizing employees and managers to put formulated strategies into action. Often considered to be the most difficult stage in strategic management, strategy implementation requires personal discipline, commitment, and sacrifice. Successful strategy implementation hinges upon managers' ability to motivate employees, which is more an art than a science. Strategies formulated but not implemented serve no useful purpose.

Interpersonal skills are especially critical for successful strategy implementation. Strategy-implementation activities affect all employees and managers in an organization. Every division and department must decide on answers to questions, such as "What must we do to implement our part of the organization's strategy?" and "How best can we get the job done?" The challenge of implementation is to stimulate managers and employees throughout an organization to work with pride and enthusiasm toward achieving stated objectives.

Strategy evaluation is the final stage in strategic management. Managers desperately need to know when particular strategies are not working well; strategy evaluation is the primary means for obtaining this information. All strategies are subject to future modification because external and internal factors are constantly changing. Three fundamental strategy-evaluation activities are (1) reviewing external and internal factors that are the bases for current strategies, (2) measuring performance, and (3) taking corrective actions. Strategy evaluation is needed because success today is no guarantee of success tomorrow! Success always creates new and different problems; complacent organizations experience demise.

Strategy formulation, implementation, and evaluation activities occur at three hierarchical levels in a large organization: corporate, divisional or strategic business unit, and functional. By fostering communication and interaction among managers and employees across hierarchical levels, strategic management helps a firm function as a competitive team. Most small businesses and some large businesses do not have divisions or strategic business units; they have only the corporate and functional levels. Nevertheless, managers and employees at these two levels should be actively involved in strategic-management activities.

Peter Drucker says the prime task of strategic management is thinking through the overall mission of a business:

> ". . . that is, of asking the question, "What is our Business?" This leads to the setting of objectives, the development of strategies, and the making of today's decisions for tomorrow's results. This clearly must be done by a part of the organization that can see the entire business; that can balance objectives and the needs of today against the needs of tomorrow; and that can allocate resources of men and money to key results.[2]

VISIT THE NET

Provides a nice narrative regarding strategy formulation and implementation at Southern Polytechnic State University. http://www.spsu.edu/ planassess/strategic.htm.

Integrating Intuition and Analysis

The strategic-management process can be described as an objective, logical, systematic approach for making major decisions in an organization. It attempts to organize qualitative and quantitative information in a way that allows effective decisions to be made under conditions of uncertainty. Yet strategic management is not a pure science that lends itself to a nice, neat, one-two-three approach.

Based on past experiences, judgment, and feelings, most people recognize that *intuition* is essential to making good strategic decisions. Intuition is particularly useful for making decisions in situations of great uncertainty or little precedent. It is also helpful when highly interrelated variables exist or when it is necessary to choose from several plausible alternatives. Some managers and owners of businesses profess to have extraordinary abilities for using intuition alone in devising brilliant strategies. For example, Will Durant, who organized General Motors Corporation, was described by Alfred Sloan as "a man who would proceed on a course of action guided solely, as far as I could tell, by some intuitive flash of brilliance. He never felt obliged to make an engineering hunt for the facts. Yet at times, he was astoundingly correct in his judgment."[3] Albert Einstein acknowledged the importance of intuition when he said, "I believe in intuition and inspiration. At times I feel certain that I am right while not knowing the reason. Imagination is more important than knowledge, because knowledge is limited, whereas imagination embraces the entire world."[4]

Although some organizations today may survive and prosper because they have intuitive geniuses managing them, most are not so fortunate. Most organizations can benefit from strategic management, which is based upon integrating intuition and analysis in decision making. Choosing an intuitive or analytic approach to decision making is not an either-or proposition. Managers at all levels in an organization inject their intuition and judgment into strategic-management analyses. Analytical thinking and intuitive thinking complement each other.

Operating from the I've-already-made-up-my-mind-don't-bother-me-with-the-facts mode is not management by intuition; it is management by ignorance.[5] Drucker says, "I believe in intuition only if you discipline it. 'Hunch' artists, who make a diagnosis but don't check it out with the facts, are the ones in medicine who kill people, and in management kill businesses."[6] As Henderson notes:

> The accelerating rate of change today is producing a business world in which customary managerial habits in organizations are increasingly inadequate. Experience alone was an adequate guide when changes could be made in small increments. But intuitive and experience-based management philosophies are grossly inadequate when decisions are strategic and have major, irreversible consequences.[7]

In a sense, the strategic-management process is an attempt both to duplicate what goes on in the mind of a brilliant, intuitive person who knows the business and to couple it with analysis.

Adapting to Change

The strategic-management process is based on the belief that organizations should continually monitor internal and external events and trends so that timely changes can be made as needed. The rate and magnitude of changes that affect organizations are increasing dramatically. Consider, for example, e-commerce, laser surgery, the war on terrorism, economic recession, the aging population, the Enron scandal, and merger mania. To survive, all organizations must be capable of astutely identifying and adapting to change.

VISIT THE NET

Provides titles and brief descriptions of many books relating to strategic planning. www.ccp.ca/ information/management/ planning/mgmtplan.html

VISIT THE NET

Reveals that strategies may need to be constantly changed. http://www. csuchico.edu/mgmt/ strategy/module1/ sld041.htm

The strategic-management process is aimed at allowing organizations to adapt effectively to change over the long run. As Waterman has noted:

> In today's business environment, more than in any preceding era, the only constant is change. Successful organizations effectively manage change, continuously adapting their bureaucracies, strategies, systems, products, and cultures to survive the shocks and prosper from the forces that decimate the competition.[8]

E-commerce and globalization are external changes that are transforming business and society today. On a political map, the boundaries between countries may be clear, but on a competitive map showing the real flow of financial and industrial activity, the boundaries have largely disappeared. The speedy flow of information has eaten away at national boundaries so that people worldwide readily see for themselves how other people live. People are traveling abroad more: ten million Japanese travel abroad annually. People are emigrating more: Germans to England and Mexicans to the United States are examples. As the Global Perspective indicates, U.S. firms are challenged by competitors in many industries. We are becoming a borderless world with global citizens, global competitors, global customers, global suppliers, and global distributors!

The need to adapt to change leads organizations to key strategic-management questions, such as "What kind of business should we become?" "Are we in the right field(s)?" "Should we reshape our business?" "What new competitors are entering our industry?" "What strategies should we pursue?" "How are our customers changing?" "Are new technologies being developed that could put us out of business?"

VISIT THE NET

Reveals that actual strategy results from planned strategy coupled with reactive changes.
http://www.csuchico.edu/mgmt/strategy/module1/sld032.htm

KEY TERMS IN STRATEGIC MANAGEMENT

Before we further discuss strategic management, we should define eight key terms: strategists, vision and mission statements, external opportunities and threats, internal strengths and weaknesses, long-term objectives, strategies, annual objectives, and policies.

Strategists

Strategists are the individuals who are most responsible for the success or failure of an organization. Strategists have various job titles, such as chief executive officer, president, owner, chair of the board, executive director, chancellor, dean, or entrepreneur. Jay Conger, professor of organizational behavior at the London Business School and author of *Building Leaders,* says, "All strategists have to be chief learning officers. We are in an extended period of change. If our leaders aren't highly adaptive and great models during this period, then our companies won't adapt either, because ultimately leadership is about being a role model." In 2001 and 2002, quite a few CEOs were fired or resigned, including Jacques Nasser of Ford Motor Company, Peter Bonfield of British Telecom, Lars Ramqvist of Ericsson, James Goodwin of UAL, and Shailesh Mehta of Providian.

Strategists help an organization gather, analyze, and organize information. They track industry and competitive trends, develop forecasting models and scenario analyses, evaluate corporate and divisional performance, spot emerging market opportunities, identify business threats, and develop creative action plans. Strategic planners usually serve in a support or staff role. Usually found in higher levels of management, they typically have considerable authority for decision making in the firm. The CEO is the most visible and critical strategic manager. Any manager who has responsibility for a unit or

GLOBAL PERSPECTIVE

Do U.S. Firms Dominate All Industries?

The Wall Street Journal's annual ranking of the world's largest companies reveals that U.S. firms are being challenged in many industries. The world's ten largest insurance companies and banks are listed below in rank order. Note that U.S. firms do not dominate these two industries.

Insurance Firms	Banks
Axa Group, France	Deutsche Bank, Germany
Allianz Group, Germany	UBS, Switzerland
Nippon Life, Japan	Bank of Tokyo-Mitsubishi, Japan
Zenkyoren & Prefectural Ins. Federations, Japan	Bank of America, U.S.
Dai-ichi Mutual Life, Japan	Fuji Bank, Japan
American International Group, U.S.	ABN Amro, Netherlands
Metropolitan Life Insurance, U.S.	HSBC Holdings, United Kingdom
Sumitomo Life, Japan	Credit Suisse Group, Switzerland
Zurich Financial Services Group, Switzerland	Bayerische Hypotheken & Vereinsbank, Germany
Prudential Corporation, United Kingdom	Sumitomo Bank, Japan

Source: Adapted from "See World Business" section, The Wall Street Journal (September 27, 1999): R30.

division, responsibility for profit and loss outcomes, or direct authority over a major piece of the business is a strategic manager (strategist).

Strategists differ as much as organizations themselves, and these differences must be considered in the formulation, implementation, and evaluation of strategies. Some strategists will not consider some types of strategies because of their personal philosophies. Strategists differ in their attitudes, values, ethics, willingness to take risks, concern for social responsibility, concern for profitability, concern for short-run versus long-run aims, and management style. The founder of Hershey Foods, Milton Hershey, built the company to manage an orphanage. From corporate profits, Hershey Foods today cares for over one thousand boys and girls in its School for Orphans.

Some strategists agree with Ralph Nader, who proclaims that organizations have tremendous social obligations. Others agree with Milton Friedman, the economist, who maintains that organizations have no obligation to do any more for society than is legally required. Most strategists agree that the first social responsibility of any business must be to make enough profit to cover the costs of the future, because if this is not achieved, no other social responsibility can be met. Strategists should examine social problems in terms of potential costs and benefits to the firm, and they should address social issues that could benefit the firm most.

Vision and Mission Statements

Many organizations today develop a *vision statement* that answers the question, "What do we want to become?" Developing a vision statement is often considered the first step in strategic planning, preceding even development of a mission statement. Many vision statements are a single sentence. For example, the vision statement of Stokes Eye Clinic in Florence, South Carolina, is "Our vision is to take care of your vision." The vision of the Institute of Management Accountants is "Global leadership in education, certification, and practice of management accounting and financial management."

Mission statements are "enduring statements of purpose that distinguish one business from other similar firms. A mission statement identifies the scope of a firm's operations in product and market terms."[9] It addresses the basic question that faces all strategists: "What is our business?" A clear mission statement describes the values and priorities of an organization. Developing a mission statement compels strategists to think about the nature and scope of present operations and to assess the potential attractiveness of future markets and activities. A mission statement broadly charts the future direction of an organization. An example of a mission statement is provided below for Microsoft.

> Microsoft's mission is to create software for the personal computer that empowers and enriches people in the workplace, at school and at home. Microsoft's early vision of a computer on every desk and in every home is coupled today with a strong commitment to Internet-related technologies that expand the power and reach of the PC and its users. As the world's leading software provider, Microsoft strives to produce innovative products that meet our customers' evolving needs. At the same time, we understand that long-term success is about more than just making great products. Find out what we mean when we talk about Living Our Values (**www.microsoft.com/mscorp/**).

External Opportunities and Threats

External opportunities and *external threats* refer to economic, social, cultural, demographic, environmental, political, legal, governmental, technological, and competitive trends and events that could significantly benefit or harm an organization in the future. Opportunities and threats are largely beyond the control of a single organization—thus the word *external*. The wireless revolution, biotechnology, population shifts, changing work values and attitudes, space exploration, recyclable packages, and increased competition from foreign companies are examples of opportunities or threats for companies. These types of changes are creating a different type of consumer and consequently a need for different types of products, services, and strategies. Many companies in many industries face the severe external threat of online sales capturing increasing market share in their industry. For example, online grocery shopping is expected to surge to $10.8 billion by 2003—to the dismay of traditional grocers.[10]

Other opportunities and threats may include the passage of a law, the introduction of a new product by a competitor, a national catastrophe, or the declining value of the dollar. A competitor's strength could be a threat. Unrest in the Middle East, rising energy costs, or the war against terrorism could represent an opportunity or a threat. The World Trade Center attack resulted in a sharp decline in travel and thus represented an external threat to airline, cruise line, and hotel companies. To mitigate the effect of this threat, Starwood Hotels & Resorts froze all capital expenses over $3 million, including the development of the upscale St. Regis Hotel and Towers in San Francisco. Many other hotel chains, including Motel 6, Red Roof Inn, Park Place, Caesars Palace, and Omni Hotels, also ceased expansion and retrenched.

A basic tenet of strategic management is that firms need to formulate strategies to take advantage of external opportunities and to avoid or reduce the impact of external threats. For this reason, identifying, monitoring, and evaluating external opportunities and threats is essential for success. This process of conducting research and gathering and assimilating external information is sometimes called *environmental scanning* or industry analysis. Lobbying is one activity that some organizations utilize to influence external opportunities and threats.

Internal Strengths and Weaknesses

Internal strengths and *internal weaknesses* are an organization's controllable activities that are performed especially well or poorly. They arise in the management, marketing, finance/accounting, production/operations, research and development, and management information systems activities of a business. Identifying and evaluating organizational strengths and weaknesses in the functional areas of a business is an essential strategic-management activity. Organizations strive to pursue strategies that capitalize on internal strengths and eliminate internal weaknesses.

Strengths and weaknesses are determined relative to competitors. *Relative* deficiency or superiority is important information. Also, strengths and weaknesses can be determined by elements of being rather than performance. For example, a strength may involve ownership of natural resources or a historic reputation for quality. Strengths and weaknesses may be determined relative to a firm's own objectives. For example, high levels of inventory turnover may not be a strength to a firm that seeks never to stock-out.

Internal factors can be determined in a number of ways, including computing ratios, measuring performance, and comparing to past periods and industry averages. Various types of surveys also can be developed and administered to examine internal factors such as employee morale, production efficiency, advertising effectiveness, and customer loyalty.

Long-Term Objectives

Objectives can be defined as specific results that an organization seeks to achieve in pursuing its basic mission. *Long-term* means more than one year. Objectives are essential for organizational success because they state direction; aid in evaluation; create synergy; reveal priorities; focus coordination; and provide a basis for effective planning, organizing, motivating, and controlling activities. Objectives should be challenging, measurable, consistent, reasonable, and clear. In a multidimensional firm, objectives should be established for the overall company and for each division. Minnesota Power's long-term objectives are to achieve a 13 percent return on equity (ROE) in its core electric utility, 14 percent ROE on water resource operations, and 15 percent ROE on support businesses. Minnesota Power also strives to stay in the top 25 percent of electric utilities in the United States in terms of common stock's market-to-book ratio and to maintain an annual growth in earnings per share of 5 percent.

Strategies

Strategies are the means by which long-term objectives will be achieved. Business strategies may include geographic expansion, diversification, acquisition, product development, market penetration, retrenchment, divestiture, liquidation, and joint ventures Strategies currently being pursued by Barnes & Noble, SunTrust Banks, and Yahoo! are described in Table 1–1.

Strategies are potential actions that require top management decisions and large amounts of the firm's resources. In addition, strategies affect an organization's long-term prosperity, typically for at least five years, and thus are future-oriented. Strategies have multifunctional or multidivisional consequences and require consideration of both the external and internal factors facing the firm. Boston Market and KFC battle each other these days with similar strategies for selling fast-food chicken. Boston Market is remodeling all of its 680 stores to provide booths, padded chairs, and an expanded menu. The company is adding 40 new restaurants in 2002. In late 2001, KFC launched a $200 million television advertising campaign that featured *Seinfeld* star Jason Alexander, with a new tag line: "There's fast food. Then there's KFC." KFC is eliminating paper boxes and is beginning to serve food on black plastic plates; this is similar to what Boston Market

TABLE 1.1   Three Organizations' Strategies in 2002

BARNES & NOBLE

Barnes & Noble, the large bookseller, hesitated with an online strategy, while upstart Amazon.com captured a huge market share in online bookselling. Despite huge capital expenditures and massive advertising in recent years, Barnes & Noble still remains barely more than one-tenth Amazon's size online. Barnes & Noble initially did not want to "cannibalize" its own core franchise. The lesson for other businesses may be that the Internet does not tolerate caution and hesitation. Many brick-and-mortar companies today "hesitate" with an online strategy because of perceived "cannibalism" with existing walk-in sales. Caution could spell disaster.

SUNTRUST BANKS

SunTrust Banks is aggressively pursuing a horizontal integration strategy by acquiring other banks. SunTrust acquired all the Florida business of Huntington Bancshares in late 2001 after losing out in efforts to acquire Wachovia earlier that year. Instead, First Union acquired Wachovia. The Huntington acquisition boosts SunTrust's market share in Florida from 10 percent to 12 percent, placing it third in Florida behind Bank of America (22 percent) and Wachovia (15 percent). Based in Atlanta, SunTrust obtained 143 Huntington branches in Florida with the acquisition to complement its 400 existing branches in that state.

YAHOO!

Yahoo!'s strategy is to shift from obtaining 80 percent of its revenue from advertising to obtaining more revenue from customers who pay for services. Yahoo! has devised a new strategy to offer services such as personalized Web pages, audio subscriptions, and music videos for a fee. Historically, Yahoo! provided free services to get customers and obtained revenue from company advertisers. Analysts, who are skeptical that Yahoo!'s new strategy can succeed, drove down the company stock price from a high of $88.75 in late 2000 to a low of $9.90 in late 2001. Yahoo! laid off 20 percent of its staff—or roughly one thousand employees—in 2001. Yahoo! also is forming strategic alliances, such as its new agreement with SBC Communications to jointly offer high-speed Internet access over SBC's phone lines using Yahoo!'s brand name and Web service. Strategic-alliance formation is a major new strategic management thrust in the 2000s (to be discussed fully in Chapter 5).

does. KFC is also renovating all of its 5,300 stores in the United States by providing track lighting and café-style tables. Employees of the two companies depend on the respective top management teams to pursue effective strategies; otherwise, demise could be in the offing due to fierce competition.[11] (Alternative types of strategies are discussed fully in Chapter 5).

Annual Objectives

Annual objectives are short-term milestones that organizations must achieve to reach long-term objectives. Like long-term objectives, annual objectives should be measurable, quantitative, challenging, realistic, consistent, and prioritized. They should be established at the corporate, divisional, and functional levels in a large organization. Annual objectives should be stated in terms of management, marketing, finance/accounting, production/operations, research and development, and management information systems (MIS) accomplishments. A set of annual objectives is needed for each long-term objective. Annual objectives are especially important in strategy implementation, whereas long-term objectives are particularly important in strategy formulation. Annual objectives represent the basis for allocating resources.

Campbell Soup Corporation has an annual objective to achieve 20 percent growth in earnings, a 20 percent ROE, and a 20 percent return on invested cash. The company calls this ERC, for earnings, returns, and cash.

Policies

Policies are the means by which annual objectives will be achieved. Policies include guidelines, rules, and procedures established to support efforts to achieve stated objectives. Policies are guides to decision making and address repetitive or recurring situations.

Policies are most often stated in terms of management, marketing, finance/accounting, production/operations, research and development, and computer information systems activities. Policies can be established at the corporate level and apply to an entire organization at the divisional level and apply to a single division, or at the functional level and apply to particular operational activities or departments. Policies, like annual objectives, are especially important in strategy implementation because they outline an organization's expectations of its employees and managers. Policies allow consistency and coordination within and between organizational departments.

Substantial research suggests that a healthier workforce can more effectively and efficiently implement strategies. The National Center for Health Promotion estimates that more than 80 percent of all American corporations have No Smoking policies. No Smoking policies are usually derived from annual objectives that seek to reduce corporate medical costs associated with absenteeism and to provide a healthy workplace.

THE STRATEGIC-MANAGEMENT MODEL

The strategic-management process can best be studied and applied using a model. Every model represents some kind of process. The framework illustrated in Figure 1–1 is a widely accepted, comprehensive model of the strategic-management process.[12] This model does not guarantee success, but it does represent a clear and practical approach for formulating, implementing, and evaluating strategies. Relationships among major components of the strategic-management process are shown in the model, which appears in all subsequent chapters with appropriate areas shaped to show the particular focus of each chapter.

Identifying an organization's existing vision, mission, objectives, and strategies is the logical starting point for strategic management because a firm's present situation and condition may preclude certain strategies and may even dictate a particular course of action. Every organization has a vision, mission, objectives, and strategy, even if these elements are not consciously designed, written, or communicated. The answer to where an organization is going can be determined largely by where the organization has been!

The strategic-management process is dynamic and continuous. A change in any one of the major components in the model can necessitate a change in any or all of the other components. For instance, a shift in the economy could represent a major opportunity and require a change in long-term objectives and strategies; a failure to accomplish annual objectives could require a change in policy; or a major competitor's change in strategy could require a change in the firm's mission. Therefore, strategy formulation, implementation, and evaluation activities should be performed on a continual basis, not

FIGURE 1–1

A Comprehensive Strategic-Management Model

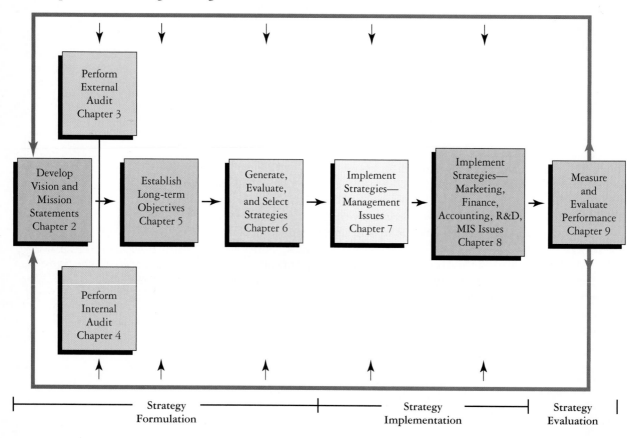

Source: Fred R. David, "How Companies Define Their Mission," *Long Range Planning* 22, no. 3 (June 1988): 40.

just at the end of the year or semi-annually. The strategic-management process never really ends.

The strategic-management process is not as cleanly divided and neatly performed in practice as the strategic-management model suggests. Strategists do not go through the process in lockstep fashion. Generally, there is give-and-take among hierarchical levels of an organization. Many organizations conduct formal meetings semiannually to discuss and update the firm's vision/mission, opportunities/threats, strengths/weaknesses, strategies, objectives, policies, and performance. These meetings are commonly held off-premises and are called *retreats*. The rationale for periodically conducting strategic-management meetings away from the work site is to encourage more creativity and candor from participants. Good communication and feedback are needed throughout the strategic-management process.

Application of the strategic-management process is typically more formal in larger and well-established organizations. Formality refers to the extent that participants, responsibilities, authority, duties, and approach are specified. Smaller businesses tend to be less formal. Firms that compete in complex, rapidly changing environments, such as technology companies, tend to be more formal in strategic planning. Firms that have many divisions, products, markets, and technologies also tend to be more formal in applying strategic-management concepts. Greater formality in applying the strategic-management process is usually positively associated with the cost, comprehensiveness, accuracy, and success of planning across all types and sizes of organizations.[13]

BENEFITS OF STRATEGIC MANAGEMENT

Strategic management allows an organization to be more proactive than reactive in shaping its own future; it allows an organization to initiate and influence (rather than just respond to) activities—and thus to exert control over its own destiny. Small business owners, chief executive officers, presidents, and managers of many for-profit and nonprofit organizations have recognized and realized the benefits of strategic management.

Historically, the principal benefit of strategic management has been to help organizations formulate better strategies through the use of a more systematic, logical, and rational approach to strategic choice. This certainly continues to be a major benefit of strategic management, but research studies now indicate that the process, rather than the decision or document, is the more important contribution of strategic management.[14] *Communication is a key to successful strategic management.* Through involvement in the process, managers and employees become committed to supporting the organization. Dialogue and participation are essential ingredients. The chief executive officer of Rockwell International explains, "We believe that fundamental to effective strategic management is fully informed employees at all organizational levels. We expect every business segment to inform every employee about the business objectives, the direction of the business, the progress towards achieving objectives, and our customers, competitors and product plans."

The manner in which strategic management is carried out is thus exceptionally important. A major aim of the process is to achieve the understanding of and commitment from all managers and employees. Understanding may be the most important benefit of strategic management, followed by commitment. When managers and employees understand what the organization is doing and why, they often feel that they are a part of the firm and become committed to assisting it. This is especially true when employees also understand linkages between their own compensation and organizational performance. Managers and employees become surprisingly creative and innovative when they understand and support the firm's mission, objectives, and strategies. A great benefit of strategic management, then, is the opportunity that the process provides to empower individuals. *Empowerment* is the act of strengthening employees' sense of effectiveness by encouraging and rewarding them to participate in decision making and to exercise initiative and imagination.

More and more organizations are decentralizing the strategic-management process, recognizing that planning must involve lower-level managers and employees. The notion of centralized staff planning is being replaced in organizations by decentralized line-manager planning. The process is a learning, helping, educating, and supporting activity, not merely a paper-shuffling activity among top executives. Strategic-management dialogue is more important than a nicely bound strategic-management document.[15] The worst thing strategists can do is develop strategic plans themselves and then present them to operating managers to execute. Though involvement in the process, line managers become "owners" of the strategy. Ownership of strategies by the people who have to execute them is a key to success!

Although making good strategic decisions is the major responsibility of an organization's owner or chief executive officer, both managers and employees must also be

VISIT THE NET

Explains in detail how to develop a strategic plan and compares this document to a business plan. http://www. planware.org/strategy. htm#1

involved in strategy formulation, implementation, and evaluation activities. Participation is a key to gaining commitment for needed changes.

An increasing number of corporations and institutions are using strategic management to make effective decisions. But strategic management is not a guarantee for success; it can be dysfunctional if conducted haphazardly.

Financial Benefits

Research indicates that organizations using strategic-management concepts are more profitable and successful than those that do not.[16] Businesses using strategic-management concepts show significant improvement in sales, profitability, and productivity compared to firms without systematic planning activities. High-performing firms tend to do systematic planning to prepare for future fluctuations in their external and internal environments. Firms with planning systems more closely resembling strategic-management theory generally exhibit superior long-term financial performance relative to their industry.

High-performing firms seem to make more informed decisions with good anticipation of both short- and long-term consequences. On the other hand, firms that perform poorly often engage in activities that are shortsighted and do not reflect good forecasting of future conditions. Strategists of low-performing organizations are often preoccupied with solving internal problems and meeting paperwork deadlines. They typically underestimate their competitors' strengths and overestimate their own firm's strengths. They often attribute weak performance to uncontrollable factors such as a poor economy, technological change, or foreign competition.

Dun & Bradstreet reports that more than 100,000 businesses in the United States fail annually. Business failures include bankruptcies, foreclosures, liquidations, and court-mandated receiverships. Although many factors besides a lack of effective strategic management can lead to business failure, the planning concepts and tools described in this text can yield substantial financial benefits for any organization. An excellent Web site for businesses engaged in strategic planning is **www.checkmateplan.com**.

Nonfinancial Benefits

Besides helping firms avoid financial demise, strategic management offers other tangible benefits, such as an enhanced awareness of external threats, an improved understanding of competitors' strategies, increased employee productivity, reduced resistance to change, and a clearer understanding of performance-reward relationships. Strategic management enhances the problem-prevention capabilities of organizations because it promotes interaction among managers at all divisional and functional levels. Firms that have nurtured their managers and employees, shared organizational objectives with them, empowered them to help improve the product or service, and recognized their contributions can turn to them for help in a pinch because of this interaction.

In addition to empowering managers and employees, strategic management often brings order and discipline to an otherwise floundering firm. It can be the beginning of an efficient and effective managerial system. Strategic management may renew confidence in the current business strategy or point to the need for corrective actions. The strategic-management process provides a basis for identifying and rationalizing the need for change to all managers and employees of a firm; it helps them view change as an opportunity rather than as a threat.

Greenley stated that strategic management offers the following benefits:

1. It allows for identification, prioritization, and exploitation of opportunities.
2. It provides an objective view of management problems.

3. It represents a framework for improved coordination and control of activities.

4. It minimizes the effects of adverse conditions and changes.

5. It allows major decisions to better support established objectives.

6. It allows more effective allocation of time and resources to identified opportunities.

7. It allows fewer resources and less time to be devoted to correcting erroneous or ad hoc decisions.

8. It creates a framework for internal communication among personnel.

9. It helps integrate the behavior of individuals into a total effort.

10. It provides a basis for clarifying individual responsibilities.

11. It encourages forward thinking.

12. It provides a cooperative, integrated, and enthusiastic approach to tackling problems and opportunities.

13. It encourages a favorable attitude toward change.

14. It gives a degree of discipline and formality to the management of a business.[17]

 ## WHY SOME FIRMS DO NO STRATEGIC PLANNING

Some firms do not engage in strategic planning, and some firms do strategic planning but receive no support from managers and employees. Some reasons for poor or no strategic planning are as follows:

- *Poor Reward Structures*—When an organization assumes success, it often fails to reward success. When failure occurs, then the firm may punish. In this situation, it is better for an individual to do nothing (and not draw attention) than to risk trying to achieve something, fail, and be punished.

- *Fire-Fighting*—An organization can be so deeply embroiled in crisis management and fire-fighting that it does not have time to plan.

- *Waste of Time*—Some firms see planning as a waste of time since no marketable product is produced. Time spent on planning is an investment.

- *Too Expensive*—Some organizations are culturally opposed to spending resources.

- *Laziness*—People may not want to put forth the effort needed to formulate a plan.

- *Content with Success*—Particularly if a firm is successful, individuals may feel there is no need to plan because things are fine as they stand. But success today does not guarantee success tomorrow.

- *Fear of Failure*—By not taking action, there is little risk of failure unless a problem is urgent and pressing. Whenever something worthwhile is attempted, there is some risk of failure.

- *Overconfidence*—As individuals amass experience, they may rely less on formalized planning. Rarely, however, is this appropriate. Being overconfident or overestimating experience can bring demise. Forethought is rarely wasted and is often the mark of professionalism.

- *Prior Bad Experience*—People may have had a previous bad experience with planning, that is, cases in which plans have been long, cumbersome, impractical, or inflexible. Planning, like anything else, can be done badly.

VISIT THE NET

Gives reasons why some organizations avoid strategic planning. http://www.mindtools.com/plfailpl.html

- *Self-Interest*—When someone has achieved status, privilege, or self-esteem through effectively using an old system, he or she often sees a new plan as a threat.
- *Fear of the Unknown*—People may be uncertain of their abilities to learn new skills, of their aptitude with new systems, or of their ability to take on new roles.
- *Honest Difference of Opinion*—People may sincerely believe the plan is wrong. They may view the situation from a different viewpoint, or they may have aspirations for themselves or the organization that are different from the plan. Different people in different jobs have different perceptions of a situation.
- *Suspicion*—Employees may not trust management.[18]

PITFALLS IN STRATEGIC PLANNING

Strategic planning is an involved, intricate, and complex process that takes an organization into unchartered territory. It does not provide a ready-to-use prescription for success; instead, it takes the organization through a journey and offers a framework for addressing questions and solving problems. Being aware of potential pitfalls and being prepared to address them is essential to success.

Some pitfalls to watch for and avoid in strategic planning are provided below:

- Using strategic planning to gain control over decisions and resources
- Doing strategic planning only to satisfy accreditation or regulatory requirements
- Too hastily moving from mission development to strategy formulation
- Failing to communicate the plan to employees, who continue working in the dark
- Top managers making many intuitive decisions that conflict with the formal plan
- Top managers not actively supporting the strategic-planning process
- Failing to use plans as a standard for measuring performance
- Delegating planning to a "planner" rather than involving all managers
- Failing to involve key employees in all phases of planning
- Failing to create a collaborative climate supportive of change
- Viewing planning to be unnecessary or unimportant
- Becoming so engrossed in current problems that insufficient or no planning is done
- Being so formal in planning that flexibility and creativity are stifled[19]

GUIDELINES FOR EFFECTIVE STRATEGIC MANAGEMENT

Failing to follow certain guidelines in conducting strategic management can foster criticisms of the process and create problems for the organization. An integral part of strategy evaluation must be to evaluate the quality of the strategic-management process. Issues such as "Is strategic management in our firm a people process or a paper process?" should be addressed.

Even the most technically perfect strategic plan will serve little purpose if it is not implemented. Many organizations tend to spend an inordinate amount of time, money, and effort on developing the strategic plan, treating the means

VISIT THE NET

Provides nice discussion of the limitations of strategic planning process within an organization. http://www.des.calstate.edu/limitations.html

and circumstances under which it will be implemented as afterthoughts!
Change comes through implementation and evaluation, not through the plan.
A technically imperfect plan that is implemented well will achieve more than
the perfect plan that never gets off the paper on which it is typed.[20]

Strategic management must not become a self-perpetuating bureaucratic mechanism. Rather, it must be a self-reflective learning process that familiarizes managers and employees in the organization with key strategic issues and feasible alternatives for resolving those issues. Strategic management must not become ritualistic, stilted, orchestrated, or too formal, predictable, and rigid. Words supported by numbers, rather than numbers supported by words, should represent the medium for explaining strategic issues and organizational responses. A key role of strategists is to facilitate continuous organizational learning and change.

R. T. Lenz offered some important guidelines for effective strategic management:

Keep the strategic-management process as simple and nonroutine as possible.
Eliminate jargon and arcane planning language. Remember, strategic management is a process for fostering learning and action, not merely a formal system
for control. To avoid routinized behavior, vary assignments, team membership,
meeting formats, and the planning calendar. The process should not be totally
predictable, and settings must be changed to stimulate creativity. Emphasize
word-oriented plans with numbers as back-up material. If managers cannot
express their strategy in a paragraph or so, they either do not have one or do not
understand it. Stimulate thinking and action that challenge the assumptions
underlying current corporate strategy. Welcome bad news. If strategy is not
working, managers desperately need to know it. Further, no pertinent information should be classified as inadmissible merely because it cannot be quantified.
Build a corporate culture in which the role of strategic management and its
essential purposes are understood. Do not permit "technicians" to co-opt the
process. It is ultimately a process for learning and action. Speak of it in these
terms. Attend to psychological, social, and political dimensions, as well as the
information infrastructure and administrative procedures supporting it.[21]

An important guideline for effective strategic management is open-mindedness. A willingness and eagerness to consider new information, new viewpoints, new ideas, and new possibilities is essential; all organizational members must share a spirit of inquiry and learning. Strategists such as chief executive officers, presidents, owners of small businesses, and heads of government agencies must commit themselves to listen to and understand managers' positions well enough to be able to restate those positions to the managers' satisfaction. In addition, managers and employees throughout the firm should be able to describe the strategists' positions to the satisfaction of the strategists. This degree of discipline will promote understanding and learning.

No organization has unlimited resources. No firm can take on an unlimited amount of debt or issue an unlimited amount of stock to raise capital. Therefore, no organization can pursue all the strategies that potentially could benefit the firm. Strategic decisions thus always have to be made to eliminate some courses of action and to allocate organizational resources among others. Most organizations can afford to pursue only a few corporate-level strategies at any given time. It is a critical mistake for managers to pursue too many strategies at the same time, thereby spreading the firm's resources so thin that all strategies are jeopardized. Joseph Charyk, CEO of the Communication Satellite Corporation (Comsat), said, "We have to face the cold fact that Comsat may not be able to do all it wants. We must make hard choices on which ventures to keep and which to fold."

Strategic decisions require trade-offs such as long-range versus short-range considerations or maximizing profits versus increasing shareholders' wealth. There are ethics issues too. Strategy trade-offs require subjective judgments and preferences. In many cases, a lack of objectivity in formulating strategy results in a loss of competitive posture and profitability. Most organizations today recognize that strategic-management concepts and techniques can enhance the effectiveness of decisions. Subjective factors such as attitudes toward risk, concern for social responsibility, and organizational culture will always affect strategy-formulation decisions, but organizations need to be as objective as possible in considering qualitative factors.

BUSINESS ETHICS AND STRATEGIC MANAGEMENT

VISIT THE NET

Describes "Why Have a Code of Ethics" and gives "Guidelines on Writing a Code of Ethics." www.ethicsweb.ca/codes

VISIT THE NET

Gives example codes of business ethics for companies such as Halliburton and Johnson & Johnson. http://www.ethics. ubc.ca/resources/business/ codes.html

Business ethics can be defined as principles of conduct within organizations that guide decision making and behavior. Good business ethics is a prerequisite for good strategic management; good ethics is just good business!

A rising tide of consciousness about the importance of business ethics is sweeping America and the world. Strategists are the individuals primarily responsible for ensuring that high ethical principles are espoused and practiced in an organization. All strategy formulation, implementation, and evaluation decisions have ethical ramifications.

Newspapers and business magazines daily report legal and moral breaches of ethical conduct by both public and private organizations. Managers and employees of firms must be careful not to become scapegoats blamed for company environmental wrongdoings. Harming the natural environment is unethical, illegal, and costly. When organizations today face criminal charges for polluting the environment, firms increasingly are turning on their managers and employees to win leniency for themselves. Employee firings and demotions are becoming common in pollution-related legal suits. Managers being fired at Darling International, Inc. and Niagara Mohawk Power Corporation for being indirectly responsible for their firms' polluting water exemplifies this corporate trend. Therefore, managers and employees today must be careful not to ignore, conceal, or disregard a pollution problem, or they may find themselves personally liable.

A new wave of ethics issues related to product safety, employee health, sexual harassment, AIDS in the workplace, smoking, acid rain, affirmative action, waste disposal, foreign business practices, cover-ups, takeover tactics, conflicts of interest, employee privacy, inappropriate gifts, security of company records, and layoffs has accented the need for strategists to develop a clear code of business ethics. United Technologies Corporation has issued a twenty-one-page Code of Ethics and named a new vice president of business ethics. Baxter Travenol Laboratories, IBM, Caterpillar Tractor, Chemical Bank, Exxon/Mobil, Dow Corning, and Celanese are firms that have formal codes of business ethics. A *code of business ethics* can provide a basis on which policies can be devised to guide daily behavior and decisions at the work site.

The explosion of the Internet into the workplace has raised many new ethical questions in organizations today. For example, United Parcel Service (UPS) caught an employee actually running a personal business from his computer. A Lockheed Martin employee recently sent a religious e-mail to sixty thousand fellow employees that disabled company networks for more than six hours. Boeing is an example of a company that seemingly has accepted the inevitable by instituting a policy specifically allowing employees to use company faxes, e-mail, and the Internet for personal reasons for "reasonable duration and frequency without embarrassment to the company." In contrast, Ameritech has a policy that says "computers and other company equipment are to be used only to provide service to customers and for other business purposes."

E-COMMERCE PERSPECTIVE

e·biz

Business Ethics and the Internet

May employees use the Internet at work to conduct day-trading of personal stocks? May employees send e-mail to personal friends and relatives from the workplace? Is it ethical for employees to shop online while at work? May employees hunt for a new job while online at work? May employees play games online while at work? Before answering these questions, consider the following facts:

- Employee productivity can suffer immensely when many workers surf the Web at work.

- Unlike phone calls, e-mail can often be retrieved months or years later and can be used against the company in litigation.

- When employees surf the Web at work, they drag the company's name along with them everywhere. This could be harmful to the company if employees visit certain sites such as racist chat rooms or pornographic material.

- Software packages are now available to companies that report Web site visits by individual employees. Companies such as Telemate.Net Software Inc. in Atlanta produce software that tells managers who went to what sites at what times and for how long.

- Some 27 percent of large U.S. firms have begun checking employee e-mail, up from 15 percent in 1997. BellSouth employees must regularly click OK to a message warning them against misuse of e-mail and the Internet, and alerting them that their actions can be monitored.

- Many companies such as Boeing grant Internet usage to employees as a perk, but many of those firms are finding that this "fringe benefit" must be managed.

Lockheed Martin now directs its employees onto the Internet for extensive training sessions on topics that include business ethics, legal compliance, sexual harassment, and day-trading. Lockheed even has an Internet ethics game, Ethics Challenge, which every single employee and manager must play once a year. During a recent six-month period, Lockheed discharged 25 employees for ethics violations, suspended 14 others, gave a written reprimand to 51 persons, and an oral reprimand to 146 employees.

Soon after installing the Telemate software, Wolverton & Associates learned that broadcast.com was the company's third-most visited site; people download music from that site. And E*TRADE was the company's eighth-most visited site; people day-trade stocks at that site.

Recent research reveals that 38 percent of companies today choose to store and review employees' e-mail messages; this represents a rise of 15 percent since 1997. In addition, 54 percent of companies also monitor employees' Internet connections, with 29 percent blocking access to unauthorized or inappropriate Web sites.[22]

Sources: Adapted from Michael McCarthy, "Virtual Morality: A New Workplace Quandary," *The Wall Street Journal* (October 21, 1999): B1; Michael McCarthy. "Now the Boss Knows Where You're Clicking," *The Wall Street Journal* (October 21, 1999); and Michael McCarthy, "How One Firm Tracks Ethics Electronically," *The Wall Street Journal* (October 21, 1999): B1.

The E-Commerce Perspective focuses on business ethics issues related to the Internet. Merely having a code of ethics, however, is not sufficient to ensure ethical business behavior. A code of ethics can be viewed as a public relations gimmick, a set of platitudes, or window dressing. To ensure that the code is read, understood, believed, and remembered, organizations need to conduct periodic ethics workshops to sensitize people to workplace circumstances in which ethics issues may arise.[23] If employees see examples of punishment for violating the code and rewards for upholding the code, this helps reinforce the importance of a firm's code of ethics.

Internet privacy is an ethical issue of immense proportions. There is a national push for industry assurances that children have parental permission before giving out their names, ages, and other private details to companies that run Web sites. Privacy

VISIT THE NET

An excellent Web site to obtain additional information regarding business ethics is www.ethicsweb.ca/codes; *it describes "Why Have a Code of Ethics" and gives "Guidelines on Writing a Code of Ethics."*

advocates increasingly argue for new government regulations to enforce protection of young users.

Millions of computer users are worried about privacy on the Internet and want the U.S. government to pass laws about how data can be collected and used. Advertisers, marketers, companies, and people with various reasons to snoop on other people now can discover easily on the Internet others' buying preferences, hobbies, incomes, medical data, social security numbers, addresses, previous addresses, sexual preferences, credit card purchases, traffic tickets, divorce settlements, and much more. Many Internet users are ready for what they call "some law and order" in cyberspace.

NATURAL ENVIRONMENT PERSPECTIVE

Combating Terrorism

In light of the World Trade Center, Pentagon, and anthrax attacks, there is much that businesses can and should do to help in the global war to combat terrorism. As part of their ongoing concern for natural environment issues, businesses should include decision and expense consideration for combating biological or chemical terrorism because it may impact their corporations. After anthrax-tainted mail began arriving at government and business offices, firms began to implement security measures such as wearing gloves in mailrooms, securing air ducts in buildings, and establishing hotlines for obtaining antibiotics. Post offices and corporate mailrooms are the first line of defense against bioterrorism.

According to the Centers for Disease Control, the biggest terrorist threat that could impact business operations comes from the following seven agents: anthrax, smallpox, pneumonic plague, botulinum toxin, tularemia, filoviruses such as ebola, and arenaviruses such as Lassa fever. Pathogens or toxins could be sprayed from an airplane or placed in air-conditioning or water systems of buildings or manufacturing plants. Methods for dispensing deadly biological agents are almost unlimited. Viruses considered to be hazardous agents under the Antiterrorism and Effective Death Penalty Act include equine morbillvirus, Venezuelan equine encephalitis virus, marburg virus, Rift Valley fever virus, and yellow fever virus. The act also includes the following bacteria: Yersinia pestis (plague), anthrax, burkholderia pseudomallei, and Clostridium botulinum.

There are also numerous chemical weapons that also could destroy the natural environment and life, including mustard gas, nitrogen dioxide, and nerve toxins such as sarin. Some companies are more vulnerable than others, and these businesses need to be

much more proactive in taking steps to safeguard themselves and their operations against natural environment terrorism. No industry or company is immune to this threat, but the following two industries are especially vulnerable:

- Transportation: Airlines, Railroads, Trucks, and Cruise Lines—Airport security has quadrupled due to the special vulnerability of this mode of transportation, and passengers are again becoming comfortable with the idea of flying. Railroads have stepped up the inspection of tracks, equipment, tunnels, and telecommunications centers. Transportation-oriented firms have increased their communication with federal agencies regarding security and intelligence. Trucking companies have tightened security at terminals. Truck drivers now stay with their trucks as much as possible. Closer screening of drivers and employees among trucking companies and cruise operators is common practice.

- Chemical: Pharmaceutical and Agricultural—Terrorists could target chemical-oriented facilities and operations, especially those that deal with deadly agents, such as pharmaceutical and agricultural companies. Enhanced security on, near, and above particular operations is necessary. Firms should reevaluate the amount of chemical information they provide on their Web sites. Closer screening of all employees is warranted.

Sources: Adapted from Laura Johannes and Marilyn Chase, "Experts Say Bioterrorism Threat Is Real, Yet Likelihood Is Uncertain," *Wall Street Journal* (September 28, 2001): B1, B6; Ted Bridis, "State of the Union: America the Vulnerable?" *Wall Street Journal* (September 28, 2001): B1 and B4.

Given the global nature of e-commerce, any U.S. government regulations to inhibit the free flow of information will not carry much weight in places such as Moldova, home of a phone-porn scam. But perhaps the United States at least should set a standard for e-commerce rules and regulations that other countries could consider adopting.

An ethics "culture" needs to permeate organizations! To help create an ethics culture, Citicorp developed a business ethics board game that is played by forty thousand employees in forty-five countries. Called The Work Ethic, this game asks players business ethics questions, such as, how do you deal with a customer who offers you football tickets in exchange for a new, backdated IRA? Diana Robertson at The Wharton School of business believes the game is effective because it is interactive. Many organizations, such as Prime Computer and Kmart, have developed a code-of-conduct manual outlining ethical expectations and giving examples of situations that commonly arise in their businesses. Harris Corporation's managers and employees are warned that failing to report an ethical violation by others could bring discharge.

One reason strategists' salaries are high compared to those of other individuals in an organization is that strategists must take the moral risks of the firm. Strategists are responsible for developing, communicating, and enforcing the code of business ethics for their organizations. Although primary responsibility for ensuring ethical behavior rests with a firm's strategists, an integral part of the responsibility of all managers is to provide ethics leadership by constant example and demonstration. Managers hold positions that enable them to influence and educate many people. This makes managers responsible for developing and implementing ethical decision making. Gellerman and Drucker, respectively, offer some good advice for managers:

> All managers risk giving too much because of what their companies demand from them. But the same superiors, who keep pressing you to do more, or to do it better, or faster, or less expensively, will turn on you should you cross that fuzzy line between right and wrong. They will blame you for exceeding instructions or for ignoring their warnings. The smartest managers already know that the best answer to the question "How far is too far?" is don't try to find out.[24]
>
> A man (or woman) might know too little, perform poorly, lack judgment and ability, and yet not do too much damage as a manager. But if that person lacks character and integrity—no matter how knowledgeable, how brilliant, how successful—he destroys. He destroys people, the most valuable resource of the enterprise. He destroys spirit. And he destroys performance. This is particularly true of the people at the head of an enterprise. For the spirit of an organization is created from the top. If an organization is great in spirit, it is because the spirit of its top people is great. If it decays, it does so because the top rots. As the proverb has it, "Trees die from the top." No one should ever become a strategist unless he or she is willing to have his or her character serve as the model for subordinates.[25]

No society anywhere in the world can compete very long or successfully with people stealing from one another or not trusting one another, with every bit of information requiring notarized confirmation, with every disagreement ending up in litigation, or with government having to regulate businesses to keep them honest. Being unethical is a recipe for headaches, inefficiency, and waste. History has proven that the greater the trust and confidence of people in the ethics of an institution or society, the greater its economic strength. Business relationships are built mostly on mutual trust and reputation. Short-term decisions based on greed and questionable ethics will preclude the necessary self-respect to gain the trust of others. More and more firms believe that ethics training and an ethics culture create strategic advantage.

VISIT THE NET

The Web site http://www.ethics.ubc.ca/resources/business/codes.html *gives example codes of business ethics for companies such as Halliburton and Johnson & Johnson.*

Some business actions considered to be unethical include misleading advertising or labeling, causing environmental harm, poor product or service safety, padding expense accounts, insider trading, dumping banned or flawed products in foreign markets, lack of equal opportunities for women and minorities, overpricing, hostile takeovers, moving jobs overseas, and using nonunion labor in a union shop.[26]

Internet fraud, including hacking into company computers and spreading viruses, has become a major unethical activity that plagues every sector of online commerce from banking to shopping sites. More than three hundred Web sites now show individuals how to hack into computers; this problem has become endemic nationwide and around the world.

Ethics training programs should include messages from the CEO emphasizing ethical business practices, the development and discussion of codes of ethics, and procedures for discussing and reporting unethical behavior. Firms can align ethical and strategic decision making by incorporating ethical considerations into long-term planning, by integrating ethical decision making into the performance appraisal process, by encouraging whistle-blowing or the reporting of unethical practices, and by monitoring departmental and corporate performance regarding ethical issues.

In a final analysis, ethical standards come out of history and heritage. Our fathers, mothers, brothers, and sisters of the past left us with an ethical foundation to build upon. Even the legendary football coach Vince Lombardi knew that some things were worth more than winning, and he required his players to have three kinds of loyalty: to God, to their families, and to the Green Bay Packers, "in that order."

COMPARING BUSINESS AND MILITARY STRATEGY

A strong military heritage underlies the study of strategic management. Terms such as *objectives, mission, strengths*, and *weaknesses* first were formulated to address problems on the battlefield. According to *Webster's New World Dictionary*, strategy is "the science of planning and directing large-scale military operations, of maneuvering forces into the most advantageous position prior to actual engagement with the enemy." The word *strategy* comes from the Greek *strategos*, which refers to a military general and combines *stratos* (the army) and *ago* (to lead). The history of strategic planning began in the military. A key aim of both business and military strategy is "to gain competitive advantage." In many respects, business strategy is like military strategy, and military strategists have learned much over the centuries that can benefit business strategists today. Both business and military organizations try to use their own strengths to exploit competitor's weaknesses. If an organization's overall strategy is wrong (ineffective), then all the efficiency in the world may not be enough to allow success. Business or military success is generally not the happy result of accidental strategies. Rather, success is the product of both continuous attention to changing external and internal conditions and the formulation and implementation of insightful adaptations to those conditions. The element of surprise provides great competitive advantages in both military and business strategy; information systems that provide data on opponents' or competitors' strategies and resources are also vitally important.

Of course, a fundamental difference between military and business strategy is that business strategy is formulated, implemented, and evaluated with an assumption of *competition*, whereas military strategy is based on an assumption of *conflict*. Nonetheless, military conflict and business competition are so similar that many strategic-management techniques apply equally to both. Business strategists have access to valuable insights that military thinkers have refined over time. Superior strategy formulation and implementation can overcome an opponent's superiority in numbers and resources.

Both business and military organizations must adapt to change and constantly improve to be successful. Too often, firms do not change their strategies when their environment and competitive conditions dictate the need to change. Gluck offered a classic military example of this:

> When Napoleon won, it was because his opponents were committed to the strategy, tactics, and organization of earlier wars. When he lost—against Wellington, the Russians, and the Spaniards—it was because he, in turn, used tried-and-true strategies against enemies who thought afresh, who were developing the strategies not of the last war but of the next.[27]

Similarities can be construed from Sun Tzu writings to the practice of formulating and implementing strategies among businesses today. Table 1–2 provides narrative excerpts from *The Art of War*. As you read through Table 1–2, consider which of the principles of war apply to business strategy as companies today compete aggressively to survive and grow.

THE NATURE OF GLOBAL COMPETITION

For centuries before Columbus discovered America and surely for centuries to come, businesses have searched and will continue to search for new opportunities beyond their national boundaries. There has never been a more internationalized and economically competitive society than today's. Some American industries, such as textiles, steel, and consumer electronics, are in complete disarray as a result of the international challenge.

Organizations that conduct business operations across national borders are called *international firms* or *multinational corporations*. The term *parent company* refers to a firm investing in international operations, while *host country* is the country where that business is conducted. The strategic-management process is conceptually the same for multinational firms as for purely domestic firms; however, the process is more complex for international firms because of the presence of more variables and relationships. The social, cultural, demographic, environmental, political, governmental, legal, technological, and competitive opportunities and threats that face a multinational corporation are almost limitless, and the number and complexity of these factors increase dramatically with the number of products produced and the number of geographic areas served.

More time and effort are required to identify and evaluate external trends and events in multinational corporations, than in domestic corporations. Geographical distance, cultural and national differences, and variations in business practices often make communication between domestic headquarters and overseas operations difficult. Strategy implementation can be more difficult because different cultures have different norms, values, and work ethics.

The global war on terrorism and advancements in telecommunications are drawing countries, cultures, and organizations worldwide closer together. Foreign revenue as a percent of total company revenues already exceeds 50 percent in hundreds of U.S. firms, including Exxon/Mobil, Gillette, Dow Chemical, Citicorp, Colgate-Palmolive, and Texaco. Joint ventures and partnerships between domestic and foreign firms are becoming the rule rather than the exception!

Fully 95 percent of the world's population lives outside the United States, and this group is growing 70 percent faster than the American population! The lineup of competitors in virtually all industries today is global. Global competition is more than a management fad. General Motors, Ford, and Chrysler compete with Toyota and Hyundai. General Electric and Westinghouse battle Siemens and Mitsubishi. Caterpillar

VISIT THE NET

Provides a nice account of strategic planning, tracing history back to the military. http://www.des.calstate.edu/history.html

VISIT THE NET

An excellent Web site that describes Sun Tzu's famous The Art of War writings is provided at http://www.ccs.neu.edu/home/thigpen/html/art_of_war.html

TABLE 1-2 **Excerpts from Sun Tzu's *The Art of War* Writings**
(Note: Substitute the words *strategy* or *strategic planning* for *war* or *warfare*)

- War is a matter of vital importance to the state; a matter of life or death, the road either to survival or ruin. Hence, it is imperative that it be studied thoroughly.

- Warfare is based on deception. When near the enemy, make it seem that you are far away; when far away, make it seem that you are near. Hold out baits to lure the enemy. Strike the enemy when he is in disorder. Avoid the enemy when he is stronger. If your opponent is of choleric temper, try to irritate him. If he is arrogant, try to encourage his egotism. If enemy troops are well prepared after reorganization, try to wear them down. If they are united, try to sow dissension among them. Attack the enemy where he is unprepared, and appear where you are not expected. These are the keys to victory for a strategist. It is not possible to formulate them in detail beforehand.

- A speedy victory is the main object in war. If this is long in coming, weapons are blunted and morale depressed. When the army engages in protracted campaigns, the resources of the state will fall short. Thus, while we have heard of stupid haste in war, we have not yet seen a clever operation that was prolonged.

- Generally, in war the best policy is to take a state intact; to ruin it is inferior to this. To capture the enemy's entire army is better than to destroy it; to take intact a regiment, a company, or a squad is better than to destroy it. For to win one hundred victories in one hundred battles is not the acme of skill. To subdue the enemy without fighting is the supreme excellence. Those skilled in war subdue the enemy's army without battle.

- The art of using troops is this—When ten to the enemy's one, surround him. When five times his strength, attack him. If double his strength, divide him. If equally matched, you may engage him with some good plan. If weaker, be capable of withdrawing. And if in all respects unequal, be capable of eluding him.

- Know your enemy and know yourself, and in a hundred battles you will never be defeated. When you are ignorant of the enemy but know yourself, your chances of winning or losing are equal. If ignorant both of your enemy and of yourself, you are sure to be defeated in every battle.

- He who occupies the field of battle first and awaits his enemy is at ease, and he who comes later to the scene and rushes into the fight is weary. And therefore, those skilled in war bring the enemy to the field of battle and are not brought there by him. Thus, when the enemy is at ease, be able to tire him; when well fed, be able to starve him; when at rest, be able to make him move.

- Analyze the enemy's plans so that you will know his shortcomings as well as his strong points. Agitate him in order to ascertain the pattern of his movement. Lure him out to reveal his dispositions and to ascertain his position. Launch a probing attack in order to learn where his strength is abundant and where deficient. It is according to the situation that plans are laid for victory, but the multitude does not comprehend this.

- An army may be likened to water, for just as flowing water avoids the heights and hastens to the lowlands, so an army should avoid strength and strike weakness. And as water shapes its flow in accordance with the ground, so an army manages its victory in accordance with the situation of the enemy. And as water has no constant form, there are in warfare no constant conditions. Thus, one able to win the victory by modifying his tactics in accordance with the enemy situation may be said to be divine.

- If you decide to go into battle, do not announce your intentions or plans. Project "business as usual."

- Unskilled leaders work out their conflicts in courtrooms and an battlefields. Brilliant strategists rarely go to battle or to court; they generally achieve their objectives through tactical positioning well in advance of any confrontation.

- When you do decide to challenge another company (or army), much calculating, estimating, analyzing, and positioning brings triumph. Little computation brings defeat.

- Skillful leaders do not let a strategy inhibit creative counter-movement. Nor should commands from those at a distance interfere with spontaneous maneuvering in the immediate situation.

- When a decisive advantage is gained over a rival, skillful leaders do not press on. They hold their position and give their rivals the opportunity to surrender or merge. They do not allow their forces to be damaged by those who have nothing to lose.

- Brillant strategists forge ahead with illusion, obscuring the area(s) of major confrontation, so that opponents divide their forces in an attempt to defend many areas. Create the appearance of confusion, fear, or vulnerability so the opponent is helplessly drawn toward this illusion of advantage.

Source: Adapted from *The Art of War* and from the Web site **www.ccs.neu.edu/home/thigpen/html/art_of_war.html.**

and John Deere compete with Komatsu. Goodyear battles Michelin, Bridgestone/ Firestone, and Pirelli. Boeing competes with Airbus. Only a few U.S. industries, such as furniture, printing, retailing, consumer packaged goods, and retail banking, are not yet greatly challenged by foreign competitors. But many products and components in these industries too are now manufactured in foreign countries.

International operations can be as simple as exporting a product to a single foreign country, or as complex as operating manufacturing, distribution, and marketing facilities in many countries. U.S. firms are acquiring foreign companies and forming joint ventures with foreign firms, and foreign firms are acquiring U.S. companies and forming joint ventures with U.S. firms. This trend is accelerating dramatically. AT&T's former Chief Executive Officer, Robert Allen, said, "The phrase *global markets* is not empty rhetoric. Foreign competitors are here. And we must be there." Many U.S. firms have been spoiled by the breadth and number of home markets and remain ignorant of foreign languages and culture. For example, Hershey Foods, the leading chocolate producer in the United States, derives less than 15 percent of its total revenues from outside the United States.

Advantages and Disadvantages of International Operations

Firms have numerous reasons for formulating and implementing strategies that initiate, continue, or expand involvement in business operations across national borders. Perhaps the greatest advantage is that firms can gain new customers for their products and services, thus increasing revenues. Growth in revenues and profits is a common organizational objective and often an expectation of shareholders because it is a measure of organizational success.

In addition to seeking growth, firms have the following potentially advantageous reasons to initiate, continue, and expand international operations:

1. Foreign operations can absorb excess capacity, reduce unit costs, and spread economic risks over a wider number of markets.

2. Foreign operations can allow firms to establish low-cost production facilities in locations close to raw materials and/or cheap labor.

3. Competitors in foreign markets may not exist, or competition may be less intense than in domestic markets.

4. Foreign operations may result in reduced tariffs, lower taxes, and favorable political treatment in other countries.

5. Joint ventures can enable firms to learn the technology, culture, and business practices of other people and to make contacts with potential customers, suppliers, creditors, and distributors in foreign countries.

6. Many foreign governments and countries offer varied incentives to encourage foreign investment in specific locations.

7. Economies of scale can be achieved from operation in global rather than solely domestic markets. Larger-scale production and better efficiencies allow higher sales volumes and lower price offerings.

A firm's power and prestige in domestic markets may be significantly enhanced with various stakeholder groups if the firm competes globally. Enhanced prestige can translate into improved negotiating power among creditors, suppliers, distributors, and other important groups.

There are also numerous potential disadvantages of initiating, continuing, or expanding business across national borders. One risk is that foreign operations could be seized by nationalistic factions. Other disadvantages include the following:

1. Firms confront different and often little-understood social, cultural, demographic, environmental, political, governmental, legal, technological, economic, and competitive forces when doing business internationally. These forces can make communication difficult between the parent firm and subsidiaries.

2. Weaknesses of competitors in foreign lands are often overestimated, and strengths are often underestimated. Keeping informed about the number and nature of competitors is more difficult when doing business internationally.

3. Language, culture, and value systems differ among countries, and this can create barriers to communication and problems managing people.

4. Gaining an understanding of regional organizations such as the European Economic Community, the Latin American Free Trade Area, the International Bank for Reconstruction and Development, and the International Finance Corporation is difficult but is often required in doing business internationally.

5. Dealing with two or more monetary systems can complicate international business operations.

6. The availability, depth, and reliability of economic and marketing information in different countries vary extensively, as do industrial structures, business practices, and the number and nature of regional organizations.

CONCLUSION

All firms have a strategy, even if it is informal, unstructured, and sporadic. All organizations are heading somewhere, but unfortunately some organizations do not know where they are going. The old saying "If you do not know where you are going, then any road will lead you there!" accents the need for organizations to use strategic-management concepts and techniques. The strategic-management process is becoming more widely used by small firms, large companies, nonprofit institutions, governmental organizations, and multinational conglomerates alike. The process of empowering managers and employees has almost limitless benefits.

Organizations should take a proactive rather than a reactive approach in their industry, and they should strive to influence, anticipate, and initiate rather than just respond to events. The strategic-management process embodies this approach to decision making. It represents a logical, systematic, and objective approach for determining an enterprise's future direction. The stakes are generally too high for strategists to use intuition alone in choosing among alternative courses of action. Successful strategists take the time to think about their businesses, where they are with the businesses, and what they want to be as organizations—and then to implement programs and policies to get from where they are to where they want to be in a reasonable period of time.

It is a known and accepted fact that people and organizations that plan ahead are much more likely to become what they want to become than those that do not plan at all. A good strategist plans and controls his or her plans, while a bad strategist never plans and then tries to control people! This textbook is devoted to providing you with the tools necessary to be a good strategist.

Success in business increasingly depends upon offering products and services that are competitive on a world basis, not just on a local basis. If the price and quality of a firm's products and services are not competitive with those available elsewhere in the world, the firm may soon face extinction. Global markets have become a reality in all but the most remote areas of the world. Certainly throughout the United States, even in small towns, firms feel the pressure of world competitors. Nearly half of all the automobiles sold in the United States, for example, are made in Japan and Germany.

We invite you to visit the David page on the Prentice Hall Companion Website at www.prenhall.com/david for this chapter's World Wide Web exercises.

KEY TERMS AND CONCEPTS

Annual Objectives (p. 12)

Business Ethics (p. 20)

Code of Business Ethics (p. 20)

Empowerment (p. 15)

Environmental Scanning (p. 10)

External Opportunities (p. 10)

External Threats (p. 10xx)

Host Country (p. 25)

Internal Strengths (p. 11)

Internal Weaknesses (p. 11)

International Firms (p. 25)

Intuition (p. 7)

Long-Range Planning (p. 5)

Long-Term Objectives (p. 11)

Mission Statements (p. 10)

Multinational Corporations (p. 25)

Policies (p. 13)

Strategic Management (p. 5)

Strategic-Management Model (p. 13)

Strategic-Management Proces (p. 5)

Strategies (p. 5)

Strategists (p. 5)

Strategy Evaluation (p. 6)

Strategy Formulation (p. 5)

Strategy Implementation (p. 6)

Vision Statement (p. 9)

ISSUES FOR REVIEW AND DISCUSSION

1. Explain why Business Policy often is called a "capstone course."
2. Read one of the suggested readings at the end of this chapter. Prepare a one-page written summary that includes your personal thoughts on the subject.
3. What aspect of strategy formulation do you think requires the most time? Why?
4. Why is strategy implementation often considered the most difficult stage in the strategic-management process?
5. Why is it so important to integrate intuition and analysis in strategic management?
6. Explain the importance of a vision and mission statement.
7. Discuss relationships among objectives, strategies, and policies.
8. Why do you think some chief executive officers fail to use a strategic-management approach to decision making?
9. Discuss the importance of feedback in the strategic-management model.
10. How can strategists best ensure that strategies will be effectively implemented?
11. Give an example of a recent political development that changed the overall strategy of an organization.
12. Who are the major competitors of your college or university? What are their strengths and weaknesses? What are their strategies? How successful are these institutions compared to your college?

13. If you owned a small business, would you develop a code of business conduct? If yes, what variables would you include? If no, how would you ensure that ethical business standards were being followed by your employees?
14. Would strategic-management concepts and techniques benefit foreign businesses as much as domestic firms? Justify your answer.
15. What do you believe are some potential pitfalls or risks in using a strategic-management approach to decision making?
16. In your opinion, what is the single major benefit of using a strategic-management approach to decision making? Justify your answer.
17. Compare business strategy and military strategy.
18. What do you feel is the relationship between personal ethics and business ethics? Are they—or should they be—the same?
19. Why is it important for all business majors to study strategic management since most students will never become a chief executive officer nor even a top manager in a large company?
20. Explain why consumption patterns are becoming similar worldwide. What are the strategic implications of this trend?
21. What are the advantages and disadvantages of beginning export operations in a foreign country?

NOTES

1. KEVIN MANEY, "The Net Effect: Evolution or Revolution?" *USA Today* (August 9, 1999): B1.
2. PETER DRUCKER, *Management: Tasks, Responsibilities, and Practices* (New York: Harper & Row, 1974): 611.
3. ALFRED SLOAN, JR., *Adventures of the White Collar Man* (New York: Doubleday, 1941): 104.
4. Quoted in Eugene Raudsepp, "Can You Trust Your Hunches?" *Management Review* 49, no. 4 (April 1960): 7.
5. STEPHEN HARPER, "Intuition: What Separates Executives from Managers," *Business Horizons* 31, no. 5 (September–October 1988): 16.
6. RON NELSON, "How to Be a Manager," *Success* (July–August 1985): 69.
7. BRUCE HENDERSON, *Henderson on Corporate Strategy* (Boston: Abt Books, 1979): 6.
8. ROBERT WATERMAN, JR., *The Renewal Factor: How the Best Get and Keep the Competitive Edge* (New York: Bantam, 1987). See also *Business Week* (September 14, 1987): 100. Also, see *Academy of Management Executive* 3, no. 2 (May 1989): 115.
9. JOHN PEARCE II and FRED DAVID, "The Bottom Line on Corporate Mission Statements," *Academy of Management Executive* 1, no. 2 (May 1987): 109.
10. LORRIE GRANT, "Grocery Chore No More," *USA Today* (July 21, 1999): p. B1.
11. SHIRLEY LEUNG, "Competition Heats Up Between Boston Market and KFC," *Wall Street Journal* (November 6, 2001): p. B4.
12. FRED R. DAVID, "How Companies Define Their Mission," *Long Range Planning* 22, no. 1 (February 1989): 91.
13. JACK PEARCE and RICHARD ROBINSON, *Strategic Management,* 7th ed. (New York: McGraw-Hill, 2000): p. 8.
14. ANN LANGLEY, "The Roles of Formal Strategic Planning," *Long Range Planning* 21, no. 3 (June 1988): 40.
15. BERNARD REIMANN, "Getting Value from Strategic Planning," *Planning Review* 16, no. 3 (May–June 1988): 42.
16. G. L. SCHWENK and K. SCHRADER, "Effects of Formal Strategic Planning in Financial Performance in Small Firms: A Meta-Analysis," *Entrepreneurship and Practice* 3, no. 17 (1993): 53–64. Also, C. C. Miller and L. B. Cardinal, "Strategic Planning and Firm Performance: A Synthesis of More than Two Decades of Research," *Academy of Management Journal* 6, no. 27 (1994): 1649–1665. Also, Michael Peel and John Bridge, "How Planning and Capital Budgeting Improve SME Performance," *Long Range Planning* 31, no. 6 (October 1998): 848–856. Also, Julia Smith, "Strategies for Start-Ups," *Long Range Planning* 31, no. 6 (October 1998): 857–872.
17. GORDON GREENLEY, "Does Strategic Planning Improve Company Performance?" *Long Range Planning* 19, no. 2 (April 1986): 106.
18. Adapted from: **www.mindtools.com/plreschn.html**.
19. Adapted from the Web sites: **www.des.calstate.edu/limitations.html** and **www.entarga.com/stratplan/purposes.html**.
20. DALE MCCONKEY, "Planning in a Changing Environment," *Business Horizons* (September–October 1988): 66.
21. R. T. LENZ, "Managing the Evolution of the Strategic Planning Process," *Business Horizons* 30, no. 1 (January–February 1987): 39.
22. SAUL GELLERMAN, "Managing Ethics from the Top Down," *Sloan Management Review* (Winter 1989): 77.
23. JOANN GRECO, "Privacy—Whose Right Is It Anyhow?" *Journal of Business Strategy* (January/February 2001): 32.
24. SAUL GELLERMAN, "Why 'Good' Managers Make Bad Ethical Choices," *Harvard Business Review* 64, no. 4 (July–August 1986): 88.
25. DRUCKER, 462, 463.
26. GENE LACZNIAK, MARVIN BERKOWITZ, RUSSELL BROOKER, and JAMES HALE, "The Ethics of Business: Improving or Deteriorating?" *Business Horizons* 38, no. 1 (January–February 1995): 43.
27. FREDERICK GLUCK, "Taking the Mystique Out of Planning," *Across the Board* (July–August 1985): 59.

CURRENT READINGS

AHLSTROM, DAVID, GARRY D. BRUTON, and STEVEN S. Y. LUI. "Navigating China's Changing Economy: Strategies for Private Firms." *Business Horizons* 43, no. 1 (January–February 2000): 5.

ALVAREZ, SHARON A., and JAY B. BARNEY. "How Entrepreneurial Firms Can Benefit from Alliances with Large Partners." *Academy of Management Executive* 15, no. 1 (February 2001): 139.

AMIT, R., and C. ZOTT. "Value Creation in E-Business." *Strategic Management Journal* 22, no. 6–7 (June–July 2001):

BARNEY, JAY B. "Is the Resource-Based 'View' a Useful Perspective for Strategic Management Research? Yes." *Academy of Management Journal* 26, no. 1 (January 2001): 41.

BOSSIDY, LARRY. "The Job No CEO Should Delegate." *Harvard Business Review* (March 2001): 46.

BOWMAN, E. H., and C. E. HELFAT. "Does Corporate Strategy Matter?" *Strategic Management Journal* 22, no. 1 (January 2001): 1.

BRUSH, CANDIDA G., PATRICIA G. GREENE, and MYRA M. HART. "From Initial Idea to Unique Advantage: The Entrepreneurial Challenge of Constructing a Resource

Base." *Academy of Management Executive* 15, no. 1 (February 2001): 64.

CANNELLA, ALBERT, A., JR., and KENNETH STARKEY. "Donald Hambrick on Executives and Strategy." *Academy of Management Executive* 15, no. 3 (August 2001): 36.

CARPENTER, MASON A., and JAMES W. FREDICKSON. "Top Management Teams, Global Strategic Posture, and the Moderating Role of Uncertainty." *Academy of Management Journal* 44, no. 3 (June 2001): 533.

CHAN, RICKY Y. K. "An Emerging Green Market in China: Myth or Reality?" *Business Horizons* 43, no. 2 (Mar.–April 2000): 55.

CHANG, S. J., and P. M. ROSENZWEIG. "The Choice of Entry Mode in Sequential Foreign Direct Investment." *Strategic Management Journal* 22, no. 8 (August 2001): 747.

CLEMONS, ERIC K., and JASON A. SANTAMARIA. "Maneuver Warfare: Can Modern Military Strategy Lead You to Victory?" *Harvard Business Review* (April 2002): 56.

DRUCKER, PETER F. "They're Not Employees, They're People." *Harvard Business Review* (February 2002): 70.

FORD, CAMERON M., and DENNIS GIOIA. "Factors Influencing Creativity in the Domain of Managerial Decision Making." *Journal of Management* 26, no. 4 (2000): 685.

GIBSON, KEVIN. "Excuses, Excuses: Moral Slippage in the Workplace." *Business Horizons* 43, no. 6 (November–December 2000): 65.

HARPER, STEPHEN C. "Timing—The Bedrock of Anticipatory Management." *Business Horizons* 43, no. 1 (January–February 2000): 75.

HAYASHI, ALDEN M. "When to Trust Your Gut." *Harvard Business Review* (February 2001): 59.

IRELAND, R. DUANE, MICHAEL A. HITT, S. MICHAEL CAMP, and DONALD L. SEXTON. "Integrating Entrepreneurship and Strategic Management Actions to Create Firm Wealth." *Academy of Management Executive* 15, no. 1 (February 2001): 49.

KELLY, EILEEN P., and HUGH C. ROWLAND. "Ethical and Online Privacy Issues in Electronic Commerce." *Business Horizons* 43, no. 3 (May–June 2000): 3.

KOVACH, KENNETH A., SANDRA J. CONNER, TAMAR LIVNEH, KEVIN M. SCALLAN, and ROY L. SCHWARTZ. "Electronic Communication in the Workplace—Something's Got to Give." *Business Horizons* 43, no. 4 (July–August 2000): 59.

KRAATZ, MATTHEW S., and JAMES H. MOORE. "Executive Migration and Institutional Change." *Academy of Management Journal* 45, no. 1 (February 2002): 120.

LI, ZHAN G., and NURIT GERY. "E-tailing—For All Products?" *Business Horizons* 43, no. 6 (November–December 2000): 49.

LYON, DOUGLAS W., G. T. LUMPKIN, and GREGORY G. DESS. "Enhancing Entrepreneurial Orientation Research: Operationalizing and Measuring a Key Strategic Decision Making Process." *Journal of Management* 26, no. 5 (2000): 1055.

MINTZBERG, HENRY, and CONSTANTINOS MARKIDES. "Henry Mintzberg and Constantinos Markides on Strategy and Management." *Academy of Management Journal* 14, no. 3 (August 2000): 31.

MOULSON, TOM, and GEORGE SPROLES. "Styling Strategy." *Business Horizons* 43, no. 5 (September–October 2000): 45.

PORTER, MICHAEL E. "Strategy and the Internet." *Harvard Business Review* (March 2001): 62.

PRIEM, RICHARD L., and JOHN E. BUTLER. "Is the Resource-Based 'View' a Useful Perspective for Strategic Management Research?" *Academy of Management Journal* 26, no. 1 (January 2001): 22.

ROSEN, CHRISTINE MEISNER. "Environmental Strategy and Competitive Advantage: An Introduction." *California Management Review* 43, no. 3 (Spring 2001): 8.

ROWE, W. GLENN. "Creating Wealth in Organizations: The Role of Strategic Leadership." *Academy of Management Executive* 15, no. 1 (February 2001): 81.

SORCHER, MELVIN, and JAME BRANT. "Are You Picking the Right Leaders?" *Harvard Business Review* (February 2002): 78.

SOULE, EDWARD. "Managerial Moral Strategies—In Search of a Few Good Principles." *Academy of Management Review* 27, no. 1 (January 2002): 114.

WALDMAN, DAVID A., GABRIEL G. RAMIREZ, ROBERT J. HOUSE, and PHANISH PURANAM. "Does Leadership Matter? CEO Leadership Attributes and Profitability Under Conditions of Perceived Environmental Uncertainty." *Academy of Management Journal* 44, no. 1 (February 2001): 134.

WEAVER, GARY R., and BRADLEY R. AGLE. "Religiosity and Ethical Behavior in Organizations: A Symbolic Interactionist Perspective." *Academy of Management Review* 27, no. 1 (January 2002): 77.

YOFFIE, DAVID B., and MARY KWAK. "Playing by the Rules: How Intel Avoids Antitrust Litigation." *Harvard Business Review* (June 2001): 119.

COHESION CASE

AMERICAN AIRLINES—2002
Fred R. David
Francis Marion University
AMR
www.AA.com
www.amrcorp.com

OVERVIEW

The largest airline in the world, American Airlines (AMR), makes forty-one hundred flights daily to forty-one countries, but it is in trouble. As the first quarter of 2002 ends, AMR continues to be adversely affected by the September 11, 2001, terrorist attacks. The parent company of AMR Investments, American Cargo, AMR Training Group, American Eagle, and American Airlines, AMR's first quarter 2002 revenues showed a $624 million (13.1 percent) decline from the prior year's first quarter, while net income for this period was a negative $575 million compared to a negative $43 million the prior year.

In addition to the threat of terrorism, AMR's poor performance is also due to a weak economy, the decline in both business and vacation air travel, and increased airfare price competition. American is reportedly losing $10 to $15 million per day. CEO Don Carty calls this "the worst financial crisis in the history of the company." After September 11, 2001, and through early 2002, AMR has:

- Reduced the number of flights by 20 percent
- Grounded and accelerated the retirement of some airplanes
- Cut 2001 and 2002 capital spending by $2.5 billion, partly by delaying the delivery of 29 airplanes on order from Boeing
- Closed 105 travel centers, six Admiral's Clubs, and five Platinum Centers
- Cut in-flight food and beverages
- Laid off twenty thousand employees
- Asked for voluntary pay cuts (the Board of Directors and the CEO volunteered to work without pay)
- Requested and received government assistance
- Borrowed approximately $800 million in cash from American's credit line
- Borrowed an additional $200 million on Wall Street using aircraft as collateral[1]

Founded in 1982, AMR acquired Trans World Airlines (TWA) in 2001, and today it provides jet service to more than 161 destinations throughout North America, Latin America, the Caribbean, Canada, Europe, and the Pacific. American is one of the largest freight and mail-service carriers in the world. AMR's operating revenues from foreign operations were approximately 28 percent, 30 percent, and 29 percent of the firm's total operating revenues in 2001, 2000, and 1999, respectively.

INTERNAL ISSUES

Airplanes

American Airline's average aircraft age is 9.9 years, down from 10.8 years on March 31, 2001. American Eagle's average aircraft age is 6.6 years, up from 6.5 years last year. AMR's operating aircraft as of March 31, 2002, are as follows:

AMERICAN AIRLINES

Aircraft	Number of Aircrafts
Airbus A300-600R	34
Boeing 717-200	11
Boeing 727-200	15
Boeing 737-800	77
Boeing 757-200	150
Boeing 767-200	8
Boeing 767-200 Extended Range	21
Boeing 767-300 Extended Range	58
Boeing 777-200 Extended Range	42
Fokker 100	74
McDonnell Douglas MD-11	4
McDonnell Douglas MD-80	362
Total	717

AMERICAN EAGLE

Aircraft	Number of Aircraft
ATR 42	29
Embraer 135	40
Embraer 140	22
Embraer 145	56
Super ATR	42
Saab 340	66
Saab 340B Plus	25
Bombardier CRJ-700	3
Total	283

Hub and Spoke

All of the major airlines have what is known as a hub-and-spoke operation, which allows an airline to route most of its passengers through one or more centralized locations in order to reduce costs. American Airlines operates five hubs: Dallas/Fort Worth, Chicago O'Hare, Miami, St. Louis, and San Juan, Puerto Rico. AMR's two largest competitors, Delta Air Lines and United, have hub operations at Dallas/Fort Worth and Chicago O'Hare, respectively. American Eagle serves smaller markets in the United States and feeds customers to American's hubs. American has contracts with three other regional airlines called American Connection to provide connecting service through its St. Louis hub.

Global Alliances and Code Sharing

Airports outside the United States are subject to widely varying government regulations, which often change depending on the relationship between the U.S. government and the foreign government. One way to limit an airline's global expansion is to place restrictions on slots. Slots are takeoff and landing authorizations. In most nondomestic airports, slots are needed before a carrier can begin to offer services. Since a carrier cannot be assured that it will be able to obtain slots, it may be locked out of certain markets. Slots may be purchased or traded in some countries, but some foreign governments restrict slot availability.

To gain access to different international airports, AMR has entered into alliances with other airlines to utilize each other's facilities and marketing efforts. As indicated in Exhibit 1, there are currently five major global airline alliances: Star Alliance, anchored by United Airlines and Lufthansa; Oneworld, with American Airlines and British Airways; Qualiflyer Group, with 11 foreign airlines as members; the SkyTeam alliance that unites Delta and Air France; and Wings, which comprises Continental, KLM, and Northwest. Each alliance involves several secondary carriers. SkyTeam is shaping up to be a stronger-than-anticipated alliance. Although Delta lost Austrian Airlines, Sabena, and Swissair, it has won AeroMexico and Korean Airlines. Star Alliance, which had fifteen members in early 2002, is perhaps the strongest of the lot.

AMR has entered into code-sharing programs with many foreign and domestic airlines. Code-sharing is an agreement which allows an airline to put its identification code on the flights of another airline. Airlines that share codes also coordinate other aspects of travel, like connection times and baggage checking. These alliances and code-sharing programs have greatly expanded American's network in areas where it would be prohibitively expensive or impossible to expand by merger or purchase. American Airlines currently has code-sharing programs with Aer Lingus, Air Pacific, Alaska Airlines, Asiana Airlines, China Eastern Airlines, EVA Air, Finnair, Gulf Air, Hawaiian Airlines, Iberia, Japan Airlines, LanChile, LOT Polish Airlines, Qantas Airways, SNCF, TACA Group, the TAM Group, TAP Air Portugal, Thalys, and Turkish Airlines. American Eagle also has code-sharing programs with Continental, Delta, Midwest Express, and Northwest; in addition, it has code-sharing arrangements with some of American's code-share partners. Certain of these relationships also include reciprocity between American and the other airlines' frequent flyer programs. In addition, AMR expects to implement code shares with Cathay Pacific Airways and Vietnam Airlines pending regulatory approval. In the coming years, AMR expects to develop these programs further and to evaluate new alliances with other carriers. AMR's most recent code-sharing agreement is with Swissair.

EXHIBIT 1 — Airline Alliances

Star Alliance	Oneworld	Qualiflyer Group	SkyTeam	Wings
http://www.star-alliance.com	http://www.oneworldallance.com	http://www.qualiflyergroup.com	http://www.skyteam.com	
Air Canada	Aer Lingus	Air Europe	AeroMexico	KLM
Air New Zeland	**American Airlines**	Air Liberte	Air France	Northwest
All Nippon Airways	British Airways	Air Littoral	Alitalia	Continental
Ansett Australia	Cathay Pacific Airways	Crossair	Czech Airlines	
Austrian Airlines	Finnair	**LOT Polish Airlines**	Delta Airlines	
British Midland	Iberia	Portugalia	Korean Air	
Lauda Air	LANChile	Sabena		
Lufthansa	Quantas Airways	Swissair		
Mexicana		TAP Air Portugal		
Scandinavian		Turkish Airlines		
Singapore Airlines		Volare Airlines		
Thai				
Tyrolean				
United Airlines				

Source: **www.AA.com.**

American Airlines and British Airways (BA), the largest airline in Europe, seek antitrust immunity for an alliance that would enable them to cooperate more fully with each other and give them the ability to better serve their customers. American Airlines and British Airways have not been allowed to code-share or integrate their networks beyond a rudimentary marketing level. Not surprisingly, all of the major competitors in the market have opposed the alliance. American and BA have insisted that such an alliance would lead to an "open skies" arrangement between the two countries, which would lead to reduced regulations on their operations. Their opponents make the claim that the agreement would be strongly anticompetitive and would dominate the market for air service between the United States and the United Kingdom. Government regulators in the United States and the United Kingdom in mid-2002 are on the verge of approving the AMR/BA alliance.

Operating Statistics

Revenue passenger-miles (RPMs) is an indicator that measures the total number of passengers carried by the industry's airlines, multiplied by the number of miles flown. The RPM numbers are available on a monthly basis from the Air Transport Association (ATA), an industry trade group. For the industry as a whole, RPMs declined 7.7 percent in 2001, to 561.3 billion. This is in contrast to the industry's ten-year growth rate of about 4 percent.

Available seats per mile (ASM) is an indicator that measures the total number of seats in the active fleet, multiplied by the number of miles flown, for either an individual airline or the entire industry. The ATA compiles an industrywide figure on a monthly basis. Changes in ASMs are influenced by the net addition of aircraft to the industry's fleet, the seating mix of aircraft, seat pitch (or spacing), as well as by how quickly the industry turns around its aircraft between flights. ASMs for the major airlines totaled 795.2 billion in 2001, a decline of 4.4 percent from 2000's total. The decline reflects the large number of flights taken out of service after the September 11, 2001, terrorist attacks as well as actions by American and United to remove seats to provide more legroom.

AMR's domestic revenue per available seat mile (RASM) decreased 15.4 percent in the first quarter of 2002. The company's overall international RASM declined 10.6 percent due to a 14.1 percent RASM decline in travel to Europe, an 11.9 percent decrease in Latin America travel, and a 9 percent increase in travel to the Pacific Far East. AMR Eagle's passenger revenues declined 13.8 percent, while American Cargo revenues declined 23.9 percent in the first quarter of 2002. However, due to labor union problems, AMR's outlays for wages, salaries, and benefits increased 19.1 percent for the quarter.

Load factor is an indicator, compiled monthly by the ATA, that measures the percentage of available seating capacity that is filled with passengers. It may be calculated as a percentage of a single airline's seats, or of all seats in the industry. Once AMR's load factor exceeds its breakeven point, profit margins can expand dramatically as an ever-larger percentage of incremental revenue filters down to the bottom line. Load factor can also be calculated by dividing a carrier's revenue passenger-miles (RPMs) by its total available seats per mile (ASMs).

Exhibit 2 provides operating statistics for American Airlines (excluding TWA) and American Eagle for the years ending December 31, 2001, 2000, and 1999.

Exhibit 3 provides operating statistics for American Airlines (excluding TWA) and American Eagle for March 31, 2002, and March 31, 2001.

Marketing

AMR's advertising expenses were $202 million, $221 million, and $206 million for 2001, 2000, and 1999, respectively. One of the company's newer commercials promotes

EXHIBIT 2   AMR's Annual Operating Statistics

	2001	2000	1999
AMERICAN AIRLINES			
Revenue passenger miles (RPM) (in millions)	106,224	116,594	112,067
Available seats per mile (in millions)	153,035	161,030	161,211
Cargo ton miles (in millions)	2,058	2,280	2,068
Passenger load factor	69.4%	72.4%	69.5%
Breakeven load factor	78.1%	65.9%	63.8%
Passenger revenue yield per passenger mile (cents)	13.28	14.06	3.14
Passenger revenue per available seat mile (cents)	9.22	10.18	9.13
Cargo revenue yield per ton mile (cents)	0.24	31.31	30.70
Operating expenses per available seat mile (cents)	1.14	10.48	9.50
Operating aircraft at year-end	712	717	697
AMERICAN EAGLE			
Revenue passenger miles (in millions)	3,725	3,731	3,371
Available seats per mile (in millions)	6,471	6,256	5,640
Passenger load factor	57.6%	59.6%	59.8%
Operating aircraft at year-end	276	261	268

Source: **www.AA.com.**

EXHIBIT 3   AMR's Quarterly Operating Statistics

	March 31, 2002	March 31, 2001
AMERICAN AIRLINES		
Revenue passenger miles (in millions)	27,817	26,452
Available seats per mile (in millions)	40,089	38,977
Cargo ton miles (in millions)	463	549
Passenger load factor	87.4%	68.2%
Breakeven load factor	87.1%	65.4%
Passenger revenue yield per passenger mile (cents)	12.52	14.88
Passenger revenue per available seat mile (cents)	8.69	10.10
Cargo revenue yield per ton mile (cents)	28.74	31.68
Operating expenses per available seat mile (cents)	11.30	11.26
Fuel consumption (gallons, in millions)	745	743
Fuel price per gallon (cents)	61.2	87.6
Fuel price per gallon, excluding fuel taxes (cents)	61.7	82.0
Operating aircraft at period-end	852	719
AMERICAN EAGLE		
Revenue passenger miles (in millions)	919	860
Available seats per mile (in millions)	1,567	1,588
Passenger load factor	58.6%	54.2%
Operating aircraft at period-end	283	267

Source: **www.AA.com.**

the new "More Room Throughout Coach" feature of AMR flights. A key AMR marketing tool, the AAdvantage frequent flyer program, was created to develop passenger loyalty by offering awards to travelers for their continued patronage. The largest such program in the United States, AAdvantage members earn mileage credits for flights on American, American Eagle, and certain other participating airlines, or by utilizing services of other program participants, including hotels, car rental companies, and bank credit card issuers. American sells mileage credits and related services to the other companies participating in the program.

American has entered into a marketing alliance with America Online to offer AOL AAdvantage miles. The miles can be earned through services that AOL owns or promotes and can also be traded for retail products through AOL. Members can also earn miles from hotel and car rental companies as well as from participating retail and financial service organizations. Awards include travel prizes, upgrades, car rentals, special services, and retail purchases.

Price competition is a key marketing weapon that airlines commonly use to win a greater share of the leisure market. Fare differentials of just a few dollars can persuade leisure travelers to select one airline over another or to make their journeys by a different mode. To attract leisure travelers, airlines advertise deeply discounted fares. Analysts expect average fares to rise modestly in 2002 over 2001 levels as both the industry and the economy improve later in the year, a development which should help to stimulate demand.

The airline industry distributes tickets primarily through travel agents. However, it also books flights directly through company clerks and via the Internet. Travel agents generate about 70 percent to 80 percent of total airline bookings. Some 135,000 travel agents and 29,000 travel agencies operate in the United States. These numbers have been declining due to a more difficult operating environment—airlines have been reducing their commissions and competition from the Internet has been growing.

The fees paid to travel agents vary from airline to airline. In late 2001, most major airlines, including AMR, cut their commission rates to 5 percent of fares, with a $20 cap on domestic roundtrip fares ($100 cap for international); previously, the commission rate was 8 percent of fares with a $50 cap. As might be expected, this change led to a sharp decline in commissions paid in the fourth quarter of the year, a development which should continue in 2002 as the cut takes its toll. Total commissions paid in 2001 accounted for about 4.0 percent of airline industry costs, down from 6.2 percent in 2000 and as much as 10.9 percent in 1993. The majority of the tickets for travel on American and American Eagle are sold by travel agents.

E-commerce

Ever on the lookout for ways to cut costs, airlines have enthusiastically embraced "ticketless travel"—the practice of issuing electronic tickets, or e-tickets, to customers. E-tickets are booked in the conventional manner, through a travel agent or directly through the airline, though no paper ticket is issued. Instead, passengers obtain boarding passes at the airport check-in counter or from an automated dispensing machine, which is activated with a credit card or frequent-flyer card. Currently, e-tickets may account for close to 50 percent of all tickets, although Southwest issues 75 percent of its tickets electronically. According to United Airlines, electronic ticketing costs just 50 cents per ticket, versus $8 for paper tickets, because it eliminates fourteen accounting and processing procedures. Much of the savings comes from not having to mail actual tickets. Travelers can get a receipt and itinerary via fax or e-mail, or they can pick them up these items at the airport.

The continued boom in Internet travel purchases, combined with the lower commissions required by Internet travel providers, has greatly reduced American's distribution costs. American has formed agreements with several travel Web sites, including Travelocity.com, Expedia.com, Hotwire.com, Priceline.com, and Orbitz. However, American's own Internet distribution system, **www.AA.com**, continues to be the foundation of AMR's e-commerce strategy. AMR continues to expand the capabilities of AA.com. Not only can you plan and book your flight online, but flight status information is also available either online or by e-mail to your phone. AA.com seeks to be the consumer's one-stop source for travel planning and sales. AMR offers online travel resources such as maps as well as assistance for those, who reserve hotels and automobiles through its Car and Hotel Wizards. The AA.com site offers travel tips, news, and other information about air travel in its Travel Information Center. AA.com received over 10 million site visits each month in 2001. In addition, over 1.5 million consumers receive American's Net SAAver e-mails each week, which offer information about American's sales, specials, and programs. The base commission for sales through Internet travel providers is lower than through traditional travel agencies.

Orbitz ranks third behind Expedia and Travelocity in online travel bookings, and it displays all airline inventories, including special discounted Internet fares. At present, not all airlines participate in all computer reservation systems (CRSs), and not all online travel agents subscribe to all CRSs. Currently, about 45 airlines have signed up for Orbitz's service, including AMR. (Southwest Airlines does not do business with Orbitz, Expedia, or Travelocity.) Orbitz offers lower fares than other online travel agents do because it undercuts their commissions, often 3.5 percent of the fare. Travelocity and Expedia have an aggregate 30 percent of the online airline booking market.

Natural Environment and Social Responsibility

AMR was the first airline to formally adopt the CERES principles (**www.ceres.org**), which require an annual self-evaluation of how well the company addresses environmental issues, such as a reduction in and the disposal of waste, conservation, environmental restoration, and management commitment. American has been identified by the EPA as a potentially responsible party (PRP) at the Operating Industries, Inc., Superfund Site in California. American has also been identified as a PRP at the Beede Waste Oil Superfund Site in New Hampshire. Both American Airlines and American Eagle have a pollution problem at Miami International Airport (MIA), which is funding the remediation costs through landing fees and various cost-recovery methods.

American and Executive Airlines, along with other tenants at Luis Munoz Marin International Airport in San Juan, have been named as PRPs for environmental claims at the airport. American Eagle Airlines, Inc., has been notified of its potential liability under New York law at an inactive hazardous waste site in Poughkeepsie, New York.

American has been the recipient of many awards for its commitment to diversity. In 2001, American received recognition and awards from *Equal Employment Magazine*, *Hispanic Magazine*, the Women's Business Enterprise National Council, Gay Financial Network, and the Gay and Lesbian Values Index.

Fuel Concerns

Airlines are energy-intensive operations; in 2001, fuel costs accounted for about 14.9 percent of total airline expenses. One of the few positives for the industry in the wake of September 11, 2001, has been declining fuel costs. Domestic jet fuel reached a high of

91.0 cents per gallon in December 2000, 45 percent higher than the year-earlier period. For 2000, it averaged 78.7 cents per gallon, a 52 percent hike from 1999. In 2001, even before the attacks, a combination of lower crude oil prices, reduced consumption, and oil cartel overproduction helped push the price down. In August 2001, jet fuel prices had fallen to 76.5 cents per gallon. After the attacks, reduced demand for jet fuel pushed the price down even farther. Domestic jet fuel hit 66.0 cents per gallon in November 2001 and continued to drop into early 2002.

AMR has a fuel hedging program in which it enters into jet fuel, heating oil, and crude swap and option contracts to protect against increases in jet fuel prices, which has had the effect of reducing the firm's average cost per gallon. During 2001 and 2000, AMR's fuel hedging program reduced the firm's fuel expense by approximately $29 million and $545 million, respectively. To reduce the impact of potential fuel price increases in 2002, AMR has hedged approximately 40 percent of its estimated 2002 fuel requirements. Based on projected fuel usage, AMR estimates that a 10 percent increase in the price per gallon of fuel would result in an increase to aircraft fuel expense of approximately $169 million in 2002. AMR's fuel costs and consumption for the years 1999 through 2001 are provided in Exhibit 4.

Finance Issues

AMR's income statements and balance sheets for 2001 and 2000 are provided in Exhibit 5 and Exhibit 6, respectively. AMR's capital expenditures in 2001 totaled $3.6 billion, compared to $3.7 billion in 2000 and $3.5 billion in 1999. In 2001, American took delivery of 26 Boeing 737-800s, 13 Boeing 777-200ERs, and 16 Boeing 757-200s. AMR Eagle took delivery of 15 Embraer 140s, 7 Embraer 135s, 6 Embraer 145s, and 1 Bombardier CRJ-700 aircraft. These expenditures were financed primarily through secured mortgage and debt agreements. Ten Boeing 737-800 aircraft were financed through sale-leaseback transactions, and as a result, AMR received approximately $352 million in cash. Proceeds from the sale of equipment and property and other investments of $401 million included the proceeds received upon the delivery of five McDonnell Douglas MD-11 aircraft to FedEx.

In late 2001, AMR reached an agreement with Boeing for aircraft delivery deferrals, substitutions, and limited additional aircraft orders. As a direct result of the agreement with Boeing, AMR's 2002 and 2003 aircraft commitment amounts have been reduced, in the aggregate, by approximately $700 million. Following this agreement, at year-end 2001, AMR had commitments to acquire the following aircraft: 47 Boeing 737-800s, 14 Boeing 777-200ERs, 9 Boeing 767-300ERs, 7 Boeing 757-200s, 124 Embraer regional jets, and 24 Bombardier CRJ-700s. Deliveries of all aircraft

EXHIBIT 4	AMR's Fuel Costs		
Year	Gallons Consumed (in millions)	Total Cost (in millions)	Average Cost per Gallon (in cents)
1999	3,084	$1,696	55.0
2000	3,197	2,495	78.1
2001	3,461	2,888	81.4

Source: www.AA.com.

EXHIBIT 5   AMR Corporation—Consolidated Statements of Operations (in millions, except per-share amounts)

	Year Ended December 31,		
	2001	2000	1999
REVENUES			
Passenger—American Airlines	$15,780	$16,394	$14,724
AMR Eagle	1,378	1,452	1,294
Cargo	662	721	643
Other revenues	1,143	1,136	1,069
Total operating revenues	$18,963	$19,703	$17,730
EXPENSES			
Wages, salaries, and benefits	$8,032	$6,783	$6,120
Aircraft fuel	2,888	2,495	1,696
Depreciation and amortization	1,404	1,202	1,092
Other rentals and landing fees	1,197	999	942
Maintenance, materials, and repairs	1,165	1,095	1,003
Commissions to agents	835	1,037	1,162
Aircraft rentals	829	607	630
Food service	778	777	740
Other operating expenses	3,695	3,327	3,189
Special charges, net of U.S. government grant	610	–	–
Total operating expenses	$21,433	$18,322	$16,574
Operating income (loss)	(2,470)	1,381	1,156
OTHER INCOME (EXPENSE)			
Interest income	110	154	95
Interest expense	(538)	(467)	(393)
Interest capitalized	144	151	118
Miscellaneous—net	(2)	68	30
Total Other Income	(286)	(94)	(150)
Income (loss) from continuing operations before income taxes and extraordinary loss	(2,756)	1,287	1,006
Income tax provision (benefit)	(994)	508	350
Income (loss) from continuing operations before extraordinary loss	(1,762)	779	656
Income from discontinued operations, net of applicable income taxes and minority interest	–	43	265
Gain on sale of discontinued operations, net of applicable income taxes	–	–	64
Income (loss) before extraordinary loss	(1,762)	822	985
Extraordinary loss, net of applicable income taxes	–	(9)	–
Net earnings (loss)	$ (1,762)	$813	$985
Earnings (loss) applicable to common shares earnings (loss) per share	$ (1,762)	$813	$985
Basic			
Income (loss) from continuing operations	$ (11.43)	$5.20	$4.30
Discontinued operations	–	0.30	2.16
Extraordinary loss	–	(0.07)	–
Net earnings (loss)	$ (11.43)	$5.43	$6.46
Diluted			
Income (loss) from continuing operations	$ (11.43)	$4.81	$4.17
Discontinued operations	–	0.27	2.09
Extraordinary loss	–	(0.05)	–
Net earnings (loss)	$ (11.43)	$5.03	$6.26

Source: **www.AA.com.**

EXHIBIT 6   AMR Corporation—Consolidated Balance Sheets
                   (in millions, except shares and par value)

	December 31,	
	2001	*2000*
ASSETS		
CURRENT ASSETS		
Cash	$120	$89
Short-term investments	2,872	2,144
Receivables, less allowance for uncollectible		
accounts (2001—$52; 2000—$27)	1,414	1,303
Inventories, less allowance for obsolescence (2001—$383; 2000—$332)	822	757
Deferred income taxes	790	695
Other current assets	522	191
Total current assets	6,540	5,179
EQUIPMENT AND PROPERTY		
Flight equipment, at cost	21,707	20,041
Less accumulated depreciation	6,727	6,320
	14,980	13,721
Purchase deposits for flight equipment	929	1,700
Other equipment and property, at cost	4,202	3,639
Less accumulated depreciation	2,123	1,968
Subtotal	2,079	1,671
	17,988	17,092
EQUIPMENT AND PROPERTY UNDER CAPITAL LEASES		
Flight equipment	2,658	2,618
Other equipment and property	163	159
Subtotal	2,821	2,777
Less accumulated amortization	1,154	1,233
Subtotal	1,667	1,544
OTHER ASSETS		
Route acquisition costs and airport operating and gate lease rights,		
less accumulated amortization (2001—$556; 2000—$498)	1,325	1,143
Goodwill, less accumulated amortization (2001—$110; 2000—$83)	1,392	385
Other	3,929	870
	6,646	2,398
TOTAL ASSETS	$32,841	$26,213
LIABILITIES AND STOCKHOLDERS' EQUITY		
CURRENT LIABILITIES		
Accounts payable	$1,785	$1,267
Accrued salaries and wages	721	955
Accrued liabilities	1,471	1,276
Air traffic liability	2,763	2,696
Current maturities of long-term debt	556	569
Current obligations under capital leases	216	227
Total current liabilities	7,512	6,990
Long-term debt, less current maturities	8,310	4,151
Obligations under capital leases, less current obligations	1,524	1,323

EXHIBIT 6   **AMR Corporation—Consolidated Balance Sheets**
                   (in millions, except shares and par value) (*continued*)

| | *December 31,* | |
	2001	2000
LIABILITIES AND STOCKHOLDERS' EQUITY (*continued*)		
OTHER LIABILITIES AND CREDITS		
Deferred income taxes	1,627	2,385
Deferred gains	520	508
Postretirement benefits	2,538	1,706
Other liabilities and deferred credits	5,437	1,974
TOTAL	$10,122	$6,573
COMMITMENTS AND CONTINGENCIES		
STOCKHOLDERS' EQUITY		
Preferred stock–20,000,000 shares authorized; none issued	–	–
Common stock—$1 par value; 750,000,000 shares authorized;		
182,278,766 shares issued	182	182
Additional paid-in capital	2,865	2,911
Treasury shares at cost: 2001—27,794,380; 2000—30,216,218	(1,716)	(1,865)
Accumulated other comprehensive loss	(146)	(2)
Retained earnings	4,188	5,950
TOTAL	5,373	7,176
Total liabilities and stockholders' equity	$32,841	$26,213

Source: **www.AA.com**.

extend through 2008. Future payments for all aircraft, including the estimated amounts for price escalation will approximate $1.3 billion in 2002, $1.7 billion in 2003, $1.2 billion in 2004 and an aggregate of approximately $1.9 billion in 2005 through 2008. AMR's financial commitments to be paid in 2002 and 2003 are as follows:

NATURE OF COMMITMENT (IN MILLIONS)

	2002	2003
Operating lease payments for aircraft and facility obligations (*)	$1,336	$1,276
Firm aircraft commitments	1,300	1,700
Long-term debt (**)	556	296
Capital lease obligations (**)	326	243
Total obligations and commitments	$3,518	$3,515

Source: AMR's 2001 *Annual Report*.

AMR has announced that it will remove from service its remaining Boeing 717-200 fleet by June 2002 and its Boeing 727-200 fleet will be removed from service by May 2003. AMR has agreed to sell its McDonnell Douglas MD-11s to FedEx Corporation (FedEx), with delivery to be completed by the third quarter of 2002. The ten McDonnell Douglas DC-10 aircraft are currently being leased to Hawaiian Airlines, Inc. (Hawaiian), but upon termination of the lease agreement with Hawaiian, AMR has agreed to sell these aircraft to FedEx also. Deliveries began in early 2002. AMR is actively marketing its remaining non-operating aircraft and does not anticipate bringing these aircraft back into its operations.

Labor Issues

In 2001, American commenced negotiations with the Allied Pilots Association (APA). The AMR/APA contract limits the number of ASMs and block hours flown by American's regional carriers when pilots from American are on furlough. American Eagle continues to accept previously ordered regional jets. This will cause the ASM cap to be reached in the first half of 2002, necessitating actions to comply with that cap. American is working with its regional partners to ensure that it is in compliance with this provision. Toward that end, American Eagle is reducing the number of ASMs flown by its carriers, including, but not limited to (1) the removal of seats from its Saab and ATR aircraft, (2) the reduction in the number of turboprop aircraft, and (3) the reduction in the frequency of flights and/or its withdrawal from several routes across its network.

The Association of Flight Attendants (AFA), which represents the flight attendants of the Eagle carriers, reached an agreement with American Eagle, effective March 2, 1998, to have all flight attendants of the American Eagle carriers covered by a single contract. The agreement became amendable on September 2, 2001. However, the parties agreed to commence negotiations over amendments to the agreement in March 2001. The parties are still engaged in direct negotiations. The other union employees at the American Eagle carriers are covered by separate agreements with the Transport Workers Union, which were effective April 28, 1998, and are amendable April 28, 2003.

EXTERNAL ISSUES

For 2001, airline industry losses were a record $11 billion, and most U.S. airlines now face a severe liquidity crisis, have large new debt burdens, and have used up their credit lines. Investors are increasingly worried about airline balance sheet stability, especially in the wake of the Enron Corporation collaspe. For example, AMR Corp. ended 2001 with total debt of $16.1 billion and a debt to total capital ratio of 76 percent, both sharply higher than at the end of 2000. US Airways also had a sharp increase in debt, which totaled $3.7 billion at the end of 2001, and pushed its debt-to-total capital ratio well over 100 percent. The most recent U.S. airline to file for bankruptcy protection was Midway Airlines, which did so on August 13, 2001. A month later, Midway announced that it would permanently cease operations (liquidate).

In emergency mode after the September 11, 2001, terrorist attacks most U.S. airlines cut both capacity (scheduled takeoffs and landings) and staffing. According to the ATA, domestic carriers reduced head count by 80,300 employees after September 11. American and United led the group by furloughing 20,000 employees each, followed by US Airways (11,000), Northwest Airlines Corp. (10,000), and Continental Airlines Inc. (8,500). Of the major carriers, only Southwest Airlines and Alaska Air Group Inc. did not announce layoffs. United ended 2001 as the industry leader in terms of revenue passenger miles, but it was significantly behind American in terms of passenger revenues.

Standard & Poor's estimates that the U.S. airline industry took in revenues of $116.5 billion in 2001, a 10 percent decline from the $129.5 billion in revenues the industry recorded in 2000. About 72 percent of this total is derived from passenger fares. The remaining revenues derived from mail and cargo transport, and in-flight sales. Income from frequent flyer programs delivered another $35.9 billion. Domestic travel accounts for about 79 percent of passenger revenues, while international travel accounts for about 21 percent.

Competitors

Airlines are subject to vigorous competition, which often leads to cutthroat pricing and razor-thin margins. The largest domestic airline in 2001, based on carrier revenues, was

American Airlines, a unit of AMR Corp. American reported 2001 operating revenues of almost $19.0 billion (including its American Eagle unit), which equaled approximately 16 percent of total industry revenues. United Airlines, a unit of UAL Corp., took second place with revenues of $16.1 billion (about 14 percent). Delta Air Lines Inc. followed with $13.9 billion (approximately 12 percent). In terms of traffic, according to DOT data, the top ten carriers logged an estimated 590.0 billion RPMs in 2001. United was number one, tallying 116.6 billion RPMs. American ranked second, with 108.4 billion RPMs, followed by Delta with 97.3 billion RPMs.

AMR faces intense competition from other airlines, including Alaska Airlines, America West Airlines, Continental Airlines, Delta, Northwest Airlines, Southwest Airlines, United, and US Airways, all as well as from of their affiliated regional carriers. Of the nine major airlines, only Southwest posted a profit in 2001. Southwest earned $511 million in 2001, a 19 percent decline from the $627 million profit the company posted in 2000. Southwest was the only carrier that kept its capacity and employee count intact after September 11, a development made possible by the airline's high efficiency levels, low-cost operating structure, and profitable route schedule. Southwest remains profitable in 2002.

AMR also competes with cargo and charter air carriers and as well as with automobiles, buses, and the Amtrak rail system. Amtrak fares are partly subsidized by the U.S. government (though Amtrak has been mandated to reach self-sufficiency by December 2, 2002). While Amtrak operates some long-distance routes, its passengers use it for an average journey length of about 280 miles. Intercity bus travel, although much more popular than railroads, rarely competes directly with air travel because the typical bus journey is just 140 miles.

Airlines compete aggressively with each other in both service and price. For business travelers, flight frequency and reliability are critical; frequent-flyer programs, cuisine, and other amenities also are influential. Small airlines that cannot obtain gate space during peak travel periods have difficulty attracting business travelers.

Security Issues

Although the U.S. government federalized all airport security screening as of February 17, 2002, airline security costs have risen dramatically in the past year. Security today ranges from the securing of all cockpit doors to the opening of extra security lanes to ease the logjam caused by stricter screening requirements. Airlines are now required either to screen all bags for explosives or to make sure each bag on a plane is matched up to a passenger seated on that flight; both of these requirements are time-consuming and expensive. By the end of 2002, all checked bags will have to pass through bomb detection machines, which cost up to $1 million each and are currently in short supply. While necessary to ensure passenger safety and to ease fears, these expenses will cut into airline profits for the foreseeable future.

Effective February 1, 2002, a $2.50 per enplanement security service fee (a $5 oneway maximum fee) is collected by all air carriers and submitted to the government to pay for enhanced security measures. Additionally, air carriers may soon be required to submit to the government an amount equal to the amount the air carriers paid for screening passengers and property in 2000. After that, this fee may be assessed based on the air carrier's market share.

Much secrecy has surrounded the Federal Air Marshal Program, which was sent into overdrive following the September 11, 2001, terrorist attacks. Operated by the Federal Aviation Administration (FAA), the program deploys specially trained, armed teams of security specialists on both domestic and international flights. While the number of total marshals in place and their itineraries remain unknown, the FAA says that it has taken steps to sharply increase the number of marshals on flights.

Regional Jet Services

Regional jet services have grown rapidly in recent years. The Regional Air Service Initiative (RASI), a Web site that tracks these operations, estimated that by the end of 2001, some 800 regional jets were in operation in the United States. In 1997, there were 137. RASI reports that 946 regional jets are on firm or conditional order, while 1,193 units are under option. This implies that future growth in regional jets should be strong. Including turboprop planes, the nation's total regional fleet was 2,300 aircraft in early 2002, a total that has remained relatively unchanged over the previous two years.

More than a dozen low-fare startup carriers currently operate, and a half-dozen others are in the planning stages. JetBlue Airways, which is the biggest threat to industry price stability since the emergence of Southwest Airlines, began flying out of New York City's Kennedy International Airport in February 2000. JetBlue is well capitalized, uses spanking new jets, and has been generating high load factors since its launch.

Regional jets can be credited with getting people out of cars, buses, and trains, and onto planes. According to Bombardier, regional jets are used to supplement existing regional service (44 percent), create new nonstop regional service (33 percent), replace mainline jet service (15 percent), and replace turboprop service (8 percent). With its low purchase and operating costs, the regional jet has made short-haul markets, previously abandoned by major airlines, into viable destinations. The regional jet also offers greater comfort and range than does the turboprop plane. It can handle routes of 1,300 miles, up to 2,300 nautical miles in some cases, while most propeller planes are confined to flights of 350 miles or less.

The regional affiliates of major airlines use regional jets to provide off-peak service when demand is insufficient to warrant a standard one-hundred-plus seat aircraft. Regional jets can be profitable for such service because their breakeven point is a 50 percent load factor, versus about 63 percent for large jets. By offering round-the-clock service in this manner, an airline will appeal to business travelers, who account for 70 percent of regional jet passengers. With regional jets gaining in passenger capacity (seventy or more seats) and range, they are increasingly being used not only to feed passengers into hub airports but also to provide point-to-point competition against carriers employing full-sized jets.

Having recognized the value of the regional carriers, the major airlines have taken steps to increase their control over such companies. Many have acquired partial or total equity positions in carriers with a strong regional jet presence. Among the majors, Delta is perhaps the most active player in the regional market. In early 2000, Delta acquired Comair, whose entire fleet consists of regional jets and Atlantic Southeast Airlines (ASA). AMR owns the largest regional carrier, American Eagle, which is the holding company for Executive Airlines, Flagship Airlines, Simmons Airlines, and Wings West Airlines. The FAA predicts that the nation's regional aircraft fleet will reach twenty-five hundred by 2006, up from twenty-three hundred in 2002.

All pilot contracts have scope clauses, which establish the definition (scope) of a pilot's jobs and stipulates who may and may not perform those jobs. Scope clauses in existing labor contracts will severely limit the ability of some airlines to participate in the regional jet market boom. American Eagle, for instance, can fly regional jets, but its scope clause limits such aircraft to forty-five seats or fewer. In April 2000, US Airways' new pilots' contract doubled the number of regional jets the airline could operate to seventy. The company, however, would like to operate four hundred. Delta Air Lines can operate as many regional jets as it likes, provided none has more than seventy seats. In March 2000, Delta ordered nearly 400 regional jet aircraft, worth $10 billion. Although this move may enable the carrier to step boldly into regional operations, Delta may also have bought itself some labor trouble, as its mainline pilots insist on limiting the carrier's use of regional jets.

The only airlines whose labor contracts carry no restrictions on aircraft use are Continental Airlines (which flies regional jets through its 100 percent-owned Continental Express affiliate), Alaska Air, America West, and Southwest. All airlines with restrictive scope clauses in their pilots' agreements are working to get relief. As pilot contracts come up for renewal, the airlines are trying to gain more flexibility with regard to flying regional jets. Many observers see the biggest emerging segment of the regional jet market in 70–100 seat aircraft, which are just now beginning to roll out of the assembly lines. However, pilots at mainline carriers, who make substantially higher salaries than those at regional operators, worry that their routes will be displaced by regional affiliates operating these larger jets.

Technology and Internet Issues

The air travel industry is capital-, labor-, and technology-intensive. Despite the Internet's considerable size and commercial potential, accurate measurements of the amount of air travel being booked online are hard to come by. Jupiter Communications, a New York-based research firm covering the consumer online industry, estimates that the percentage of airline tickets sold online will reach 11 percent by 2003, up from an estimated 7 percent in 2001. Forrester Research, a technology research firm headquartered in Cambridge, Massachusetts, estimates that total online travel bookings (which includes cruises, hotels, and car rentals as well as air travel) will reach $29 billion by 2003, up from $14.2 billion in 2001.

Southwest Airlines has for years led the industry in this area, obtaining 40 percent of its revenues from Internet sales. Southwest's secret is to offer customers one free round-trip ticket for every four round-trip tickets booked through its Web site. America West does about 12 percent of its business online, whereas Continental Airlines and United are the industry laggards at only 3 percent and 4 percent, respectively.

The Internet's appeal for airlines is apparent. A commercial Web site can be kept open for business twenty-four hours a day, seven days a week. It allows an airline to reduce the number of customer service agents, since fewer such employees are needed to field flight information questions. Southwest Airlines reported in 2002 that each Internet booking cost it about $1, whereas its cost to book with a travel agent is between $6 and $8. Tickets booked through Southwest's own agents cost several dollars. Indeed, a big incentive for airlines to distribute tickets via the Internet is the fact that such transactions allow them to eliminate travel agent commissions.

On the down side, the Internet may hurt airlines by making travelers very price-sensitive. With airfares changing at lightning speed and the Internet keeping customers apprised of such fares, airlines must respond quickly to match rivals' fare cuts. Consequently, the range of fares that competing airlines can charge on a point-to-point route will tend to be extremely compressed.

Globalization

While U.S. airlines still see international markets as an avenue for growth, a slowdown in Asia/Pacific markets has not allowed that growth to materialize in recent years. International travel, defined here as flights between the United States and a second nation, encompasses both business and leisure travel. In 2001, international travel accounted for 11.4 percent of enplanements for U.S. airlines, versus 11.0 percent in 2000, according to the ATA. Because the average stage (or flight) length is nearly four times longer for international than for domestic flights, international travel generates a disproportionately high level of revenue: 20.8 percent of the industry's total passenger revenues in 2000 (latest available) and 20.4 percent of 1999 total passenger revenues.

Many foreign nations see increased airline competition as a way to boost tourism and commerce because it lowers the cost of air travel. Nations such as China, with state-controlled airlines, have been more reluctant to enter open skies agreements than those with privately owned commercial aviation systems. By early 2002, 97 nations had signed agreements with the United States, the most recent being Sri Lanka in November 2001. Not all of these aviation pacts provide for unfettered competition, but all move strongly in that direction, providing for phased-in deregulation. These agreements provide for reduced economic regulation and unrestricted code-sharing between international carriers, the formation of alliances, and at least partial ownership rights.

The European Union (EU) objects to the piecemeal approach the United States takes to airline deregulation. Instead, if favors the negotiation of a single bilateral aviation agreement between the United States and the European Union and the elimination of individual aviation treaties between the United States and European nations. The European Court of Justice will issue a final ruling later in 2002.

Business Before Pleasure

The airline industry has turned the commercial world into one big marketplace. Many businesspeople use air travel to make sales trips, visit far-flung factories, and attend industry conventions. Because business trips are often scheduled within seven days of the flight, business travelers tend to pay full fare, whether in coach or first class. Because their firms pick up the tab, these travelers tend to be relatively price-insensitive. However, corporations have become more cost-conscious in recent years as business fares have climbed significantly faster than leisure fares.

Airlines actively solicit the business traveler. Many larger aircraft contain designated business sections with roomy seats and premium food service. Recently, airlines have expanded their business-class sections. Airlines compete for business passengers by offering priority check-in, expedited baggage handling, luxurious airport lounges, and in-flight amenities such as faxes, telephones, and power outlets for recharging laptop computers. To appeal to this class of traveler, airlines must provide frequent flights, reliable on-time performance, and top safety records.

In marked contrast to the business traveler, the leisure traveler is highly price-sensitive. The cheaper fares resulting from deregulation have allowed people from all walks of life to travel by air to visit distant friends and relatives or to take more frequent vacations. Leisure travelers can secure discount fares in two ways. First, low fares are available to individuals who book flights at least twenty-one days in advance. Second, deeply discounted fares are also available (mainly through the Internet) a few days before departure. Commonly, leisure travelers defer making any trip arrangements until a fare sale is offered. The upshot of these patterns is that over short periods, leisure travel can be erratic. Over the longer term, leisure travel is more cyclical than business travel; it waxes and wanes together with consumer sentiment and disposable income levels.

Cargo and Cocktails

All passenger aircraft also are capable of carrying cargo, but most freight tends to move on wide-body jets on long stage lengths. Major airlines carry significantly more mail and cargo in the belly space under the passenger cabin than do regional and commuter airlines. Passenger airlines view freight transport as a byproduct of their main business, and they charge discounted rates compared with those charged by specialized air freight carriers. Lacking sales forces to pursue this business, the airlines often accept freight from only a few air forwarders. Some airlines, having more cargo demand than belly space, lease freighter aircraft to their customers. Among passenger airlines, Northwest generated the most revenue from cargo in 2001—about $715 million. This represented about 7 percent of the carrier's 2001 revenues. Cargo and mail together accounted for just 3.7 percent of the industry's total revenues in 2001.

In addition to income from fares and freight, airlines generate revenues from the sale of in-flight alcoholic beverages and various amenities and services. The "other" revenue category may also include income from international code-sharing programs. On long-haul flights, most carriers provide telephone, automated teller machine (ATM), fax, and television and entertainment services for a fee. Some international flights even offer video gambling. Although such supplementary sales carry high margins, they account for a relatively small portion of industry revenues.

Labor Unions

Labor is the industry's largest single airline expense, accounting for about 48 percent of total costs in 2001, up sharply from 34.9 percent in 2000. Labor costs should decline sharply both on an absolute basis and as a percentage of revenues in 2002. More than eighty-thousand employees were laid off by the airlines in late 2001, and the airlines are negotiating concessions with most major unions to help them through the current downturn.

Employment can be divided into several broad craft positions: flight crews (pilots and engineers), flight attendants, ground service (including baggage handlers), dispatchers, maintenance, and customer service (bookings and boardings). Most airline workers belong to one of a dozen major unions. The larger unions include the Association of Flight Attendants, the Allied Pilots Association, and the International Association of Machinists and Aerospace Workers. At any given time, a half-dozen or more contracts may be in negotiation.

The downsizing of the U.S. Air Force—the main if not the sole source of experienced pilots—is reducing the number of pilots who are available to fly civilian planes. The resulting shortage of qualified pilots has led to outsized gains in recent pilot union contracts. For example, in October 2000, United's pilots won a four-year pact giving them a 23.8 percent raise retroactive to April of that year, with an additional 4.5 percent raise to come in each of the subsequent years. The contract pushed United's pilots to the top of the industry pay scale. First-year pension contributions increased from 1 percent of pay under the old contract to 11 percent in the new contract.

To lure new pilots to their ranks, major airlines are raiding lower-paid pilots at regional carriers. Airlines also hope to alleviate the shortage by getting Congress to raise the mandatory retirement age to sixty-five from sixty. Unless this happens, pilot pay will continue to experience upward pressure. In addition, because pilot contracts tend to set the pattern for other craft unions in the industry, labor unrest will increase as other workers demand comparable percentages in their own pay hikes.

Regulation

Federal regulation of domestic airline fares and markets ended with the Airline Deregulation Act of 1978. However, the DOT and its affiliated agency, the FAA, continue to regulate the industry with regard to safety, labor, operating procedures, and aircraft fitness and emission levels. The International Civil Aviation Organization (ICAO), an entity affiliated with the United Nations, proposes noise standards, although the standards aren't legally binding in a given country unless the country has formally agreed to them.

CONCLUSION

Standard & Poor's puts a low probability on future merger deals being struck between any of the nation's largest air carriers. Given the industry's overcapacity, weakened balance sheets, and high debt levels, analysts feel that the largest airlines will seek to shrink capacity, conserve cash, and restore profitability before seeking to acquire other firms. The industry's dramatic downturn after the September 11, 2001, terrorist attacks has focused management attention on restoring industry profitability rather than on mergers. However, the American/TWA merger was completed in December 2001, and there are airlines now that could be acquired at bargain prices.

The airline industry has extremely high fixed costs. When revenue declines, expenses stay close to constant. When there is a gradual decline in passenger traffic, management has time to gradually reduce costs. But after September 11, 2001, the gradual decline due to an economic slowdown was converted into a plummeting fall. AMR and other airlines are now in a very tenuous financial position. Survival of AMR itself is dependent upon an effective strategic plan.

With industry load factors far below industry breakeven load factors, it is apparent that there will be dramatic changes in the airline industry. Reductions in capacity and employee layoffs have not reversed continuing losses. Other measures must be taken. Should AMR cut more routes? How many should be cut? If AMR cuts too deeply, it will lose needed revenue. If it does not cut enough, then high fixed costs could sink the company. Route decisions are hampered by the fact that it is difficult to determine when a route will return to profitability. A route currently losing money may become profitable in the next quarter. If capacity is cut further, AMR may not have the infrastructure (planes, slots, gates, people) to provide services if demand increases.

Perhaps AMR should view the current situation as a growth opportunity and take advantage of the failure other airlines. Should AMR expand routes as others abandon routes and buy planes as others sell planes? CEO Donald Carty announced in April 2002 that AMR will recall about forty-five hundred workers by the end of the year. He announced in June 2002 that AMR is adding service from Boston to Port-au-Prince, Haiti, and to the Turks and Caicos Islands in the Caribbean; it is also adding service from New York to Grand Cayman. AMR also just added new nonstop service from New York to Tokyo.

With billion-dollar annual losses and billion-dollar debt obligations, AMR is indeed in trouble. AMR's traffic decreased another 15.9 percent in April 2002 on a capacity decrease of 13.3 percent. Without a clear strategic plan and successful implementation, AMR will perish, and thousands of people will be out of work. Then terrorists, who do not like the name American anyway, could claim another victory if AMR fails. Develop a clear strategic plan for AMR's CEO Donald Carty.

NOTES

1. AMR's 2001 *Annual Report.*
2. Parts of this section are taken from S&P Airline *Industry Surveys,* March 28, 2002. Used with permission of S&P.

EXPERIENTIAL EXERCISES

**EXPERIENTIAL
EXERCISE 1A** ▶

Strategy Analysis for
American Airlines
(AMR)

PURPOSE

The purpose of this exercise is to give you experience identifying an organization's opportunities, threats, strengths, and weaknesses. This information is vital to generating and selecting among alternative strategies.

INSTRUCTIONS

Step 1   Identify what you consider to be AMR's major opportunities, threats, strengths, and weaknesses. On a separate sheet of paper, list these key factors under separate headings. Describe each factor in specific terms.

Step 2   Through class discussion, compare your lists of external and internal factors to those developed by other students. From the discussion, add to your lists of factors. Keep this information for use in later exercises.

**EXPERIENTIAL
EXERCISE 1B** ▶

Developing a Code of
Business Ethics for
American Airlines
(AMR)

PURPOSE

This exercise can give you practice in developing a code of business ethics. Research was conducted to examine codes of business ethics from large manufacturing and service firms in the United States. The twenty-eight variables that follow were found to be included in a sample of more than eighty codes of business ethics. The variables are presented in order of how frequently they occurred. Thus, the first variable, "conduct business in compliance with all laws," was most often included in the sample documents; "firearms at work are prohibited" was least often included.

1.   Conduct business in compliance with all laws.
2.   Payments for unlawful purposes are prohibited.
3.   Avoid outside activities that impair duties.
4.   Comply with all antitrust and trade regulations.
5.   Comply with accounting rules and controls.
6.   Bribes are prohibited.
7.   Maintain confidentiality of records.
8.   Participate in community and political activities.
9.   Provide products and services of the highest quality.
10. Exhibit standards of personal integrity and conduct.
11. Do not propagate false or misleading information.
12. Perform assigned duties to the best of your ability.
13. Conserve resources and protect the environment.
14. Comply with safety, health, and security regulations.
15. Racial, ethnic, religious, and sexual harassment at work is prohibited.
16. Report unethical and illegal activities to your manager.
17. Convey true claims in product advertisements.
18. Make decisions without regard for personal gain.
19. Do not use company property for personal benefit.
20. Demonstrate courtesy, respect, honesty, and fairness.
21. Illegal drugs and alcohol at work are prohibited.

22. Manage personal finances well.
23. Employees are personally accountable for company funds.
24. Exhibit good attendance and punctuality.
25. Follow directives of supervisors.
26. Do not use abusive language.
27. Dress in businesslike attire.
28. Firearms at work are prohibited.[1]

INSTRUCTIONS

Step 1 On a separate sheet of paper, write a code of business ethics for AMR. Include as many variables listed above as you believe appropriate to AMR's business. Limit your document to one hundred words or less.

Step 2 Read your code of ethics to the class. Comment on why you did or did not include certain variables.

Step 3 Explain why having a code of ethics is not sufficient for ensuring ethical behavior in an organization. What else does it take?

NOTES

1. DONALD ROBIN, MICHAEL GIALLOURAKIS, FRED R. DAVID, and THOMAS E. MORITZ. "A Different Look at Codes of Ethics," *Business Horizons* 32, no. 1 (January–February 1989): 66–73.

**EXPERIENTIAL
EXPERIENTIAL
EXERCISE 1C ▶**

**The Ethics of Spying
on Competitors**

PURPOSE

This exercise gives you an opportunity to discuss ethical and legal issues in class as related to methods being used by many companies to spy on competing firms. Gathering and using information about competitors is an area of strategic management that Japanese firms do more proficiently than American firms.

INSTRUCTIONS

On a separate sheet of paper, number from 1 to 18. For the 18 spying activities listed below, indicate whether or not you believe the activity is Ethical or Unethical and Legal or Illegal. Place either an *E* for ethical or *U* for unethical, and either an *L* for legal or an *I* for illegal for each activity. Compare your answers to your classmates', and discuss any differences.

1. Buying competitors' garbage.
2. Dissecting competitors' products.
3. Taking competitors' plant tours anonymously.
4. Counting tractor-trailer trucks leaving competitors' loading bays.
5. Studying aerial photographs of competitors' facilities.
6. Analyzing competitors' labor contracts.
7. Analyzing competitors' help-wanted ads.
8. Quizzing customers and buyers about the sales of competitors' products.
9. Infiltrating customers' and competitors' business operations.
10. Quizzing suppliers about competitors' level of manufacturing.
11. Using customers to buy out phony bids.
12. Encouraging key customers to reveal competitive information.

13. Quizzing competitors' former employees.
14. Interviewing consultants who may have worked with competitors.
15. Hiring key managers away from competitors.
16. Conducting phony job interviews to get competitors' employees to reveal information.
17. Sending engineers to trade meetings to quiz competitors' technical employees.
18. Quizzing potential employees who worked for or with competitors.

EXPERIENTIAL EXERCISE 1D ▶

Strategic Planning for My University

PURPOSE

External and internal factors are the underlying bases of strategies formulated and implemented by organizations. Your college or university faces numerous external opportunities/threats and has many internal strengths/weaknesses. The purpose of this exercise is to illustrate the process of identifying critical external and internal factors.

External influences include trends in the following areas: economic, social, cultural, demographic, environmental, technological, political, legal, governmental, and competitive. External factors could include declining numbers of high school graduates; population shifts; community relations; increased competitiveness among colleges and universities; rising numbers of adults returning to college; decreased support from local, state, and federal agencies; and increasing numbers of foreign students attending American colleges.

Internal factors of a college or university include faculty, students, staff, alumni, athletic programs, the physical plant, grounds and maintenance, student housing, administration, fundraising, academic programs, food services, parking, placement, clubs, fraternities, sororities, and public relations.

INSTRUCTIONS

Step 1   On a separate sheet of paper, make four headings: External Opportunities, External Threats, Internal Strengths, and Internal Weaknesses.

Step 2   As related to your college or university, list five factors under each of the four headings.

Step 3   Discuss the factors as a class. Write the factors on the board.

Step 4   What new things did you learn about your university from the class discussion? How could this type of discussion benefit an organization?

EXPERIENTIAL EXERCISE 1E ▶

Strategic Planning at a Local Company

PURPOSE

This activity is aimed at giving you practical knowledge about how organizations in your city or town are doing strategic planning. This exercise also will give you experience interacting on a professional basis with local business leaders.

INSTRUCTIONS

Step 1   Use the telephone to contact business owners or top managers. Find an organization that does strategic planning. Make an appointment to visit with the strategist (president, chief executive officer, or owner) of that business.

Step 2   Seek answers to the following questions during the interview:

   a. How does your firm formally conduct strategic planning? Who is involved in the process?

b. Does your firm have a written mission statement? How was the statement developed? When was the statement last changed?

c. What are the benefits of engaging in strategic planning?

d. What are the major costs or problems in doing strategic planning in your business?

e. Do you anticipate making any changes in the strategic planning process at your company? If yes, please explain.

Step 3   Report your findings to the class.

EXPERIENTIAL EXERCISE 1F ▶

Does My University Recruit in Foreign Countries?

PURPOSE

A competitive climate is emerging among colleges and universities around the world. Colleges and universities in Europe and Japan are increasingly recruiting American students to offset declining enrollments. Foreign students already make up more than one-third of the student body at many American universities. The purpose of this exercise is to identify particular colleges and universities in foreign countries that represent a competitive threat to American institutions of higher learning.

INSTRUCTIONS

Step 1   Select a foreign country. Conduct research to determine the number and nature of colleges and universities in that country. What are the major educational institutions in that country? What programs are those institutions recognized for offering? What percentage of undergraduate and graduate students attending those institutions are American? Do these institutions actively recruit American students?

Step 2   Prepare a report for the class that summarizes your research findings. Present your report to the class.

EXPERIENTIAL EXERCISE 1G ▶

Getting Familiar with SMCO

PURPOSE

This exercise is designed to get you familiar with the Strategic Management Club Online (SMCO), which offers many benefits for the strategy student.

INSTRUCTIONS

Step 1   Go to the **www.strategyclub.com** Web site. Review the various sections of this site.

Step 2   Select a section of the SMCO site that you feel will be most useful to you in this class. Write a one-page summary of that section and why you feel it will benefit you most.

2

THE BUSINESS MISSION

CHAPTER OUTLINE

- What Do We Want to Become?
- What Is Our Business?
- Importance of Vision and Mission Statements
- Characteristics of a Mission Statement
- Components of a Mission Statement
- Writing and Evaluating Mission Statements

EXPERIENTIAL EXERCISE 2A
Evaluating Mission Statements

EXPERIENTIAL EXERCISE 2B
Writing a Vision and Mission Statement for American Airlines (AMR)

EXPERIENTIAL EXERCISE 2C
Writing a Vision and Mission Statement for My University

EXPERIENTIAL EXERCISE 2D
Conducting Mission Statement Research

CHAPTER OBJECTIVES

After studying this chapter, you should be able to do the following:

1. Describe the nature and role of vision and mission statements in strategic management.
2. Discuss why the process of developing a mission statement is as important as the resulting document.
3. Identify the components of mission statements.
4. Discuss how clear vision and mission statements can benefit other strategic-management activities.
5. Evaluate mission statements of different organizations.
6. Write good vision and mission statements.

NOTABLE QUOTES

A business is not defined by its name, statutes, or articles of incorporation. It is defined by the business mission. Only a clear definition of the mission and purpose of the organization makes possible clear and realistic business objectives.

PETER DRUCKER

A corporate vision can focus, direct, motivate, unify, and even excite a business into superior performance. The job of a strategist is to identify and project a clear vision.

JOHN KEANE

Where there is no vision, the people perish.

PROVERBS 29:18

Customers are first, employees second, shareholders third, and the community fourth. That's the credo at H. B. Fuller, the century-old adhesives maker in St. Paul.

PATRICIA SELLERS

For strategists, there's a trade-off between the breadth and detail of information needed. It's a bit like an eagle hunting for a rabbit. The eagle has to be high enough to scan a wide area in order to enlarge his chances of seeing prey, but he has to be low enough to see the detail—the movement and features that will allow him to recognize his target. Continually making this trade-off is the job of a strategist—it simply can't be delegated.

FREDERICK GLUCK

The best laid schemes of mice and men often go awry.

ROBERT BURNS (paraphrased)

A strategist's job is to see the company not as it is . . . but as it can become.

JOHN W. TEETS, CHAIRMAN OF GREYHOUND, INC.

That business mission is so rarely given adequate thought is perhaps the most important single cause of business frustration.

PETER DRUCKER

Vision is the art of seeing things invisible.

JONATHAN SWIFT

The very essence of leadership is that you have to have vision. You can't blow an uncertain trumpet.

THEODORE HESBURGH

Some men see things as they are and say why. I dream of things that never were and say why not.

JOHN F. KENNEDY

This chapter focuses on the concepts and tools needed to evaluate and write business vision and mission statements. A practical framework for developing mission statements is provided. Actual mission statements from large and small organizations and for-profit and nonprofit enterprises are presented and critically examined. The process of creating a vision and mission statement is discussed.

We can perhaps best understand vision and mission by focusing on a business when it is first started. In the beginning, a new business is simply a collection of ideas. Starting a new business rests on a set of beliefs that the new organization can offer some product or service to some customers, in some geographic area, using some type of technology, at a profitable price. A new business owner typically believes that the management philosophy of the new enterprise will result in a favorable public image and that this concept of the business can be communicated to, and will be adopted by, important constituencies. When the set of beliefs about a business at its inception is put into writing, the resulting document mirrors the same basic ideas that underlie the vision and mission statements. As a business grows, owners or managers find it necessary to revise the founding set of beliefs, but those original ideas usually are reflected in the revised statements of vision and mission.

Vision and mission statements often can be found in the front of annual reports. They often are displayed throughout a firm's premises and are distributed with company information sent to constituencies. The statements are part of numerous internal reports, such as loan requests, supplier agreements, labor relations contracts, business plans, and customer service agreements. In a recent study, researchers concluded that 90 percent of all companies have used a mission statement sometime in the previous five years.[1]

 ## WHAT DO WE WANT TO BECOME?

It is especially important for managers and executives in any organization to agree upon the basic vision that the firm strives to achieve in the long term. A vision statement should answer the basic question, "What do we want to become?" A clear vision provides the foundation for developing a comprehensive mission statement. Many organizations have both a vision and mission statement, but the vision statement should be established first and foremost. The vision statement should be short, preferably one sentence, and as many managers as possible should have input into developing the statement.

Several example vision statements are provided below and in Table 2–1.

VISIT THE NET

Gives an introduction to the vision concept. http://www.csuchico.edu/mgmt/strategy/module1/sld007.htm

The Vision of the National Pawnbrokers Association is to have complete and vibrant membership that enjoys a positive public and political image and is the focal organization of all pawn associations.—National Pawnbrokers Association (**http://npa.ploygon.net**)

Our Vision as an independent community financial institution is to achieve superior long-term shareholder value, exercise exemplary corporate citizenship, and create an environment which promotes and rewards employee development and the consistent delivery of quality service to our customers.—First Reliance Bank of Florence, South Carolina

At CIGNA, we intend to be the best at helping our customers enhance and extend their lives and protect their financial security. Satisfying customers is the key to meeting employee needs and shareholder expectations, and will enable CIGNA to build on our reputation as a financially strong and highly respected company. (**www.cigna.com**)

TABLE 2-1   Vision and Mission Statement Examples

THE BELLEVUE HOSPITAL

Vision Statement

The Bellevue Hospital is the LEADER in providing resources necessary to realize the community's highest level of HEALTH throughout life.

Mission Statement

The Bellevue Hospital, with *respect, compassion, integrity, and courage,* honors the individuality and confidentiality of our patients, employees, and community, and is progressive in anticipating and providing future health care services.

U.S. POULTRY & EGG ASSOCIATION

Vision Statement

A national organization which represents its members in all aspects of poultry and eggs on both a national and an international level.

Mission Statement:

1. We will partner with our affiliated state organizations to attack common problems.
2. We are committed to the advancement of all areas of research and education in poultry technology.
3. The International Poultry Exposition must continue to grow and be beneficial to both exhibitors and attendees.
4. We must always be responsive and effective to the changing needs of our industry.
5. Our imperatives must be such that we do not duplicate the efforts of our sister organizations.
6. We will strive to constantly improve the quality and safety of poultry products.

We will continue to increase the availability of poultry products.

JOHN DEERE, INC.

Vision Statement

John Deere is committed to providing Genuine Value to the company's stakeholders, including our customers, dealers, shareholders, employees, and communities. In support of that commitment, Deere aspires to:

- Grow and pursue leadership positions in each of our businesses.
- Extend our preeminent leadership position in the agricultural equipment market worldwide.
- Create new opportunities to leverage the John Deere brand globally.

Mission Statement

John Deere has grown and prospered through a long-standing partnership with the world's most productive farmers. Today, John Deere is a global company with several equipment operations and complementary service businesses. These businesses are closely interrelated, providing the company with significant growth opportunities and other synergistic benefits.

MANLEY BAPTIST CHURCH

The Vision of Manley Baptist Church is to be the people of God, on mission with God, motivated by a love for God, and a love for others.

The Mission of Manley Baptist Church is to help people in the Lakeway area become fully developed followers of Jesus Christ.

U.S. GEOLOGICAL SURVEY (USGS)

The Vision of USGS is to be a world leader in the natural sciences through our scientific excellence and responsiveness to society's needs.

The mission of USGS is to serve the Nation by providing reliable scientific information to

Continued

TABLE 2-1 **Vision and Mission Statement Examples** (*continued*)

- describe and understand the Earth
- minimize loss of life and property from natural disasters
- manage water, biological, energy, and mineral resources; and enhance and protect our quality of life

MASSACHUSETTS DIVISION OF BANKS

Vision Statement

To protect the public interest, ensure competition, accessibility and fairness within the relevant financial services industries, respond innovatively to a rapidly changing environment, and foster a positive impact on the Commonwealth's economy.

Mission Statement

To maintain a safe and sound competitive banking and financial services environment throughout the Commonwealth and ensure compliance with community reinvestment and consumer protection laws by chartering, licensing and supervising state regulated financial institutions in a professional and innovative manner.

OHIO DIVISION OF HAZARDOUS WASTE MANAGEMENT

Vision Statement

Ohio's Division of Hazardous Waste Management is recognized as a leader among state hazardous waste management programs through our expertise, effectiveness, application of sound science, and delivery of quality service to out stakeholders.

Mission Statement

The Division of Hazardous Waste Management protects and improves the environment and therefore the health of Ohio's citizens by promoting pollution prevention and the proper management and cleanup of hazardous waste. We provide quality service to our stakeholders by assisting them in understanding and complying with the hazardous waste management regulations, and by implementing our program effectively.

ATLANTA WEB PRINTERS, INC.

Vision Statement

To be the first choice in the printed communications business. The first choice is the best choice, and *being the best* is what Atlanta Web *pledges* to work hard at being—*every day!*

Mission Statement

- to make our clients feel welcome, appreciated, and worthy of our best efforts in everything we do . . . each and every day
- to be recognized as an exceptional leader in our industry and community
- to conduct all our relationships with an emphasis on long-term mutual success and satisfaction, rather than short-term gain
- to earn the trust and respect of all we work with as being a Company of honesty, integrity, and responsibility
- to provide an environment of positive attitude and action to accomplish our vision, by increasing positive feedback and recognition at all levels of the Company
- to train and motivate our employees and to develop cooperation and communication at all levels
- to use our resources, knowledge, and experience to create win/win relationships for our clients, employees, suppliers, and shareholders in terms of growing compensation, service, and value

CALIFORNIA ENERGY COMMISSION

Vision Statement

It is the vision of the California Energy Commission for Californians to have energy choices that are affordable, reliable, diverse, safe, and environmentally acceptable.

Mission Statement

It is the California Energy Commission's mission to assess, advocate, and act through public/private partnerships to improve energy systems that promote a strong economy and a healthy environment.

WHAT IS OUR BUSINESS?

Current thought on mission statements is based largely on guidelines set forth in the mid-1970s by Peter Drucker, who is often called "the father of modern management" for his pioneering studies at General Motors Corporation and for his twenty-two books and hundreds of articles. *Harvard Business Review* has called Drucker, "the preeminent management thinker of our time."

Drucker says that asking the question, "What is our business?," is synonymous with asking the question, "What is our mission?" An enduring statement of purpose that distinguishes one organization from other similar enterprises, the *mission statement* is a declaration of an organization's "reason for being." It answers the pivotal question, "What is our business?" A clear mission statement is essential for effectively establishing objectives and formulating strategies.

Sometimes called a *creed statement,* a statement of purpose, a statement of philosophy, a statement of beliefs, a statement of business principles, or a statement "defining our business," a mission statement reveals what an organization wants to be and whom it wants to serve. All organizations have a reason for being, even if strategists have not consciously transformed this reason into writing. As illustrated in Figure 2–1, carefully prepared statements of vision and mission are widely recognized by both practitioners and academicians as the first step in strategic management.

> A business mission is the foundation for priorities, strategies, plans, and work assignments. It is the starting point for the design of managerial jobs and, above all, for the design of managerial structures. Nothing may seem simpler or more obvious than to know what a company's business is. A steel mill makes steel, a railroad runs trains to carry freight and passengers, an insurance company underwrites fire risks, and a bank lends money. Actually, "What is our business?" is almost always a difficult question and the right answer is usually anything but obvious. The answer to this question is the first responsibility of strategists. Only strategists can make sure that this question receives the attention it deserves and that the answer makes sense and enables the business to plot its course and set its objectives.[2]

Some strategists spend almost every moment of every day on administrative and tactical concerns, and strategists who rush quickly to establish objectives and implement strategies often overlook the development of a vision and mission statement. This problem is widespread even among large organizations. Many corporations in America have not yet developed a formal vision or mission statement, but most do have formal mission statements.[3] An increasing number of organizations are developing these statements.

Some companies develop mission statements simply because they feel it is fashionable, rather than out of any real commitment. However, as will be described in this chapter, firms that develop and systematically revisit their vision and mission statements, treat them as living documents, and consider them to be an integral part of the firm's culture realize great benefits. Johnson & Johnson (J&J) is an example firm. J&J managers meet regularly with employees to review, reword, and reaffirm the firm's vision and mission. The entire J&J workforce recognizes the value that top management places on this exercise, and these employees respond accordingly.

Vision versus Mission

Many organizations develop both a mission statement and a vision statement. Whereas the mission statement answers the question, "What is our business," the *vision statement*

VISIT THE NET

Gives an introduction to the mission concept. http://www.csuchico.edu/mgmt/strategy/module1/sld008.htm

FIGURE 2–1

A Comprehensive Strategic-Management Model

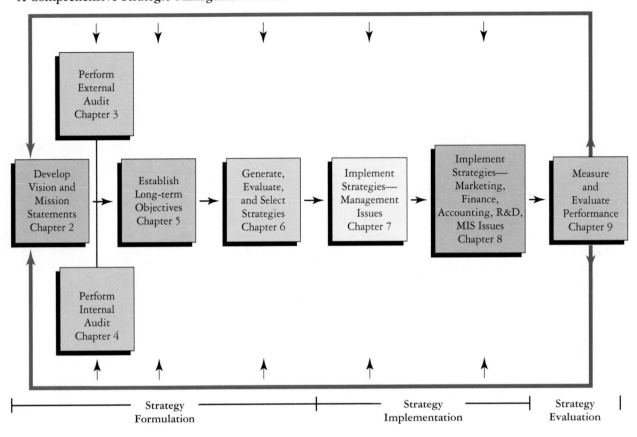

Source: Fred R. David, "How Companies Define Their Mission," *Long Range Planning* 22, no. 3 (June 1988): 40.

VISIT THE NET

Gives questions that help form an effective vision and mission statement. http://www.csuchico.edu/mgmt/strategy/module1/sld009.htm

answers the question, "What do we want to become?" Many organizations have both a mission and vision statement. Several examples are given in Table 2–1.

It can be argued that profit, not mission or vision, is the primary corporate motivator. But profit alone is not enough to motivate people.[4] Profit is perceived negatively by some employees in companies. Employees may see profit as something that they earn and management then uses and even gives away to shareholders. Although this perception is undesired and disturbing to management, it clearly indicates that both profit and vision are needed to effectively motivate a workforce.

When employees and managers together shape or fashion the vision and mission statements for a firm, the resultant documents can reflect the personal visions that managers and employees have in their hearts and minds about their own futures. Shared vision creates a commonality of interests that can lift workers out of the monotony of daily work and put them into a new world of opportunity and challenge.

The Process of Developing a Mission Statement

As indicated in the strategic-management model, a clear mission statement is needed before alternative strategies can be formulated and implemented. It is important to involve as many managers as possible in the process of developing a mission statement, because through involvement, people become committed to an organization.

A widely used approach to developing a mission statement is first to select several articles about mission statements and ask all managers to read these as background information. Then ask managers themselves to prepare a mission statement for the organization. A facilitator, or committee of top managers, should then merge these statements into a single document and distribute this draft mission statement to all managers. A request for modifications, additions, and deletions is needed next, along with a meeting to revise the document. To the extent that all managers have input into and support the final mission statement document, organizations can more easily obtain managers' support for other strategy formulation, implementation, and evaluation activities. Thus, the process of developing a mission statement represents a great opportunity for strategists to obtain needed support from all managers in the firm.

During the process of developing a mission statement, some organizations use discussion groups of managers to develop and modify the mission statement. Some organizations hire an outside consultant or facilitator to manage the process and help draft the language. Sometimes an outside person with expertise in developing mission statements and unbiased views can manage the process more effectively than an internal group or committee of managers. Decisions on how best to communicate the mission to all managers, employees, and external constituencies of an organization are needed when the document is in final form. Some organizations even develop a videotape to explain the mission statement and how it was developed.

An article by Campbell and Yeung emphasizes that the process of developing a mission statement should create an "emotional bond" and "sense of mission" between the organization and its employees.[5] Commitment to a company's strategy and intellectual agreement on the strategies to be pursued do not necessarily translate into an emotional bond; hence, strategies that have been formulated may not be implemented. These researchers stress that an emotional bond comes when an individual personally identifies with the underlying values and behavior of a firm, thus turning intellectual agreement and commitment to strategy into a sense of mission. Campbell and Yeung also differentiate between the terms *vision* and *mission*, saying that vision is "a possible and desirable future state of an organization" that includes specific goals, whereas mission is more associated with behavior and the present.

IMPORTANCE OF VISION AND MISSION STATEMENTS

The importance of vision and mission statements to effective strategic management is well documented in the literature, although research results are mixed. Rarick and Vitton found that firms with a formalized mission statement have twice the average return on shareholders' equity than those firms without a formalized mission statement; Bart and Baetz found a positive relationship between mission statements and organizational performance; *Business Week* reports that firms using mission statements have a 30 percent higher return on certain financial measures than those without such statements; O'Gorman and Doran, however, found that having a mission statement does not directly contribute positively to financial performance.[6] The extent of manager and employee involvement in developing vision and mission statements can make a difference in business success. This chapter provides guidelines for developing these important documents. In actual practice, wide variations exist in the nature, composition, and use of both vision and mission statements. King and Cleland recommend that organizations carefully develop a written mission statement for the following reasons:

1. To ensure unanimity of purpose within the organization
2. To provide a basis, or standard, for allocating organizational resources
3. To establish a general tone or organizational climate
4. To serve as a focal point for individuals to identify with the organization's purpose and direction, and to deter those who cannot from participating further in the organization's activities
5. To facilitate the translation of objectives into a work structure involving the assignment of tasks to responsible elements within the organization
6. To specify organizational purposes and then to translate these purposes into objectives in such a way that cost, time, and performance parameters can be assessed and controlled[7]

Reuben Mark, former CEO of Colgate, maintains that a clear mission increasingly must make sense internationally. Mark's thoughts on vision are as follows:

> When it comes to rallying everyone to the corporate banner, it's essential to push one vision globally rather than trying to drive home different messages in different cultures. The trick is to keep the vision simple but elevated: "We make the world's fastest computers" or "Telephone service for everyone." You're never going to get anyone to charge the machine guns only for financial objectives. It's got to be something that makes people feel better, feel a part of something.[8]

A Resolution of Divergent Views

Developing a comprehensive mission statement is important because divergent views among managers can be revealed and resolved through the process. The question, "What is our business?," can create controversy. Raising the question often reveals differences among strategists in the organization. Individuals who have worked together for a long time and who think they know each other suddenly may realize that they are in fundamental disagreement. For example, in a college or university, divergent views regarding the relative importance of teaching, research, and service often are expressed during the mission statement development process. Negotiation, compromise, and eventual agreement on important issues are needed before people can focus on more specific strategy formulation activities.

> "What is our mission?" is a genuine decision; and a genuine decision must be based on divergent views to have a chance to be a right and effective decision. Developing a business mission is always a choice between alternatives, each of which rests on different assumptions regarding the reality of the business and its environment. It is always a high-risk decision. A change in mission always leads to changes in objectives, strategies, organization, and behavior. The mission decision is far too important to be made by acclamation. Developing a business mission is a big step toward management effectiveness. Hidden or half-understood disagreements on the definition of a business mission underlie many of the personality problems, communication problems, and irritations that tend to divide a top-management group. Establishing a mission should never be made on plausibility alone, should never be made fast, and should never be made painlessly.[9]

Considerable disagreement among an organization's strategists over vision and mission statements can cause trouble if not resolved. For example, unresolved disagreement over the business mission was one of the reasons for W. T. Grant's bankruptcy and eventual liquidation. As one executive reported:

There was a lot of dissension within the company whether we should go the Kmart route or go after the Montgomery Ward and JCPenney position. Ed Staley and Lou Lustenberger (two top executives) were at loggerheads over the issue, with the upshot being we took a position between the two and that consequently stood for nothing.[10]

Too often, strategists develop vision and business mission statements only when the organization is in trouble. Of course, it is needed then. Developing and communicating a clear mission during troubled times indeed may have spectacular results and even may reverse decline. However, to wait until an organization is in trouble to develop a vision and mission statement is a gamble that characterizes irresponsible management. According to Drucker, the most important time to ask seriously, "What do we want to become?" and "What is our business?," is when a company has been successful:

Success always obsoletes the very behavior that achieved it, always creates new realities, and always creates new and different problems. Only the fairy story ends, "They lived happily ever after." It is never popular to argue with success or to rock the boat. The ancient Greeks knew that the penalty of success can be severe. The management that does not ask, "What is our mission?," when the company is successful is, in effect, smug, lazy, and arrogant. It will not be long before success will turn into failure. Sooner or later, even the most successful answer to the question, "What is our business?," becomes obsolete.[11]

In multidivisional organizations, strategists should ensure that divisional units perform strategic-management tasks, including the development of a statement of vision and mission. Each division should involve its own managers and employees in developing a vision and mission statement that is consistent with and supportive of the corporate mission.

An organization that fails to develop a vision statement as well as a comprehensive and inspiring mission statement loses the opportunity to present itself favorably to existing and potential stakeholders. All organizations need customers, employees, and managers, and most firms need creditors, suppliers, and distributors. The vision and mission statements are effective vehicles for communicating with important internal and external stakeholders. The principal value of these statements as tools of strategic management is derived from their specification of the ultimate aims of a firm:

They provide managers with a unity of direction that transcends individual, parochial, and transitory needs. They promote a sense of shared expectations among all levels and generations of employees. They consolidate values over time and across individuals and interest groups. They project a sense of worth and intent that can be identified and assimilated by company outsiders. Finally, they affirm the company's commitment to responsible action, which is symbiotic with its need to preserve and protect the essential claims of insiders for [the] sustained survival, growth, and profitability of the firm.[12]

CHARACTERISTICS OF A MISSION STATEMENT

A Declaration of Attitude

A mission statement is more than a statement of specific details; it is a declaration of attitude and outlook. It usually is broad in scope for at least two major reasons. First, a good mission statement allows for the generation and consideration of a range of feasible alternative objectives and strategies without unduly stifling management creativity. Excess specificity would limit the potential of creative growth for the organization. On the other hand, an overly general statement that does not exclude any strategy alternatives could be dysfunctional. Apple Computer's mission statement, for example, should not open the possibility for diversification into pesticides—or Ford Motor Company's into food processing. As indicated in the Global Perspective box, French mission statements are more general than British mission statements.

Second, a mission statement needs to be broad to effectively reconcile differences among and appeal to an organization's diverse *stakeholders,* the individuals and groups of individuals who have a special stake or claim on the company. Stakeholders include employees, managers, stockholders, boards of directors, customers, suppliers, distributors, creditors, governments (local, state, federal, and foreign), unions, competitors, environmental groups, and the general public. Stakeholders affect and are affected by an organization's strategies, yet the claims and concerns of diverse constituencies vary and often conflict. For example, the general public is especially interested in social responsibility, whereas stockholders are more interested in profitability. Claims on any business

GLOBAL PERSPECTIVE

Concern About Company Mission Across Continents

Researchers recently studied the mission statements of British and French firms. The results are summarized here.

Researchers found that a highly participative (French) approach to developing a mission statement is more effective in gaining employee commitment than a less participative (British) approach. Differences between British and French statements are rooted in or attributable to different cultural, social, and economic factors in the two countries. For example, in Britain, because of the predominance of equity financing, lead companies are frequently bought and sold like commodities. In contrast, the traditions of family ownership are stronger in France, providing a sense of community and a better basis for the development of shared mission statements.

British mission statements tend to be short and specific, and they are generally developed by top managers, whereas French mission statements tend to be long and general, and they are generally developed by all managers and employees.

A large study of chief executive officers (CEOs) around the world revealed management challenges. The table below provides the percentage of CEOs in each area that consider various topics to be a management challenge. Note that 38 percent of Japanese CEOs considered "engaging employees in the company mission" to be a major management challenge.

Major Management Challenge in 2000	United States	Europe	Japan
Customer Loyalty	44%	28%	3%
Managing Mergers, Acquisitions, Alliances	30	42	16
Reducing Costs	29	32	41
Engaging Employees in Company's Mission	28	32	38
Competing for Talent	26	9	3
Increasing Flexibility and Speed	24	39	31

Sources: Adapted from Julienne Brabet and Mary Klemm, "Sharing the Vision: Company Mission Statements in Britain and France," *Long Range Planning* (February 1994): 84–94; adapted from Anne Carey and Alejandro Gonzalez, "What's Troubling CEOs?" *USA Today* (August 12, 1999): B1.

literally may number in the thousands, and they often include clean air, jobs, taxes, investment opportunities, career opportunities, equal employment opportunities, employee benefits, salaries, wages, clean water, and community services. All stakeholders' claims on an organization cannot be pursued with equal emphasis. A good mission statement indicates the relative attention that an organization will devote to meeting the claims of various stakeholders. Many firms are environmentally proactive in response to the concerns of stakeholders, as indicated in the Natural Environment Perspective box.

NATURAL ENVIRONMENT PERSPECTIVE

Is Your Firm Environmentally Proactive?

Conducting business in a way that preserves the natural environment is more than just good public relations; it is good business. Preserving the environment is a permanent part of doing business for the following reasons:

1. Consumer demand for environmentally safe products and packages is high.

2. Public opinion demanding that firms conduct business in ways that preserve the natural environment is strong.

3. Environmental advocacy groups now have over twenty million Americans as members.

4. Federal and state environmental regulations are changing rapidly and becoming more complex.

5. More lenders are examining the environmental liabilities of businesses seeking loans.

6. Many consumers, suppliers, distributors, and investors shun doing business with environmentally weak firms.

7. Liability suits and fines against firms having environmental problems are on the rise.

More firms are becoming environmentally proactive, which means they are taking the initiative to develop and implement strategies that preserve the environment while enhancing their efficiency and effectiveness. The old undesirable alternative is to be environmentally reactive—waiting until environmental pressures are thrust upon a firm by law or consumer pressure. A reactive environmental policy often leads to high cleanup costs, numerous liability suits, loss in market share, reduced customer loyalty, and higher medical costs. In contrast, a proactive policy views environmental pressures as opportunities and includes such actions as developing green products and packages, conserving energy, reducing waste, recycling, and creating a corporate culture that is environmentally sensitive.

A proactive policy forces a company to innovate and upgrade process; this leads to reduced waste, improved efficiency, better quality, and greater profits. Successful firms today assess "the profit in preserving the environment" in decisions ranging from developing a mission statement to determining plant location, manufacturing technology, design, products, packaging, and consumer relations. A proactive environmental policy is simply good business. However, the *Wall Street Journal* reports that consumer interest in buying environmentally-friendly products has declined significantly since 2000. The *Journal* says "Eco-marketing is fading faster than the ozone over Antarctica." Many companies now conclude that "green" sales pitches do not sell. Consumers today "leave their conscience at the landfill when they head to the store." More than 40 percent of consumers "don't buy green products because they fear the products won't work as well." The remaining consumers focus on price and convenience. Recycling rates for plastic bottles dropped 66 percent in the United States from 1995 to 2002. Even New York City is considering elimation of all metal, glass, and plastic recycling services to save $57 million annually.

Sources: Adapted from "The Profit in Preserving America," *Forbes* (November 11, 1991): 181–189; and Forest Beinhardt, "Bringing the Environment Down to Earth," *Harvard Business Review* (July–August 1999): 149–158; Christine Rosen, "Environmental Strategy and Competitive Advantage," *California Management Review* 43, 3 (Spring 2001): 8–15; and Geoffrey Fowler, "Green Sales Pitch Isn't Moving Many Products," *Wall Street Journal* (March 6, 2002): B1 and B4.

Reaching the fine balance between specificity and generality is difficult to achieve, but it is well worth the effort. George Steiner offers the following insight on the need for a mission statement to be broad in scope:

> Most business statements of mission are expressed at high levels of abstraction. Vagueness nevertheless has its virtues. Mission statements are not designed to express concrete ends, but rather to provide motivation, general direction, an image, a tone, and a philosophy to guide the enterprise. An excess of detail could prove counterproductive since concrete specification could be the base for rallying opposition. Precision might stifle creativity in the formulation of an acceptable mission or purpose. Once an aim is cast in concrete, it creates a rigidity in an organization and resists change. Vagueness leaves room for other managers to fill in the details, perhaps even to modify general patterns. Vagueness permits more flexibility in adapting to changing environments and internal operations. It facilitates flexibility in implementation.[13]

An effective mission statement should not be too lengthy. Less than 200 words is a recommended length. An effective mission statement also arouses positive feelings and emotions about an organization; it is inspiring in the sense that it motivates readers to action. An effective mission statement generates the impression that a firm is successful, has direction, and is worthy of time, support, and investment—from all socio-economic groups of people.

It reflects judgments about future growth directions and strategies that are based upon forward-looking external and internal analyses. A business mission should provide useful criteria for selecting among alternative strategies. A clear mission statement provides a basis for generating and screening strategic options. The statement of mission should be dynamic in orientation, allowing judgments about the most promising growth directions and those considered less promising.

A Customer Orientation

A good mission statement describes an organization's purpose, customers, products or services, markets, philosophy, and basic technology. According to Vern McGinnis, a mission statement should (1) define what the organization is and what the organization aspires to be, (2) be limited enough to exclude some ventures and broad enough to allow for creative growth, (3) distinguish a given organization from all others, (4) serve as a framework for evaluating both current and prospective activities, and (5) be stated in terms sufficiently clear to be widely understood throughout the organization.[14]

A good mission statement reflects the anticipations of customers. Rather than developing a product and then trying to find a market, the operating philosophy of organizations should be to identify customers' needs and then provide a product or service to fulfill those needs. Good mission statements identify the utility of a firm's products to its customers. This is why AT&T's mission statement focuses on communication rather than on telephones; it is why Exxon/Mobil's mission statement focuses on energy rather than on oil and gas; it is why Union Pacific's mission statement focuses on transportation rather than on railroads; it is why Universal Studio's mission statement focuses on entertainment rather than on movies. The following utility statements are relevant in developing a mission statement:

Do not offer me things.

Do not offer me clothes. Offer me attractive looks.

E-COMMERCE PERSPECTIVE

Is the Internet Revolution Bypassing the Poor and Minorities?

YES. The U.S. Department of Commerce recently conducted a massive study that concluded the Internet revolution in America is largely bypassing the poor, minorities, rural areas, and inner cities. This fact is resulting in a widening gap between the rich and the poor in this country and a widening gap between the educated and uneducated.

Nearly 90 percent of all shares of common stock of American companies are held by the wealthiest 10 percent of Americans. The wealthiest 10 percent of Americans hold 73.2 percent of this country's net worth today, up from 68.2 percent in 1983. Stock ownership disparity between rich and poor Americans exemplifies growing separation between economic classes.

The *Wall Street Journal* reported in 2002 that Web usage is growing slowest among poor and minority citizens. The so-called digital divide in Internet access between the rich and poor in America is widening. President Bush opposes Democratic proposals for tax incentives for companies that bring broadband Internet access to poor and rural areas. The percentage gap between Americans making $25,000 or less per year who use the Internet versus Americans making over $75,000 annually has grown from 35 percent to 50 percent between 1997 and 2002—despite progress in both groups.

Sources: Adapted from David Lieberman, "Internet Gap Widening—Study: Revolution Bypassing Poor; Minorities," *USA Today* (July 9, 1999): 1A; Jacob Schlesinger, "Wealth Gap Grows: Why Does It Matter," *The Wall Street Journal* (September 13, 1999); A1 Alejandro Gonzalez, "Average Net Worth for U.S. Families," *USA Today* (October 12, 1999): 5A; Yochi Dreazen, "White House Takes Aim at Technology Programs," *Wall Street Journal* (February 27, 2002): A22.

Do not offer me shoes. Offer me comfort for my feet and the pleasure of walking.

Do not offer me a house. Offer me security, comfort, and a place that is clean and happy.

Do not offer me books. Offer me hours of pleasure and the benefit of knowledge.

Do not offer me records. Offer me leisure and the sound of music.

Do not offer me tools. Offer me the benefits and the pleasure that come from making beautiful things.

Do not offer me furniture. Offer me comfort and the quietness of a cozy place.

Do not offer me things. Offer me ideas, emotions, ambience, feelings, and benefits.

Please, do not offer me *things*.

A major reason for developing a business mission statement is to attract customers who give meaning to an organization. Hotel customers today want to use the Internet, so more and more hotels are providing Internet service. A classic description of the purpose of a business reveals the relative importance of customers in a statement of mission:

It is the customer who determines what a business is. It is the customer alone whose willingness to pay for a good or service converts economic resources into wealth and things into goods. What a business thinks it produces is not of first importance, especially not to the future of the business and to its success. What the customer thinks he/she is buying, what he/she considers value, is decisive—it determines what a business is, what it produces, and whether it will prosper. And what the customer buys and considers value is never a product. It is always utility, meaning what a product or service does for him or her. The customer is the foundation of a business and keeps it in existence.[15]

A Declaration of Social Policy

The term *social policy* embraces managerial philosophy and thinking at the highest levels of an organization. For this reason, social policy affects the development of a business mission statement. Social issues mandate that strategists consider not only what the organization owes its various stakeholders but also what responsibilities the firm has to consumers, environmentalists, minorities, communities, and other groups. After decades of debate on the topic of social responsibility, many firms still struggle to determine appropriate social policies. As indicated in the E-Commerce Perspective, there is a growing gap in economic well-being between the poor and the rich in America.

The issue of social responsibility arises when a company establishes its business mission. The impact of society on business and vice versa is becoming more pronounced each year. Social policies directly affect a firm's customers, products and services, markets, technology, profitability, self-concept, and public image. An organization's social policy should be integrated into all strategic-management activities, including the development of a mission statement. Corporate social policy should be designed and articulated during strategy formulation, set and administered during strategy implementation, and reaffirmed or changed during strategy evaluation.[16] The emerging view of social responsibility holds that social issues should be attended to both directly and indirectly in determining strategies. In 2002, the *Wall Street Journal* rated the top companies for social responsibility to be as follows:[17]

1. Johnson & Johnson
2. Coca-Cola
3. Wal-Mart
4. Anheuser Busch
5. Hewlett-Packard
6. Walt Disney
7. Microsoft
8. IBM
9. McDonald's
10. 3M
11. UPS
12. FedEx
13. Target
14. Home Depot
15. General Electric

VISIT THE NET

Provides example mission and vision statements that can be critiqued.

http://www.csuchico.edu/mgmt/strategy/module1/sld015.htm;
http://www.csuchico.edu/mgmt/strategy/module1/sld014.htm;
http://www.csuchico.edu/mgmt/strategy/module1/sld017.htm

Firms should strive to engage in social activities that have economic benefits. For example, Merck & Co. recently developed the drug, ivermectin, for treating river blindness, a disease caused by a fly-borne parasitic worm endemic in poor, tropical areas of Africa, the Middle East, and Latin America. In an unprecedented gesture that reflected its corporate commitment to social responsibility, Merck then made ivermectin available at no cost to medical personnel throughout the world. Merck's action highlights the dilemma of orphan drugs, which offer pharmaceutical companies no economic incentive for development and distribution.

Despite differences in approaches, most American companies try to assure outsiders that they conduct their businesses in socially responsible ways. The mission statement is an effective instrument for conveying this message.

 ## COMPONENTS OF A MISSION STATEMENT

Mission statements can and do vary in length, content, format, and specificity. Most practitioners and academicians of strategic management feel that an effective statement exhibits nine characteristics or components. Because a mission statement is often the most visible and public part of the strategic-management process, it is important that it includes all of these essential components:

1. *Customers:* Who are the firm's customers?
2. *Products or services:* What are the firm's major products or services?
3. *Markets:* Geographically, where does the firm compete?
4. *Technology:* Is the firm technologically current?
5. *Concern for survival, growth, and profitability:* Is the firm committed to growth and financial soundness?
6. *Philosophy:* What are the basic beliefs, values, aspirations, and ethical priorities of the firm?
7. *Self-concept:* What is the firm's distinctive competence or major competitive advantage?
8. *Concern for public image:* Is the firm responsive to social, community, and environmental concerns?
9. *Concern for employees:* Are employees a valuable asset of the firm?

Excerpts from the mission statements of different organizations are provided in Table 2–2 to exemplify the nine essential mission statement components.

WRITING AND EVALUATING MISSION STATEMENTS

Perhaps the best way to develop a skill for writing and evaluating mission statements is to study actual company missions. Therefore, six mission statements are presented in Table 2–3. These statements are then evaluated in Table 2–4 based on the nine criteria presented above.

There is no one best mission statement for a particular organization, so good judgment is required in evaluating mission statements. In Table 2–4, a *Yes* indicates that the given mission statement answers satisfactorily the question posed in Table 2–2 for the respective evaluative criteria. Some individuals are more demanding than others in rating mission statements in this manner. For example, if a statement includes the word *employees* or *customer,* is that alone sufficient for the respective component? Some companies answer this question in the affirmative and some in the negative. You may ask yourself this question: "If I worked for this company, would I have done better with regard to including a particular component in its mission statement." Perhaps the important issue here is that mission statements include each of the nine components in some manner.

As indicated in Table 2–4, the Dell Computer mission statement was rated to be the best among the six statements evaluated. Note, however, that the Dell Computer statement lacks inclusion of the "Philosophy" and the "Concern for Employees" components. The PepsiCo mission statement was evaluated as the worst because it included only three of the nine components. Note that only one of these six statements included the "Technology" component in their document.

VISIT THE NET

Provides the NIH Clinical Center's vision and mission statements and its overall strategic plan. http://www.cc.nih.gov/od/strategic/index.html

TABLE 2-2   **Examples of the Nine Essential Components of a Mission Statement**

1. CUSTOMERS

We believe our first responsibility is to the doctors, nurses, patients, mothers, and all others who use our products and services. (Johnson & Johnson)

To earn our customers' loyalty, we listen to them, anticipate their needs, and act to create value in their eyes. (Lexmark International)

2. PRODUCTS OR SERVICES

AMAX's principal products are molybdenum, coal, iron ore, copper, lead, zinc, petroleum and natural gas, potash, phosphates, nickel, tungsten, silver, gold, and magnesium. (AMAX Engineering Company)

Standard Oil Company (Indiana) is in business to find and produce crude oil, natural gas, and natural gas liquids; to manufacture high-quality products useful to society from these raw materials; and to distribute and market those products and to provide dependable related services to the consuming public at reasonable prices. (Standard Oil Company)

3. MARKETS

We are dedicated to the total success of Corning Glass Works as a worldwide competitor. (Corning Glass Works)

Our emphasis is on North American markets, although global opportunities will be explored. (Blockway)

4. TECHNOLOGY

Control Data is in the business of applying micro-electronics and computer technology in two general areas: computer-related hardware; and computing-enhancing services, which include computation, information, education, and finance. (Control Data)

We will continually strive to meet the preferences of adult smokers by developing technologies that have the potential to reduce the health risks associated with smoking. (RJ Reynolds)

5. CONCERN FOR SURVIVAL, GROWTH, AND PROFITABILITY

In this respect, the company will conduct its operations prudently and will provide the profits and growth which will assure Hoover's ultimate success. (Hoover Universal)

To serve the worldwide need for knowledge at a fair profit by adhering, evaluating, producing, and distributing valuable information in a way that benefits our customers, employees, other investors, and our society. (McGraw-Hill)

6. PHILOSOPHY

Our world-class leadership is dedicated to a management philosophy that holds people above profits. (Kellogg)

It's all part of the Mary Kay philosophy—a philosophy based on the golden rule. A spirit of sharing and caring where people give cheerfully of their time, knowledge, and experience. (Mary Kay Cosmetics)

7. SELF-CONCEPT

Crown Zellerbach is committed to leapfrogging ongoing competition within 1,000 days by unleashing the constructive and creative abilities and energies of each of its employees. (Crown Zellerbach)

8. CONCERN FOR PUBLIC IMAGE

To share the world's obligation for the protection of the environment. (Dow Chemical)

To contribute to the economic strength of society and function as a good corporate citizen on a local, state, and national basis in all countries in which we do business. (Pfizer)

Continued

TABLE 2-2   **Examples of the Nine Essential Components of a Mission Statement** (*continued*)

9. CONCERN FOR EMPLOYEES

To recruit, develop, motivate, reward, and retain personnel of exceptional ability, character, and dedication by providing good working conditions, superior leadership, compensation on the basis of performance, an attractive benefit program, opportunity for growth, and a high degree of employment security. (The Wachovia Corporation)

To compensate its employees with remuneration and fringe benefits competitive with other employment opportunities in its geographical area and commensurate with their contributions toward efficient corporate operations. (Public Service Electric & Gas Company)

TABLE 2-3   **Mission Statements of Six Organizations**

PepsiCo's mission is to increase the value of our shareholders' investment. We do this through sales growth, cost controls, and wise investment resources. We believe our commercial success depends upon offering quality and value to our consumers and customers; providing products that are safe, wholesome, economically efficient, and environmentally sound; and providing a fair return to our investors while adhering to the highest standards of integrity.

Ben & Jerry's mission is to make, distribute, and sell the finest quality all-natural ice cream and related products in a wide variety of innovative flavors made from Vermont dairy products. To operate the Company on a sound financial basis of profitable growth, increasing value for our shareholders, and creating career opportunities and financial rewards for our employees. To operate the Company in a way that actively recognizes the central role that business plays in the structure of society by initiating innovative ways to improve the quality of life of a broad community—local, national, and international.

The Mission of the Institute of Management Accountants (IMA) is to provide to members personal and professional development opportunities through education, association with business professionals, and certification in management accounting and financial management skills. The IMA is globally recognized by the financial community as a respected institution influencing the concepts and ethical practices of management accounting and financial management.

The Mission of Genentech, Inc., is to be the leading biotechnology company, using human genetic information to develop, manufacture, and market pharmaceuticals that address significant unmet medical needs. We commit ourselves to high standards of integrity in contributing to the best interests of patients, the medical profession, and our employees, and to seek significant returns to our stockholders based on the continued pursuit of excellent science.

The Mission of Barrett Memorial Hospital is to operate a high-quality health care facility, providing an appropriate mix of services to the residents of Beaverhead County and surrounding areas. Service is given with ultimate concern for patients, medical staff, hospital staff, and the community. Barrett Memorial Hospital assumes a strong leadership role in the coordination and development of health-related resources within the community.

Dell Computer's mission is to be the most successful computer company in the world at delivering the best customer experience in markets we serve. In doing so, Dell will meet customer expectations of highest quality; leading technology; competitive pricing; individual and company accountability; best-in-class service and support; flexible customization capability; superior corporate citizenship; financial stability.

TABLE 2-4   An Evaluation Matrix of Mission Statements

COMPONENTS

Organization	Customers	Products/ Services	Markets	Technology	Concern for Survival, Growth, Profitability
PepsiCo	Yes	No	No	No	Yes
Ben & Jerry's	No	Yes	Yes	No	Yes
Institute of Management Accountants	Yes	Yes	Yes	No	No
Genentech, Inc.	Yes	Yes	No	No	Yes
Barrett Memorial Hospital	Yes	Yes	Yes	No	No
Dell Computer	Yes	Yes	Yes	Yes	Yes

Organization	Philosophy	Self-Concept	Concern for Public Image	Concern for Employees
PepsiCo	Yes	No	No	No
Ben & Jerry's	No	Yes	Yes	Yes
Institute of Management Accountants	Yes	Yes	Yes	No
Genentech, Inc.	Yes	Yes	Yes	Yes
Barrett Memorial Hospital	No	Yes	Yes	Yes
Dell Computer	No	Yes	Yes	No

CONCLUSION

VISIT THE NET

Provides the strategic plan for Kansas State University, including its vision and mission statements.
www.ksu.edu/provost/
planning/

Every organization has a unique purpose and reason for being. This uniqueness should be reflected in vision and mission statements. The nature of a business vision and mission can represent either a competitive advantage or disadvantage for the firm. An organization achieves a heightened sense of purpose when strategists, managers, and employees develop and communicate a clear business vision and mission. Drucker says that developing a clear business vision and mission is the "first responsibility of strategists."

A good mission statement reveals an organization's customers; products or services; markets; technology; concern for survival, growth, and profitability; philosophy; self-concept; concern for public image; and concern for employees. These nine basic components serve as a practical framework for evaluating and writing mission statements. As the first step in strategic management, the vision and mission statements provide direction for all planning activities.

Well-designed vision and mission statements are essential for formulating, implementing, and evaluating strategy. Developing and communicating a clear business vision and mission is one of the most commonly overlooked tasks in strategic management. Without clear statements of vision and mission, a firm's short-term actions can be counterproductive to long-term interests. Vision and mission statements always should be subject to revision, but, if carefully prepared, they will require infrequent major changes. Organizations usually reexamine their vision and mission statements annually. Effective mission statements stand the test of time.

Vision and mission statements are essential tools for strategists, a fact illustrated in a short story told by Porsche former CEO Peter Schultz:

> Three people were at work on a construction site. All were doing the same job, but when each was asked what his job was, the answers varied: "Breaking rocks," the first replied; "Earning a living," responded the second; "Helping to build a cathedral," said the third. Few of us can build cathedrals. But to the extent we can see the cathedral in whatever cause we are following, the job seems more worthwhile. Good strategists and a clear mission help us find those cathedrals in what otherwise could be dismal issues and empty causes.[18]

We invite you to visit the David page on the Prentice Hall Companion Website at **www.prenhall.com/david** for this chapter's World Wide Web exercise.

KEY TERMS AND CONCEPTS

Concern for Employees (p. 69)

Concern for Public Image (p. 69)

Concern for Survival, Growth, and Profitability (p. 69)

Creed Statement (p. 59)

Customers (p. 69)

Markets (p. 69)

Mission Statement (p. 59)

Mission Statement Components (p. 69)

Philosophy (p. 69)

Products or Services (p. 69)

Self-Concept (p. 69)

Social Policy (p. 68)

Stakeholders (p. 64)

Technology (p. 69)

Vision Statement (p. 59)

ISSUES FOR REVIEW AND DISCUSSION

1. Compare and contrast vision statements with mission statements in terms of composition and importance.

2. Do local service stations need to have written vision and mission statements? Why or why not?

3. Why do you think organizations that have a comprehensive mission tend to be high performers? Does having a comprehensive mission cause high performance?

4. Explain why a mission statement should not include strategies and objectives.

5. What is your college or university's self-concept? How would you state that in a mission statement?

6. Explain the principal value of a vision and a mission statement.

7. Why is it important for a mission statement to be reconciliatory?

8. In your opinion, what are the three most important components that should be included when writing a mission statement? Why?

9. How would the mission statements of a for-profit and a nonprofit organization differ?

10. Write a vision and mission statement for an organization of your choice.

11. Go to www.altavista.com and conduct a search with the keywords *vision statement* and *mission statement*. Find various company vision and mission statements and evaluate the documents.

12. Who are the major stakeholders of the bank that you do business with locally? What are the major claims of those stakeholders?

13. Select one of the current readings at the end of this chapter. Look up that article in your college library, and give a five-minute oral report to the class summarizing the article.

NOTES

1. Barbara Bartkus, Myron Glassman, and Bruce McAfee, "Mission Statements: Are They Smoke and Mirrors?" *Business Horizons* (November–December 2000): 23.

2. Peter Drucker, *Management: Tasks, Responsibilities, and Practices* (New York: Harper & Row, 1974): 61.

3. Fred David, "How Companies Define Their Mission," *Long Range Planning* 22, no. 1 (February 1989): 90–92; John Pearce II and Fred David, "Corporate Mission Statements: The Bottom Line," *Academy of Management Executive* 1, no. 2 (May 1987): 110.

4. Joseph Quigley, "Vision: How Leaders Develop It, Share It and Sustain It," *Business Horizons* (September–October 1994): 39.

5. Andrew Campbell and Sally Yeung, "Creating a Sense of Mission," *Long Range Planning* 24, no. 4 (August 1991): 17.

6. Charles Rarick and John Vitton, "Mission Statements Make Cents," *Journal of Business Strategy* 16 (1995): 11. Also, Christopher Bart and Mark Baetz, "The Relationship Between Mission Statements and Firm Performance: An Exploratory Study," *Journal of Management Studies* 35 (1998): 823; "Mission Possible," *BusinessWeek* (August 1999): F12.

7. W. R. King and D. I. Cleland, *Strategic Planning and Policy* (New York: Van Nostrand Reinhold, 1979): 124.

8. Brian Dumaine, "What the Leaders of Tomorrow See," *Fortune* (July 3, 1989): 50.

9. DRUCKER: 78, 79.

10. "How W. T. Grant Lost $175 Million Last Year," *BusinessWeek* (February 25, 1975): 75.

11. DRUCKER, 88.

12. JOHN PEARCE II, "The Company Mission as a Strategic Tool," *Sloan Management Review* 23, no. 3 (Spring 1982): 74.

13. GEORGE STEINER, *Strategic Planning: What Every Manager Must Know* (New York: The Free Press, 1979): 160.

14. VERN MCGINNIS, "The Mission Statement: A Key Step in Strategic Planning," *Business* 31, no. 6 (November–December 1981): 41.

15. DRUCKER, 61.

16. ARCHIE CARROLL and FRANK HOY, "Integrating Corporate Social Policy into Strategic Management," *Journal of Business Strategy* 4, no. 3 (Winter 1984): 57.

17. RONALD ALSOP, "Perits of Corporate Philanthropy," *Wall Street Journal* (January 16, 2002): p. 81.

18. ROBERT WATERMAN, JR., *The Renewal Factor: How the Best Get and Keep the Competitive Edge* (New York: Bantam, 1987); *Business Week* (September 14, 1987): 120.

CURRENT READINGS

BAETZ, MARK C., and CHRISTOPHER K. BART, "Developing Mission Statements Which Work." *Long Range Planning* 29, no. 4 (August 1996): 526–533.

BARTKUS, BARBARA, MYRON GLASSMAN, and R. BRUCE MCAFEE. "Mission Statements: Are They Smoke and Mirrors?" *Business Horizons* 43, no. 6 (November–December 2000): 23.

BARTLETT, CHRISTOPHER A., and SUMANTRA GHOSHAL. "Changing the Role of Top Management: Beyond Strategy to Purpose." *Harvard Business Review* (November–December 1994): 79–90.

BRABET, JULIENNE, and MARY KLEMM. "Sharing the Vision: Company Mission Statements in Britain and France." *Long Range Planning* (February 1994): 84–94.

CIULLA, JOANNE B. "The Importance of Leadership in Shaping Business Values." *International Journal of Strategic Management* 32, no. 2 (April 1999): 166–172.

COLLINS, JAMES C., and JERRY I. PORRAS. "Building a Visionary Company." *California Management Review* 37, no. 2 (Winter 1995): 80–100.

COLLINS, JAMES C., and JERRY I. PORRAS. "Building Your Company's Vision." *Harvard Business Review* (September–October 1996): 65–78.

CUMMINGS, STEPHEN, and JOHN DAVIES. "Brief Case—Mission, Vision, Fusion." *Long Range Planning* 27, no. 6 (December 1994): 147–150.

DAVIES, STUART W., and KEITH W. GLAISTER. "Business School Mission Statements—The Bland Leading the Bland?" *Long Range Planning* 30, no. 4 (August 1997): 594–604.

GRATTON, LYNDA. "Implementing a Strategic Vision—Key Factors for Success." *Long Range Planning* 29, no. 3 (June 1996): 290–303.

GRAVES, SAMUEL B., and SANDRA A. WADDOCK. "Institutional Owners and Corporate Social Performance." *Academy of Management Journal* 37, no. 4 (August 1994): 1034–1046.

HEMPHILL, THOMAS A. "Legislating Corporate Social Responsibility." *Business Horizons* 40, no. 2 (March–April 1997): 53–63.

JONES, IAN W., and MICHAEL G. POLLITT. "Putting Values into Action: Lessons from Best Practice." *International Journal of Strategic Management* 32, no. 2 (April 1999): 162–165.

LARWOOD, LAURIE, CECILIA M. FALBE, MARK P. KRIGER, and PAUL MIESING. "Structure and Meaning of Organizational Vision." *Academy of Management Journal* 38, no. 3 (June 1995): 740–769.

LISSAK, MICHAEL, and JOHAN ROOS. "Be Coherent, Not Visionary." *Long Range Planning* 34, no. 1 (February 2001): 53.

MCTAVISH, RON. "One More Time: What Business Are You In?" *Long Range Planning* 28, no. 2 (April 1995): 49–60.

MARKOCZY, L. "Consensus Formation During Strategic Change." *Strategic Management Journal* 22, no. 11 (November 2001): 1013.

MARTIN, ROGER L. "The Virtue Matrix: Calculating the Return on Corporate Responsibility." *Harvard Business Review* (March 2002): 68.

MITOFF, IAN I., and ELIZABETH A. DENTON. "A Study of Spirituality in the Workplace." *Sloan Management Review* 40, no. 4 (Summer 1999): 83–92.

NASSER, JAC "Ford Motor Company's CEO Jac Nasser on Transformational Change, E-business, and Environmental Responsibility." *Academy of Management Journal* 14, no. 3 (August 2000): 46.

OSBORNE, RICHARD L. "Strategic Values: The Corporate Performance Engine." *Business Horizons* 39, no. 5 (September–October 1996): 41–47.

OSWALD, S. L., K. W. MOSSHOLDER, and S. G. HARRIS. "Vision Salience and Strategic Involvement: Implications for Psychological Attachment to Organization and Job." *Strategic Management Journal* 15, no. 6 (July 1994): 477–490.

ROUNDTABLE DISCUSSION. "Business as a Living System: The Value of Industrial Ecology." *California Management Review* 43, no. 3 (Spring 2001): 16.

SHANKLIN, WILLIAM L. "Creatively Managing for Creative Destruction." *Business Horizons* 43, no. 6 (November–December 2000): 29.

SNYDER, NEIL H., and MICHELLE GRAVES. "The Editor's Chair/Leadership and Vision." *Business Horizons* 37, no. 1 (January–February 1994): 1–7.

SWANSON, DIANE L. "Addressing a Theoretical Problem by Reorienting the Corporate Social Performance Model." *Academy of Management Review* 20, no. 1 (January 1995): 43–64.

SWANSON, DIANE L. "Toward an Integrative Theory of Business and Society: A Research Strategy for Corporate Social Performance." *Academy of Management Review* 24, no. 3 (July 1999): 506–521.

EXPERIENTIAL EXERCISES

EXPERIENTIAL EXERCISE 2A ▶

Evaluating Mission Statements

PURPOSE

A business mission statement is an integral part of strategic management. It provides direction for formulating, implementing, and evaluating strategic activities. This exercise will give you practice evaluating mission statements, a skill that is prerequisite to writing a good mission statement.

INSTRUCTIONS

Step 1   Your instructor will select some or all of the following mission statements to evaluate. On a separate sheet of paper, construct an evaluation matrix like the one presented in Table 2–4. Evaluate the mission statements based on the nine criteria presented in the chapter.

Step 2   Record a *yes* in appropriate cells of the evaluation matrix when the respective mission statement satisfactorily meets the desired criteria. Record a *no* in appropriate cells when the respective mission statement does not meet the stated criteria.

MISSION STATEMENTS

Criterion Productions, Inc.

The mission statement of Criterion Productions, Inc., is to increase the success of all who avail themselves of our products and services by providing image enhancement and a medium that communicates our customer's corporate identity and unique message to a targeted audience. In this, our tenth year of business, Criterion Productions, Inc., pledges to offer a distinct advantage and a superior value in all of your video production needs. We will assist our customers in their endeavors to grow and prosper through celebrity associations that are "effectively appropriate" to their industry, and/or who possess the qualities and characteristics most respected by our customers.

Mid-America Plastics, Inc.

"Continuous Improvement Every Day, In Everything We Do."
In order for us to accomplish our mission, every employee must be "Committed to Excellence" in everything he or she does by performing his or her job right the first time.

Hatboro Area YMCA

To translate the principles of the YMCA's Christian heritage into programs that nurture children, strengthen families, build strong communities, and develop healthy minds, bodies, and spirits for all.

Integrated Communications, Inc.

Our mission is to be perceived by our customers as providing the highest quality of customer service and salesmanship, delivered with a sense of ownership, friendliness, individual pride, and team spirit. We will accomplish this with the quality of our Wireless Products that supply complete solutions to our customers needs. And, through unyielding loyalty to our customers and suppliers, ICI will provide opportunities and security to our employees as well as [maximize] our long-term financial growth.

American Counseling Association (ACA)

The Mission of ACA is to promote public confidence and trust in the counseling profession.

Idaho Hospital Association

The mission of the Idaho Hospital Association is to provide representation, advocacy and assistance for member hospitals, healthcare systems and the healthcare services they provide. The Association, through leadership and collaboration among healthcare providers and others, promotes quality healthcare that is adequately financed and accessible to all Idahoans.

EXPERIENTIAL EXERCISE 2B ▶

Writing a Vision and Mission Statement for American Airlines (AMR)

PURPOSE

There is no one best vision or mission statement for a given organization. Analysts feel that AMR needs a clear vision and mission statement to survive. Writing a mission statement that includes desired components—and at the same time is inspiring and reconciliatory—requires careful thought. Mission statements should not be too lengthy; statements under two-hundred words are desirable.

INSTRUCTIONS

Step 1   Take 15 minutes to write vision and mission statements for AMR. Scan the case for needed details as you prepare your statements.

Step 2   Join with three other classmates to form a group of four people. Read each other's statements silently. As a group, select the best vision statement and best mission statement from your group.

Step 3   Read those best statements to the class.

EXPERIENTIAL EXERCISE 2C ▶

Writing a Vision and Mission Statement for My University

PURPOSE

Most universities have a vision and mission statement. The purpose of this exercise is to give you practice writing a vision and mission statement for a nonprofit organization such as your own university.

INSTRUCTIONS

Step 1   Take 15 minutes to write a vision statement and a mission statement for your university. Your mission statement should not exceed two hundred words.

Step 2   Read your vision and mission statements to the class.

Step 3   Determine whether your institution has a vision and/or mission statement. Look in the front of the college handbook. If your institution has a written statement, contact an appropriate administrator of the institution to inquire as to how and when the statement was prepared. Share this information with the class. Analyze your college's mission statement in light of concepts presented in this chapter.

EXPERIENTIAL EXERCISE 2D ►

Conducting Mission Statement Research

PURPOSE

This exercise gives you the opportunity to study the nature and role of vision and mission statements in strategic management.

INSTRUCTIONS

Step 1   Call various organizations in your city or county to identify firms that have developed a formal vision and/or mission statement. Contact nonprofit organizations and government agencies in addition to small and large businesses. Ask to speak with the director, owner, or chief executive officer of one organization. Explain that you are studying vision and mission statements in class and are conducting research as part of a class activity.

Step 2   Ask several executives the following four questions, and record their answers.

1. When did your organization first develop its vision and/or mission statement? Who was primarily responsible for its development?

2. How long have your current statements existed? When were they last modified? Why were they modified at that point in time?

3. By what process are your firm's vision and mission statements altered?

4. How are your vision and mission statements used in the firm? How do they affect the firm's strategic-planning process?

Step 3   Provide an overview of your findings to the class.

3

THE EXTERNAL ASSESSMENT

CHAPTER OUTLINE

- The Nature of an External Audit
- Economic Forces
- Social, Cultural, Demographic, and Environmental Forces.
- Political, Governmental, and Legal Forces
- Technological Forces
- Competitive Forces
- Competitive Analysis: Porter's Five-Forces Model
- Sources of External Information
- Forecasting Tools and Techniques
- The Global Challenge
- Industry Analysis: The External Factor Evaluation (EFE) Matrix
- The Competitive Profile Matrix (CPM)

EXPERIENTIAL EXERCISE 3A
Developing an EFE Matrix for American Airlines (AMR)

EXPERIENTIAL EXERCISE 3B
The Internet Search

EXPERIENTIAL EXERCISE 3C
Developing an EFE Matrix for My University

EXPERIENTIAL EXERCISE 3D
Developing a Competitive Profile Matrix for American Airlines (AMR)

EXPERIENTIAL EXERCISE 3E
Developing a Competitive Profile Matrix for My University

CHAPTER OBJECTIVES

After studying this chapter, you should be able to do the following:

1. Describe how to conduct an external strategic-management audit.
2. Discuss ten major external forces that affect organizations: economic, social, cultural, demographic, environmental, political, governmental, legal, technological, and competitive.
3. Identify key sources of external information, including the Internet.
4. Discuss important forecasting tools used in strategic management.
5. Discuss the importance of monitoring external trends and events.
6. Explain how to develop an EFE Matrix.
7. Explain how to develop a Competitive Profile Matrix.
8. Discuss the importance of gathering competitive intelligence.
9. Describe the trend toward cooperation among competitors.
10. Discuss the political environment in Russia.
11. Discuss the global challenge facing American firms.

NOTABLE QUOTES

If you're not faster than your competitor, you're in a tenuous position, and if you're only half as fast, you're terminal.

GEORGE SALK

The opportunities and threats existing in any situation always exceed the resources needed to exploit the opportunities or avoid the threats. Thus, strategy is essentially a problem of allocating resources. If strategy is to be successful, it must allocate superior resources against a decisive opportunity.

WILLIAM COHEN

Organizations pursue strategies that will disrupt the normal course of industry events and forge new industry conditions to the disadvantage of competitors.

IAN C. MACMILLAN

The idea is to concentrate our strength against our competitor's relative weakness.

BRUCE HENDERSON

There was a time in America when business was easier. We set the pace for the rest of the world. We were immune to serious foreign competition. Many of us were regulated [and] therefore protected. No longer. Today's leaders must recreate themselves and their ways of doing business in order to stay on top and stay competitive.

ROBERT H. WATERMAN, JR.

If everyone is thinking alike, then somebody isn't thinking.

GEORGE PATTON

Prediction is very difficult, especially about the future.

NEILS BOHR

The best preparation for good work tomorrow is to do good work today.

ELBERT HUBBARD

This chapter examines the tools and concepts needed to conduct an external strategic management audit (sometimes called *environmental scanning* or *industry analysis*). An *external audit* focuses on identifying and evaluating trends and events beyond the control of a single firm, such as increased foreign competition, population shifts to the Sunbelt, an aging society, consumer fear of traveling, and stock market volatility. An external audit reveals key opportunities and threats confronting an organization so that managers can formulate strategies to take advantage of the opportunities and avoid or reduce the impact of threats. This chapter presents a practical framework for gathering, assimilating, and analyzing external information.

THE NATURE OF AN EXTERNAL AUDIT

The purpose of an *external audit* is to develop a finite list of opportunities that could benefit a firm and threats that should be avoided. As the term *finite* suggests, the external audit is not aimed at developing an exhaustive list of every possible factor that could influence the business; rather, it is aimed at identifying key variables that offer actionable responses. Firms should be able to respond either offensively or defensively to the factors by formulating strategies that take advantage of external opportunities or that minimize the impact of potential threats. Figure 3–1 illustrates how the external audit fits into the strategic-management process.

Key External Forces

External forces can be divided into five broad categories: (1) economic forces; (2) social, cultural, demographic, and environmental forces; (3) political, governmental, and legal forces; (4) technological forces; and (5) competitive forces. Relationships among these forces and an organization are depicted in Figure 3–2. External trends and events significantly affect all products, services, markets, and organizations in the world.

Changes in external forces translate into changes in consumer demand for both industrial and consumer products and services. External forces affect the types of products developed, the nature of positioning and market segmentation strategies, the types of services offered, and the choice of businesses to acquire or sell. External forces directly affect both suppliers and distributors. Identifying and evaluating external opportunities and threats enables organizations to develop a clear mission, to design strategies to achieve long-term objectives, and to develop policies to achieve annual objectives.

The increasing complexity of business today is evidenced by more countries developing the capacity and will to compete aggressively in world markets. Foreign businesses and countries are willing to learn, adapt, innovate, and invent to compete successfully in the marketplace. There are more competitive new technologies in Europe and the Far East today than ever before. American businesses can no longer beat foreign competitors with ease.

The Process of Performing an External Audit

The process of performing an external audit must involve as many managers and employees as possible. As emphasized in earlier chapters, involvement in the strategic management process can lead to understanding and commitment from organizational members. Individuals appreciate having the opportunity to contribute ideas and to gain a better understanding of their firm's industry, competitors, and markets.

FIGURE 3–1

A Comprehensive Strategic-Management Model

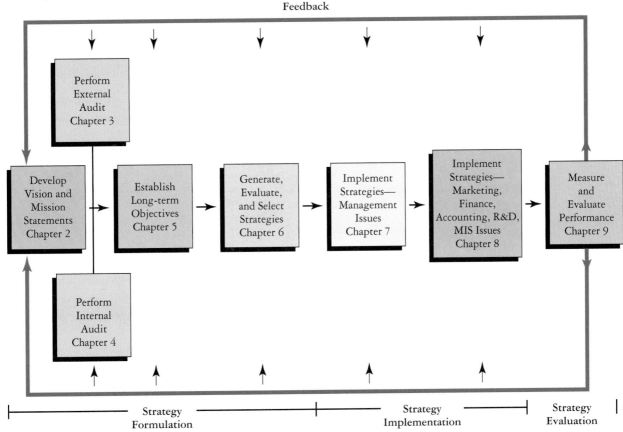

To perform an external audit, a company first must gather competitive intelligence and information about economic, social, cultural, demographic, environmental, political, governmental, legal, and technological trends. Individuals can be asked to monitor various sources of information, such as key magazines, trade journals, and newspapers. These persons can submit periodic scanning reports to a committee of managers charged with performing the external audit. This approach provides a continuous stream of timely strategic information and involves many individuals in the external-audit process. The Internet provides another source for gathering strategic information, as do corporate, university, and public libraries. Suppliers, distributors, salespersons, customers, and competitors represent other sources of vital information.

Once information is gathered, it should be assimilated and evaluated. A meeting or series of meetings of managers is needed to collectively identify the most important opportunities and threats facing the firm. These key external factors should be listed on flip charts or a blackboard. A prioritized list of these factors could be obtained by requesting that all managers rank the factors identified, from 1 for the most important opportunity/threat to 20 for the least important opportunity/threat. These key external factors can vary over time and by industry. Relationships with suppliers or distributors are often a critical success factor. Other variables commonly used include market share,

VISIT THE NET

Describes the external audit process in a university setting.

http://horizon.unc.edu/ projects/seminars/ futuresresearch/stages.asp

FIGURE 3–2

Relationships Between Key External Forces and an Organization

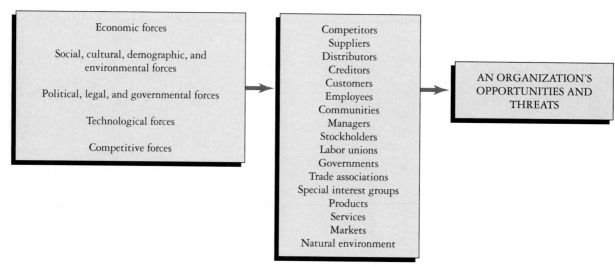

breadth of competing products, world economies, foreign affiliates, proprietary and key account advantages, price competitiveness, technological advancements, population shifts, interest rates, and pollution abatement.

Freund emphasized that these key external factors should be (1) important to achieving long-term and annual objectives, (2) measurable, (3) applicable to all competing firms, and (4) hierarchical in the sense that some will pertain to the overall company and others will be more narrowly focused on functional or divisional areas.[1] A final list of the most important key external factors should be communicated and distributed widely in the organization. Both opportunities and threats can be key external factors.

ECONOMIC FORCES

As domestic and global economies slowly recover from recession, consumer confidence and disposable income are the lowest in a decade, whereas unemployment and consumer debt are the highest in a decade. Stock prices, interest rates, corporate profits, exports, and imports are all very low in the United States and abroad. Foreign direct investment among countries fell by nearly 50 percent in 2001, the sharpest decline in thirty years. The number and value of cross-country mergers in 2001 fell to less than one-third the volume of the year before, as the overall downturn in international investment worsened following the September 11, 2001, terrorist attacks.

Increasing numbers of two-income households is an economic trend in America. As affluence increases, individuals place a premium on time. Improved customer service, immediate availability, trouble-free operation of products, and dependable maintenance and repair services are becoming more important. Americans today are more willing than ever to pay for good service if it limits inconvenience.

Economic factors have a direct impact on the potential attractiveness of various strategies. For example, when interest rates rise, funds needed for capital expansion become more costly or unavailable. Also, when interest rates rise, discretionary income declines, and the demand for discretionary goods falls. When stock prices increase, the desirability of equity as a source of capital for market development increases. Also, when the market rises, consumer and business wealth expands. A summary of economic variables that often represent opportunities and threats for organizations is provided in Table 3–1.

Trends in the dollar's value have significant and unequal effects on companies in different industries and in different locations. For example, the pharmaceutical, tourism, entertainment, motor vehicle, aerospace, and forest products industries benefit greatly when the dollar falls against the yen and euro. Agricultural and petroleum industries are hurt by the dollar's rise against the currencies of Mexico, Brazil, Venezuela, and Australia. Generally, a strong or high dollar makes American goods more expensive in overseas markets. This worsens America's trade deficit. When the value of the dollar falls, tourism-oriented firms benefit because Americans do not travel abroad as much when the value of the dollar is low; rather, foreigners visit and vacation more in the United States.

A low value of the dollar means lower imports and higher exports; it helps U.S. companies' competitiveness in world markets. Recent years have seen the U.S. dollar gaining against virtually every other currency. One benefit of this trend is that consumers pay less for imported goods such as cars and computer memory chips. Domestic firms that manufacture extensively outside the United States also benefit from the rising value of the dollar. The euro lost nearly a quarter of its value against the dollar in 2000 and 2001. As the value of the dollar declines, prices of products the United States imports increase, which can result in higher inflation and interest rates domestically.

Every business day, thousands of American workers learn that they will lose their jobs. More than 500,000 annual employee layoffs by U.S. firms in the 1990s led to terms such as *downsizing, rightsizing,* and *decruiting* becoming common. European firms, too, are beginning to downsize. The U.S. and world economies face a sustained period of slow, low-inflationary expansion, global overcapacity, high unemployment, price wars, and increased competitiveness. Thousands of laid-off workers are being forced to become entrepreneurs to make a living. The United States is becoming more entrepreneurial every day.

VISIT THE NET

Provides excellent narrative on NASA's strategic-management process, especially its external assessment activities. Provides NASA's entire strategic plan with outstanding narrative and illustrations about how to do strategic planning. http://www.hq.nasa.gov/office/nsp/toc.htm

TABLE 3–1   **Key Economic Variables to Be Monitored**

Shift to a service economy in the United States	Demand shifts for different categories of goods and services
Availability of credit	Income differences by region and consumer groups
Level of disposable income	
Propensity of people to spend	Price fluctuations
Interest rates	Export of labor and capital from the United States
Inflation rates	
Money market rates	Monetary policies
Federal government budget deficits	Fiscal policies
Gross domestic product trend	Tax rates
Consumption patterns	European Economic Community (ECC) policies
Unemployment trends	
Worker productivity levels	Organization of Petroleum Exporting Countries (OPEC) policies
Value of the dollar in world markets	
Stock market trends	Coalitions of Lesser Developed Countries (LDC) policies
Foreign countries' economic conditions	
Import/export factors	

Deregulation of industries worldwide is acting to restrain inflation worldwide. Deregulation in the utility and telecommunications industries, for example, is lowering electricity and phone prices worldwide. Energy deregulation worldwide contributes to keeping inflation in check in most industrialized countries of the world. Global cross-border mergers and alliances, too, serve to increase competitiveness within industries, thus lowering prices and also lessening inflation pressures worldwide.

The 15-nation European Union (EU) is Iran's biggest trading partner, with imports exceeding $5 billion annually. To the dismay of U.S. officials, the EU is close to signing an economic trade pact with Iran, despite the fact that the Khatami government in Iran supports some Mideast terrorist groups, such as Hezbollah and Hamas, in their fight against Israel. U.S. companies are today banned from investing in or trading with Iran, while the EU looks to further its trade ties.

The North American Free Trade Agreement (NAFTA) has spurred economic trade between the United States and Mexico. For example, since the United States signed the treaty, its exports to Mexico have increased 170 percent, far above the 68 percent gain for overall U.S. exports. In 2000, the United States ran a $25 billion trade deficit with Mexico, compared to $84 billion with China and $81 billion with Japan. More than $85 billion of investment has gone into the Mexican economy since NAFTA was born. However, in 2001, as a result of the recession that had struck the U.S. and world economies, more than 60,000 individuals were laid off from work along the Mexican border with the United States.[2]

Russia's Economy

The Russian economy is in trouble. Many companies are bankrupt and out of cash but keep operating. Many employees are not paid in cash but keep working. Many companies do not pay their electricity bills yet rarely face power cutoffs. *Business Week* magazine calls the Russian economy bizarre because real money, goods, and output play such a small role.[3] Most business between companies and individuals is done through IOUs known as *veksel* and barter. Noncash forms of payment now make up 45 percent of most companies' and cities' budget. Some companies rely totally on barter, such as Velta Company, a bicycle factory on the outskirts of the Western Russia city of Perm, which pays its employees in bicycles.

The major barriers to increased U.S. exports to Russia are a substantial value-added tax, high import duties, and onerous Russian excise levies. In addition, the government has imposed strict quality and safety standards on the majority of goods entering Russia. However, Russian standards authorities have permitted only a tightly circumscribed number of groups to perform this testing in the United States. The customs clearance process at Russian border points is frequently cumbersome and unpredictable. Local transportation problems also complicate the process of getting goods to the Russian market.

SOCIAL, CULTURAL, DEMOGRAPHIC, AND ENVIRONMENTAL FORCES

Social, cultural, demographic, and environmental changes have a major impact upon virtually all products, services, markets, and customers. Small, large, for-profit and non-profit organizations in all industries are being staggered and challenged by the opportunities and threats arising from changes in social, cultural, demographic, and environmental variables. In every way, the United States is much different today than it was yesterday, and tomorrow promises even greater changes.

The United States is getting older and less Caucasian. The oldest members of America's 76 million baby boomers plan to retire in 2011, and this has lawmakers and younger taxpayers deeply concerned about who will pay their social security, Medicare, and Medicaid. Individuals age 65 and older in the United States as a percent of the population will rise to 18.5 percent by 2025.

By the year 2075, the United States will have no racial or ethnic majority. This forecast is aggravating tensions over issues such as immigration and affirmative action. Hawaii, California, and New Mexico already have no majority race or ethnic group.

Population of the world passed 6 billion on October 12, 1999; the United States has less than 300 million people. That leaves billions of people outside the United States who may be interested in the products and services produced through domestic firms. Remaining solely domestic is an increasingly risky strategy, especially as the world population continues to grow to estimated numbers of 7 billion in 2013, 8 billion in 2028, and 9 billion in 2054.

Social, cultural, demographic, and environmental trends are shaping the way Americans live, work, produce, and consume. New trends are creating a different type of consumer and, consequently, a need for different products, different services, and different strategies. There are now more American households with people living alone or with unrelated people than there are households consisting of married couples with children. Census data suggest that Americans are not returning to traditional lifestyles. Church membership fell substantially during the 1980s for nearly all religious denominations, except for Southern Baptists and Mormons. It is interesting to note that Protestant churches in the United States take in over $7 billion in donations annually. The eight largest U.S. church denominations are (in millions of members) Roman Catholic (60.3), Southern Baptist (15.7), National Baptist (11.7), United Methodist (8.5), Lutheran (5.2), Mormon (4.7), Presbyterian (3.7), and Episcopalian (3.5).

Significant trends for the 2000s include consumers becoming more educated, the population aging, minorities becoming more influential, people looking for local rather than federal solutions to problems, and fixation on youth decreasing. The United States Census Bureau projects that the number of Hispanics will increase to 15 percent of the population by 2021, when they will become a larger minority group than African Americans in America. The percentage of African Americans in the U.S. population is expected to increase to 14 percent by 2021. Many states currently have more than 500,000 Hispanics as registered voters, including California, New Mexico, Arizona, Texas, Florida, New York, Illinois, and New Jersey. The Hispanic population in the United States increased by over 40 percent in the 1990s. States with the largest percentage increase of Hispanics during that period were Arkansas (149%), Nevada (124%), North Carolina (110%), Georgia (103%), and Nebraska (96%).

During the 1990s, the number of individuals age fifty and over increased 18.5 percent—to 76 million. In contrast, the number of Americans under age fifty grew by just 3.5 percent. The trend toward an older America is good news for restaurants, hotels, airlines, cruise lines, tours, resorts, theme parks, luxury products and services, recreational vehicles, home builders, furniture producers, computer manufacturers, travel services, pharmaceutical firms, automakers, and funeral homes. Older Americans are especially interested in healthcare, financial services, travel, crime prevention, and leisure. The world's longest-living people are the Japanese, with Japanese women living to 86.3 years and men living to 80.1 years on average. By 2050, the Census Bureau projects that the number of Americans age one hundred and older will increase to over 834,000 from just under 100,000 centenarians in the United States in 2000. Senior citizens are also senior executives at hundreds of American companies. Examples include eighty-seven-year-old William Dillard at Dillard's Department Stores; seventy-nine-year-old Sumner Redstone, CEO of Viacom; seventy-one-year-old Ellen Gordon, president of Tootsie Roll Industries; seventy-seven-year-old Richard Jacobs, CEO of the Cleveland Indians; seventy-six-year-old Leslie Quick, CEO of Quick & Reilly; eighty-three-year-old Ralph

Roberts, chairman of Comcast; and seventy-six-year-old Alan Greenspan, chairman of the Federal Reserve. Americans age sixty-five and over will increase from 12.6 percent of the U.S. population in 2000 to 20.0 percent by the year 2050.

The aging American population affects the strategic orientation of nearly all organizations. Apartment complexes for the elderly, with one meal a day, transportation, and utilities included in the rent, have increased nationwide. Called *lifecare facilities,* these complexes now exceed two million. Some well-known companies building these facilities include Avon, Marriott, and Hyatt. By the year 2005, individuals age sixty-five and older in the United States will rise to 13 percent of the total population; Japan's elderly population ratio will rise to 17 percent, and Germany's to 19 percent.

Americans are on the move in a population shift to the South and West (Sunbelt) and away from the Northeast and Midwest (Frost Belt). The Internal Revenue Service provides the Census Bureau with massive computer files of demographic data. By comparing individual address changes from year to year, the Census Bureau publishes extensive information about population shifts across the country. For example, Nevada is the fastest-growing state. Arizona, Colorado, and Florida are close behind. States incurring the greatest loss of people are North Dakota, West Virginia, Iowa, Louisiana, and Pennsylvania. This type of information can be essential for successful strategy formulation, including where to locate new plants and distribution centers and where to focus marketing efforts.

Americans are becoming less interested in fitness and exercise. Fitness participants declined in the United States by 3.5 percent annually in the 1990s. Makers of fitness products, such as Nike, Reebok International, and CML Group—which makes NordicTrack—are experiencing declines in sales growth. American Sports Data in Hartsdale, New York, reports that "the one American in five who exercises regularly is now outnumbered by three couch potatoes."

Except for terrorism, no greater threat to business and society exists than the voracious, continuous decimation and degradation of our natural environment. The U.S. Clean Air Act went into effect in 1994. The U.S. Clean Water Act went into effect in 1984. As indicated in the Natural Environment Perspective box, air and water pollution causes great anguish worldwide. A summary of important social, cultural, demographic, and environmental variables that represent opportunities or threats for virtually all organizations is given in Table 3–2.

The U.S.–Mexican Border

Stretching 2,100 miles from the Pacific Ocean to the Gulf of Mexico, this 180-mile-wide strip of land is North America's fastest-growing region. With 11 million people and $150 billion in output, this region's economy is larger than Poland's. For the 6.1 million residents on the U.S. side, the average hourly wage plus benefits is $7.71, but for the 5.1 million residents on the Mexican side, the average is $1.36. The developed and developing nations meet along this border, which features shantytowns just down the street from luxury residential neighborhoods.

There are now over fifteen hundred *maquiladoras* (assembly plants) on the Mexican side of the border. Many analysts contend that the *maquiladoras* are a vital key to continued U.S. global competitiveness. Mexico now ranks only behind China as global investors' favorite location for establishing business in the developing world. Amid the swelter of economic activity, deep disparities and contrasts are likely to persist. But the two sides of the border are now so interdependent that they can only move forward together.

Tijuana, fifteen minutes from San Diego, is the television-manufacturing capital of the world. Plants of Sony, Samsung, Matsushita, and others produce fourteen million units annually. Per capita income in San Diego is $25,000; in Tijuana, it is $3,200.

TABLE 3-2   **Key Social, Cultural, Demographic, and Environmental Variables**

Childbearing rates	Attitudes toward retirement
Number of special interest groups	Attitudes toward leisure time
Number of marriages	Attitudes toward product quality
Number of divorces	Attitudes toward customer service
Number of births	Pollution control
Number of deaths	Attitudes toward foreign peoples
Immigration and emigration rates	Energy conservation
Social security programs	Social programs
Life expectancy rates	Number of churches
Per capita income	Number of church members
Location of retailing, manufacturing, and service businesses	Social responsibility
	Attitudes toward careers
Attitudes toward business	Population changes by race, age, sex, and level of affluence
Lifestyles	
Traffic congestion	Attitudes toward authority
Inner-city environments	Population changes by city, county, state, region, and country
Average disposable income	
Trust in government	Value placed on leisure time
Attitudes toward government	Regional changes in tastes and preferences
Attitudes toward work	Number of women and minority workers
Buying habits	Number of high school and college graduates by geographic area
Ethical concerns	
Attitudes toward saving	Recycling
Sex roles	Waste management
Attitudes toward investing	Air pollution
Racial equality	Water pollution
Use of birth control	Ozone depletion
Average level of education	Endangered species
Government regulation	

Cuidad Juarez, midway between the Pacific Ocean and the Gulf of Mexico and just 15 minutes from El Paso, has 235 factories employing 178,000, the largest concentration of *maquiladoras* anywhere along the border. General Motors alone has 17 auto parts plants. But explosive industrial growth and uncontrolled urban expansion have far surpassed municipal services such as sewers and street paving. Juarez and El Paso share the worst air pollution anywhere on the border.

Nuevo Laredo, fifteen minutes from Laredo, Texas, is home to the largest rail and truck crossings of the Rio Grande River from Mexico into the United States. More than 4,000 loaded trucks cross the Rio Grande daily at Nuevo Laredo, which is home to Wal-Mart's largest distribution center.

 POLITICAL, GOVERNMENTAL, AND LEGAL FORCES

Federal, state, local, and foreign governments are major regulators, deregulators, subsidizers, employers, and customers of organizations. Political, governmental, and legal factors, therefore, can represent key opportunities or threats for both small and large organizations.

NATURAL ENVIRONMENT PERSPECTIVE

Is Your Business Polluting the Air or Water?

AIR

More than 1.5 billion people around the world live in urban areas with dangerous levels or air pollution. Alarmingly, cities are growing too rapidly to reverse this trend. Seven of the ten worst cities for sulfur dioxide and carbon monoxide are in developing countries. These and other pollutants cause acute and chronic lung disease, heart disease, lung cancer, and lead-induced neurological damage in children. Lung cancer alone kills over one million people annually, and more than a million new cases of lung cancer are diagnosed annually. In the European Union countries, a 33 percent increase in female lung cancer cases is predicted by 2005. There is no effective treatment for lung cancer—only 10 percent of patients are alive five years after diagnosis. Polluted air knows no city, state, country or continent boundaries.

The Environmental Protection Agency (EPA) wants to expand air pollution regulations in the United States to cover microscopic particles as tiny as 2.5 microns, down from the current standard of 10 microns. The EPA says this will cut premature deaths in the United States by 20,000; cases or aggravated asthma by 250,000; cases of acute childhood respiratory problems by 250,000; bronchitis cases by 60,000; hospital admissions by 9,000; and cases of major breathing problems by 1.5 million. The total savings of these benefits would exceed $115 billion. Critics say the proposed new regulations will cost U.S. companies and cities too much.

Source: Adapted from William Miller, "Clean-Air Contention," *Industry Week* (May 5, 1997): 14. Also, *World Health Organization Report* (1997).

WATER

Is your business polluting the water? Contaminated water is blamed for as much as 80 percent of all disease in developing countries. Well over one billion people in the world still are without safe water to drink, bathe, cook, and clean. Less than 2 percent of the domestic and industrial wastewater generated in developing countries receives any kind of treatment; it just runs into rivers and groundwater resources, thus poisoning populations, the environment, and the planet. Unsafe drinking water is a prime cause of diarrhea, malaria, cancer, infant deformities, and infant mortality. A few statistics reveal the severity, harshness, and effect of water pollution.

- More than five million babies born in developing countries die annually in the first month of life, mainly because of polluted water.
- About four million babies are born with deformities annually.
- Diarrhea and dysentery kill 2.5 million people annually.
- Malaria kills 2.1 million people annually.

Industrial discharge, a major water problem even in the United States, contributes significantly to the dramatic rise in cancer both here and abroad. More than 10 million new cases of cancer are diagnosed annually, and about 6.5 million people die of cancer annually. More than 1.2 billion of these deaths are caused by stomach and colon cancer, two types often associated with poor water and eating habits. Besides deaths, the anguish, sickness, suffering, and expense inflicted upon people directly or indirectly because of contaminated water is immeasurably high even in the United States. Dangerous industrial chemicals are used here as fertilizers, pesticides, solvents, food additives, fuels, medicines, cosmetics, and in a wide range of manufacturing processes.

The EPA's most recent proposal for the Great Lakes would reduce by 91 percent the twenty-two toxic chemicals comprising about ninety thousand pounds being dumped each year into those waters. The chemicals include mercury, dioxin, chlordane, DDT, and mirex.

Source: Adapted from *World Health Organization Report* (1997). John Jones, "EPA Proposes to Limit PCBs In Great Lakes," *The Wall Street Journal* (September 27, 1999): B19G.

E-COMMERCE PERSPECTIVE

e·biz

Should Internet Sales Remain Tax Free?

Currently, nobody pays sales taxes when they buy books, clothing, cars, or anything else on the Internet. The average sales tax nationwide is 6.3 percent, so the absence of any tax on Internet sales means that state and local governments are giving e-business a huge subsidy. Currently about 49 percent of all state tax revenues are from sales taxes, more than individual and corporate taxes combined. Those revenues are used for schools, law enforcement, highway repair and other work of governments. Traditional retail stores argue that it will soon be impossible for them to compete with e-tailers if Internet sales remain tax free.

A thorny question thus looms on the horizon in terms of whether to tax Internet sales. With online sales rising 300 percent a year and topping $1 trillion in 2003, advocates pro and con debate whether those sales taxes should go uncollected. The national moratorium on new Internet taxes was renewed for three years in October 2001. Grover Norquist, president of Americans for Tax Reform says, "Any business guy stupid enough to participate in leading the charge to tax the Internet is going to find that tax named after him or his company." And surely no state or federal legislator wants an Internet tax named for him or her.

Some considerations and contentions regarding taxing Internet sales are as follows:

- Keeping Internet sales tax-free will help the economy grow faster.

- Traditional merchants contend that online shopping with no sales tax robs them of customers.

- Local and state governments contend those sales tax dollars are needed for schools and public safety.

- Americans may buy from foreign companies if sales taxes are imposed on Internet shopping.

- Consumers in other countries may bypass U.S. products if sales taxes are imposed.

- Imposing a sales tax on Internet shopping will slow the growth of Internet shopping, thus hutting online businesses.

- Neither state nor federal legislators want to be responsible for tax increases.

- Currently there are over sixty-six hundred sales tax jurisdictions in the United States; taxing Internet sales could logistically be a nightmare for interstate retailers who would have to calculate these rates.

- Research concludes that online spending would drop by 30 percent or more if taxes were suddenly imposed. This would cripple many marginal Internet businesses.

Source: Adapted from: Mike France, "A Web Sales Tax: Not If, But When," *Business Week* (June 21, 1999): 104–106. Also, Richard Wolf, "Taxes on Internet Sales Opposed," *USA Today* (September 14, 1999): 6A.

Mexican companies laid off almost half a million employees during the first ten months of 2001; these companies included ADC Telecommunications (4,300 in Chihuahua), Goodyear (1,559 in Tultitlán), Selectron (2,000 in Guadalajara), General Motors (600 in Ramos Arizpe), and Vtech (3,000 in Guadalajara). Mexico has very strict regulations that penalize employers with expensive severance packages who lay off employees. For example, when Goodyear Tire & Rubber fired nearly 1,600 workers from a factory outside Mexico City recently, the company paid more that $48 million in severance pay— an average of $31,000 per worker. Federal government decisions regarding taxation of Internet sales is an important factor, as indicated in the E-Commerce Perspective box.

For industries and firms that depend heavily on government contracts or subsidies, political forecasts can be the most important part of an external audit. Changes in patent laws, antitrust legislation, tax rates, and lobbying activities can affect firms significantly. The U.S. Justice Department offers excellent information at its Web site (**www.usdoj. gov**) on such topics.

In the world of biopolitics, Americans are still deeply divided over issues such as assisted suicide, genetic testing, genetic engineering, cloning, stem-cell research, and abortion. Such political issues have great ramifications for companies in many industries, ranging from pharmaceuticals to computers.

The increasing global interdependence among economies, markets, governments, and organizations makes it imperative that firms consider the possible impact of political variables on the formulation and implementation of competitive strategies. A number of nationally known firms forecast political, governmental, and legal variables. Some of the best Web sites for finding legal help on the Internet are listed below:[4]

> www.findlaw.com
> www.lawguru.com
> www.freeadvice.com
> www.nolo.com
> www.lectlaw.com
> www.abanet.org

Political forecasting can be especially critical and complex for multinational firms that depend on foreign countries for natural resources, facilities, the distribution of products, special assistance, or customers. Strategists today must possess skills that enable them to deal more legalistically and politically than previous strategists, whose attention was directed more toward economic and technical affairs of the firm. Strategists today are spending more time anticipating and influencing public policy actions. They spend more time meeting with government officials, attending hearings and government-sponsored conferences, giving public speeches, and meeting with trade groups, industry associations, and government agency directors. Before entering or expanding international operations, strategists need a good understanding of the political and decision-making processes in countries where their firms may conduct business. For example, republics that made up the former Soviet Union differ greatly in wealth, resources, language, and lifestyle.

Increasing global competition accents the need for accurate political, governmental, and legal forecasts. Many strategists will have to become familiar with political systems in Europe, Africa, and Asia and with trading currency futures. East Asian countries already have become world leaders in labor-intensive industries. A world market has emerged from what previously was a multitude of distinct national markets, and the climate for international business today is much more favorable than yesterday. Mass communication and high technology are creating similar patterns of consumption in diverse cultures worldwide. This means that many companies may find it difficult to survive by relying solely on domestic markets.

> It is no exaggeration that in an industry that is, or is rapidly becoming, global, the riskiest possible posture is to remain a domestic competitor. The domestic competitor will watch as more aggressive companies use this growth to capture economies of scale and learning. The domestic competitor will then be faced with an attack on domestic markets using different (and possibly superior) technology, product design, manufacturing, marketing approaches, and economies of scale. A few examples suggest how extensive the phenomenon of world markets has already become. Hewlett-Packard's manufacturing chain reaches halfway around the globe, from well-paid, skilled engineers in California to low-wage assembly workers in Malaysia. General Electric has survived as a manufacturer of inexpensive audio products by centralizing its world production in Singapore.[5]

Local, state, and federal laws, regulatory agencies, and special interest groups can have a major impact on the strategies of small, large, for-profit, and nonprofit organizations. Many companies have altered or abandoned strategies in the past because of political or governmental actions. Other federal regulatory agencies include the Food and Drug Administration (FDA), the National Highway Traffic and Safety Administration (NHTSA), the Occupational Safety and Health Administration (OSHA), the Consumer Product Safety Commission (CPSC), the Federal Trade Commission (FTC), the Securities and Exchange Commission (SEC), the Equal Employment Opportunity Commission (EEOC), the Federal Communications Commission (FCC), the Federal Maritime Commission (FMC), the Interstate Commerce Commission (ICC), the Federal Energy Regulatory Commission (FERC), the National Labor Relations Board (NLRB), and the Civil Aeronautics Board (CAB). A summary of political, governmental, and legal variables that can represent key opportunities or threats to organizations is provided in Table 3–3.

Russia

Russia's gross domestic product grew 8.3 percent in 2000 and another 5 percent in 2001 due partly to high world commodity prices. Despite economic growth in Russia, the country's debt payments as a proportion of GDP are growing—to 5.4 percent in 2003 from 4.7 percent in 2001. Russia has announced it cannot repay upcoming loans on international capital markets.

However Russia is the last large country outside of the World Trade Organization and is prepared to make big concessions to join the WTO. Russia has agreed to open its markets in banking, insurance, and agriculture, but not in the automobile and aircraft industries. The Russian parliament is currenting passing legislation to pave the way for WTO rules and policies.

The Russian government has failed at one of its primary responsibilities—collecting taxes. The government has no money to send to regional governments for social services or the military, or to pay government employees. It has no money to run the judicial system or to enforce federal laws. Many Russian people have lost trust in their government, their banking system, their legal system, and their currency. Law and order itself is in jeopardy in Russia as a result of a crippled economy. Mismanagement of the economy and corruption have so severely discredited democracy in the eyes of ordinary Russian people that communist and organized-crime approaches to government are the rule rather than the exception. President Putin promises to crack down on organized crime, revamp the Russian tax code, strengthen the judiciary, and maintain democratic freedoms.

The climate for business in Russia is poor because of the continued devaluation of the ruble, high unemployment, organized crime, high inflation, and skyrocketing taxes.

TABLE 3–3   Some Political, Governmental, and Legal Variables

Government regulations or deregulations	Sino-American relationships
Changes in tax laws	Russian-American relationships
Special tariffs	European-American relationships
Political action committees	African-American relationships
Voter participation rates	Import-export regulations
Number, severity, and location of government protests	Government fiscal and monetary policy changes
Number of patents	Political conditions in foreign countries
Changes in patent laws	Special local, state, and federal laws
Environmental protection laws	Lobbying activities
Level of defense expenditures	Size of government budgets
Legislation on equal employment	World oil, currency, and labor markets
Level of government subsidies	Location and severity of terrorist activities
Antitrust legislation	Local, state, and national elections

Russian tax laws are among the world's most punitive and confusing, so firms keep business off the books to avoid paying out about 90 percent of their profits to the government. Tax receipts by the Russian government are far lower than expected or needed to run the country.

It is almost impossible today to run a business in Russia legally. Racketeering, money laundering, financial scams, and organized criminal activity plague businesses. Russian organized crime operations have been so successful within the country that they now aggressively infiltrate governments and businesses worldwide.

The risk of business investments in Russia decreases from south to north and west to east. Thus, investments in Siberia and along the Pacific coast are more stable and much less corrupt than those near Moscow or the Russian areas bordering Europe. Because the ruble is virtually of no value in Russia, companies need to pay their workers with something besides money, such as apartments, healthcare, and medical and food products. Bartering is an excellent way to motivate Russian workers.

Since the war on terrorism began in late 2001, Russia and the United States have become much better friends, and implications suggest that trade and cooperation between the two countries are improving rapidly. President Bush and President Putin realize that they and their countries need each other, and rapport between the two leaders is excellent. *Business Week* says, "As the United States and Russia become allies determined to defeat the same foe, their political and economic interests are starting to converge. Putin has recently pushed through the Duma a broad array of reform legislation that makes U.S. investments in Russia much more attractive."[6] In contrast to the early 1990s and earlier, more and more Russian businesses are succeeding today through good management and high quality products rather than through bribery and crime. Russia's gross national product grew 8.4 percent in 2000 and 5.5 percent in 2001, making it one of the world's fastest growing economies.

 ## TECHNOLOGICAL FORCES

Revolutionary technological changes and discoveries are having a dramatic impact on organizations. Superconductivity advancements alone, which increase the power of electrical products by lowering resistance to current, are revolutionizing business operations, especially in the transportation, utility, healthcare, electrical, and computer industries.

The *Internet* is acting as a national and even global economic engine that is spurring productivity, a critical factor in a country's ability to improve living standards. The Internet is saving companies billions of dollars in distribution and transaction costs from direct sales to self-service systems. For example, the familiar Hypertext Markup Language (HTML) is being replaced by Extensible Markup Language (XML). XML is a programming language based on "tags," whereby a number represents a price, an invoice, a date, a zip code, or whatever. XML is forcing companies to make a major strategic decision in terms of whether to open their information to the world in the form of catalogs, inventories, prices and specifications, or to attempt to withhold their data to preserve some perceived advantage.[7] XML is reshaping industries, reducing prices, accelerating global trade, and revolutionizing all commerce. Microsoft and other software companies reoriented most of its software development around XML, replacing HTML.

The Internet is changing the very nature of opportunities and threats by altering the life cycles of products, increasing the speed of distribution, creating new products and services, erasing limitations of traditional geographic markets, and changing the historical trade-off between production standardization and flexibility. The Internet is altering economies of scale, changing entry barriers, and redefining the relationship between industries and various suppliers, creditors, customers, and competitors.

To effectively capitalize on e-commerce, a number of organizations are establishing two new positions in their firms: *chief information officer (CIO)* and *chief technology officer (CTO)*. This trend reflects the growing importance of *information technology (IT)* in strategic management. A CIO and CTO work together to ensure that information needed to formulate, implement, and evaluate strategies is available where and when it is needed. These individuals are responsible for developing, maintaining, and updating a company's information database. The CIO is more a manager, managing the overall external-audit process; the CTO is more a technician, focusing on technical issues such as data acquisition, data processing, decision-support systems, and software and hardware acquisition.

Technological forces represent major opportunities and threats that must be considered in formulating strategies. Technological advancements can dramatically affect organizations' products, services, markets, suppliers, distributors, competitors, customers, manufacturing processes, marketing practices, and competitive position. Technological advancements can create new markets, result in a proliferation of new and improved products, change the relative competitive cost positions in an industry, and render existing products and services obsolete. Technological changes can reduce or eliminate cost barriers between businesses, create shorter production runs, create shortages in technical skills, and result in changing values and expectations of employees, managers, and customers. Technological advancements can create new *competitive advantages* that are more powerful than existing advantages. No company or industry today is insulated against emerging technological developments. In high-tech industries, identification and evaluation of key technological opportunities and threats can be the most important part of the external strategic-management audit.

Organizations that traditionally have limited technology expenditures to what they can fund after meeting marketing and financial requirements urgently need a reversal in thinking. The pace of technological change is increasing and literally wiping out businesses every day. An emerging consensus holds that technology management is one of the key responsibilities of strategists. Firms should pursue strategies that take advantage of technological opportunities to achieve sustainable, competitive advantages in the marketplace.

> Technology-based issues will underlie nearly every important decision that strategists make. Crucial to those decisions will be the ability to approach technology planning analytically and strategically. . . . technology can be planned and managed using formal techniques similar to those used in business and capital investment planning. An effective technology strategy is built on a penetrating analysis of technology opportunities and threats, and an assessment of the relative importance of these factors to overall corporate strategy.[8]

In practice, critical decisions about technology too often are delegated to lower organizational levels or are made without an understanding of their strategic implications. Many strategists spend countless hours determining market share, positioning products in terms of features and price, forecasting sales and marker size, and monitoring distributors; yet too often, technology does not receive the same respect.

Not all sectors of the economy are affected equally by technological developments. The communications, electronics, aeronautics, and pharmaceutical industries are much more volatile than the textile, forestry, and metals industries. For strategists in industries affected by rapid technological change, identifying and evaluating technological opportunities and threats can represent the most important part of an external audit.

For example, in the office supply industry, business customers find that purchasing supplies over the Internet to be more convenient than shopping in a store. Office Depot was the first office supply company to establish a Web site for this purpose and remains the largest Internet office supply retailer, with close to $1 billion in sales. Staples, Inc., has recently also entered the Internet office supply business with its **staples.com** Web site, but it has yet to make a profit on these operations, although revenue growth from the site is growing dramatically.

 # COMPETITIVE FORCES

VISIT THE NET

Provides information regarding the importance of gathering information about competitors. This Web site offers audio answers to key questions about intelligence systems.
www.fuld.com

The top five U.S. competitors in four different industries are identified in Table 3–4. An important part of an external audit is identifying rival firms and determining their strengths, weaknesses, capabilities, opportunities, threats, objectives, and strategies.

Collecting and evaluating information on competitors is essential for successful strategy formulation. Identifying major competitors is not always easy because many firms have divisions that compete in different industries. Most multidivisional firms generally do not provide sales and profit information on a divisional basis for competitive reasons. Also, privately held firms do not publish any financial or marketing information.

However, many businesses use the Internet to obtain most of their information on competitors. The Internet is fast, thorough, accurate, and increasingly indispensable in this regard. Addressing questions about competitors such as those presented in Table 3–5 is important in performing an external audit.

Competition in virtually all industries can be described as intense—and sometimes as cutthroat. For example, when United Parcel Service (UPS) employees were on strike in 1997, competitors such as FedEx, Greyhound, Roadway, and United Airlines lowered prices, doubled advertising efforts, and locked new customers into annual contracts in efforts to leave UPS customer-less when the strike ended. If a firm detects weakness in a competitor, no mercy at all is shown in capitalizing on its problems.

Seven characteristics describe the most competitive companies in America: (1) Market share matters; the 90th share point isn't as important as the 91st, and nothing is more dangerous than falling to 89; (2) Understand and remember precisely what business you are in; (3) Whether it's broke or not, fix it—make it better; not just products, but the whole company, if necessary; (4) Innovate or evaporate; particularly in technology-driven businesses, nothing quite recedes like success; (5) Acquisition is essential to growth; the most successful purchases are in niches that add a technology or a related market; (6) People make a difference; tired of hearing it? Too bad; (7) There is no substitute for quality and no greater threat than failing to be cost-competitive on a global basis; these are complementary concepts, not mutually exclusive ones.[9]

Competitive Intelligence Programs

What is competitive intelligence? *Competitive intelligence,* as formally defined by the Society of Competitive Intelligence Professionals (SCIP), is a systematic and ethical process for gathering and analyzing information about the competition's activities and general business trends to further a business' own goals (SCIP Web site).

Good competitive intelligence in business, as in the military, is one of the keys to success. The more information and knowledge a firm can obtain about its competitors,

TABLE 3-4   The Top Five U.S. Competitors in Four Different Industries in 2002

	2001 SALES (IN $ MILLIONS)	PERCENTAGE CHANGE (FROM 2000)	2001 PROFITS (IN $ MILLIONS)	PERCENTAGE CHANGE FROM 2000
AEROSPACE				
Boeing	58,198	+13	2,826	+33
United Technologies	27,897	+5	1,938	+7
Lockheed Martin	23,990	−2	79	NM
Northrop Grumman	13,558	+78	427	−32
General Dynamics	12,163	+17	943	+5
FOREST PRODUCTS				
International Paper	26,363	−6	−1,142	NM
Georgia-Pacific	25,016	13	−255	NM
Weyerhaeuser	14,545	−9	354	−58
Boise Cascade	7,422	−5	−42	NM
Loussiana-Pacific	2,359	−20	−171	NM
COMPUTERS				
IBM	85,866	−3	7,723	−5
Hewlett-Packard	44,211	−11	712	−77
Compaq Computer	33,554	−21	−563	NM
Dell Computer	31,168	−2	1,246	−44
Xerox	19,228	−1	1,424	+143
PUBLISHING & BROADCASTING				
AOL Time Warner	38,234	NM	−4,921	NM
Walt Disney	24,884	−4	316	−63
Viacom	23,222	+16	−219	NM
Comcast	9,674	+18	226	−89
Gannett	6,344	+2	831	−14

Source: Adapted from Industry Rankings of the S&P 500, *Business Week* (Spring 2002): 87–113.
NM: Not Measurable.

the more likely it is that it can formulate and implement effective strategies. Major competitors' weaknesses can represent external opportunities; major competitors' strengths may represent key threats.

According to *Business Week*, there are more than five thousand corporate spies now actively engaged in intelligence activities, and nine out of ten large companies have employees dedicated solely to gathering competitive intelligence.[10] The article contends that many large U.S. companies spend more than $1 million annually tracking their competitors. Evidence suggests that the benefits of corporate spying include increased revenues, lower costs, and better decision making.

The global war on terrorism has even led countries to place more emphasis on gathering and sharing intelligence. Even former foes—such as the United States, Russia, China, and even Iran—share intelligence to reach common goals. Do you feel that intelligence sharing among countries will spur increased intelligence sharing among rival companies?

TABLE 3-5   Key Questions About Competitors

1. What are the major competitors' strengths?
2. What are the major competitors' weaknesses?
3. What are the major competitors' objectives and strategies?
4. How will the major competitors most likely respond to current economic, social, cultural, demographic, environmental, political, governmental, legal, technological, and competitive trends affecting our industry?
5. How vulnerable are the major competitors to our alternative company strategies?
6. How vulnerable are our alternative strategies to successful counterattack by our major competitors?
7. How are our products or services positioned relative to major competitors?
8. To what extent are new firms entering and old firms leaving this industry?
9. What key factors have resulted in our present competitive position in this industry?
10. How have the sales and profit rankings of major competitors in the industry changed over recent years? Why have these rankings changed that way?
11. What is the nature of supplier and distributor relationships in this industry?
12. To what extent could substitute products or services be a threat to competitors in this industry?

Unfortunately, the majority of U.S. executives grew up in times when American firms dominated foreign competitors so much that gathering competitive intelligence seemed not worth the effort. Too many of these executives still cling to these attitudes—to the detriment of their organizations today. Even most MBA programs do not offer a course in competitive and business intelligence, thus reinforcing this attitude. As a consequence, three strong misperceptions about business intelligence prevail among American executives today:

1. Running an intelligence program requires lots of people, computers, and other resources.
2. Collecting intelligence about competitors violates antitrust laws; business intelligence equals espionage.
3. Intelligence gathering is an unethical business practice.[11]

VISIT THE NET

Provides the strategic plan for the University of Hawaii, including its Planning Assumptions.
www2.hawaii.edu/uhhilo/strategic

All three of these perceptions are totally misguided. Any discussions with a competitor about price, market, or geography intentions could violate antitrust statutes, but this fact must not lure a firm into underestimating the need for and benefits of systematically collecting information about competitors for the purpose of enhancing a firm's effectiveness. The Internet has become an excellent medium for gathering competitive intelligence. Information gathering from employees, managers, suppliers, distributors, customers, creditors, and consultants also can make the difference between having superior or just average intelligence and overall competitiveness.

Firms need an effective competitive intelligence *(CI)* program. The three basic missions of a CI program are (1) to provide a general understanding of an industry and its competitors, (2) to identify areas in which competitors are vulnerable and to assess the impact strategic actions would have on competitors, and (3) to identify potential moves that a competitor might make that would endanger a firm's position in the market.[12] Competitive information is equally applicable for strategy formulation, implementation, and evaluation decisions. An effective CI program allows all areas of a firm to access consistent and verifiable information in making decisions. All members of an organization—from the chief executive officer to custodians—are valuable intelligence agents and should feel themselves to be a part of the CI process. Special characteristics of a successful CI program include flexibility, usefulness, timeliness, and cross-functional cooperation.

The increasing emphasis on *competitive analysis* in the United States is evidenced by corporations putting this function on their organizational charts under job titles such as Director of Competitive Analysis, Competitive Strategy Manager, Director of Information Services, or Associate Director of Competitive Assessment. The responsibilities of a *director of competitive analysis* include planning, collecting data, analyzing data, facilitating the process of gathering and analyzing data, disseminating intelligence on a timely basis, researching special issues, and recognizing what information is important and who needs to know. Competitive intelligence is not corporate espionage because 95 percent of the information a company needs in order to make strategic decisions is available and accessible to the public. Sources of competitive information include trade journals, want ads, newspaper articles, and government filings, as well as customers, suppliers, distributors, competitors themselves, and the Internet.

Unethical tactics such as bribery, wiretapping, and computer break-ins should never be used to obtain information. Marriott and Motorola—two American companies that do a particularly good job of gathering competitive intelligence—agree that all the information you could wish for can be collected without resorting to unethical tactics. They keep their intelligence staffs small, usually under five people, and spend less than $200,000 per year on gathering competitive intelligence.

Unilever recently sued Procter & Gamble (P&G) over that company's corporate-espionage activities to obtain the secrets of its Unilever hair-care business. After spending $3 million to establish a team to find out about competitors in the domestic hair-care industry, P&G allegedly took roughly eighty documents from garbage bins outside Unilever's Chicago offices. P&G produces Pantene and Head & Shoulders shampoos, while Unilver has hair-care brands such as ThermaSilk, Suave, Salon Selectives, and Finesse. Similarly, Oracle Corp. recently admitted that detectives it hired paid janitors to go through Microsoft Corp.'s garbage, looking for evidence to use in court.

The security software company McAfee estimates that cybertheft and cybervandalism cost U.S. companies $20 billion annually. More and more companies are, therefore, using new weapons to combat cyber-attacks, including "honey pots" and tracers. A honey pot is a fake server set up to trap the unwitting intruder and to monitor the hacker's every keystroke and method of entry. Tracers are surveillance algorithms powerful enough to trace a hacker's entry back to its origin. The Nimda computer virus in late 2001 crippled more than one million computers in the United States, Europe, and Asia, and it cost firms more than the earlier Code Red virus. The Code Red virus cost firms an estimated $2.4 billion in cleanup expenses.[13]

Cooperation Among Competitors

Strategies that stress cooperation among competitors are being used more. For example, Lockheed teamed up with British Aerospace PLC to compete against Boeing Company to develop the next-generation U.S. fighter jet. Lockheed's cooperative strategy with a profitable partner in the Airbus Industrie consortium encourages broader Lockheed-European collaboration as Europe's defense industry consolidates. The British firm offers Lockheed special expertise in the areas of short takeoff and vertical landing technologies, systems integration, and low-cost design and manufacturing.

Cooperative agreements between competitors are even becoming popular. For example, Boeing and Lockheed are working together to modernize the United States' overburdened air-traffic-control system. Northrop Grumman, also a competitor in the defense industry, may join the cooperative agreement too. For collaboration between

VISIT THE NET

Gives the National Oceanic and Atmospheric Administration (NOAA) Strategic Plan, including its external assessment.

http://www.strategic.noaa.gov/

competitors to succeed, both firms must contribute something distinctive, such as technology, distribution, basic research, or manufacturing capacity. But a major risk is that unintended transfers of important skills or technology may occur at organizational levels below where the deal was signed.[14] Information not covered in the formal agreement often gets traded in the day-to-day interactions and dealings of engineers, marketers, and product developers. Firms often give away too much information to rival firms when operating under cooperative agreements! Tighter formal agreements are needed.

Renault SA and Nissan Motor Company are forming a joint venture company solely to develop joint strategies whereby the two rival firms can cooperate more effectively. Renault already owns 36.8 percent of Nissan, and under the new company, Nissan may take part ownership of Renault. When cooperation among rival firms reaches high levels, part ownership between involved companies can be an effective strategy.

Two other fierce competitors, ABC and CBS, have formed a strategic alliance to share satellite-uplink facilities in Pakistan and another alliance with Fox News to share raw news footage. Satellite-uplink equipment costs up to $500,000, so sharing this expense benefits both firms. However, the two companies will not share stories or producers, and they remain fierce rivals; yet they desire to become "permanent partners" in mutually beneficial areas.

The idea of joining forces with a competitor is not easily accepted by Americans, who often view cooperation and partnerships with skepticism and suspicion. Indeed, joint ventures and cooperative arrangements among competitors demand a certain amount of trust if companies are to combat paranoia about whether one firm will injure the other. However, multinational firms are becoming more globally cooperative, and increasing numbers of domestic firms are joining forces with competitive foreign firms to reap mutual benefits. Kathryn Harrigan at Columbia University says, "Within a decade, most companies will be members of teams that compete against each other."

American companies often enter alliances primarily to avoid investments, being more interested in reducing the costs and risks of entering new businesses or markets than in acquiring new skills. In contrast, *learning from the partner* is a major reason why Asian and European firms enter into cooperative agreements. American firms, too, should place learning high on the list of reasons to cooperative with competitors. American companies often form alliances with Asian firms to gain an understanding of their manufacturing excellence, but Asian competence in this area is not easily transferable. Manufacturing excellence is a complex system that includes employee training and involvement, integration with suppliers, statistical process controls, value engineering, and design. In contrast, American know-how in technology and related areas more easily can be imitated. American firms thus need to be careful not to give away more intelligence than they receive in cooperative agreements with rival Asian firms.

COMPETITIVE ANALYSIS: PORTER'S FIVE-FORCES MODEL

As illustrated in Figure 3–3, *Porter's Five-Forces Model* of competitive analysis is a widely used approach for developing strategies in many industries. The intensity of competition among firms varies widely across industries. Table 3–6 reveals the average return on equity for firms in twenty-four different industries in 2001. Intensity of competition is highest in lower-return industries. According to Porter, the nature of competitiveness in a given industry can be viewed as a composite of five forces:

FIGURE 3-3

The Five-Forces Model of Competition

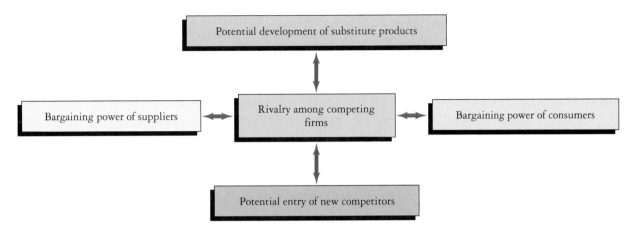

TABLE 3-6   Intensity of Competition Among Firms in Different Industries—2001 Results Provided

RANK	INDUSTRY	2001 AVERAGE RETURN ON EQUITY/ AVERAGE EARNINGS PER SHARE
1	Consumer Products	26.7/1.91
2	Healthcare	22.5/1.34
3	Conglomerates	18.1/1.45
4	Fuel	16.4/2.40
5	Food	15.2/1.21
6	Aerospace and Defense	13.0/2.31
7	Housing and Real Estate	12.6/2.17
8	Nonbank Financial	12.4/2.11
9	Discount and Fashion Retailing	12.2/0.98
10	Utilities and Power	11.7/2.10
11	Banks	11.4/1.84
12	Manufacturing	10.9/1.36
13	Chemicals	9.3/1.13
14	Leisure Time Industries	8.0/0.74
15	Containers and Packaging	7.4/0.90
16	Service Industries	6.0/0.46
17	Publishing and Broadcasting	2.6/0.33
18	Office Equipment and Computers	−1.0/−0.10
19	Paper and Forest Products	−2.6/−0.62
20	Transportation	−2.7/−0.43
21	Metals and Mining	−7.6/−0.83
22	Automotive	−9.1/−1.20
23	Telecommunications	−9.3/−0.91
24	Electrical and Electronics	−44.6/−3.14

Source: Adapted from "Corporate Scoreboard," *Business Week* (February 25, 2002): 63–102.

1. Rivalry among competing firms
2. Potential entry of new competitors
3. Potential development of substitute products
4. Bargaining power of suppliers
5. Bargaining power of consumers

Rivalry Among Competing Firms

Rivalry among competing firms is usually the most powerful of the five competitive forces. The strategies pursued by one firm can be successful only to the extent that they provide competitive advantage over the strategies pursued by rival firms. Changes in strategy by one firm may be met with retaliatory countermoves, such as lowering prices, enhancing quality, adding features, providing services, extending warranties, and increasing advertising.

In the Internet world, competitiveness is fierce. Amazon.com watches in dismay as customers use its site's easy-to-use format, in-depth reviews, expert recommendations— and then bypass the cash register as they click their way over to deep-discounted sites such as Buy.com to make their purchases. Buy.com's CEO says, "The Internet is going to shrink retailers' margins to the point where they will not survive." Price-comparison Web sites allow consumers to efficiently find the lowest-priced seller on the Internet. Kate Delhagen of Forrester Research says, "If you're a consumer and you're thinking about any kind of researched purchase, you're leaving thousands of dollars on the table if you don't at least look online."[15] The costs of setting up a great e-commerce site are nothing compared to the cost of acquiring real estate for building retail stores— or even printing and mailing catalogs.

Free-flowing information on the Internet is driving down prices and inflation worldwide. The Internet, coupled with the common currency in Europe, enables consumers to easily make price comparisons across countries. Just for a moment, consider the implications for car dealers who used to know everything about a new car's pricing, while you, the consumer, knew very little. You could bargain, but being in the dark, you rarely could win. Now you can go to Web sites such as CarPoint or Edmunds.com and know more about new car prices than the car salesperson, and you can even shop online in a few hours at every dealership within five hundred miles to find the best price and terms. So you, the consumer, can win. This is true in many, if not most, business-to-consumer and business-to-business sales transactions today.

The intensity of rivalry among competing firms tends to increase as the number of competitors increases, as competitors become more equal in size and capability, as demand for the industry's products declines, and as price cutting becomes common. Rivalry also increases when consumers can switch brands easily; when barriers to leaving the market are high; when fixed costs are high; when the product is perishable; when rival firms are diverse in strategies, origins, and culture; and when mergers and acquisitions are common in the industry. As rivalry among competing firms intensifies, industry profits decline, in some cases to the point where an industry becomes inherently unattractive.

Potential Entry of New Competitors

Whenever new firms can easily enter a particular industry, the intensity of competitiveness among firms increases. Barriers to entry, however, can include the need to gain economies of scale quickly, the need to gain technology and specialized know-how, the lack of experience, strong customer loyalty, strong brand preferences, large capital requirements, lack of adequate distribution channels, government regulatory policies, tariffs, lack of access to raw materials, possession of patents, undesirable locations, counterattack by entrenched firms, and potential saturation of the market.

Despite numerous barriers to entry, new firms sometimes enter industries with higher-quality products, lower prices, and substantial marketing resources. The strategist's job, therefore, is to identify potential new firms entering the market, to monitor the new rival firms' strategies, to counterattack as needed, and to capitalize on existing strengths and opportunities.

Potential Development of Substitute Products

In many industries, firms are in close competition with producers of substitute products in other industries. Examples are plastic container producers competing with glass, paperboard, and aluminum can producers, and acetaminophen manufacturers competing with other manufacturers of pain and headache remedies. The presence of substitute products puts a ceiling on the price that can be charged before consumers will switch to the substitute product.

Competitive pressures arising from substitute products increase as the relative price of substitute products declines and as consumers' switching costs decrease. The competitive strength of substitute products is best measured by the inroads into the marketshare those products obtain, as well as those firms' plans for increased capacity and market penetration.

Bargaining Power of Suppliers

The bargaining power of suppliers affects the intensity of competition in an industry, especially when there is a large number of suppliers, when there are only a few good substitute raw materials, or when the cost of switching raw materials is especially costly. It is often in the best interest of both suppliers and producers to assist each other with reasonable prices, improved quality, development of new services, just-in-time deliveries, and reduced inventory costs, thus enhancing long-term profitability for all concerned.

Firms may pursue a backward integration strategy to gain control or ownership of suppliers. This strategy is especially effective when suppliers are unreliable, too costly, or not capable of meeting a firm's needs on a consistent basis. Firms generally can negotiate more favorable terms with suppliers when backward integration is a commonly used strategy among rival firms in an industry.

Bargaining Power of Consumers

When customers are concentrated or large, or buy in volume, their bargaining power represents a major force affecting the intensity of competition in an industry. Rival firms may offer extended warranties or special services to gain customer loyalty whenever the bargaining power of consumers is substantial. Bargaining power of consumers also is higher when the products being purchased are standard or undifferentiated. When this is the case, consumers often can negotiate selling price, warranty coverage, and accessory packages to a greater extent. Even for a huge company such as Wal-Mart, the drastic increase in bargaining power of consumers caused by Internet usage is a major external threat.

SOURCES OF
EXTERNAL INFORMATION

A wealth of strategic information is available to organizations from both published and unpublished sources. Unpublished sources include customer surveys, market research, speeches at professional and shareholders' meetings, television programs, interviews, and

TABLE 3-7   **Excellent Internet Sources of Information**

I. INVESTMENT RESEARCH

Strategic Management Club Online → www.strategyclub.com
American Stock Exchange → www.amex.com
DBC Online → www.esignal.com
Hoover's Online → www.hoovers.com
InvestorGuide → www.investorguide.com
Wall Street Research Net → www.wsrn.com
Market Guide → www.marketguide.com
Money Search—Find It! → www.moneysearch.com
NASDAQ → www.nasdaq.com
New York Stock Exchange → www.nyse.com/public/home.html
PC Financial Network → www.csfbdirect.com
Quote.Com → www.quote.com
Stock Smart → www.stocksmart.com
Wright Investors' Service on the World Wide Web → www.wisi.com
Zacks Investment Research → www.zacks.com

II. SEARCH ENGINES

Alta Vista → www.altavista.com
Deja News → www.dejanews.com
DogPile → www.dogpile.com
Excite → www.excite.com
HotBot → www.hotbot.com
InfoSeek → www.go.com
Lycos → www.lycos.com
Metacrawler → www.metacrawler.com
WebCrawler → www.webcrawler.com
Yahoo! → www.yahoo.com

III. DIRECTORIES

Argus Clearinghouse → www.clearinghouse.net
BigBook → www.bigbook.com
ComFind → www.allbusiness.com
Thomas Publishing Co. → www.thomaspublishing.com
Competitive Intelligence Guide → www.fuld.com

IV. NEWS, MAGAZINES, AND NEWSPAPERS

PR Newswire → www.prnewswire.com
American Demographics → www.marketingtools.com
Barron's Magazine → www.barrons.com
Business Week → www.businessweek.com
CNNfn → www.cnnfn.com/search
Financial Times → www.ft.com
Forbes Magazine On-line → www.forbes.com
Fortune Magazine → www.fortune.com
USA Today → www.usatoday.com
Wall Street Journal → www.wsj.com
Washington Post Online → www.washingtonpost.com

V. U.S. GOVERNMENT

Better Business Bureau → www.bbb.org
Census Bureau → www.census.gov

Continued

TABLE 3-7   **Excellent Internet Sources of Information (*continued*)**

Federal Trade Commission → **www.ftc.gov**
FreeEDGAR → **www.freeedgar.com**
Edgar-Online → **www.edgar-online.com**
General Printing Office → **www.gpo.gov**
Internal Revenue Service → **www.irs.ustreas.gov**
Library of Congress → **www.loc.gov**
SEC's Edgar Database → **www.sec.gov/edgarhp.htm**
Small Business Administration → **www.sba.gov**
U.S. Department of Commerce → **www.doc.gov**
U.S. Department of the Treasury → **www.ustreas.gov**
Environmental Protection Agency → **www.epa.gov**
National Aeronautics and Space Administration → **www.hq.nasa.gov**

conversations with stakeholders. Published sources of strategic information include periodicals, journals, reports, government documents, abstracts, books, directories, newspapers, and manuals. Computerization and the Internet have made it easier today for firms to gather, assimilate, and evaluate information.

Internet
Millions of people today use other online services for both business and personal purposes. *America Online* and other leading commercial online services are expanding their menus of available services to include everything from online access to most major television networks, newspapers, and magazines to online interviews with celebrities, and they offer access to the furthermost boundaries of the Internet. These companies harness the power of multimedia, combining sound, video, and graphics with text. Excellent sources of strategic management and case research information on the *World Wide Web* are provided in Table 3–7. Table 3–8 provides selected academic and consulting strategic planning Web sites.

The Internet offers consumers and businesses a widening range of services and information resources from all over the world. Interactive services offer users not only access to information worldwide but also the ability to communicate with the person or company that created the information. Historical barriers to personal and business success—time zones and diverse cultures—are being eliminated. The Internet has become as important to our society as television and newspapers.

FORECASTING TOOLS AND TECHNIQUES

Forecasts are educated assumptions about future trends and events. Forecasting is a complex activity because of factors such as technological innovation, cultural changes, new products, improved services, stronger competitors, shifts in government priorities, changing social values, unstable economic conditions, and unforeseen events. Managers often must rely upon published forecasts to identify key external opportunities and threats effectively.

A sense of the future permeates all action and underlies every decision a person makes. People eat expecting to be satisfied and nourished—in the future. People sleep assuming that in the future they will feel rested. They invest energy, money, and time because they believe their efforts will be rewarded in the future. They build highways

VISIT THE NET

Dr. Porter today heads the Institute for Strategy and Competitiveness at Harvard Business School in Boston, Massachusetts. Michael Porter's home Web page can be found at http://www.people.hbs.edu/oporter/

TABLE 3-8   Important Strategic Planning Web Sites

I. ACADEMIC

1. *STRATEGIC MANAGEMENT SOCIETY*—**www.virtual-indiana.com/sms/**
   This is a non-profit, professional society composed of nearly two thousand academic, business, and consulting members from forty-five countries. This group publishes the *Strategic Management Journal* and offers annual meetings and conferences. The Web site is well designed and outlines the society's services and resources.

2. *AMERICAN MANAGEMENT ASSOCIATION*—**www.amanet.org**
   AMA provides educational forums worldwide for business to learn practical business skills. This Web site is comprehensive in providing access to all AMA seminars, videos, and courses worldwide, including strategic planning products. AMA publishes *Management Review*.

3. *ACADEMY OF MANAGEMENT ONLINE*—**www.aom.pace.edu**
   This non-profit organization is the leading professional association for management research and education in the United States. Almost ten thousand members from businesses and universities around the world participate. About twenty-five hundred of these members specify business policy and strategy as their primary interest. This site provides a search engine to locate and contact all these members. Many links and personal Web pages are provided. This organization publishes *Academy of Management Executive, Academy of Management Review*, and *Academy of Management Journal*.

4. *STRATEGIC LEADERSHIP FORUM*—**www.slfnet.org**
   This is an international organization of executives focusing on strategic management and planning. The Web site is outstanding. Many excellent strategic planning links are provided. The Forum publishes *Strategy and Leadership* (formerly *Planning Review*).

II. CONSULTANTS

1. *STRATEGIC PLANNING SYSTEMS*—**www.checkmateplan.com**
   This site provides *CheckMATE*, the industry leader in strategic planning software worldwide. This software is Windows-based and easy to use. The new version released in mid-2002 is improved ten-fold over prior versions.

2. *MIND TOOLS*—**www.mindtools.com/planpage.html**
   This is an excellent Web site for providing strategic planning information. More than thirty pages of narrative about how and why to do strategic planning are provided. Planning templates are provided.

3. *PALO ALTO SOFTWARE*—**www.bizplans.com**
   This Web site offers a model of the business planning process with excellent narrative as well as seven example business plans from real firms. This is one of the two best sites available for business planning information. (The other is the Small Business Administration Web site.)

4. *CENTER FOR STRATEGIC MANAGEMENT*—**www.csmweb.com**
   This Web site describes strategic management training, seminars, and facilitation services. The site also provides excellent links to other strategic planning academic and government sites.

5. *BOSTON CONSULTING GROUP (BCG)*—**www.bcg.com**
   This is perhaps the best-known strategic planning consulting firm. The Web site offers some nice discussion of strategic planning but focuses mostly on getting a job with BCG rather than on strategic planning information.

Continued

TABLE 3-8   **Important Strategic Planning Web Sites** (*continued*)

6. *FULD & COMPANY*—**www.fuld.com**

This Web site specializes in competitive intelligence. Nice links are provided regarding the importance of gathering information about competitors. This site offers audio answers to key questions about intelligence systems.

assuming that automobiles and trucks will need them in the future. Parents educate children on the basis of forecasts that they will need certain skills, attitudes, and knowledge when they grow up. The truth is we all make implicit forecasts throughout our daily lives. The question, therefore, is not whether we should forecast but rather how we can best forecast to enable us to move beyond our ordinarily unarticulated assumptions about the future. Can we obtain information and then make educated assumptions (forecasts) to better guide our current decisions to achieve a more desirable future state of affairs. We should go into the future with our eyes and our minds open, rather than stumbling into the future with our eyes closed.[16]

Many publications and sources on the Internet forecast external variables. Several published examples include *Industry Week*'s "Trends and Forecasts," *Business Week*'s "Investment Outlook," and Standard & Poor's *Industry Survey*. The reputation and continued success of these publications depend partly on accurate forecasts, so published sources of information can offer excellent projections.

Sometimes organizations must develop their own projections. Most organizations forecast (project) their own revenues and profits annually. Organizations sometimes forecast market share or customer loyalty in local areas. Because forecasting is so important in strategic management and because the ability to forecast (in contrast to the ability to use a forecast) is essential, selected forecasting tools are examined further here.

Forecasting tools can be broadly categorized into two groups: quantitative techniques and qualitative techniques. Quantitative forecasts are most appropriate when historical data are available and when the relationships among key variables are expected to remain the same in the future. *Linear regression*, for example, is based on the assumption that the future will be just like the past—which, of course, it never is. As historical relationships become less stable, quantitative forecasts becomes less accurate.

No forecast is perfect, and some forecasts are even wildly inaccurate. This fact accents the need for strategists to devote sufficient time and effort to study the underlying bases for published forecasts and to develop internal forecasts of their own. Key external opportunities and threats can be effectively identified only through good forecasts. Accurate forecasts can provide major competitive advantages for organizations. Forecasts are vital to the strategic-management process and to the success of organizations.

Making Assumptions

Planning would be impossible without assumptions. McConkey defines assumptions as the "best present estimates of the impact of major external factors, over which the manager has little if any control, but which may exert a significant impact on performance or the ability to achieve desired results.[17] Strategists are faced with countless variables and imponderables that can be neither controlled nor predicted with 100 percent accuracy.

By identifying future occurrences that could have a major effect on the firm and by making reasonable assumptions about those factors, strategists can carry the strategic-management process forward. Assumptions are needed only for future trends and events that are most likely to have a significant effect on the company's business. Based on the best information at the time, assumptions serve as checkpoints on the validity of strategies. If future occurrences deviate significantly from assumptions, strategists know that corrective actions may be needed. Without reasonable assumptions, the strategy-formulation process could not proceed effectively. Firms that have the best information generally make the most accurate assumptions, which can lead to major competitive advantages.

THE GLOBAL CHALLENGE

Foreign competitors are battering U.S. firms in many industries. In its simplest sense, the international challenge faced by U.S. business is twofold: (1) how to gain and maintain exports to other nations and (2) how to defend domestic markets against imported goods. Few companies can afford to ignore the presence of international competition. Firms that seem insulated and comfortable today may be vulnerable tomorrow; for example, foreign banks do not yet compete or operate in most of the United States.

America's economy is becoming much less American. A world economy and monetary system is emerging. Corporations in every corner of the globe are taking advantage of the opportunity to share in the benefits of worldwide economic development. Markets are shifting rapidly and in many cases converging in tastes, trends, and prices. Innovative transport systems are accelerating the transfer of technology, and shifts in the nature and location of production systems are reducing the response time to changing market conditions.

More and more countries around the world are welcoming foreign investment and capital. As a result, labor markets have steadily become more international. East Asian countries have become market leaders in labor-intensive industries, Brazil offers abundant natural resources and rapidly developing markets, and Germany offers skilled labor and technology. The drive to improve the efficiency of global business operations is leading to greater functional specialization. This is not limited to a search for the familiar low-cost labor in Latin America or Asia. Other considerations include the cost of energy, availability of resources, inflation rates, existing tax rates, and the nature of trade regulations.

Multinational Corporations

Multinational corporations (MNCs) face unique and diverse risks, such as expropriation of assets, currency losses through exchange rate fluctuations, unfavorable foreign court interpretations of contracts and agreements, social/political disturbances, import/export restrictions, tariffs, and trade barriers. Strategists in MNCs are often confronted with the need to be globally competitive and nationally responsive at the same time. With the rise in world commerce, government and regulatory bodies are more closely monitoring foreign business practices. The United States Foreign Corrupt Practices Act, for example, defines corrupt practices in many areas of business. A sensitive issue is that some MNCs sometimes violate legal and ethical standards of the home country, but not of the host country.

Before entering international markets, firms should scan relevant journals and patent reports, seek the advice of academic and research organizations, participate in international trade fairs, form partnerships, and conduct extensive research to broaden their contacts and diminish the risk of doing business in new markets. Firms can also reduce the risks of doing business internationally by obtaining insurance from the U.S. government's Overseas Private Investment Corporation (OPIC). Note in the Global Perspective that U.S. firms are doing more extensive research today before entering particular global markets.

Globalization

Globalization is a process of worldwide integration of strategy formulation, implementation, and evaluation activities. Strategic decisions are made based on their impact upon global profitability of the firm, rather than on just domestic or other individual country

GLOBAL PERSPECTIVE

The Old Way versus the New Way to Take a Company Global

The old way to take a company global was to get in fast, do minimal research, strike deals with top officials, make quick acquisitions, focus on upscale consumers, and watch local customers begin buying up the company's products. That approach, however, failed more often that it succeeded.

The new, more effective approach to taking a company global is to do extensive homework regarding culture, distributors, suppliers, and customers before placing operations in a foreign land. Successful globalization today requires investing time and energy to understand the nature of business in those countries and to methodically build a presence from the ground up. Companies successfully going global today work closely with bureaucrats, entrepreneurs, social groups, and other potential customers at the grassroots level. These companies are also targeting individuals in countries where the average income is low yet whose numbers far exceed those of the richest 10 percent of countries and customers. These companies have come to realize that developing nations are growing much faster than the industrial nations. Fully four billion people who earn the equivalent of

$1,500 or less annually live in developing nations, and this group is growing more rapidly than well-to-do citizens and countries.

A number of companies are using this new approach to be successful globally. Hewlett-Packard is presently marketing its products heavily in Central America and Africa. Citibank also is following this new approach by persuading its corporate customers in developing countries to set up retail bank accounts for their entire staffs—from janitors to top managers. Kodak also is following this new approach for being successful globally. Kodak has struggled in the United States recently, but the company's sales in Asia are up nicely. The company has increased its number of Kodak Express photo supply shops in China from 6,000 in early 2001 to 10,000 in 2002. A final example of a company using this new approach to be successful globally is Whirlpool, which invested fourteen months of research in the effort before rolling out what has become the leading brand of washing machines in India.

Source: Adapted from "Smart Globalization," *Business Week* (August 27, 2001): 132–137.

---

considerations. A global strategy seeks to meet the needs of customers worldwide, with the highest value at the lowest cost. This may mean locating production in countries with the lowest labor costs or abundant natural resources, locating research and complex engineering centers where skilled scientists and engineers can be found, and locating marketing activities close to the markets to be served. A global strategy includes designing, producing, and marketing products with global needs in mind, instead of considering individual countries alone. A global strategy integrates actions against competitors into a worldwide plan.

Globalization of industries is occurring for many reasons, including a worldwide trend toward similar consumption patterns, the emergence of global buyers and sellers, and e-commerce and the instant transmission of money and information across continents. The European Economic Community (EEC), religions, the Olympics, the World Bank, world trade centers, the Red Cross, the Internet, environmental conferences, telecommunications, and economic summits all contribute to global interdependencies and the emerging global marketplace.

It is clear that different industries become global for different reasons. The need to amortize massive R&D investments over many markets is a major reason why the aircraft manufacturing industry became global. Monitoring globalization in one's industry is an important strategic-management activity. Knowing how to use that information for one's competitive advantage is even more important. For example, firms may look around the world for the best technology and select one that has the most promise for the largest number of markets. When firms design a product, they design it to be marketable in as many countries as possible. When firms manufacture a product, they select the lowest cost source, which may be Japan for semiconductors, Sri Lanka for textiles, Malaysia for simple electronics, and Europe for precision machinery. MNCs design manufacturing systems to accommodate world markets. One of the riskiest strategies for a domestic firm is to remain solely a domestic firm in an industry that is rapidly becoming global.

China: Opportunities and Threats

U.S. firms increasingly are doing business in China as market reforms create a more businesslike arena daily. Foreign direct investment in China is about $50 billion annually. This places China second behind the United States. Motorola is investing $6.6 billion in China between 2002–2006, even as the firm cuts its workforce elsewhere. Hitachi Ltd. and Intel are doubling their investment in Shanghai during this same time.

Risks that still restrain firms from initiating business with China include the following:

- Poor infrastructure
- Disregard for the natural environment
- Absence of a legal system
- Rampant corruption
- Lack of freedom of press, speech, and religion
- Severe human-rights violations
- Little respect for parents, copyrights, brands, and logos
- Counterfeiting, fraud, and pirating of products
- Little respect for legal contracts
- No generally accepted accounting principles

The minimum wage in China is twelve cents per hour, but many firms pay even less. Chinese workers usually have no healthcare and no compensation for injury. Few factories have fire extinguishers. Bribes are often paid to officials to avoid fines and shutdowns. Labor unions are illegal and nonexistent in China. Child labor is commonplace. Political and religious oppression and imprisonment occur. Levi Strauss has pulled all its business operations out of China to protest its human rights violations.

Business Week offers the following formula for success in doing business with China:

Pick partners wisely. Avoid forming ventures with inefficient state-owned enterprises. Search for entrepreneurial companies owned by local governments—or go it alone. Insist on management control.

Focus on fundamentals. Capitalize on China rapidly becoming a market economy by executing the basics, such as marketing, distribution, and service.

Guard know-how. Do not hand over state-of-the-art technology just to get an agreement. Aggressively fight theft of intellectual property because China wants to shed its bad reputation in this regard.

Fly low. Begin with a series of small ventures rather than big, costly, high-profile projects that often get snarled in bureaucratic red tape and politics.[18]

Hong Kong is the centerpiece of China's efforts to reform, privatize, and expand imports and exports worldwide. The map in Figure 3–4 illustrates Hong Kong's strategic location for China. With its 6.3 million people, magnificent harbor, financial wealth, 500 banks from 43 countries, the world's eighth-largest stock market, and minimum taxation, Hong Kong serves as the gateway to a fast-growing China. U.S. companies alone have 178 regional headquarters in Hong Kong and $10.5 billion in direct investment.

Much of Hong Kong's economic base is shifting north thirty miles to Shenzhen on mainland China. Shenzhen has a vast new shipping port and offers greatly reduced prices for retail goods and home ownership. China is actually melding Hong Kong and Shenzhen into one economic region under Chinese rules and regulations, such as arbitrary arrests and few legal protections. The people of Hong Kong had previously enjoyed freedom for decades prior to this slow unification with Shenzhen.[19]

Both the European community and the United States have approved China's membership in the World Trade Organization. This action integrates the world's most populated country into the global trading order. Some key changes in China resulting from this action are as follows:

1. Foreign companies can take increased stakes in mobile phone companies.
2. Tariffs on high-tech products will be phased out and eliminated by 2005.
3. Import tariffs on automobiles will drop to 25 percent by mid-2006 from 90 percent today.
4. Foreign banks may conduct domestic currency business with Chinese firms.
5. Foreign banks may do business anywhere in China by 2006.
6. Foreign firms will be allowed a 49 percent stake in securities joint ventures by 2004.
7. Foreign insurance firms may own operations in China.
8. Retail oil distribution will open in China by 2004.[20]

However, entry into the World Trade Organization may not be enough to revive China's worsening economy. China exports 20 percent of its products to the United States, and these sales declined greatly in late 2001 and early 2002. The United States is second behind Japan in buying Chinese products, which mostly are cheap consumer goods such as televisions, toys, and textiles.

As the twenty-first century begins, Hong Kong is still an attractive city to establish business operations, but China is moving Hong Kong more toward regulation, government control, and a China-like culture. For example, schools now must adopt Chinese as the main language of instruction, whereas English proficiency previously was required

FIGURE 3–4

Hong Kong's Strategic Location

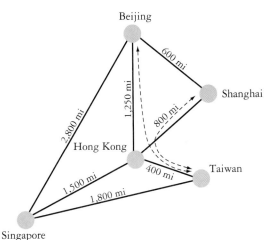

at schools. The Hong Kong government awarded various companies rights to develop government land without public bids, which previously was the accepted democratic way to do business. The government previously was a regulator of the Hong Kong stock market but now is its biggest investor and controller. The government is making decisions that trample longstanding principles of free markets and consistent rule of law. The Heritage Foundation has lowered Hong Kong's rating as a free economy to one notch below that of Singapore "unless it sees the error of its ways and reverses course."[21]

However, Taiwan and mainland China are cooperating more and more on economic issues, which is good for the region and indeed the world. Companies in the two separate countries recently agreed to jointly explore the Taiwan Strait for oil and gas under the Taiwan Basin. This unprecedented contract marks the first major commercial agreement between state-owned companies from the two countries. The involved companies are China National Offshore Oil, which is China's No. 3 oil producer, and Taiwan's China Petroleum, which has excellent refining capabilities.

Fifty years of separation between China and Taiwan has pushed the two countries so far apart politically, socially, and culturally that it is hard to even imagine them ever being part of the same whole. Further indication that commercial relations between Taipei and Beijing are improving is that China Airlines of Taiwan has signed an agreement to invest in China's first all-cargo airline, China Cargo Airlines. China Airlines soon expects to feed traffic from China Cargo into Taipei. Taiwan and China thus are beginning to engage in direct trade and transportation, something Taiwan has banned since the two sides separated in 1949 after a civil war. China's civil aviation authority is now holding technical talks with Taiwan's air-traffic controllers. The global economic recession has been the spark to help normalize relations between these two countries, which actually have much to offer each other in trade and travel. Taiwanese companies, such as Microtek, now view China as a primary market for their products, rather than viewing the mainland as simply a base for its manufacturing operations.

INDUSTRY ANALYSIS: THE EXTERNAL FACTOR EVALUATION (EFE) MATRIX

An *External Factor Evaluation (EFE) Matrix* allows strategists to summarize and evaluate economic, social, cultural, demographic, environmental, political, governmental, legal, technological, and competitive information. Illustrated in Table 3–9, the EFE Matrix can be developed in five steps:

1. List key external factors as identified in the external-audit process. Include a total of from ten to twenty factors, including both opportunities and threats, that affect the firm and its industry. List the opportunities first and then the threats. Be as specific as possible, using percentages, ratios, and comparative numbers whenever possible.

2. Assign to each factor a weight that ranges from 0.0 (not important) to 1.0 (very important). The weight indicates the relative importance of that factor to being successful in the firm's industry. Opportunities often receive higher weights than threats, but threats too can receive high weights if they are especially severe or threatening. Appropriate weights can be determined by comparing successful with unsuccessful competitors or by discussing the factor and reaching a group consensus. The sum of all weights assigned to the factors must equal 1.0.

3. Assign a 1-to-4 rating to each key external factor to indicate how effectively the firm's current strategies respond to the factor, where 4 = *the response is superior,*

TABLE 3-9   An Example External Factor Evaluation Matrix for
             UST, Inc.

KEY EXTERNAL FACTORS	WEIGHT	RATING	WEIGHTED SCORE
Opportunities			
1. Global markets are practically untapped by smokeless tobacco market	.15	1	.15
2. Increased demand caused by public banning of smoking	.05	3	.15
3. Astronomical Internet advertising growth	.05	1	.05
4. Pinkerton is leader in discount tobacco market	.15	4	.60
5. More social pressure to quit smoking, thus leading users to switch to alternatives	.10	3	.30
Threats			
1. Legislation against the tobacco industry	.10	2	.20
2. Production limits on tobacco increases competition for production	.05	3	.15
3. Smokeless tobacco market is concentrated in southeast region of United States	.05	2	.10
4. Bad media exposure from the FDA	.10	2	.20
5. Clinton administration	.20	1	.20
TOTAL	1.00		2.10

3 = *the response is above average*, 2 = *the response is average*, and 1 = *the response is poor*. Ratings are based on effectiveness of the firm's strategies. Ratings are thus company-based, whereas the weights in Step 2 are industry-based. It is important to note that both threats and opportunities can receive a 1, 2, 3, or 4.

4. Multiply each factor's weight by its rating to determine a weighted score.

5. Sum the weighted scores for each variable to determine the total weighted score for the organization.

Regardless of the number of key opportunities and threats included in an EFE Matrix, the highest possible total weighted score for an organizations is 4.0 and the lowest possible total weighted score is 1.0. The average total weighted score is 2.5. A total weighted score of 4.0 indicates that an organization is responding in an outstanding way to existing opportunities and threats in its industry. In other words, the firm's strategies effectively take advantage of existing opportunities and minimize the potential adverse effects of external threats. A total score of 1.0 indicates that the firm's strategies are not capitalizing on opportunities or avoiding external threats.

An example of an EFE Matrix is provided in Table 3–9 for UST, Inc., the manufacturer of Skoal and Copenhagen smokeless tobacco. Note that the Clinton administration was considered to be the most important factor affecting this industry, as indicated by the weight of 0.20. UST was not pursuing strategies that effectively capitalize on this opportunity, as indicated by the rating of 1.0. The total weighted score of 2.10 indicates that UST is below average in its effort to pursue strategies that capitalize on external opportunities and avoid threats. It is important to note here that a thorough understanding of the factors being used in the EFE Matrix is more important than the actual weights and ratings assigned.

THE COMPETITIVE PROFILE MATRIX (CPM)

The *Competitive Profile Matrix (CPM)* identifies a firm's major competitors and its particular strengths and weaknesses in relation to a sample firm's strategic position. The weights and total weighted scores in both a CPM and EFE have the same meaning. However, *critical success* factors in a CPM include both internal and external issues; therefore, the ratings refer to strengths and weaknesses, where 4 = major strength, 3 = minor strength, 2 = minor weakness, and 1 = major weakness. There are some important differences between the EFE and CPM. First of all, the critical success factors in a CPM are broader, they do not include specific or factual data and even may focus on internal issues. The critical success factors in a CPM also are not grouped into opportunities and threats as they are in an EFE. In a CPM, the ratings and total weighted scores for rival firms can be compared to the sample firm. This comparative analysis provides important internal strategic information.

A sample Competitive Profile Matrix is provided in Table 3–10. In this example, advertising and global expansion are the most important critical success factors, as indicated by a weight of 0.20. Avon's and L'Oreal's product quality is superior, as evidenced by a rating of 4; L'Oreal's "financial position" is good, as indicated by a rating of 3; Procter & Gamble is the weakest firm overall, as indicated by a total weighted score of 2.80.

Other than the critical success factors listed in the example CPM, factors often included in this analysis include breadth of product line, effectiveness of sales distribution, proprietary or patent advantages, location of facilities, production capacity and efficiency, experience, union relations, technological advantages, and e-commerce expertise.

A word on interpretation: Just because one firm receives a 3.2 rating and another receives a 2.8 rating in a Competitive Profile Matrix, it does not follow that the first firm is 20 percent better than the second. Numbers reveal the relative strengths of firms, but their implied precision is an illusion. Numbers are not magic. The aim is not to arrive at a single number, but rather to assimilate and evaluate information in a meaningful way that aids in decision making.

TABLE 3-10   An Example Competitive Profile Matrix

CRITICAL SUCCESS FACTORS	WEIGHT	AVON RATING	AVON SCORE	L'OREAL RATING	L'OREAL SCORE	PROCTER & GAMBLE RATING	PROCTER & GAMBLE SCORE
Advertising	0.20	1	0.20	4	0.80	3	0.60
Product Quality	0.10	4	0.40	4	0.40	3	0.30
Price Competitiveness	0.10	3	0.30	3	0.30	4	0.40
Management	0.10	4	0.40	3	0.30	3	0.30
Financial Position	0.15	4	0.60	3	0.45	3	0.45
Customer Loyalty	0.10	4	0.40	4	0.40	2	0.20
Global Expansion	0.20	4	0.80	2	0.40	2	0.40
Market Share	0.05	1	0.05	4	0.20	3	0.15
TOTAL	1.00		3.15		3.25		2.80

Note: (1) The ratings values are as follows: 1 = major weakness, 2 = minor weakness, 3 = minor strength, 4 = major strength. (2) As indicated by the total weighted score of 2.8, Competitor 3 is weakest. (3) Only eight critical success factors are included for simplicity; this is too few in actuality.

CONCLUSION

Increasing turbulence in markets and industries around the world means the external audit has become an explicit and vital part of the strategic-management process. This chapter provides a framework for collecting and evaluating economic, social, cultural, demographic, environmental, political, governmental, legal, technological, and competitive information. Firms that do not mobilize and empower their managers and employees to identify, monitor, forecast, and evaluate key external forces may fail to anticipate emerging opportunities and threats and, consequently, may pursue ineffective strategies, miss opportunities, and invite organizational demise. Firms not taking advantage of the Internet are falling behind technologically.

A major responsibility of strategists is to ensure development of an effective external-audit system. This includes using information technology to devise a competitive intelligence system that works. The external-audit approach described in this chapter can be used effectively by any size or type of organization. Typically, the external-audit process is more informal in small firms, but the need to understand key trends and events is no less important for these firms. The EFE Matrix and Porter's Five-Forces Model can help strategists evaluate the market and industry, but these tools must be accompanied by good intuitive judgment. Multinational firms especially need a systematic and effective external-audit system because external forces among foreign countries vary so greatly.

We invite you to visit the David page on the Prentice Hall Companion Website at **www.prenhall.com/david** for this chapter's World Wide Web exercises.

KEY TERMS AND CONCEPTS

America Online (p. 103)

Chief Information Officer (CIO) (p. 93)

Chief Technology Officer (CTO) (p. 93)

Competitive Advantages (p. 93)

Competitive Analysis (p. 97)

Competitive Intelligence (CI) (p. 94)

Competitive Profile Matrix (CPM) (p. 112)

Decruiting (p. 83)

Director of Competitive Analysis (p. 97)

Downsizing (p. 83)

Environmental Scanning (p. 80)

External Audit (p. 80)

External Factor Evaluation (EFE) Matrix (p. 110)

External Forces (p. 80)

Industry Analysis (p. 80)

Information Technology (IT) (p. 93)

Internet (p. 92)

Learning from the Partner (p. 98)

Linear Regression (p. 105)

Lifecare Facilities (p. 86)

Porter's Five-Forces Model (p. 98)

Rightsizing (p. 83)

World Wide Web (p. 103)

ISSUES FOR REVIEW AND DISCUSSION

1. Explain how to conduct an external strategic-management audit.
2. Identify a recent economic, social, political, or technological trend that significantly affects financial institutions.
3. Discuss the following statement: Major opportunities and threats usually result from an interaction among key environmental trends rather than from a single external event or factor.

4. Identify two industries experiencing rapid technological changes and three industries that are experiencing little technological change. How does the need for technological forecasting differ in these industries? Why?
5. Use Porter's Five-Forces Model to evaluate competitiveness within the U.S. banking industry.
6. What major forecasting techniques would you use to identify (1) economic opportunities and threats

and (2) demographic opportunities and threats? Why are these techniques most appropriate?

7. How does the external audit affect other components of the strategic-management process?

8. As the owner of a small business, explain how you would organize a strategic-information scanning system. How would you organize such a system in a large organization?

9. Construct an EFE Matrix for an organization of your choice.

10. Make an appointment with a librarian at your university to learn how to use online databases. Report your findings in class.

11. Give some advantages and disadvantages of cooperative versus competitive strategies.

12. As strategist for a local bank, explain when you would use qualitative versus quantitative forecasts.

13. What is your forecast for interest rates and the stock market in the next several months? As the stock market moves up, do interest rates always move down? Why? What are the strategic implications of these trends?

14. Explain how information technology affects strategies of the organization where you worked most recently.

15. Let's say your boss develops an EFE Matrix that includes sixty-two factors. How would you suggest reducing the number of factors to twenty?

16. Select one of the current readings at the end of this chapter. Prepare a one-page written summary that includes your personal opinion of the article.

17. Discuss the ethics of gathering competitive intelligence.

18. Discuss the ethics of cooperating with rival firms.

19. Visit the SEC Web site at **www.sec.gov**, and discuss the benefits of using information provided there.

20. What are the major differences between U.S. and multinational operations that affect strategic management?

21. Why is globalization of industries a common factor today?

22. Discuss the opportunities and threats a firm faces in doing business in China.

NOTES

1. YORK FREUND, "Critical Success Factors," *Planning Review* 16, no. 4 (July–August 1988): 20.

2. CHARLES WHALEN "NAFTA's Scorecard: So Far, So Good." *Business Week* (July 9, 2001): 54–55.

3. EMILY THORTON, "Russia—What Happens When Markets Fail," *Business Week* (April 26, 1999): 50–52.

4. SUSAN DECKER, "Where to Find Legal Help On the Net," *USA Today* (October 18, 1999): 8B.

5. FREDERICK GLUCK, "Global Competition in the 1990s," *Journal of Business Strategy* (Spring 1983): 22, 24.

6. STAN CROCK, "From Evil Empire to Strategic Ally," *Business Week* (November 12, 2001): 76.

7. DAVID BANK, "Internet Learns New Lingo, XML, and the Hype Is On," *The Wall Street Journal* (September 16, 1999): A10.

8. JOHN HARRIS, ROBERT SHAW, JR., and WILLIAM SOMMERS, "The Strategic Management of Technology," *Planning Review* 11, no. 11 (January–February 1983): 28, 35.

9. BILL SAPORITO, "Companies That Compete Best," *Fortune* (May 22, 1989): 36.

10. LOUIS LAVELLE, "The Case of the Corporate Spy," *Business Week* (November 26, 2001): 56–57.

11. KENNETH SAWKA, "Demystifying Business Intelligence," *Management Review* (October 1996): 49.

12. JOHN PRESCOTT and DANIEL SMITH, "The Largest Survey of 'Leading-Edge' Competitor Intelligence Managers," *Planning Review* 17, no. 3 (May–June 1989): 6–13.

13. JON SWARTZ, "Nimda Called Most Serious Internet Attack on Business," *USA Today* (September 26, 2001): 5B. See also Srikumar Rao, "Counterspy," *Forbes* (February 5, 2001): 130.

14. GARY HAMEL, YVES DOZ, and C. K. PRAHALAD, "Collaborate with Your Competitors—and Win," *Harvard Business Review* 67, no. 1 (January–February 1989): 133.

15. DAVID BANK, "A Site-Eat-Site World," *The Wall Street Journal* (July 12, 1999): R8.

16. http://horizon.unc.edu/projects/seminars/futures research/rationale.asp.

17. DALE MCCONKEY, "Planning in a Changing Environment," *Business Horizons* 31, no. 5 (September–October 1988): 67.

18. "How Can You Win in China?" *Business Week* (May 26, 1997): 65.

19. GEORGE MELLOAN, "Hong Kong Is Gradually Melding with the Mainland," *Wall Street Journal* (September 11, 2001): A27.

20. GEOFF WINESTOCK and KARBY LEGGETT, "China to Enter WTO: Dispute on Insurance to Be First Test," *Wall Street Journal* (September 18, 2001): A14.

21. ERIK GUYOT, "Reined In: For Years, Hong Kong was the Poster Child for Laissez-faire Economics. No Longer," *The Wall Street Journal* (September 27, 1999): R20.

CURRENT READINGS

BERGH, D. D. and J. F. FAIRBANK. "Measuring and Testing Change in Strategic Management Research." *Strategic Management Journal* 23, no. 4 (April 2002): 359.

BIRKINSHAW, JULIAN and NEIL HOOD. "Unleash Innovation in Foreign Subsidiaries." *Harvard Business Review* (March 2001): 131.

BONABEAU, ERIC. "Predicting the Unpredictable." *Harvard Business Review* (March 2002): 109.

BONABEAU, ERIC and CHRISTOPHER MEYER. "Swarm Intelligence: A Whole New Way to Think About Business." *Harvard Business Review* (May 2001): 106.

CHATTOPADHYAY, PRITHVIRAJ, WILLIAM H. GLICK, and GEORGE P. HUBER. "Organizational Actions in Response to Threats and Opportunities." *Academy of Management Journal* 44, no. 5 (October 2001): 937.

CLAMPITT, PHILLIP G., ROBERT J. DEKOCH, and THOMAS CASHMAN. "A Strategy for Communicating About Uncertainty." *Academy of Management Executive* 14, no. 4 (November 2000): 41.

FERRIER, WALTER J. "Navigating the Competitive Landscape: The Drivers and Consequences of Competitive Aggressiveness." *Academy of Management Journal* 44, no. 4 (August 2001): 858.

GHEMAWAT, PANKAJ. "Distance Still Matters: The Hard Reality of Global Expansion." *Harvard Business Review* (September 2001): 137.

MICHAILOVA, SNEJINA. "Contrasts in Culture: Russian and Western Perspectives on Organizational Change." *Academy of Management Executive* 14, no. 4 (November 2000): 99.

PITT, LEYLAND F., MICHAEL T. EWING, and PIERRE BERTHON. "Turning Competitive Advantage into Customer Equity." *Business Horizons* 43, no. 5 (September–October 2000): 11.

POWELL, T. C. "Competitive Advantage: Logical and Philosophical Considerations." *Strategic Management Journal* 22, no. 9 (September 2001): 875.

PRESTON, LYNELLE. "Sustainability at Hewlett-Packard: From Theory to Practice." *California Management Review* 43, no. 3 (Spring 2001): 26.

RAMAMURTI, RAVI and DEVESH KAPUR. "India's Emerging Competitive Advantages in Services." *Academy of Management Executive* 15, no. 2 (May 2001): 20.

SHAMA, AVRAHAM. "After the Meltdown: A Survey of International Firms in Russia." *Business Horizons* 43, no. 4 (July–August 2000): 73.

SLATER, STANLEY F. and ERIC M. OLSON. "A Fresh Look at Industry and Market Analysis." *Business Horizons* 45, no. 1 (January-February 2002): 15.

VIBERT, CONOR. "Secrets of Online Sleuthing." *Journal of Business Strategy* 22, no. 3 (May/June 2001): 39.

EXPERIENTIAL EXERCISES

PURPOSE

This exercise will give you practice developing an EFE Matrix. An EFE Matrix summarizes the results of an external audit. This is an important tool widely used by strategists.

INSTRUCTIONS

Step 1   Join with two other students in class, and jointly prepare an EFE Matrix for American Airlines. Refer back to the Cohesion Case and to Experiential Exercise 1A, if necessary, to identify external opportunities and threats.

Step 2   All three-person teams participating in this exercise should record their EFE total weighted scores on the board. Put your initials after your score to identify it as your team's.

Step 3   Compare the total weighted scores. Which team's score came closest to the instructor's answer? Discuss reasons for variation in the scores reported on the board.

PURPOSE

This exercise will help you become familiar with important sources of external information available in your college library. A key part of preparing an external audit is searching the Internet and examining published sources of information for relevant economic, social, cultural, demographic, environmental, political, governmental, legal, technological, and competitive trends and events. External opportunities and threats must be identified and evaluated before strategies can be formulated effectively.

INSTRUCTIONS

Step 1   Select a company or business. Conduct an external audit for this company. Find opportunities and threats in recent issues of newspapers and magazines. Search for information using the Internet.

Step 2   On a separate sheet of paper, list ten opportunities and ten threats that face this company. Be specific in stating each factor.

Step 3   Include a bibliography to reveal where you found the information.

Step 4   Share your information with a manager of that company. Ask for his or her comments and additions.

Step 5   Write a three-page summary of your findings, and submit it to your teacher.

PURPOSE

More colleges and universities are embarking upon the strategic-management process. Institutions are consciously and systematically identifying and evaluating external opportunities and threats facing higher education in your state, the nation, and the world.

INSTRUCTIONS

Step 1   Join with two other individuals in class, and jointly prepare an EFE Matrix for your institution.

Step 2 Go to the board and record your total weighted score in a column that includes the scores of all three-person teams participating. Put your initials after your score to identify it as your team's.

Step 3 Which team viewed your college's strategies most positively? Which team viewed your college's strategies most negatively? Discuss the nature of the differences.

EXPERIENTIAL EXERCISE 3D ▶

Developing a Competitive Profile Matrix for American Airlines (AMR)

PURPOSE

Monitoring competitors' performance and strategies is a key aspect of an external audit. This exercise is designed to give you practice evaluating the competitive position of organizations in a given industry and assimilating that information in the form of a Competitive Profile Matrix.

INSTRUCTIONS

Step 1 Turn back to the Cohesion Case and review the section on competitors.

Step 2 On a separate sheet of paper, prepare a Competitive Profile Matrix that includes American Airlines (AMR) and United Airlines (UAL).

Step 3 Turn in your Competitive Profile Matrix for a classwork grade.

EXPERIENTIAL EXERCISE 3E ▶

Developing a Competitive Profile Matrix for My University

PURPOSE

Your college or university competes with all other educational institutions in the world, especially those in your own state. State funds, students, faculty, staff, endowments, gifts, and federal funds are areas of competitiveness. The purpose of this exercise is to give you practice thinking competitively about the business of education in your state.

INSTRUCTIONS

Step 1 Identify two colleges or universities in your state that compete directly with your institution for students. Interview several persons who are aware of particular strengths and weaknesses of those universities. Record information about the two competing universities.

Step 2 Prepare a Competitive Profile Matrix that includes your institution and the two competing institutions. Include the following factors in your analysis:

1. Tuition costs
2. Quality of faculty
3. Academic reputation
4. Average class size
5. Campus landscaping
6. Athletic programs
7. Quality of students
8. Graduate programs
9. Location of campus
10. Campus culture

Step 3 Submit your Competitive Profile Matrix to your instructor for evaluation.

4 THE INTERNAL ASSESSMENT

CHAPTER OUTLINE

CHAPTER OBJECTIVES

After studying this chapter, you should be able to do the following:

1. Describe how to perform an internal strategic-management audit.

2. Discuss key interrelationships among the functional areas of business.

3. Compare and contrast culture in America with other countries.

4. Identify the basic functions or activities that make up management, marketing, finance/accounting, production/operations, research and development, and management information systems.

5. Explain how to determine and prioritize a firm's internal strengths and weaknesses.

6. Explain the importance of financial ratio analysis.

7. Discuss the nature and role of management information systems in strategic management.

8. Develop an Internal Factor Evaluation (IFE) Matrix.

NOTABLE
QUOTES

Like a product or service, the planning process itself must be managed and shaped, if it is to serve executives as a vehicle for strategic decision-making.

ROBERT LENZ

The difference between now and five years ago is that information systems had limited function. You weren't betting your company on it. Now you are.

WILLIAM GRUBER

Weak leadership can wreck the soundest strategy.

SUN ZI

A firm that continues to employ a previously successful strategy eventually and inevitably falls victim to a competitor.

WILLIAM COHEN

An organization should approach all tasks with the idea that they can be accomplished in a superior fashion.

THOMAS WATSON, JR.

By 2010, managers will have to handle greater cultural diversity. Managers will have to understand that employees don't think alike about such basics as "handling confrontation" or even what it means "to do a good day's work."

JEFFREY SONNENFELD

Sad but true, U.S. businesspeople have the lowest foreign language proficiency of any major trading nation. U.S. business schools do not emphasize foreign languages, and students traditionally avoid them.

RONALD DULEK

Great spirits have always encountered violent opposition from mediocre minds.

ALBERT EINSTEIN

This chapter focuses on identifying and evaluating a firm's strengths and weaknesses in the functional areas of business, including management, marketing, finance/accounting, production/operations, research and development, and management information systems. Relationships among these areas of business are examined. Strategic implications of important functional area concepts are examined. The process of performing an internal audit is described.

THE NATURE OF AN INTERNAL AUDIT

VISIT THE NET

Excellent strategic planning quotes. http://www. planware.org/quotes.htm#3

All organizations have strengths and weaknesses in the functional areas of business. No enterprise is equally strong or weak in all areas. Maytag, for example, is known for excellent production and product design, whereas Procter & Gamble is known for superb marketing. Internal strengths/weaknesses, coupled with external opportunities/threats and a clear statement of mission, provide the basis for establishing objectives and strategies. Objectives and strategies are established with the intention of capitalizing upon internal strengths and overcoming weaknesses. The internal-audit part of the strategic-management process is illustrated in Figure 4–1.

Key Internal Forces

It is not possible in a business policy text to review in depth all the material presented in courses such as marketing, finance, accounting, management, management information systems, and production/operations; there are many subareas within these functions, such as customer service, warranties, advertising, packaging, and pricing under marketing.

For different types of organizations, such as hospitals, universities, and government agencies, the functional business areas, of course, differ. In a hospital, for example, functional areas may include cardiology, hematology, nursing, maintenance, physician support, and receivables. Functional areas of a university can include athletic programs, placement services, housing, fundraising, academic research, counseling, and intramural programs. Within large organizations, each division has certain strengths and weaknesses.

VISIT THE NET

Gives excellent information about the need for planning. http://www. mindtools.com/plintro.html

A firm's strengths that cannot be easily marched or imitated by competitors are called *distinctive competencies.* Building competitive advantages involves taking advantage of distinctive competencies. For example, 3M exploits its distinctive competence in research and development by producing a wide range of innovative products. Strategies are designed in part to improve on a firm's weaknesses, turning them into strengths—and maybe even into distinctive competencies.

Some researchers emphasize the importance of the internal audit part of the strategic-management process by comparing it to the external audit. Robert Grant concluded that the internal audit is more important, saying:

> In a world where customer preferences are volatile, the identity of customers is changing, and the technologies for serving customer requirements are continually evolving; an externally focused orientation does not provide a secure foundation for formulating long-term strategy. When the external environment is in a state of flux, the firm's own resources and capabilities may be a much more stable basis on which to define its identity. Hence, a definition of a business in terms of what it is capable of doing may offer a more durable basis for strategy than a definition based upon the needs which the business seeks to satisfy.[1]

FIGURE 4–1

A Comprehensive Strategic-Management Model

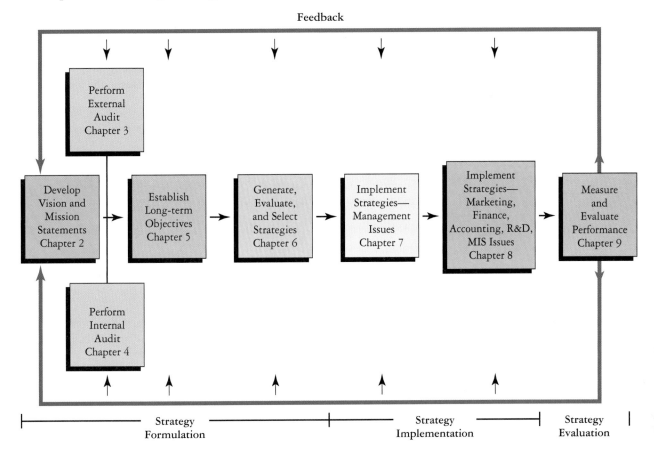

The Process of Performing an Internal Audit

The process of performing an *internal audit* closely parallels the process of performing an external audit. Representative managers and employees from throughout the firm need to be involved in determining a firm's strengths and weaknesses. The internal audit requires gathering and assimilating information about the firm's management, marketing, finance/accounting, production/operations, research and development (R&D), and management information systems operations. Key factors should be prioritized as described in Chapter 3 so that the firm's most important strengths and weaknesses can be determined collectively.

Compared to the external audit, the process of performing an internal audit provides more opportunity for participants to understand how their jobs, departments, and divisions fit into the whole organization. This is a great benefit because managers and employees perform better when they understand how their work affects other areas and activities of the firm. For example, when marketing and manufacturing managers jointly discuss issues related to internal strengths and weaknesses, they gain a better appreciation of the issues, problems, concerns, and needs of all the functional areas. In organizations that do not use strategic management, marketing, finance, and manufacturing managers often do not interact with each other in significant ways. Performing an internal audit thus is an excellent vehicle or forum for improving the process of communication in the organization. Communication may be the most important word in management.

Performing an internal audit requires gathering, assimilating, and evaluating information about the firm's operations. Critical success factors, consisting of both strengths and weaknesses, can be identified and prioritized in the manner discussed in Chapter 3. According to William King, a task force of managers from different units of the organization, supported by staff, should be charged with determining the ten to twenty most important strengths and weaknesses that should influence the future of the organization. He says:

> The development of conclusions on the 10 to 20 most important organizational strengths and weaknesses can be, as any experienced manager knows, a difficult task, when it involves managers representing various organizational interests and points of view. Developing a 20-page list of strengths and weaknesses could be accomplished relatively easily, but a list of the 10 to 15 most important ones involves significant analysis and negotiation. This is true because of the judgments that are required and the impact which such a list will inevitably have as it is used in the formulation, implementation, and evaluation of strategies.[2]

VISIT THE NET

Provides the complete strategic plan for the Wyoming Insurance Department Agency, including its list of strengths and weaknesses.
http://www.state.wy.us/state/strategy/insurance.html

Strategic management is a highly interactive process that requires effective coordination among management, marketing, finance/accounting, production/operations, R&D, and management information systems managers. Although the strategic-management process is overseen by strategists, success requires that managers and employees from all functional areas work together to provide ideas and information. Financial managers, for example, may need to restrict the number of feasible options available to operations managers, or R&D managers may develop products that marketing managers need to set higher objectives. A key to organizational success is effective coordination and understanding among managers from all functional business areas. Through involvement in performing an internal strategic-management audit, managers from different departments and divisions of the firm come to understand the nature and effect of decisions in other functional business areas in their firm. Knowledge of these relationships is critical for effectively establishing objectives and strategies.

A failure to recognize and understand relationships among the functional areas of business can be detrimental to strategic management, and the number of those relationships that must be managed increases dramatically with a firm's size, diversity, geographic dispersion, and the number of products or services offered. Governmental and nonprofit enterprises traditionally have not placed sufficient emphasis on relationships among the business functions. Some firms place too great an emphasis on one function at the expense of others. Ansoff explained:

> During the first fifty years, successful firms focused their energies on optimizing the performance of one of the principal functions: production/operations, R&D, or marketing. Today, due to the growing complexity and dynamism of the environment, success increasingly depends on a judicious combination of several functional influences. This transition from a single function focus to a multifunction focus is essential for successful strategic management.[3]

Financial ratio analysis exemplifies the complexity of relationships among the functional areas of business. A declining return on investment or profit margin ratio could be the result of ineffective marketing, poor management policies, research and development errors, or a weak management information system. The effectiveness of strategy formulation, implementation, and evaluation activities hinges upon a clear understanding of how major business functions affect one another. For strategies to succeed, a coordinated effort among all the functional areas of business is needed. In the case of planning, George wrote:

> We may conceptually separate planning for the purpose of theoretical discussion and analysis, but in practice, neither is it a distinct entity nor is it capable of being separated. The planning function is mixed with all other business functions and, like ink once mixed with water, it cannot be set apart. It is spread throughout and is a part of the whole of managing an organization.[4]

INTEGRATING STRATEGY AND CULTURE

Relationships among a firm's functional business activities perhaps can be exemplified best by focusing on organizational culture, an internal phenomenon that permeates all departments and divisions of an organization. *Organizational culture* can be defined as "a pattern of behavior [that has been] developed by an organization as it learns to cope with its problem of external adaptation and internal integration, [and] that has worked well enough to be considered valid and to be taught to new members as the correct way to perceive, think, and feel."[5] This definition emphasizes the importance of matching external with internal factors in making strategic decisions.

Organizational culture captures the subtle, elusive, and largely unconscious forces that shape a workplace. Remarkably resistant to change, culture can represent a major strength or weakness for the firm. It can be an underlying reason for strengths or weaknesses in any of the major business functions.

Defined in Table 4–1, *cultural products* include values, beliefs, rites, rituals, ceremonies, myths, stories, legends, sagas, language, metaphors, symbols, heroes, and heroines. These products or dimensions are levers that strategists can use to influence and direct strategy formulation, implementation, and evaluation activities. An organization's culture compares to an individual's personality in the sense that no two organizations have the same culture and no two individuals have the same personality. Both culture and personality are fairly enduring and can be warm, aggressive, friendly, open, innovative, conservative, liberal, harsh, or likable.

Dimensions of organizational culture permeate all the functional areas of business. It is something of an art to uncover the basic values and beliefs that are deeply buried in an organization's rich collection of stories, language, heroes, and rituals, but cultural products can represent both important strengths and weaknesses. Culture is an aspect of an organization that can no longer be taken for granted in performing an internal strategic-management audit because culture and strategy must work together.

The strategic-management process takes place largely within a particular organization's culture. Lorsch found that executives in successful companies are emotionally committed to the firm's culture, but he concluded that culture can inhibit strategic management in two basic ways. First, managers frequently miss the significance of changing external conditions-because they are blinded by strongly held beliefs. Second, when a particular culture has been effective in the past, the natural response is to stick with it in the future, even during times of major strategic change.[6] An organization's culture must support the collective commitment of its people to a common purpose. It must foster competence and enthusiasm among managers and employees.

Organizational culture significantly affects business decisions and thus must be evaluated during an internal strategic-management audit. If strategies can capitalize on

VISIT THE NET

Provides excellent narrative on how the state of Missouri does strategic planning, including its internal assessment.
http://www.mri.state.mo.us/SP/model.htm

TABLE 4-1   **Cultural Products and Associated Definitions**

Rites	Relatively elaborate, dramatic, planned sets of activities that consolidate various forms of cultural expressions into one event, carried out through social interactions, usually for the benefit of an audience
Ceremonial	A system of several rites connected with a single occasion or event
Ritual	A standardized, detailed set of techniques and behaviors that manage anxieties, but seldom produce intended, technical consequences of practical importance
Myth	A dramatic narrative of imagined events, usually used to explain origins or transformations of something. Also, an unquestioned belief about the practical benefits of certain techniques and behaviors that is not supported by facts
Saga	A historical narrative describing the unique accomplishments of a group and its leaders, usually in heroic terms
Legend	A handed-down narrative of some wonderful event that is based on history but has been embellished with fictional details
Story	A narrative based on true events, sometimes a combination of truth and fiction
Folktale	A completely fictional narrative
Symbol	Any object, act, event, quality, or relation that serves as a vehicle for conveying meaning, usually by representing another thing
Language	A particular form or manner in which members of a group use sounds and written signs to convey meanings to each other
Metaphors	Shorthand words used to capture a vision or to reinforce old or new values
Values	Life-directing attitudes that serve as behavioral guidelines
Belief	An understanding of a particular phenomenon
Heroes/Heroines	Individuals whom the organization has legitimized to model behavior for others

Source: Adapted from H. M. Trice and J. M. Beyer, "Studying Organizational Cultures through Rites and Ceremonials," *Academy of Management Review* 9, no. 4 (October 1984): 655.

cultural strengths, such as a strong work ethic or highly ethical beliefs, then management often can implement changes swiftly and easily. However, if the firm's culture is not supportive, strategic changes may be ineffective or even counterproductive. A firm's culture can become antagonistic to new strategies, with the result being confusion and disorientation. An organization's culture should infuse individuals with enthusiasm for implementing strategies. Allarie and Firsirotu emphasized the need to understand culture:

> Culture provides an explanation for the insuperable difficulties a firm encounters when it attempts to shift its strategic direction. Not only has the "right" culture become the essence and foundation of corporate excellence, it is also claimed that success or failure of reforms hinges on management's sagacity and ability to change the firm's driving culture in time and in time with required changes in strategies.[7]

The potential value of organizational culture has not been realized fully in the study of strategic management. Ignoring the effect that culture can have on relationships among the functional areas of business can result in barriers to communication, lack of coordination, and an inability to adapt to changing conditions. Some tension between culture and a firm's strategy is inevitable, but the tension should be monitored so that it does not reach a point at which relationships are severed and the culture becomes antagonistic. The resulting disarray among members of the organization would disrupt strategy formulation, implementation, and evaluation. On the other hand, a supportive organizational culture can make managing much easier.

Internal strengths and weaknesses associated with a firm's culture sometimes are overlooked because of the interfunctional nature of this phenomenon. It is important, therefore, for strategists to understand their firm as a sociocultural system. Success is often determined by linkages between a firm's culture and strategies. The challenge of strategic management today is to bring about the changes in organizational culture and individual mind-sets that are needed to support the formulation, implementation, and evaluation of strategies.

American versus Foreign Cultures

To successfully compete in world markets, U.S. managers must obtain a better knowledge of historical, cultural, and religious forces that motivate and drive people in other countries. In Japan, for example, business relations operate within the context of *Wa*, which stresses group harmony and social cohesion. In China, business behavior revolves around *guanxi*, or personal relations. In Korea, activities involve concern for *inhwa*, or harmony based on respect of hierarchical relationships, including obedience to authority.[8] Note in the Global Perspective box that it is important to be sensitive to foreign business cultures.

In Europe, it is generally true that the farther north on the continent, the more participatory the management style. Most European workers are unionized and enjoy

GLOBAL PERSPECTIVE

American versus Foreign Communication Differences

As Americans increasingly interact with managers in other countries, it is important to be sensitive to foreign business cultures. Americans too often come across as intrusive, manipulative, and garrulous, and this impression reduces their effectiveness in communication. *Forbes* recently provided the following cultural hints from Charis Intercultural Training:

1. Italians, Germans, and French generally do not soften up executives with praise before they criticize. Americans do soften up folks, and this practice seems manipulative to Europeans.
2. Israelis are accustomed to fast-paced meetings and have little patience for American informality and small talk.
3. British executives often complain that American executives chatter too much. Informality, egalitarianism, and spontaneity from Americans in business settings jolt many foreigners.

4. Europeans feel they are being treated like children when asked to wear name tags by Americans.
5. Executives in India are used to interrupting one another. Thus, when American executives listen without asking for clarification or posing questions, they are viewed by Indians as not paying attention.
6. When negotiating orally with Malaysian or Japanese executives, periodically allow for a time of silence. However, do not pause when negotiating in Israel.

Refrain from asking foreign managers questions such as "How was your weekend?" That is intrusive to foreigners, who tend to regard their business and private lives as totally separate.

Source: Adapted from Lalita Khosla, "You Say Tomato," *Forbes* (May 21, 2001): 36.

more frequent vacations and holidays than U.S. workers. A ninety-minute lunch break plus twenty-minute morning and afternoon breaks are common in European firms. Guaranteed permanent employment is commonly a part of employment contracts in Europe. In socialist countries such as France, Belgium, and the United Kingdom, the only ground for immediate dismissal from work is a criminal offense. A six-month trial period at the beginning of employment is usually part of the contract with a European firm. Many Europeans resent pay-for-performance, commission salaries, and objective measurement and reward systems. This is true especially of workers in southern Europe. Many Europeans also find the notion of team spirit difficult to grasp because the unionized environment has dichotomized worker-management relations throughout Europe.

A weakness that U.S. firms have in competing with Pacific Rim firms is a lack of understanding of Far Eastern cultures, including how Asians think and behave. Spoken Chinese, for example, has more in common with spoken English than with spoken Japanese or Korean. Managers around the world face the responsibility of having to exert authority while at the same time trying to be liked by subordinates. U.S. managers consistently put more weight on being friendly and liked, whereas Asian and European managers exercise authority often without this concern. Americans tend to use first names instantly in business dealings with foreigners, but foreigners find this presumptuous. In Japan, for example, first names are used only among family members and intimate friends; even long-time business associates and coworkers shy away from the use of first names. Other cultural differences or pitfalls that U.S. managers need to know about are given in Table 4–2.

U.S. managers have a low tolerance for silence, whereas Asian managers view extended periods of silence as important for organizing and evaluating one's thoughts. U.S. managers are much more action-oriented than their counterparts around the world; they rush to appointments, conferences, and meetings—and then feel the day has been

TABLE 4-2   Cultural Pitfalls That You Need to Know

Waving is a serious insult in Greece and Nigeria, particularly if the hand is near someone's face.

Making a "good-bye" wave in Europe can mean "no," but it means "come here" in Peru.

In China, last names are written first.

A man named Carlos Lopez-Garcia should be addressed as Mr. Lopez in Latin America, but as Mr. Garcia in Brazil.

Breakfast meetings are considered uncivilized in most foreign countries.

Latin Americans average being twenty minutes late to business appointments.

Direct eye contact is impolite in Japan.

Don't cross your legs in Arab or many Asian countries—it's rude to show the sole of your shoe.

In Brazil, touching your thumb and first finger—an American "OK" sign—is the equivalent of raising your middle finger.

Nodding or tossing your head back in southern Italy, Malta, Greece, and Tunisia means "no." In India, this body motions means "yes."

Snapping your fingers is vulgar in France and Belgium.

Folding your arms across your chest is a sign of annoyance in Finland.

In China, leave some food on your plate to show that your host was so generous that you couldn't finish.

Do not eat with your left hand when dining with clients from Malaysia or India.

One form of communication works the same worldwide. It's the smile—so take that along wherever you go.

productive. But for foreign managers, resting, listening, meditating, and thinking is considered productive. Sitting through a conference without talking is unproductive in the United States, but it is viewed as positive in Japan if one's silence helps preserve unity.

U.S. managers also put greater emphasis on short-term results than foreign managers do. In marketing, for example, Japanese managers strive to achieve "everlasting customers," whereas many Americans strive to make a one-time sale. Marketing managers in Japan see making a sale as the beginning, not the end, of the selling process. This is an important distinction. Japanese managers often criticize U.S. managers for worrying more about shareholders, whom they do not know, than employees, whom they do know. Americans refer to "hourly employees," whereas many Japanese companies still refer to "lifetime employees."

Rose Knotts recently summarized some important cultural differences between U.S. and foreign managers:[9]

1. Americans place an exceptionally high priority on time, viewing time as an asset. Many foreigners place more worth on relationships. This difference results in foreign managers often viewing U.S. managers as "more interested in business than people."

2. Personal touching and distance norms differ around the world. Americans generally stand about three feet from each other when carrying on business conversations, but Arabs and Africans stand about one foot apart. Touching another person with the left hand in business dealings is taboo in some countries. American managers need to learn the personal space rules of foreign managers with whom they interact in business.

3. People in some cultures do not place the same significance on material wealth as American managers often do. Lists of the "largest corporations" and "highest-paid" executives abound in the United States. "More is better" and "bigger is better" in the United States, but not everywhere. This can be a consideration in trying to motivate individuals in other countries.

4. Family roles and relationships vary in different countries. For example, males are valued more than females in some cultures, and peer pressure, work situations, and business interactions reinforce this phenomenon.

5. Language differs dramatically across countries, even in countries where people speak the same language. Words and expressions commonly used in one country may be disrespectful in another.

6. Business and daily life in some societies is governed by religious factors. Prayer times, holidays, daily events, and dietary restrictions, for example, need to be respected by American managers not familiar with these practices in some countries.

7. Time spent with the family and the quality of relationships are more important in some cultures than the personal achievement and accomplishments espoused by the traditional American manager. For example, where a person stands in the hierarchy of a firm's organizational structure, how large the firm is, and where the firm is located are much more important factors to American managers than to many foreign managers.

8. Many cultures around the world value modesty, team spirit, collectivity, and patience much more than the competitiveness and individualism that are so important in America.

9. Punctuality is a valued personal trait when conducting business in America, but it is not revered in many of the world's societies. Eating habits also differ dramatically across cultures. For example, belching is acceptable in many countries as evidence of satisfaction with the food that has been prepared. Chinese culture considers it good manners to sample a portion of each food served.

10. To prevent social blunders when meeting with managers from other lands, one must learn and respect the rules of etiquette of others. Sitting on a toilet seat is viewed as unsanitary in most countries, but not in the United States. Leaving food or drink after dining is considered impolite in some countries, but not in China. Bowing instead of shaking hands is customary in many countries. Many cultures view Americans as unsanitary for locating toilet and bathing facilities in the same area, whereas Americans view people of some cultures as unsanitary for not taking a bath or shower every day.

11. Americans often do business with individuals they do not know, but this practice is not accepted in many other cultures. In Mexico and Japan, for example, an amicable relationship is often mandatory before conducting business.

In many countries, effective managers are those who are best at negotiating with government bureaucrats rather than those who inspire workers. Many U.S. managers are uncomfortable with nepotism and bribery, which are common in many countries. In almost every country except the United States, bribery is tax-deductible.

The United States has gained a reputation for defending women from sexual harassment and minorities from discrimination, but not all countries embrace the same values. For example, in the Czech Republic, it is considered a compliment when the boss openly flirts with his female secretary and invites her to dinner. U.S. managers in the Czech Republic who do not flirt seem cold and uncaring to some employees.

American managers in China have to be careful about how they arrange office furniture because Chinese workers believe in *feng shui,* the practice of harnessing natural forces. American managers in Japan have to be careful about *nemaswashio,* whereby Japanese workers expect supervisors to alert them privately of changes rather than informing them in a meeting. Japanese managers have little appreciation for versatility, expecting all managers to be the same. In Japan, "If a nail sticks out, you hit it into the wall," says Brad Lashbrook, an international consultant for Wilson Learning.

Probably the biggest obstacle to the effectiveness of U.S. managers—or managers from any country working in another—is the fact that it is almost impossible to change the attitude of a foreign workforce. "The system drives you; you cannot fight the system or culture," says Bill Parker, president of Phillips Petroleum in Norway.

 ## MANAGEMENT

The *functions of management* consist of five basic activities: planning, organizing, motivating, staffing, and controlling. An overview of these activities is provided in Table 4–3.

Planning

The only thing certain about the future of any organization is change, and *planning* is the essential bridge between the present and the future that increases the likelihood of achieving desired results. Planning is the process by which one determines whether to attempt a task, works out the most effective way of reaching desired objectives, and prepares to overcome unexpected difficulties with adequate resources. Planning is the start

TABLE 4-3   The Basic Functions of Management

FUNCTION	DESCRIPTION	STAGE OF STRATEGIC-MANAGEMENT PROCESS WHEN MOST IMPORTANT
Planning	Planning consists of all those managerial activities related to preparing for the future. Specific tasks include forecasting, establishing objectives, devising strategies, developing policies, and setting goals.	Strategy Formulation
Organizing	Organizing includes all those managerial activities that result in a structure of task and authority relationships. Specific areas include organizational design, job specialization, job descriptions, job specifications, span of the control, unity of command, coordination, job design, and job analysis.	Strategy Implementation
Motivating	Motivating involves efforts directed toward shaping human behavior. Specific topics include leadership, communication, work groups, behavior modification, delegation of authority, job enrichment, job satisfaction, needs fulfillment, organizational change, employee morale, and managerial morale.	Strategy Implementation
Staffing	Staffing activities are centered on personnel or human resource management. Included are wage and salary administration, employee benefits, interviewing, hiring, firing, training, management development, employee safety, affirmative action, equal employment opportunity, union relations, career development, personnel research, discipline policies, grievance procedures, and public relations.	Strategy Implementation
Controlling	Controlling refers to all those managerial activities directed toward ensuring that actual results are consistent with planned results. Key areas of concern include quality control, financial control, sales control, inventory control, expense control, analysis of variances, rewards, and sanctions.	Strategy Evaluation

of the process by which an individual or business may turn empty dreams into achievements. Planning enables one to avoid the trap of working extremely hard but achieving little.

Planning is an up-front investment in success. Planning helps a firm achieve maximum effect from a given effort. Planning enables a firm to take into account relevant factors and focus on the critical ones. Planning helps ensure that the firm can be prepared for all reasonable eventualities and for all changes that will be needed. Planning enables a firm to gather the resources needed and carry out tasks in the most efficient way possible. Planning enables a firm to conserve its own resources, avoid wasting ecological resources, make a fair profit, and be seen as an effective, useful firm. Planning enables a firm to identify precisely what is to be achieved and to detail precisely the who, what, when, where, why, and how needed to achieve desired objectives. Planning enables a firm to assess whether the effort, costs, and implications associated with achieving desired objectives are warranted.[10] Planning is the cornerstone of effective strategy formulation. But even though it is considered the foundation of management, it is commonly the task that managers neglect most. Planning is essential for successful strategy implementation and strategy evaluation, largely because organizing, motivating, staffing, and controlling activities depend upon good planning.

The process of planning must involve managers and employees throughout an organization. The time horizon for planning decreases from two to five years for top-level to less than six months for lower-level managers. The important point is that all managers do planning and should involve subordinates in the process to facilitate employee understanding and commitment.

Planning can have a positive impact on organizational and individual performance. Planning allows an organization to identify and take advantage of external opportunities as well as minimize the impact of external threats. Planning is more than extrapolating from the past and present into the future. It also includes developing a mission, forecasting future events and trends, establishing objectives, and choosing strategies to pursue.

An organization can develop synergy through planning. *Synergy* exists when everyone pulls together as a team that knows what it wants to achieve; synergy is the 2 + 2 = 5 effect. By establishing and communicating clear objectives, employees and managers can work together toward desired results. Synergy can result in powerful competitive advantages. The strategic-management process itself is aimed at creating synergy in an organization.

Planning allows a firm to adapt to changing markets and thus to shape its own destiny. Strategic management can be viewed as a formal planning process that allows an organization to pursue proactive rather than reactive strategies. Successful organizations strive to control their own futures rather than merely react to external forces and events as they occur. Historically, organisms and organizations that have not adapted to changing conditions have become extinct. Swift adaptation is needed today more than ever before because changes in markets, economies, and competitors worldwide are accelerating.

Organizing

The purpose of *organizing* is to achieve coordinated effort by defining task and authority relationships. Organizing means determining who does what and who reports to whom. There are countless examples in history of well-organized enterprises successfully competing against—and in some cases defeating—much stronger but less-organized firms. A well-organized firm generally has motivated managers and employees who are committed to seeing the organization succeed. Resources are allocated more effectively and used more efficiently in a well-organized firm than in a disorganized firm.

The organizing function of management can be viewed as consisting of three sequential activities: breaking tasks down into jobs (work specialization), combining jobs to form departments (departmentalization), and delegating authority. Breaking tasks down into jobs requires the development of job descriptions and job specifications. These tools clarify for both managers and employees what particular jobs entail. In *Wealth of Nations,* published in 1776, Adam Smith cited the advantages of work specialization in the manufacture of pins:

> One man draws the wire, another straightens it, a third cuts it, a fourth points it, a fifth grinds it at the top for receiving the head. Ten men working in this manner can produce 48,000 pins in a single day, but if they had all wrought separately and independently, each might at best produce twenty pins in a day.[11]

Combining jobs to form departments results in an organizational structure, span of control, and a chain of command. Changes in strategy often require changes in structure because positions may be created, deleted, or merged. Organizational structure dictates how resources are allocated and how objectives are established in a firm. Allocating resources and establishing objectives geographically, for example, is much different from doing so by product or customer.

The most common forms of departmentalization are functional, divisional, strategic business unit, and matrix. These types of structure are discussed further in Chapter 7.

Delegating authority is an important organizing activity, as evidenced in the old saying "You can tell how good a manager is by observing how his or her department functions when he or she isn't there." Employees today are more educated and more capable of participating in organizational decision making than ever before. In most cases, they expect to be delegated authority and responsibility, and to be held accountable for results. Delegation of authority is embedded in the strategic-management process.

Motivating

Motivating can be defined as the process of influencing people to accomplish specific objectives.[12] Motivation explains why some people work hard and others do not. Objectives, strategies, and policies have little chance of succeeding if employees and managers are not motivated to implement strategies once they are formulated. The motivating function of management includes at least four major components: leadership, group dynamics, communication, and organizational change.

When managers and employees of a firm strive to achieve high levels of productivity, this indicates that the firm's strategists are good leaders. Good leaders establish rapport with subordinates, empathize with their needs and concerns, set a good example, and are trustworthy and fair. Leadership includes developing a vision of the firm's future and inspiring people to work hard to achieve that vision. Kirkpatrick and Locke reported that certain traits also characterize effective leaders: knowledge of the business, cognitive ability, self-confidence, honesty, integrity, and drive.[13]

Research suggests that democratic behavior on the part of leaders results in more positive attitudes toward change and higher productivity than does autocratic behavior. Drucker said:

> Leadership is not a magnetic personality. That can just as well be demagoguery. It is not "making friends and influencing people." That is flattery. Leadership is the lifting of a person's vision to higher sights, the raising of a person's performance to a higher standard, the building of a person's personality beyond its normal limitations.[14]

Group dynamics play a major role in employee morale and satisfaction. Informal groups or coalitions form in every organization. The norms of coalitions can range from being very positive to very negative toward management. It is important, therefore, that strategists identify the composition and nature of informal groups in an organization to facilitate strategy formulation, implementation, and evaluation. Leaders of informal groups are especially important in formulating and implementing strategy changes.

Communication, perhaps the most important word in management, is a major component in motivation. An organization's system of communication determines whether strategies can be implemented successfully. Good two-way communication is vital for gaining support for departmental and divisional objectives and policies. Top-down communication can encourage bottom-up communication. The strategic-management process becomes a lot easier when subordinates are encouraged to discuss their concerns, reveal their problems, provide recommendations, and give suggestions. A primary reason for instituting strategic management is to build and support effective communication networks throughout the firm.

> The manager of tomorrow must be able to get his people to commit themselves to the business, whether they are machine operators or junior vice-presidents. Ah, you say, participative management. Have a cigar. But just because most managers tug a forelock at the P word doesn't mean they know how to make it

work. Today, throwing together a few quality circles won't suffice. The key issue will be empowerment, a term whose strength suggests the need to get beyond merely sharing a little information and a bit of decision making.[15]

Staffing

The management function of *staffing,* also called *personnel management* or *human resource management,* includes activities such as recruiting, interviewing, testing, selecting, orienting, training, developing, caring for, evaluating, rewarding, disciplining, promoting, transferring, demoting, and dismissing employees, as well as managing union relations.

Staffing activities play a major role in strategy-implementation efforts, and for this reason, human resource managers are becoming more actively involved in the strategic-management process. It is important to identify strengths and weaknesses in the staffing area.

The complexity and importance of human resource activities have increased to such a degree that all but the smallest organizations now need a full-time human resource manager. Numerous court cases that directly affect staffing activities are decided each day. Organizations and individuals can be penalized severely for not following federal, state, and local laws and guidelines related to staffing. Line managers simply cannot stay abreast of all the legal developments and requirements regarding staffing. The human resources department coordinates staffing decisions in the firm so that an organization as a whole meets legal requirements. This department also provides needed consistency in administering company rules, wages, and policies.

Human resources management is particularly challenging for international companies. For example, the inability of spouses and children to adapt to new surroundings has become a major staffing problem in overseas transfers. The problems include premature returns, job performance slumps, resignations, discharges, low morale, marital discord, and general discontent. Firms such as Ford Motor and Exxon/Mobil have begun screening and interviewing spouses and children before assigning persons to overseas positions. 3M Corporation introduces children to peers in the target country and offers spouses educational benefits.

Strategists are becoming increasingly aware of how important human resources are to effective strategic management. Human resource managers are becoming more involved and more proactive in formulating and implementing strategies. They provide leadership for organizations that are restructuring, or they allow employees to work at home.

Controlling

The *controlling* function of management includes all of those activities undertaken to ensure that actual operations conform to planned operations. All managers in an organization have controlling responsibilities, such as conducting performance evaluations and taking necessary action to minimize inefficiencies. The controlling function of management is particularly important for effective strategy evaluation. Controlling consists of four basic steps:

1. Establishing performance standards
2. Measuring individual and organizational performance
3. Comparing actual performance to planned performance standards
4. Taking corrective actions

Measuring individual performance is often conducted ineffectively or not at all in organizations. Some reasons for this shortcoming are that evaluations can create confrontations that most managers prefer to avoid, can take more time than most managers are willing to give, and can require skills that many managers lack. No single approach to measuring individual performance is without limitations. For this reason, an organization should examine various methods, such as the graphic rating scale, the behaviorally anchored rating scale, and the critical incident method, and then develop or select a performance appraisal approach that best suits the firm's needs. Increasingly, firms are striving to link organizational performance with managers' and employees' pay. This topic is discussed further in Chapter 7.

Management Audit Checklist of Questions

The checklists of questions provided below can help determine specific strengths and weaknesses in the functional area of business. An answer of *no* to any question could indicate a potential weakness, although the strategic significance and implications of negative answers, of course, will vary by organization, industry, and severity of the weakness. Positive or *yes* answers to the checklist questions suggest potential areas of strength.

1. Does the firm use strategic-management concepts?
2. Are company objectives and goals measurable and well communicated?
3. Do managers at all hierarchical levels plan effectively?
4. Do managers delegate authority well?
5. Is the organization's structure appropriate?
6. Are job descriptions and job specifications clear?
7. Is employee morale high?
8. Are employee turnover and absenteeism low?
9. Are organizational reward and control mechanisms effective?

 ## MARKETING

Marketing can be described as the process of defining, anticipating, creating, and fulfilling customers' needs and wants for products and services. There are seven basic *functions of marketing:* (1) customer analysis, (2) selling products/services, (3) product and service planning (4) pricing, (5) distribution, (6) marketing research, and (7) opportunity analysis.[16] Understanding these functions helps strategists identify and evaluate marketing strengths and weaknesses.

Customer Analysis

Customer analysis—the examination and evaluation of consumer needs, desires, and wants—involves administering customer surveys, analyzing consumer information, evaluating market positioning strategies, developing customer profiles, and determining optimal market segmentation strategies. The information generated by customer analysis can be essential in developing an effective mission statement. Customer profiles can reveal the demographic characteristics of an organization's customers. Buyers, sellers, distributors, salespeople, managers, wholesalers, retailers, suppliers, and creditors can all participate in gathering information to identify customers' needs and wants successfully. Successful organizations continually monitor present and potential customers' buying patterns.

Selling Products/Services

Successful strategy implementation generally rests upon the ability of an organization to sell some product or service. *Selling* includes many marketing activities, such as advertising, sales promotion, publicity, personal selling, sales force management, customer relations, and dealer relations. These activities are especially critical when a firm pursues a market penetration strategy. The effectiveness of various selling tools for consumer and industrial products varies. Personal selling is most important for industrial goods companies, and advertising is most important for consumer goods companies. Determining organizational strengths and weaknesses in the selling function of marketing is an important part of performing an internal strategic-management audit.

With regard to advertising products and services on the Internet, a new trend is to base advertising rates exclusively on sales rates. This new accountability contrasts sharply with traditional broadcast and print advertising, which bases rates on the number of persons expected to see a given advertisement. The new cost-per-sale online advertising rates are possible because any Web site can monitor which user clicks on which advertisement and then can record whether that consumer actually buys the product. If there are no sales, then the advertisement is free.

Due to weakening consumer confidence, falling demand, and increased layoffs, total corporate advertising expenditures declined 4 percent in 2001. Company expenditures on advertising in traditional media such as television, newspapers, and magazines declined more rapidly than nontraditional junk mail and direct mail. Newspaper advertising declined 5.9 percent in 2001, television ad spending fell 3.5 percent, and magazines advertising fell 8 percent. Ad spending on television fell another 4 percent in 2002.[17]

Product and Service Planning

Product and service planning includes activities such as test marketing; product and brand positioning; devising warranties; packaging; determining product options, product features, product style, and product quality; deleting old products; and providing for customer service. Product and service planning is particularly important when a company is pursuing product development or diversification.

One of the most effective product and service planning techniques is *test marketing*. Test markets allow an organization to test alternative marketing plans and to forecast future sales of new products. In conducting a test market project, an organization must decide how many cities to include, which cities to include, how long to run the test, what information to collect during the test, and what action to take after the test has been completed. Test marketing is used more frequently by consumer goods companies than by industrial goods companies. Test marketing can allow an organization to avoid substantial losses by revealing weak products and ineffective marketing approaches before large-scale production begins.

Pricing

Five major stakeholders affect *pricing* decisions: consumers, governments, suppliers, distributors, and competitors. Sometimes an organization will pursue a forward integration strategy primarily to gain better control over prices charged to consumers. Governments can impose constraints on price fixing, price discrimination, minimum prices, unit pricing, price advertising, and price controls. For example, the Robinson-Patman Act prohibits manufacturers and wholesalers from discriminating in price among channel member purchasers (suppliers and distributors) if competition is injured.

Competing organizations must be careful not to coordinate discounts, credit terms, or condition of sale; not to discuss prices, markups, and costs at trade association meetings; and not to arrange to issue new price lists on the same date, to rotate low bids on contracts, or to uniformly restrict production to maintain high prices. Strategists should view price from both a short-run and a long-run perspective, because competitors can copy price changes with relative ease. Often a dominant firm will aggressively match all price cuts by competitors.

With regard to pricing, as the value of the dollar increases, U.S. multinational companies have a choice. They can raise prices in the local currency of a foreign country or risk losing sales and market share. Alternatively, multinational firms can keep prices steady and face reduced profit when their export revenue is reported in the United States in dollars.

The largest operator of pay telephones in the United States, Verizon Communications, increased the price of local pay-phone calls to 50 cents because of declining pay-phone revenue and increased competition from cellphones. Previously, the cost was 35 cents for local calls. Verizon operates 430,000 pay phones in 33 states.

Prices on handheld computers are falling dramatically because distributors have excess inventory due to slowing consumer demand. Analysts contend that handheld computers will soon become as inexpensive as cellphones—and eventually may be given away when a consumer purchases the company's wireless Internet service. Palm is the largest handheld-computer maker, but other competitors include Casio, Handspring, and Hewlett-Packard. While the current economic downturn has wreaked havoc for companies on Wall Street, it has benefited consumers on Main Street, who have seen lower prices almost everywhere they shop.

Distribution

Distribution includes warehousing, distribution channels, distribution coverage, retail site locations, sales territories, inventory levels and location, transportation carriers, wholesaling, and retailing. Most producers today do not sell their goods directly to consumers. Various marketing entities act as intermediaries; they bear a variety of names such as wholesalers, retailers, brokers, facilitators, agents, vendors—or simply distributors.

Distribution becomes especially important when a firm is striving to implement a market development or forward integration strategy. Some of the most complex and challenging decisions facing a firm concern product distribution. Intermediaries flourish in our economy because many producers lack the financial resources and expertise to carry out direct marketing. Manufacturers who could afford to sell directly to the public often can gain greater returns by expanding and improving their manufacturing operations. Even General Motors would find it very difficult to buy out its more than eighteen thousand independent dealers.

Successful organizations identify and evaluate alternative ways to reach their ultimate market. Possible approaches vary from direct selling to using just one or many wholesalers and retailers. Strengths and weaknesses of each channel alternative should be determined according to economic, control, and adaptive criteria. Organizations should consider the costs and benefits of various wholesaling and retailing options. They must consider the need to motivate and control channel members and the need to adapt to changes in the future. Once a marketing channel is chosen, an organization usually must adhere to it for an extended period of time.

But as indicated in the E-Commerce Perspective, furniture manufacturers are now selling direct to consumers to the dismay of their brick-and-mortar distributors. However, Federated Stores is one of many brick-and-mortar firms pulling back from Internet operations. Federated is substantially reducing its macys.com and its bloomingdales.com Internet catalog operations. Federated has found that customers shopping online are most comfortable buying hard goods, such as jewelry and gifts, than apparel. These two Federated Web sites have never been profitable, but they still remain in operation, primarily as marketing sites. Other traditional retailers are scaling back their Internet operations, including Kmart with **bluelight.com** and Wal-Mart with **walmart.com**, as well as Toys R Us and Saks Fifth Avenue.

Marketing Research

Marketing research is the systematic gathering, recording, and analyzing of data about problems relating to the marketing of goods and services. Marketing research can uncover critical strengths and weaknesses, and marketing researchers employ numerous scales, instruments, procedures, concepts, and techniques to gather information. Marketing research activities support all of the major business functions of an organization. Organizations that possess excellent marketing research skills have a definite strength in pursuing generic strategies.

> The President of PepsiCo [said], "Looking at the competition is the company's best form of market research. The majority of our strategic successes are ideas that we borrow from the marketplace, usually from a small regional or local competitor. In each case, we spot a promising new idea, improve on it, and then out-execute our competitor."[18]

E-COMMERCE PERSPECTIVE

E-Stores Replacing Brick Stores

Like many industries, retail furniture stores nationwide are intensely debating whether the Internet will destroy their business or simply add another small sales channel. Furniture retailers nationwide are demanding assurance from furniture suppliers (manufacturers) that discount Internet retailers will not be supplied with their same furniture brands. The furniture industry is crazed over this subject. Some analysts contend that all furniture stores in the United States will disappear and some say Internet furniture sales will actually spur retail furniture sales. The furniture manufacturer, Stanley Furniture Company in Stanleytown, Virginia, decided to sell its products on the Internet, but after a month of loud protests from its retail distributors, Stanley banned all online sales of its products. But two other big furniture makers, Ethan Allan Interiors in Danbury, Connecticut, and La-Z-Boy Inc. in Monroe, Michigan, both plan to distribute their products online in "cooperation" with their retailers. The nation's largest furniture manufacturer with 9 percent of the market, Furniture Brands, in St. Louis, contends that people will want to "see and touch" before purchasing furniture. However, an increasing number of discount online furniture companies, such as Benchmark Industries in Olathe,

Kansas, and JCPenney of Plano, Texas, now offer furniture online. Online furniture sales are expected to increase to nearly $4 billion by 2004 from $0.5 billion in 2000, representing a market share increase from 0.75 to 5.0.

Gone are the days when furniture stores had a geographically captive customer, when merchants had the advantage of being the only store within driving distance, and when only the merchants knew the actual costs of their brands being sold. Using the Internet, the next furniture store is only seconds away for customers. and it is open twenty-four hours a day. Cybershoppers research furniture brands and prices from any computer, anywhere, and make their purchase(s) with the click of a mouse. Various Web sites now do the furniture research for the customer. This approach is garnering an ever-increasing number of furniture customers. Traditional brick-and-mortar furniture stores must offer superior customer service, low prices, and more to have a chance to compete in this market.

Source: Adapted from James, Hagerty, "Furniture Brands May Have to Rethink Its Web Policy," *The Wall Street Journal* September 14, 1999: B4.

About twenty thousand new products are introduced by U.S. companies annually, but 85 percent of these fail within three years. Many CEOs continue to trust their own best judgment over market research; this mindset can be detrimental to a business. For example, the Greyhound Bus Company first pursued the African American market by advertising on African American radio stations. However, instead of creating a new commercial, Greyhound used its popular country & western music ad, which later was considered to have failed in that market.

 ## OPPORTUNITY ANALYSIS

The eighth function of marketing is *opportunity analysis,* which involves assessing the costs, benefits, and risks associated with marketing decisions. Three steps are required to perform a *cost/benefit analysis:* (1) compute the total costs associated with a decision, (2) estimate the total benefits from the decision, and (3) compare the total costs with the total benefits. When expected benefits exceed total costs, an opportunity becomes more attractive. Sometimes the variables included in a cost/benefit analysis cannot be quantified or even measured, but usually reasonable estimates can be made to allow the analysis to be performed. One key factor to be considered is risk. Cost/benefit analyses should also be performed when a company is evaluating alternative ways to be socially responsible.

Marketing Audit Checklist of Questions
The following questions about marketing, much like the earlier questions for management, are pertinent:

1. Are markets segmented effectively?
2. Is the organization positioned well among competitors?
3. Has the firm's market share been increasing?
4. Are present channels of distribution reliable and cost-effective?
5. Does the firm have an effective sales organization?
6. Does the firm conduct market research?
7. Are product quality and customer service good?
8. Are the firm's products and services priced appropriately?
9. Does the firm have an effective promotion, advertising, and publicity strategy?
10. Are marketing, planning, and budgeting effective?
11. Do the firm's marketing managers have adequate experience and training?

 ## FINANCE/ACCOUNTING

Financial condition is often considered the single best measure of a firm's competitive position and overall attractiveness to investors. Determining an organization's financial strengths and weaknesses is essential to formulating strategies effectively. A firm's liquidity, leverage, working capital, profitability, asset utilization, cash flow, and equity can eliminate some strategies as being feasible alternatives. Financial factors often alter existing strategies and change implementation plans.

An especially good Web site to obtain financial information about a company is **www.quicken.com**, which provides excellent financial ratio, stock, and valuation information on all publicly held companies. Simply insert the company's stock symbol when the screen first loads and a wealth of information follows. Another nice site for obtaining financial information is **www.forbes.com**. Be sure to access the Manufacturing and Service section of **www.strategy club.com** for excellent financial-related Web sites.

Finance/Accounting Functions

According to James Van Horne, the *functions of finance/accounting* comprise three decisions: the investment decision, the financing decision, and the dividend decision.[19] Financial ratio analysis is the most widely used method for determining an organization's strengths and weaknesses in the investment, financing, and dividend areas. Because the functional areas of business are so closely related, financial ratios can signal strengths or weaknesses in management, marketing, production, research and development, and management information systems activities.

The *investment decision,* also called *capital budgeting,* is the allocation and reallocation of capital and resources to projects, products, assets, and divisions of an organization. Once strategies are formulated, capital budgeting decisions are required to implement strategies successfully. The *financing decision* determines the best capital structure for the firm and includes examining various methods by which the firm can raise capital (for example, by issuing stock, increasing debt, selling assets, or using a combination of these approaches). The financing decision must consider both short-term and long-term needs for working capital. Two key financial ratios that indicate whether a firm's financing decisions have been effective are the debt-to-equity ratio and the debt-to-total-assets ratio.

Dividend decisions concern issues such as the percentage of earnings paid to stockholders, the stability of dividends paid over time, and the repurchase or issuance of stock. Dividend decisions determine the amount of funds that are retained in a firm compared to the amount paid out to stockholders. Three financial ratios that are helpful in evaluating a firm's dividend decisions are the earnings-per-share ratio, the dividends-per-share ratio, and the price-earnings ratio. The benefits of paying dividends to investors must be balanced against the benefits of retaining funds internally, and there is no set formula on how to balance this trade-off. For the reasons listed here, dividends are sometimes paid out even when funds could be better reinvested in the business or when the firm has to obtain outside sources of capital:

1. Paying cash dividends is customary. Failure to do so could be thought of as a stigma. A dividend change is considered a signal about the future.
2. Dividends represent a sales point for investment bankers. Some institutional investors can buy only dividend-paying stocks.
3. Shareholders often demand dividends, even in companies with great opportunities for reinvesting all available funds.
4. A myth exists that paying dividends will result in a higher stock price.

Many companies, such as Xerox, have recently suspended paying dividends due to consistently falling revenues and earnings.

Basic Types of Financial Ratios

Financial ratios are computed from an organization's income statement and balance sheet. Computing financial ratios is like taking a picture because the results reflect a situation at just one point in time. Comparing ratios over time and to industry averages is

FIGURE 4–2

A Financial Ratio Trend Analysis

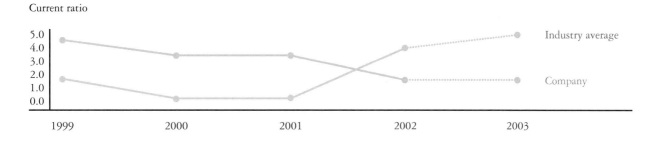

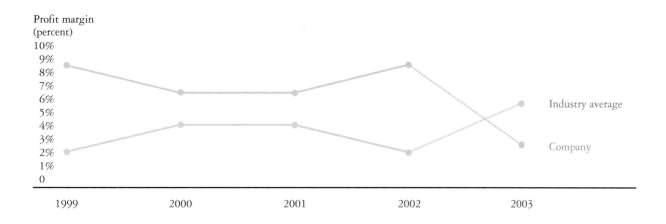

more likely to result in meaningful statistics that can be used to identify and evaluate strengths and weaknesses. Trend analysis, illustrated in Figure 4–2, is a useful technique that incorporates both the time and industry average dimensions of financial ratios. Note that the dotted lines reveal projected ratios. Some Web sites, such as Wall Street Research Net at **www.wsrn.com**, calculate financial ratios and provide data with charts. Four major sources of industry-average financial ratios follow:

1. Dun & Bradstreet's *Industry Norms and Key Business Ratios*—Fourteen different ratios are calculated in an industry-average format for eight hundred different types of businesses. The ratios are presented by Standard Industrial Classification (SIC) number and are grouped by annual sales into three size categories.

2. Robert Morris Associates' *Annual Statement Studies*—Sixteen different ratios are calculated in an industry-average format. Industries are referenced by SIC numbers published by the Bureau of the Census. The ratios are presented in four size categories by annual sales for all firms in the industry.

3. *Almanac of Business & Industrial Financial Ratios*—Twenty-two financial ratios and percentages are provided in an industry-average format for all major industries. The ratios and percentages are given for twelve different company-size categories for all firms in a given industry.

VISIT THE NET

Click on the showcase site at bottom, then enter your stock symbol in upper right, and then scroll down left column to the financial ratio comparison and click.
http://www.stockpoint.com

4. *Federal Trade Commission Reports*—The FTC publishes quarterly financial data, including ratios on manufacturing companies. FTC reports include analyses by industry group and asset size.

Table 4–4 provides a summary of key financial ratios showing how each ratio is calculated and what each ratio measures. However, all the ratios are not significant for all industries and companies. For example, accounts receivable turnover and average collection period are not very meaningful to a company that primarily does a cash receipts business. Key financial ratios can be classified into the following five types:

1. *Liquidity ratios* measure a firm's ability to meet maturing short-term obligations.
   Current ratio
   Quick (or acid-test) ratio

2. *Leverage ratios* measure the extent to which a firm has been financed by debt.
   Debt-to-total-assets ratio
   Debt-to-equity ratio
   Long-term debt-to-equity ratio
   Times-interest-earned (or coverage) ratio

3. *Activity ratios* measure how effectively a firm is using its resources.
   Inventory-turnover
   Fixed assets turnover
   Total assets turnover
   Accounts receivable turnover
   Average collection period

4. *Profitability ratios* measure management's overall effectiveness as shown by the returns generated on sales and investment.
   Gross profit margin
   Operating profit margin
   Net profit margin
   Return on total assets (ROA)
   Return on stockholders' equity (ROE)
   Earnings per share (EPS)
   Price-earnings ratio

5. *Growth ratios* measure the firm's ability to maintain its economic position in the growth of the economy and industry.
   Sales
   Net income
   Earnings per share
   Dividends per share

Financial ratio analysis is not without some limitations. First of all, financial ratios are based on accounting data, and firms differ in their treatment of such items as depreciation, inventory valuation, research and development expenditures, pension plan costs, mergers, and taxes. Also, seasonal factors can influence comparative ratios. Therefore, conformity to industry composite ratios does not establish with certainty that a firm is performing normally or that it is well managed. Likewise, departures from industry averages do not always indicate that a firm is doing especially well or badly. For example, a high inventory turnover ratio could indicate efficient inventory management and a strong working capital position, but it also could indicate a serious inventory shortage and a weak working capital position.

TABLE 4-4   A Summary of Key Financial Ratios

RATIO	HOW CALCULATED	WHAT IT MEASURES
Liquidity Ratios		
Current Ratio	$$\frac{\text{Current assets}}{\text{Current liabilities}}$$	The extent to which a firm can meet its short-term obligations
Quick Ratio	$$\frac{\text{Current assets minus inventory}}{\text{Current liabilities}}$$	The extent to which a firm can meet its short-term obligations without relying upon the sale of its inventories
Leverage Ratios		
Debt-to-Total-Assets Ratio	$$\frac{\text{Total debt}}{\text{Total assets}}$$	The percentage of total funds that are provided by creditors
Debt-to-Equity Ratio	$$\frac{\text{Total debt}}{\text{Total stockholders' equity}}$$	The percentage of total funds provided by creditors versus by owners
Long-Term Debt-to-Equity Ratio	$$\frac{\text{Long-term debt}}{\text{Total stockholders' equity}}$$	The balance between debt and equity in a firm's long-term capital structure
Times-Interest-Earned Ratio	$$\frac{\text{Profits before interest and taxes}}{\text{Total interest charges}}$$	The extent to which earnings can decline without the firm becoming unable to meet its annual interest costs
Activity Ratios		
Inventory Turnover	$$\frac{\text{Sales}}{\text{Inventory of finished goods}}$$	Whether a firm holds excessive stocks of inventories and whether a firm is selling its inventories slowly compared to the industry average
Fixed Assets Turnover	$$\frac{\text{Sales}}{\text{Fixed assets}}$$	Sales productivity and plant and equipment utilization
Total Assets Turnover	$$\frac{\text{Sales}}{\text{Total assets}}$$	Whether a firm is generating a sufficient volume of business for the size of its asset investment
Accounts Receivable Turnover	$$\frac{\text{Annual credit sales}}{\text{Accounts receivable}}$$	The average length of time it takes a firm to collect credit sales (in percentage terms)
Average Collection Period	$$\frac{\text{Accounts receivable}}{\text{Total credit sales/365 days}}$$	The average length of time it takes a firm to collect on credit sales (in days)
Profitability Ratios		
Gross Profit Margin	$$\frac{\text{Sales minus cost of goods sold}}{\text{Sales}}$$	The total margin available to cover operating expenses and yield a profit
Operating Profit Margin	$$\frac{\text{Earnings before interest and taxes (EBIT)}}{\text{Sales}}$$	Profitability without concern for taxes and interest
Net Profit Margin	$$\frac{\text{Net income}}{\text{Sales}}$$	After-tax profits per dollar of sales
Return on Total Assets (ROA)	$$\frac{\text{Net income}}{\text{Total assets}}$$	After-tax profits per dollar of assets; this ratio is also called return on investment (ROI)
Return on Stockholders' Equity (ROE)	$$\frac{\text{Net income}}{\text{Total stockholders' equity}}$$	After-tax profits per dollar of stockholders' investment in the firm
Earnings Per Share (EPS)	$$\frac{\text{Net income}}{\text{Number of shares of common stock outstanding}}$$	Earnings available to the owners of common stock
Price-earnings Ratio	$$\frac{\text{Market price per share}}{\text{Earnings per share}}$$	Attractiveness of firm on equity markets
Growth Ratios		
Sales	Annual percentage growth in total sales	Firm's growth rate in sales
Net Income	Annual percentage growth in profits	Firm's growth rate in profits
Earnings Per Share	Annual percentage growth in EPS	Firm's growth rate in EPS
Dividends Per Share	Annual percentage growth in dividends per share	Firm's growth rate in dividends per share

It is important to recognize that a firm's financial condition depends not only on the functions of finance, but also on many other factors that include (1) management, marketing, management production/operations, research and development, and management information systems decisions; (2) actions by competitors, suppliers, distributors, creditors, customers, and shareholders; and (3) economic, social, cultural, demographic, environmental, political, governmental, legal, and technological trends. Even natural environment liabilities can affect financial ratios, as indicated in the Natural Environment Perspective. So financial ratio analysis, like all other analytical tools, should be used wisely.

Finance/Accounting Audit Checklist of Questions

The following finance/accounting questions, like the similar questions about marketing and management earlier, should be examined:

1. Where is the firm financially strong and weak as indicated by financial ratio analyses?
2. Can the firm raise needed short-term capital?
3. Can the firm raise needed long-term capital through debt and/or equity?
4. Does the firm have sufficient working capital?
5. Are capital budgeting procedures effective?
6. Are dividend payout policies reasonable?

 # NATURAL ENVIRONMENT PERSPECTIVE

Environmental Liability on the Balance Sheet

Environmental liability may be the largest recognized or unrecognized liability on a company's balance sheet. More American firms are finding themselves liable for cleanup costs and damages stemming from waste disposal practices of the past—in some cases going back 100 years. Environmental liabilities associated with air and water pollution, habitat destruction, deforestation, and medical problems can be immense. For this reason, many financial institutions now inquire about environmental liabilities as part of their commercial lending procedures. Firms such as American Insurance Company specialize in providing environmental liability insurance to companies.

Environmental Protection Agency (EPA) regulations take up more than 11,000 pages; they vary with location and size of firm and are added to daily. The complexity of these regulations can translate into liabilities for the environmentally reactive firm. Proactive firms, on the other hand, are adding a "green executive" and department to oversee management of environmental policies and practices of the firm. The responsibility of green executives includes thinking through environmental regulations, marketing needs, public attitudes, consumer demands, and potential problems. Ideally, green executives should promote development of a corporate culture in which all managers and employees become "green," or environmentally sensitive. Such a culture would represent an internal strength to the firm.

The September 11, 2001, terrorist attacks and the global war on terrorism accents the need for companies to include antibiological and antichemical terrorism expenses on the firm's financial statements. Thousands of businesses today are upgrading security measures to safeguard their operations, employees, and customers from possible terrorist attacks on the natural environment.

Source: Adapted from Laura Johannes and Marilyn Chase, "Experts Say Bioterrorism Threat Is Real, Yet Likelihood Is Uncertain," *Wall Street Journal* (September 28, 2001): B1 and B6. See also Ted Bridis, "State of the Union: America the Vulnerable?" *Wall Street Journal* (September 28, 2001): B1 and B4.

7. Does the firm have good relations with its investors and stockholders?

8. Are the firm's financial managers experienced and well trained?

PRODUCTION/OPERATIONS

The *production/operations function* of a business consists of all those activities that transform inputs into goods and services. Production/operations management deals with inputs, transformations, and outputs that vary across industries and markets. A manufacturing operation transforms or converts inputs such as raw materials, labor, capital, machines, and facilities into finished goods and services. As indicated in Table 4–5, Roger Schroeder suggested that production/operations management comprises five functions or decision areas: process, capacity, inventory, workforce, and quality.

Most automakers require a thirty-day notice to build vehicles, but Toyota Motor fills a buyer's new car order in just five days. Honda Motor was considered the industry's fastest producer, filling orders in fifteen days. Automakers have for years operated under just-in-time inventory systems, but Toyota's 360 suppliers are linked to the company via computers on a virtual assembly line. The new Toyota production system was developed in the company's Cambridge, Ontario, plant and now applies to its Solara, Camry, Corolla, and Tacoma vehicles.

Capacity utilization for light trucks in the automobile industry has dropped from 107 percent in 2000 to an expected 75 percent in 2005, due to oversupply and falling demand. Light trucks, which include SUVs, minivans, and pickups, accounted for nearly all the profits for Ford, DaimlerChrysler, and General Motors in 2000 and 2001. These American automobile producers have been slow to upgrade their car models, and consequently, foreign makes of cars now comprise more than half of the market share for all

TABLE 4–5   **The Basic Functions of Production Management**

FUNCTION	DESCRIPTION
1. Process	Process decisions concern the design of the physical production system. Specific decisions include choice of technology, facility layout, process flow analysis, facility location, line balancing, process control, and transportation analysis.
2. Capacity	Capacity decisions concern determination of optimal output levels for the organization—not too much and not too little. Specific decisions include forecasting, facilities planning, aggregate planning, scheduling, capacity planning, and queuing analysis.
3. Inventory	Inventory decisions involve managing the level of raw materials, work-in-process, and finished goods. Specific decisions include what to order, when to order, how much to order, and materials handling.
4. Workforce	Workforce decisions are concerned with managing the skilled, unskilled, clerical, and managerial employees. Specific decisions include job design, work measurement, job enrichment, work standards, and motivation techniques:
5. Quality	Quality decisions are aimed at ensuring that high-quality goods and services are produced. Specific decisions include quality control, sampling, testing, quality assurance, and cost control.

Source: Adapted from R. Schroeder, *Operations Management* (New York: McGraw-Hill Book Co., 1981): 12.

cars sold in the United States. For example, General Motors is selling Saturns with an eleven-year-old design and Chevrolet Cavaliers with a seven-year-old one—and complaining that they're unprofitable.[20] In contrast, Volkswagen, Toyota, and Honda all have redesigned Beetles, Corollas, and Civics, respectively, and all of these models are profitable.

All domestic automobile makers are closing plants due to slowing consumer demand for most models of cars and trucks. The movement of supplies and parts needed for automobile manufacturing has slowed dramatically as some analysts even question whether just-in-time inventory control will ever again be the norm given shipment delays along the United States-Mexican border.

Production/operations activities often represent the largest part of an organization's human and capital assets. In most industries, the major costs of producing a product or service are incurred within operations, so production/operations can have great value as a competitive weapon in a company's overall strategy. Strengths and weaknesses in the five functions of production can mean the success or failure of an enterprise.

Many production/operations managers are finding that cross-training of employees can help their firms respond to changing markets faster. Cross-training of workers can increase efficiency, quality, productivity, and job satisfaction. For example, at General Motors's Detroit gear & axle plant, costs related to product defects were reduced 400 percent in two years as a result of cross-training workers. A shortage of qualified labor in America is another reason cross-training is becoming a common management practice.

Singapore rivals Hong Kong as an attractive site for locating production facilities in Southeast Asia. Singapore is a city-state near Malaysia. An island nation of about four million, Singapore is changing from an economy built on trade and services to one built upon information technology. A large-scale program in computer education for older (over twenty-six-year-old) residents is very popular. Singapore children receive outstanding computer training in schools. All government services are computerized nicely. Singapore lures multinational businesses with great tax breaks, world-class infrastructure, excellent courts that handle business disputes efficiently, exceptionally low tariffs, large land giveaways, impressive industrial parks, excellent port facilities, and a government very receptive to and cooperative with foreign businesses. Foreign firms now account for 70 percent of manufacturing output in Singapore.

There is much reason for concern that many organizations have not taken sufficient account of the capabilities and limitations of the production/operations function in formulating strategies. Scholars contend that this neglect has had unfavorable consequences on corporate performance in America. As shown in Table 4–6, James Dilworth outlined several types of strategic decisions that a company might make with production/operations implications of those decisions. Production capabilities and policies can also greatly affect strategies.

Production/Operations Audit
Checklist of Questions
Questions such as the following should be examined:

1. Are supplies of raw materials, parts, and subassemblies reliable and reasonable?
2. Are facilities, equipment, machinery, and offices in good condition?
3. Are inventory-control policies and procedures effective?
4. Are quality-control policies and procedures effective?
5. Are facilities, resources, and markets strategically located?
6. Does the firm have technological competencies?

TABLE 4-6   **Impact of Strategy Elements on Production Management**

POSSIBLE ELEMENTS OF STRATEGY	CONCOMITANT CONDITIONS THAT MAY AFFECT THE OPERATIONS FUNCTION AND ADVANTAGES AND DISADVANTAGES
1. Compete as low-cost provider of goods or services	Discourages competition Broadens market Requires longer production runs and fewer product changes Requires special-purpose equipment and facilities
2. Compete as high-quality provider	Often possible to obtain more total profit from a smaller volume of sales Requires more quality-assurance effort and higher operating cost Requires more precise equipment, which is more expensive Requires highly skilled workers, necessitating higher wages and greater training efforts
3. Stress customer service	Requires broader development of servicepeople and service parts and equipment Requires rapid response to customer needs or changes in customer tastes, rapid and accurate information system, careful coordination Requires a higher inventory investment
4. Provide rapid and frequent introduction of new products	Requires versatile equipment and people Has higher research and development costs Has high retraining costs and high tooling and changeover in manufacturing Provides lower volumes for each product and fewer opportunities for improvements due to the learning curve
5. Strive for absolute growth	Requires accepting some projects or products with lower marginal value, which reduces ROI Diverts talents to areas of weakness instead of concentrating on strengths
6. Seek vertical integration	Enables company to control more of the process May not have economies of scale at some stages of process May require high capital investment as well as technology and skills beyond those currently available within the organization
7. Maintain reserve capacity for flexibility	Provides ability to meet peak demands and quickly implement some contingency plans if forecasts are too low Requires capital investment in idle capacity Provides capability to grow during the lead time normally required for expansion
8. Consolidate processing (Centralize)	Can result in economies of scale Can locate near one major customer or supplier Vulnerability: one strike, fire, or flood can halt the entire operation
9. Disperse processing of service (Decentralize)	Can be near several market territories Requires more complex coordination network: perhaps expensive data transmission and duplication of some personnel and equipment at each location If each location produces one product in the line, then other products still must be transported to be available at all locations If each location specializes in a type of component for all products, the company is vulnerable to strike, fire, flood, etc. If each location provides total product line, then economies of scale may not be realized
10. Stress the use of mechanization, automation, robots	Requires high capital investment Reduces flexibility May affect labor relations Makes maintenance more crucial
11. Stress stability of employment	Serves the security needs of employees and may develop employee loyalty Helps to attract and retain highly skilled employees May require revisions of make-or-buy decisions, use of idle time, inventory, and subcontractors as demand fluctuates

Source: J. Dilworth, *Production and Operations Management: Manufacturing and Nonmanufacturing*, 2nd ed. Copyright © 1983 by Random House, Inc. Reprinted by permission of Random House, Inc.

RESEARCH AND DEVELOPMENT

The fifth major area of internal operations that should be examined for specific strengths and weaknesses is *research and development* (R&D). Many firms today conduct no R&D, and yet many other companies depend on successful R&D activities for survival. Firms pursuing a product development strategy especially need to have a strong R&D orientation.

Organizations invest in R&D because they believe that such an investment will lead to a superior product or services and will give them competitive advantages. Research and development expenditures are directed at developing new products before competitors do at improving product quality, or at improving manufacturing processes to reduce costs.

Effective management of the R&D function requires a strategic and operational partnership between R&D and the other vital business functions. A spirit of partnership and mutual trust between general and R&D managers is evident in the best-managed firms today. Managers in these firms jointly explore; assess; and decide the what, when, where, why, and how much of R&D. Priorities, costs, benefits, risks, and rewards associated with R&D activities are discussed openly and shared. The overall mission of R&D thus has become broad-based, including supporting existing businesses, helping launch new businesses, developing new products, improving product quality, improving manufacturing efficiency, and deepening or broadening the company's technological capabilities.[21]

The best-managed firms today seek to organize R&D activities in a way that breaks the isolation of R&D from the rest of the company and promotes a spirit of partnership between R&D managers and other managers in the firm. R&D decisions and plans must be integrated and coordinated across departments and divisions by having the departments share experiences and information. The strategic-management process facilitates this cross-functional approach to managing the R&D function.

Internal and External R&D

Cost distributions among R&D activities vary by company and industry, but total R&D costs generally do not exceed manufacturing and marketing startup costs. Four approaches to determining R&D budget allocations commonly are used: (1) financing as many project proposals as possible, (2) using a percentage-of-sales method, (3) budgeting about the same amount that competitors spend for R&D, or (4) deciding how many successful new products are needed and working backward to estimate the required R&D investment.

R&D in organizations can take two basic forms: (1) internal R&D, in which an organization operates its own R&D department, and/or (2) contract R&D, in which a firm hires independent researchers or independent agencies to develop specific products. Many companies use both approaches to develop new products. A widely used approach for obtaining outside R&D assistance is to pursue a joint venture with another firm. R&D strengths (capabilities) and weaknesses (limitations) play a major role in strategy formulation and strategy implementation.

Most firms have no choice but to continually develop new and improved products because of changing consumer needs and tastes, new technologies, shortened product life cycles, and increased domestic and foreign competition. A shortage of ideas for new products, increased global competition, increased market segmentation, strong special-interest groups, and increased government regulation are several factors making the successful development of new products more and more difficult, costly, and risky. In the pharmaceutical industry, for example, only one out of every few thousand drugs created in the laboratory ends up on pharmacists' shelves. Scarpello, Boulton, and Hofer emphasized that different strategies require different R&D capabilities:

> The focus of R&D efforts can vary greatly depending on a firm's competitive strategy. Some corporations attempt to be market leaders and innovators of new products, while others are satisfied to be market followers and developers of currently available products. The basic skills required to support these strategies will vary, depending on whether R&D becomes the driving force behind competitive strategy. In cases where new product introduction is the driving force for strategy, R&D activities must be extensive. The R&D unit must then be able to advance scientific and technological knowledge, exploit that knowledge, and manage the risks associated with ideas, products, services, and production requirements.[22]

Motorola recently announced that it had figured out how to combine silicon and gallium arsenide in one semiconductor chip. The company said this discovery will greatly reduce manufacturing process costs and result in smaller, faster products. The discovery is expected to yield products by the end of 2003 and may lead to cellphones as small as shirt buttons.

Intel and Microsoft are continuing to increase their expenditures on research and development. Intel spent just over $4 billion on R&D in 2001, nearly 15 percent of sales, while Microsoft spent $4.8 billion, up 37 percent from two years earlier. Both companies expect to increase R&D spending an additional $500 million in 2002. Intel is developing more powerful and smaller chips to power computers, while Microsoft is improving its Windows XP operating system.

Research and Development Audit Checklist of Questions

Questions such as the following should be asked in performing an R&D audit:

1. Does the firm have R&D facilities? Are they adequate?
2. If outside R&D firms are used, are they cost-effective?
3. Are the organization's R&D personnel well qualified?
4. Are R&D resources allocated effectively?
5. Are management information and computer systems adequate?
6. Is communication between R&D and other organizational units effective?
7. Are present products technologically competitive?

MANAGEMENT INFORMATION SYSTEMS

Information ties all business functions together and provides the basis for all managerial decisions. It is the cornerstone of all organizations. Information represents a major source of competitive management advantage or disadvantage. Assessing a firm's internal strengths and weaknesses in information systems is a critical dimension of performing an internal audit. The company motto of Mitsui, a large Japanese trading company, is "Information is the lifeblood of the company." A satellite network connects Mitsui's 200 worldwide offices.

A management information system's purpose is to improve the performance of an enterprise by improving the quality of managerial decisions. An effective information system thus collects, codes, stores, synthesizes, and presents information in such a manner that it answers important operating and strategic questions. The heart of an information system is a database containing the kinds of records and data important to managers.

A *management information system* receives raw material from both the external and internal evaluation of an organization. It gathers data about marketing, finance, production, and personnel matters internally, and social, cultural, demographic, environmental, economic, political, governmental legal, technological, and competitive factors externally. Data are integrated in ways needed to support managerial decision making.

There is a logical flow of material in a computer information system, whereby data is input to the system and transformed into output. Outputs include computer printouts, written reports, tables, chairs, graphs, checks, purchase orders, invoices, inventory records, payroll accounts, and a variety of other documents. Payoffs from alternative strategies can be calculated and estimated. *Data* become *information* only when they are evaluated, filtered, condensed, analyzed, and organized for a specific purpose, problem, individual, or time.

An effective management information system utilizes computer hardware, software, models for analysis, and a database. Some people equate information systems with the advent of the computer, but historians have traced recordkeeping and noncomputer data processing to Babylonian merchants living in 3500 B.C. Benefits of an effective information system include an improved understanding of business functions, improved communications, more informed decision making, a better analysis of problems, and improved control.

Because organizations are becoming more complex, decentralized, and globally dispersed, the function of information systems is growing in importance. Spurring this advance is the falling cost and increasing power of computers. There are costs and benefits associated with obtaining and evaluating information, just as with equipment and land. Like equipment, information can become obsolete and may need to be purged from the system. An effective information system is like a library, collecting, categorizing, and filing data for use by managers throughout the organization. Information systems are a major strategic resource, monitoring environmental changes, identifying competitive threats, and assisting in the implementation, evaluation, and control of strategy.

We are truly in an information age. Firms whose information-system skills are weak are at a competitive disadvantage. On the other hand, strengths in information systems allow firms to establish distinctive competencies in other areas. Low-cost manufacturing and good customer service, for example, can depend on a good information system.

A good executive information system provides graphic, tabulate, and textual information. Graphic capabilities are needed so current conditions and trends can be examined quickly; tables provide greater detail and enable variance analyses; textual information adds insight and interpretation to data.

Most companies today use the Internet to connect with their employees, their customers, and their suppliers. Now companies are using technology to drive better customer relationships, create new revenue streams, offer innovative services, and generate greater efficiencies.

Strategic Planning Software

Some strategic decision support systems, however, are too sophisticated, expensive, or restrictive to be used easily by managers in a firm. This is unfortunate because the strategic-management process must be a people process to be successful. People make the difference! Strategic planning software should thus be simple and unsophisticated. Simplicity allows wide participation among managers in a firm and participation is essential for effective strategy implementation.

One strategic-planning software product that parallels this text and offers managers and executives a simple yet effective approach for developing organizational strategies is *CheckMATE*. This personal computer software performs planning analyses and generates strategies a firm could pursue. *CheckMATE* incorporates the most modern strategic planning techniques. No previous experience with computers or knowledge of strategic planning is required of the user. *CheckMATE* thus promotes communication, understanding, creativity, and forward thinking among users.

CheckMATE is not a spreadsheet program or database; it is an expert system that carries a firm through strategy formulation and implementation. A major strength of the new 2002 version of *CheckMATE* strategic-planning software is its simplicity and participative approach. The user is asked appropriate questions, responses are recorded, information is assimilated, and results are printed. Individuals can work through the software independently and then the program will develop joint recommendations for the firm.

Specific analytical procedures included in the *CheckMATE* program are Strategic Position and Action Evaluation (SPACE) analysis, Threats-Opportunities-Weaknesses-Strengths (TOWS) analysis, Internal-External (IE) analysis, and Grand Strategy Matrix analysis. These widely used strategic-planning analyses are described in Chapter 6.

An individual license for *CheckMATE* costs $995. More information about *CheckMATE* can be obtained at **www.checkmateplan.com** or 843-669-6960 (phone).

Management Information Systems Audit
Checklist of Questions
Questions such as the following should be asked when conducting this audit:

1. Do all managers in the firm use the information system to make decisions?
2. Is there a chief information officer or director of information systems position in the firm?
3. Are data in the information system updated regularly?
4. Do managers from all functional areas of the firm contribute input to the information system?
5. Are there effective passwords for entry into the firm's information system?
6. Are strategists of the firm familiar with the information systems of rival firms?
7. Is the information system user-friendly?
8. Do all users of the information system understand the competitive advantages that information can provide firms?
9. Are computer training workshops provided for users of the information system?
10. Is the firm's information system continually being improved in content and user-friendliness?

THE INTERNAL FACTOR EVALUATION (IFE) MATRIX

A summary step in conducting an internal strategic-management audit is to construct an *Internal Factor Evaluation (IFE) Matrix*. This strategy-formulation tool summarizes and evaluates the major strengths and weaknesses in the functional areas of a business, and it also provides a basis for identifying and evaluating relationships among those areas. Intuitive judgments are required in developing an IFE Matrix, so the appearance of a scientific approach should not be interpreted to mean this is an all-powerful technique. A thorough understanding of the factors included is more important than the actual numbers. Similar to the EFE Matrix and Competitive Profile Matrix described in Chapter 3, an IFE Matrix can be developed in five steps:

1. List key internal factors as identified in the internal-audit process. Use a total of from ten to twenty internal factors, including both strengths and weaknesses. List strengths first and then weakness. Be as specific as possible, using percentages, ratios, and comparative numbers.

2. Assign a weight that ranges from 0.0 (not important) to 1.0 (all-important) to each factor. The weight assigned to a given factor indicates the relative importance of the factor to being successful in the firm's industry. Regardless of whether a key factor is an internal strength or weakness, factors considered to have the greatest effect on organizational performance should be assigned the highest weights. The sum of all weights must equal 1.0.

3. Assign a 1-to-4 rating to each factor to indicate whether that factor represents a major weakness (rating = 1), a minor weakness (rating = 2), a minor strength (rating = 3), or a major strength (rating = 4). Note that strengths must receive a 4 or 3 rating and weaknesses must receive a 1 or 2 rating. Ratings are thus company-based, whereas the weights in Step 2 are industry-based.

4. Multiply each factor's weight by its rating to determine a weighted score for each variable.

5. Sum the weighted scores for each variable to determine the total weighted score for the organization.

Regardless of how many factors are included in an IFE Matrix, the total weighted score can range from a low of 1.0 to a high of 4.0, with the average score being 2.5. Total weighted scores well below 2.5 characterize organizations that are weak internally, whereas scores significantly above 2.5 indicate a strong internal position. Like the EFE Matrix, an IFE Matrix should include from 10 to 20 key factors. The number of factors has no effect upon the range of total weighted scores because the weights always sum to 1.0.

When a key internal factor is both a strength and a weakness, the factor should be included twice in the IFE Matrix, and a weight and rating should be assigned to each statement. For example, the Playboy logo both helps and hurts Playboy Enterprises; the logo attracts customers *Playboy* magazine, but it keeps the Playboy cable channel out of many markets.

An example of an IFE Matrix for Mandalay Bay is provided in Table 4–7. Note that the firm's major strengths are its size, occupancy rates, property, and long-range planning as indicated by the rating of 4. The major weaknesses are locations and recent joint venture. The total weighted score of 2.75 indicates that this large gaming corporation is above average in its overall internal strength.

In multidivisional firms, each autonomous division or strategic business unit should construct an IFE Matrix. Divisional matrices then can be integrated to develop an overall corporate IFE Matrix.

CONCLUSION

Management, marketing, finance/accounting, production/operations, research and development, and management information systems represent the core operations of most businesses. A strategic-management audit of a firm's internal operations is vital to organizational health. Many companies still prefer to be judged solely on their bottom-line performance. However, an increasing number of successful organizations are using the internal audit to gain competitive advantages over rival firms.

Systematic methodologies for performing strength-weakness assessments are not well developed in the strategic-management literature, but it is clear that strategists

TABLE 4-7   **A Sample Internal Factor Evaluation Matrix for Mandalay Bay**

KEY INTERNAL FACTORS	WEIGHT	RATING	WEIGHTED SCORE
Internal Strengths			
1. Largest casino company in the United States	.05	4	.20
2. Room occupancy rates over 95% in Las Vegas	.10	4	.40
3. Increasing free cash flows	.05	3	.15
4. Owns one mile on Las Vegas Strip	.15	4	.60
5. Strong management team	.05	3	.15
6. Buffets at most facilities	.05	3	.15
7. Minimal comps provided	.05	3	.15
8. Long-range planning	.05	4	.20
9. Reputation as family-friendly	.05	3	.15
10. Financial ratios	.05	3	.15
Internal Weaknesses			
1. Most properties are located in Las Vegas	.05	1	.05
2. Little diversification	.05	2	.10
3. Family reputation, not high rollers	.05	2	.10
4. Laughlin properties	.10	1	.10
5. Recent loss of joint ventures	.10	1	.10
TOTAL	1.00		2.75

must identify and evaluate internal strengths and weaknesses in order to formulate and choose among alternative strategies effectively. The EFE Matrix, Competitive Profile Matrix, IFE Matrix, and clear statements of vision and mission provide the basic information needed to formulate competitive strategies successfully. The process of performing an internal audit represents an opportunity for managers and employees throughout the organization to participate in determining the future of the firm. Involvement in the process can energize and mobilize managers and employees.

We invite you to visit the David page on the Prentice Hall Companion Website at **www.prenhall.com/david** for this chapter's World Wide Web exercises.

KEY TERMS AND CONCEPTS

Activity Ratios (p. 140)

Capital Budgeting (p. 138)

Communication (p. 131)

Controlling (p. 132)

Cost/Benefit Analysis (p. 137)

Cultural Products (p. 123)

Customer Analysis (p. 133)

Distinctive Competencies (p. 120)

Distribution (p. 135)

Dividend Decision (p. 138)

Financial Ratio Analysis (p. 122)

Financing Decision (p. 138)

Functions of Finance/Accounting (p. 138)

Functions of Management (p. 128)

Functions of Marketing (p. 133)

Functions of Production/Operations (p. 143)

Growth Ratios (p. 140)

Human Resource Management (p. 132)

Internal Audit (p. 121)

Internal Factor Evaluation (IFE) Matrix (p. 149)

Investment Decision (p. 138)

Leverage Ratios (p. 140)

Liquidity Ratios (p. 140)

Management Information Systems (p. 148)

Marketing Research (p. 136)

Motivating (p. 131)

Opportunity Analysis (p. 137)

Organizational Culture (p. 123)

ISSUES FOR REVIEW AND DISCUSSION

1. Explain why prioritizing the relative importance of strengths and weaknesses in an IFE Matrix is an important strategic-management activity.

2. How can delegation of authority contribute to effective strategic management?

3. Diagram a formal organizational chart that reflects the following positions: a president, two executive officers, four middle managers, and eighteen lower-level managers. Now, diagram three overlapping and hypothetical informal group structures. How can this information be helpful to a strategist in formulating and implementing strategy?

4. How could a strategist's attitude toward social responsibility affect a firm's strategy? What is your attitude toward social responsibility?

5. Which of the three basic functions of finance/accounting do you feel is most important in a small electronics manufacturing concern? Justify your position.

6. Do you think aggregate R&D expenditures for American firms will increase or decrease next year? Why?

7. Explain how you would motivate managers and employees to implement a major new strategy.

8. Why do you think production/operations managers often are not directly involved in strategy-formulation activities? Why can this be a major organizational weakness?

9. Give two examples of staffing strengths and two examples of staffing weaknesses of an organization with which you are familiar.

10. Would you ever pay out dividends when your firm's annual net profit is negative? Why? What effect could this have on a firm's strategies?

11. If a firm has zero debt in its capital structure, is that always an organizational strength? Why or why not?

12. Describe the production/operations system in a police department.

13. After conducting an internal audit, a firm discovers a total of 100 strengths and 100 weaknesses. What procedures then could be used to determine the most important of these? Why is it important to reduce the total number of key factors?

14. Select one of the suggested readings at the end of this chapter. Look up that article, and give a five-minute oral report to the class that summarizes the article and your views on the topic.

15. Why do you believe cultural products affect all the functions of business?

16. Do you think cultural products affect strategy formulation, implementation, or evaluation the most? Why?

17. Identify cultural products at your college or university. Do these products, viewed collectively or separately, represent a strength or weakness for the organization?

18. Describe the management information system at your college or university.

19. Explain the difference between data and information in terms of each being useful to strategists.

20. What are the most important characteristics of an effective management information system?

NOTES

1. ROBERT GRANT, "The Resource-Based Theory of Competitive Advantage: Implications for Strategy Formulation," *California Management Review* (Spring 1991): 116.

2. Reprinted by permission of the publisher from "Integrating Strength-Weakness Analysis into Strategic Planning," by WILLIAM KING, *Journal of Business Research 2*, no. 4: p. 481. Copyright 1983 by Elsevier Science Publishing Co., Inc.

3. IGOR ANSOFF, "Strategic Management of Technology," *Journal of Business Strategy* 7, no. 3 (Winter 1987): 38.

4. CLAUDE GEORGE, JR., *The History of Management Thought*, 2nd ed. (Englewood Cliffs, N.J.: Prentice-Hall, 1972): 174.

5. EDGAR SCHEIN, *Organizational Culture and Leadership* (San Francisco: Jossey-Bass, 1985): 9.

6. JOHN LORSCH, "Managing Culture: The Invisible Barrier to Strategic Change," *California Management Review* 28, no. 2 (1986): 95–109.

7. Y. ALLARIE and M. FIRSIROTU, "How to Implement Radical Strategies in Large Organizations," *Sloan Management Review* (Spring 1985): 19.

8. JON ALSTON, "Wa, Guanxi, and Inhwa: Managerial Principles in Japan, China and Korea," *Business Horizons* 32, no. 2 (March–April 1989): 26.

9. ROSE KNOTTS, "Cross-Cultural Management: Transformations and Adaptations," *Business Horizons* (January–February 1989): 29–33.

10. http://www.mindtools.com/plfailpl.html

11. ADAM SMITH, *Wealth of Nations* (New York: Modern Library, 1937): 3–4.

12. RICHARD DAFT, *Management*, 3rd ed. (Orlando, FL: Dryden Press, 1993): 512.

13. SHELLEY KIRKPATRICK and EDWIN LOCKE, "Leadership: Do Traits Matter?" *Academy of Management Executive* 5, no. 2 (May 1991): 48.

14. PETER DRUCKER, *Management Tasks, Responsibilities, and Practice* (New York: Harper & Row, 1973): 463.

15. BRIAN DUMAINE, "What the Leaders of Tomorrow See," *Fortune* (July 3, 1989): 51.

16. J. EVANS and B. BERGMAN, *Marketing* (New York: Macmillan, 1982): 17.

17. Venessa O'Connell, "Ad-Spending Outlook Is Worsening," *Wall Street Journal* (September 4, 2001): B4.

18. Quoted in ROBERT WATERMAN, JR., "The Renewal Factor," *Business Week* (September 14, 1987): 108.

19. J. VAN HORNE, *Financial Management and Policy* (Englewood Cliffs, N.J.: Prentice-Hall, 1974): 10.

20. Robyn Meredith, "Paradise Lost," *Forbes* (May 28, 2001): 56.

21. PHILIP ROUSEBL, KAMAL SAAD, and TAMARA ERICKSON, "The Evolution of Third Generation R&D," *Planning Review* 19, no. 2 (March–April 1991): 18–26.

22. VIDA SCARPELLO, WILLIAM BOULTON, and CHARLES HOFER, "Reintegrating R&D into Business Strategy," *Journal of Business Strategy* 6, no. 4 (Spring 1986): 50, 51.

CURRENT READINGS

BAKER, WALTER, MIKE MARN, and CRAIG ZAWANDA. "Price Smarter on the Net." *Harvard Business Review* (February 2001): 122.

BEAL, REGINALD and MASOUD YASAI-ARDEKANI. "Performance Implications of Aligning CEO Functional Experiences with Competitive Strategies." *Journal of Management* 26, no. 4 (2000): 733.

BERNICK, CAROL LAVIN. "When Your Culture Needs a Makeover." *Harvard Business Review* (June 2001): 53.

DENIS, JEAN-LOUIS, LISE LAMOTHE, and ANN LANGLEY. "The Dynamics of Collective Leadership and Strategic Change in Pluralistic Organizations." *Academy of Management Journal* 44, no. 4 (August 2001): 809.

FAGENSON-ELAND, ELLEN. "The National Football League's Bill Parcells on Winning, Leading, and Turning Around Teams." *Academy of Management Executive* 15, no. 3 (August 2001): 48.

FORRESTER, RUSS. "Empowerment: Rejuvenating a Potent Idea." *Academy of Management Executive* 14, no. 3 (August 2000): 67.

GILBERT, JACQUELINE A. and JOHN M. IVANCEVICH. "Valuing Diversity: A Tale of Two Organizations." *Academy of Management Executive* 14, no. 1 (February 2000): 93.

GUPTA, ANIL K. and VIJAY GOVINDARAJAN. "Converting Global Presence into Global Competitive Advantage." *Academy of Management Executive* 15, no. 2 (May 2001): 45.

HEMPHILL, THOMAS A. "Airline Marketing Alliances and U.S. Competition Policy: Does the Consumer Benefit." *Business Horizons* 43, no. 2 (March–April 2000): 17.

KING, ADELAIDE, SALLY FOWLER, and CARL ZEITHAML. "Managing Organizational Competencies for Competitive Advantage: The Middle-Management Edge." *Academy of Management Executive* 15, no. 2 (May 2001): 95.

KIRKMAN, BRADLEY L. and DEBRA L. SHAPIRO. "The Impact of Cultural Values on Job Satisfaction and Organizational Commitment in Self-Managing Work Teams: The Mediating Role of Employee Resistance." *Academy of Management Journal* 44, no. 3 (June 2001): 557.

LUO, Y. and S. H. PARK. "Strategic Alignment and Performance of Market-Seeking MNC's in China." *Strategic Management Journal* 22, no. 2 (February 2001): 141.

PARK, S. H. and Y. LUO. "Guanxi and Organizational Dynamics: Organizational Networking in Chinese Firms." *Strategic Management Journal* 22, no. 5 (May 2001): 455.

PITT, LEYLAND F., PIERRE BERTHON, RICHARD T. WATSON, and MICHAEL EWING. "Pricing Strategy and the Net." *Business Horizons* 44, no. 2 (March–April 2001): 45.

PRATT, D. JANE. "Corporations, Communities, and Conservation: The Mountain Institute and Antamina Mining Company." *California Management Review* 43, no. 3 (Spring 2001): 38.

SCHRAGE, MICHAEL. "Playing Around with Brainstorming." *Harvard Business Review* (March 2001): 149.

YOUNG, DAVID W. "The Six Levers for Managing Organizational Culture." *Business Horizons* 43, no. 5 (September–October 2000): 19.

EXPERIENTIAL EXERCISES

EXPERIENTIAL EXERCISE 4A ▶

Performing a Financial Ratio Analysis for American Airlines (AMR)

PURPOSE

Financial ratio analysis is one of the best techniques for identifying and evaluating internal screngths and weaknesses. Potential investors and current shareholders look closely at firms' financial ratios, making detailed comparisons to industry averages and to previous periods of time. Financial ratio analyses provide vital input information for developing an IFE Matrix.

INSTRUCTIONS

Step 1   On a separate sheet of paper, number from 1 to 20. Referring to American Airline's statement of operations and balance sheet (pp. 40–42), calculate twenty financial ratios for 2001 for the company. Use Table 4–4 as a reference.

Step 2   Go to www.investor.stockpoint.com and find industry average financial ratios for the airline industry. Record the industry average values in a second column on your paper.

Step 3   In a third column, indicate whether you consider each ratio to be a strength, a weakness, or a neutral factor for AMR.

EXPERIENTIAL EXERCISE 4B ▶

Constructing an IFE Matrix for American Airlines (AMR)

PURPOSE

This exercise will give you experience in developing an IFE Matrix. Identifying and prioritizing factors to include in an IFE Matrix fosters communication among functional and divisional managers. Preparing an IFE Matrix allows human resource, marketing, production/operations, finance/accounting, R&D, and management information systems managers to articulate their concerns and thoughts regarding the business condition of the firm. This results in an improved collective understanding of the business.

INSTRUCTIONS

Step 1   Join with two other individuals to form a three-person team. Develop a team IFE Matrix for AMR.

Step 2   Compare your team's IFE Matrix to other teams' IFE Matrices. Discuss any major differences.

Step 3   What strategies do you think would allow AMR to capitalize on its major strengths? What strategies would allow AMR to improve upon its major weaknesses?

EXPERIENTIAL EXERCISE 4C ▶

Constructing an IFE Matrix for My University

PURPOSE

This exercise gives you the opportunity to evaluate your university's major strengths and weaknesses. As will become clearer in the next chapter, an organization's strategies are largely based upon striving to take advantage of strengths and improving upon weaknesses.

INSTRUCTIONS

Step 1 Join with two other individuals to form a three-person team. Develop a team IFE Matrix for your university. You may use the strengths/weaknesses determined in Experimential Exercise 1D.

Step 2 Go to the board and diagram your team's IFE Matrix.

Step 3 Compare your team's IFE Matrix to other teams' IFE Matrices. Discuss any major differences.

Step 4 What strategies do you think would allow your university to capitalize on its major strengths? What strategies would allow your university to improve upon its major weaknesses?

5

STRATEGIES IN ACTION

CHAPTER OUTLINE

CHAPTER OBJECTIVES

After studying this chapter, you should be able to do the following:

1. Discuss the value of establishing long-term objectives.
2. Identify sixteen types of business strategies.
3. Identify numerous examples of organizations pursuing different types of strategies.
4. Discuss guidelines when particular strategies are most appropriate to pursue.
5. Discuss Porter's generic strategies.
6. Describe strategic management in nonprofit, governmental, and small organizations.
7. Discuss joint ventures as a way to enter the Russian market.

NOTABLE QUOTES

Alice said, "Would you please tell me which way to go from here?" The cat said, "That depends on where you want to get to."

LEWIS CARROLL

Tomorrow always arrives. It is always different. And even the mightiest company is in trouble if it has not worked on the future. Being surprised by what happens is a risk that even the largest and richest company cannot afford, and even the smallest business need not run.

PETER DRUCKER

Planning. Doing things today to make us better tomorrow. Because the future belongs to those who make the hard decisions today.

EATON CORPORATION

One big problem with American business is that when it gets into trouble, it redoubles its effort. It's like digging for gold. If you dig down twenty feet and haven't found it, one of the strategies you could use is to dig twice as deep. But if the gold is twenty feet to the side, you could dig a long time and not find it.

EDWARD DE BONO

If you don't invest for the long term, there is no short term.

GEORGE DAVID

Even if you're on the right track, you'll get run over if you just sit there.

WILL ROGERS

We always plan too much and always think too little.

JOSHEP SCHUMPER

Behold the turtle, he makes progress only when he sticks his neck out.

BRUCE LEVIN

Hundreds of companies today, including Sears, IBM, Searle, and Hewlett-Packard, have embraced strategic planning fully in their quest for higher revenues and profits. Kent Nelson, former chair of UPS, explains why his company has created a new strategic planning department: "Because we're making bigger bets on investments in technology, we can't afford to spend a whole lot of money in one direction and then find out five years later it was the wrong direction."[1]

This chapter brings strategic management to life with many contemporary examples. Sixteen types of strategies are defined and exemplified, including Michael Porter's generic strategies: cost leadership, differentiation, and focus. Guidelines are presented for determining when it is most appropriate to pursue different types of strategies. An overview of strategic management in nonprofit organizations, governmental agencies, and small firms is provided.

 # LONG-TERM OBJECTIVES

Long-term objectives represent the results expected from pursuing certain strategies. Strategies represent the actions to be taken to accomplish long-term objectives. The time frame for objectives and strategies should be consistent, usually from two to five years.

The Nature of Long-Term Objectives

Objectives should be quantitative, measurable, realistic, understandable, challenging, hierarchical, obtainable, and congruent among organizational units. Each objective should also be associated with a time line. Objectives are commonly stated in terms such as growth in assets, growth in sales, profitability, market share, degree and nature of diversification, degree and nature of vertical integration, earnings per share, and social responsibility. Clearly established objectives offer many benefits. They provide direction, allow synergy, aid in evaluation, establish priorities, reduce uncertainty, minimize conflicts, stimulate exertion, and aid in both the allocation of resources and the design of jobs.

Long-term objectives are needed at the corporate, divisional, and functional levels of an organization. They are an important measure of managerial performance. Many practitioners and academicians attribute a significant part of U.S. industry's competitive decline to the short-term, rather than long-term, strategy orientation of managers in the United States. Arthur D. Little argues that bonuses or merit pay for managers today must be based to a greater extent on long-term objectives and strategies. A general framework for relating objectives to performance evaluation is provided in Table 5–1. A particular organization could tailor these guidelines to meet its own needs, but incentives should be attached to both long-term and annual objectives.

VISIT THE NET

Gives the basic principles of strategic planning.
http://www. eaglepointconsulting.com/ sp_principles.html

TABLE 5–1   **Varying Performance Measures by Organizational Level**

ORGANIZATIONAL LEVEL	BASIS FOR ANNUAL BONUS OR MERIT PAY
Corporate	75% based on long-term objectives
	25% based on annual objectives
Division	50% based on long-term objectives
	50% based on annual objectives
Function	25% based on long-term objectives
	75% based on annual objectives

Clearly stated and communicated objectives are vital to success for many reasons. First, objectives help stakeholders understand their role in an organization's future. They also provide a basis for consistent decision making by managers whose values and attitudes differ. By reaching a consensus on objectives during strategy-formulation activities, an organization can minimize potential conflicts later during implementation. Objectives set forth organizational priorities and stimulate exertion and accomplishment. They serve as standards by which individuals, groups, departments, divisions, and entire organizations can be evaluated. Objectives provide the basis for designing jobs and organizing activities to be performed in an organization. They also provide direction and allow for organizational synergy.

Without long-term objectives, an organization would drift aimlessly toward some unknown end. It is hard to imagine an organization or individual being successful without clear objectives. Success only rarely occurs by accident; rather, it is the result of hard work directed toward achieving certain objectives.

Not Managing by Objectives

An unknown educator once said, "If you think education is expensive, try ignorance." The idea behind this saying also applies to establishing objectives. Strategists should avoid the following alternative ways to "not managing by objectives."

- Managing by Extrapolation—adheres to the principle "If it ain't broke, don't fix it." The idea is to keep on doing about the same things in the same ways because things are going well.

- Managing by Crisis—based on the belief that the true measure of a really good strategist is the ability to solve problems. Because there are plenty of crises and problems to go around for every person and every organization, strategists ought to bring their time and creative energy to bear on solving the most pressing problems of the day. Managing by crisis is actually a form of reacting rather than acting and of letting events dictate the whats and when of management decisions.

- Managing by Subjectives—built on the idea that there is no general plan for which way to go and what to do; just do the best you can to accomplish what you think should be done. In short, "Do your own thing, the best way you know how" (sometimes referred to as *the mystery approach to decision making* because subordinates are left to figure out what is happening and why).

- Managing by Hope—based on the fact that the future is laden with great uncertainty, and that if we try and do not succeed, then we hope our second (or third) attempt will succeed. Decisions are predicted on the hope that they will work and the good times are just around the corner, especially if luck and good fortune are on our side![2]

 ## TYPES OF STRATEGIES

The model illustrated in Figure 5–1 provides a conceptual basis for applying strategic management. Defined and exemplified in Table 5–2, alternative strategies that an enterprise could pursue can be categorized into thirteen actions—forward integration, backward integration, horizontal integration, market penetration, market development, product development, concentric diversification, conglomerate diversification, horizontal diversification, joint venture/partnering, retrenchment, divestiture, and liquidation. Each alternative strategy has countless variations. For example, market penetration can

VISIT THE NET

Provides good narrative on why to do strategic planning.
http://www.orggrow.co.uk/gap/plan.html

FIGURE 5–1

A Comprehensive Strategic-Management Model

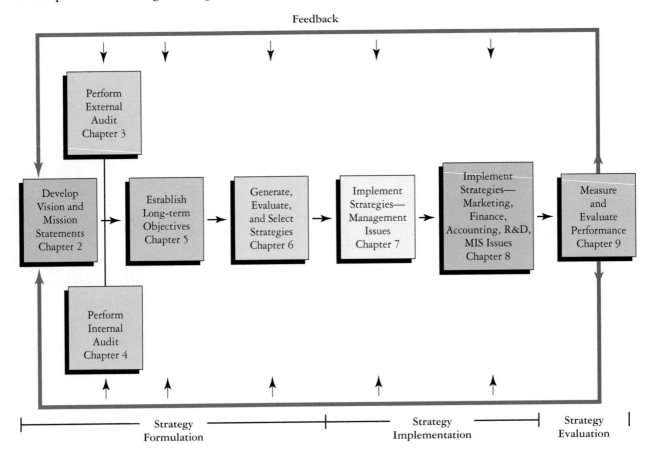

include adding salespersons, increasing advertising expenditures, couponing, and using similar actions to increase market share in a given geographic area.

Many, if not most, organizations pursue a combination of two or more strategies simultaneously, but a *combination strategy* can be exceptionally risky if carried too far. No organization can afford to pursue all the strategies that might benefit the firm. Difficult decisions must be made. Priority must be established. Organizations, like individuals, have limited resources. Both organizations and individuals must choose among alternative strategies and avoid excessive indebtedness.

Organizations cannot do too many things well because resources and talents get spread thin and competitors gain advantage. In large diversified companies, a combination strategy is commonly employed when different divisions pursue different strategies. Also, organizations struggling to survive may employ a combination of several defensive strategies, such as divestiture, liquidation, and retrenchment, simultaneously.

 ## INTEGRATION STRATEGIES

Forward integration, backward integration, and horizontal integration are sometimes collectively referred to as *vertical integration* strategies. Vertical integration strategies allow a firm to gain control over distributors, suppliers, and/or competitors.

TABLE 5-2   **Alternative Strategies Defined and Exemplified**

STRATEGY	DEFINITION	EXAMPLE
Forward Integration	Gaining ownership or increased control over distributors or retailers	Gateway Computer Company opening its own chain of retail computer stores.
Backward Integration	Seeking ownership or increased control of a firm's suppliers	Financial firms such as JP. Morgan are outsourcing their technology operations to firms such as EDS and IBM.
Horizontal Integration	Seeking ownership or increased control over competitors	Reader's Digest Association acquired Reiman Publications LLC.
Market Penetration	Seeking increased market share for present products or services in present markets through greater marketing efforts	American Express launched a $100 million+ advertising campaign in 2002 to boost its lead over Citigroup in the credit card industry.
Market Development	Introducing present products or services into new geographic area	South African Breweries PLC is trying to acquire Miller Brewing Company for about $5 billion.
Product Development	Seeking increased sales by improving present products or services or developing new ones	Miller Brewing developed the new Skyy Blue citrus and "vodka-flavored" malt beverage.
Concentric Diversification	Adding new but related products or services	Hilton Hotels is now selling time shares to fill rooms. The Hilton in New York City is selling off the two top floors of rooms.
Horizontal Diversification	Adding new, unrelated products or services for present customers	The New York Yankees baseball team is merging business operations with the New Jersey Nets basketball team.
Retrenchment	Regrouping through cost and asset reduction to reverse declining sales and profit	Net2Phone in 2002 cut 110 jobs, or 28 percent of its workforce, as part of its restructuring plan.
Divestiture	Selling a division or part of an organization	Tyco International is selling off its plastics division, which accounts for about 4 percent of Tyco's sales.
Liquidation	Selling all of a company's assets, in parts, for their tangible worth	Service Merchandise liquidated in 2002, closing all of its 216 stores in 32 states. The firm had been operating for three years under Chapter 11 bankruptcy.

Forward Integration

Forward integration involves gaining ownership or increased control over distributors or retailers. Increasing numbers of manufacturers (suppliers) today are pursuing a forward integration strategy by establishing Web sites to sell products directly to consumers. This strategy is causing turmoil in some industries. For example, Home Depot warned its suppliers not to compete with them in selling products online. Many manufacturers are reluctant to offend their distributors (retailers) by selling online, but low relative costs in selling online versus retail stores makes forward integration a very tempting strategy for many suppliers. Manufacturer Joe Boxer sells underwear on Macy's Web site, but this degree of cooperation between supplier and distributor is the exception rather than the rule.

The external threat of online sales, perhaps from suppliers eroding its catalog market share, is a primary reason why L.L. Bean opened its first full-line retail store in eighty-seven years. The store is located in McLean, Virginia. L.L. Bean is pursuing forward integration out of concern that online stores will further erode catalog sales, which are slowing. Other catalog retailers such as Delia's and J. Jill have opened retail stores for the first time in their history.

Brick-and-mortar retailers such as Wal-Mart, Sharper Image, and The Right Start are rapidly combating the purely online retailers by mobilizing a multichannel attack selling via stores and the Internet. Many traditional retailers are adding catalogs too and offering auctions to further enhance their distribution network. **Wal-Mart.com** is aimed at becoming the leading Internet discounter. Even Amway has a new online division named Quixtar to sell its and other companies' products. "We're looking at the biggest change in forty years," said Amway executive Ken McDonald. Amway's sales force continues to sell products to friends and family but now also has the option to sell products online for Quixtar.

Both Sears and Home Depot are employing forward integration to battle for American homeowners' decorating dollars. The two retailers are rushing to open their own freestanding home-décor stores. As part of its effort to expand beyond its do-it-yourself warehouses, Home Depot plans to have 200 Expo Design Center stores by 2005, while Sears is opening 150 The Great Indoors stores by 2003.

Oakland, California-based Dreyers Ice Cream has used forward integration to gain 18 percent of the U.S. market share for ice cream, followed by its major competitor Breyers with 15 percent. Dreyers' competitive advantage in this industry is its outstanding distribution system, led by a new fleet of 1,100 trucks and a new computerized form of delivery and ordering. Dreyers' distribution system is so efficient that competitors such as Ben & Jerry's, Häagen-Dazs, and Godiva all use Dreyers for distribution. Breyers, however, does not use Dreyers, even though both Breyers and Ben & Jerry's are divisions of Unilever.[3]

Toronto-Dominion (TD) Bank of Canada is pursuing forward integration by beginning to offer banking services at 100 Wal-Mart supercenter stores beginning in 2002. This strategy enables the Toronto-based bank to build a retail-banking presence without investing in its own distribution or branch network. While Wal-Mart already offers banking services, no single bank has operations in as many Wal-Mart stores as TD will have. Wal-Mart had tried to diversify into the banking business in 1999 by acquiring a small savings bank, but that move was blocked by Congress. Wal-Mart will not own or operate the TD operations in its stores. Congress is determined to see that banking and commerce in the United States should stay separate.

An effective means of implementing forward integration is *franchising*. Approximately two thousand companies in about fifty different industries in the United States use franchising to distribute their products or services. Businesses can expand rapidly by franchising because costs and opportunities are spread across many individuals. Total sales by franchises in the United States are about $1 trillion annually.

Six guidelines when forward integration may be an especially effective strategy are:[4]

- When an organization's present distributors are especially expensive, or unreliable, or incapable of meeting the firm's distribution needs.
- When the availability of quality distributors is so limited as to offer a competitive advantage to those firms that integrate forward.
- When an organization competes in an industry that is growing and is expected to continue to grow markedly; this is a factor because forward integration reduces an organization's ability to diversify if its basic industry falters.
- When an organization has both the capital and human resources needed to manage the new business of distributing its own products.

- When the advantages of stable production are particularly high; this is a consideration because an organization can increase the predictability of the demand for its output through forward integration.

- When present distributors or retailers have high profit margins; this situation suggests that a company profitably could distribute its own products and price them more competitively by integrating forward.

Backward Integration

Both manufacturers and retailers purchase needed materials from suppliers. *Backward integration* is a strategy of seeking ownership or increased control of a firm's suppliers. This strategy can be especially appropriate when a firm's current suppliers are unreliable, too costly, or cannot meet the firm's needs.

When you buy a box of Pampers diapers at Wal-Mart, a scanner at the store's checkout counter instantly zaps an order to Procter & Gamble Company. In contrast, in most hospitals, reordering supplies is a logistical nightmare. Inefficiency caused by lack of control of suppliers in the healthcare industry is, however, rapidly changing as many giant health-care purchasers, such as the U.S. Defense Department and Columbia/HCA Healthcare Corporation, move to require electronic bar codes on every supply item purchased. This allows instant tracking and recording without invoices and paperwork. Of the estimated $83 billion spent annually on hospital supplies, industry reports indicate that $11 billion can be eliminated through more effective backward integration.

Some industries in the United States (such as the automotive and aluminum industries) are reducing their historical pursuit of backward integration. Instead of owning their suppliers, companies negotiate with several outside suppliers. Ford and Daimler-Chrysler buy over half of their components parts from outside suppliers such as TRW, Eaton, General Electric, and Johnson Controls. Deintegration makes sense in industries that have global sources of supply. *Outsourcing,* whereby companies use outside suppliers, shop around, play one seller against another, and go with the best deal, is becoming widely practiced. Small steel manufacturers such as Arrowhead Steel Company and Worthington Steel Company are pursuing backward integration today through the use of the Internet. Owners of most small steel firms now click on Web sites such as MetalSite LP, based in Pittsburgh, or e-Steel Corporation, based in New York, to find the lowest-priced supplier of scrap steel that they need. These two sites give buyers and sellers of steel the opportunity to trade, buy, and sell metal from a variety of companies. Many steel companies now have Web sites to capitalize on backward integration opportunities in the industry.

Global competition is also spurring firms to reduce their number of suppliers and to demand higher levels of service and quality from those they keep. Although traditionally relying on many suppliers to ensure uninterrupted supplies and low prices, American firms now are following the lead of Japanese firms, which have far fewer suppliers and closer, long-term relationships with those few. "Keeping track of so many suppliers is onerous," says Mark Shimelonis, formerly of Xerox.

Seven guidelines when backward integration may be an especially effective strategy are:[5]

- When an organization's present suppliers are especially expensive, or unreliable, or incapable of meeting the firm's needs for parts, components, assemblies, or raw materials.

- When the number of suppliers is small and the number of competitors is large.

- When an organization competes in an industry that is growing rapidly; this is a factor because integrative-type strategies (forward, backward, and horizontal) reduce an organization's ability to diversify in a declining industry.

VISIT THE NET

Read about the Immigration and Naturalization Strategic Management Process.
www.ins.usdoj.gov/text/
aboutins/insmission/
dojplan.htm

- When an organization has both capital and human resources to manage the new business of supplying its own raw materials.

- When the advantages of stable prices are particularly important; this is a factor because an organization can stabilize the cost of its raw materials and the associated price of its product(s) through backward integration.

- When present supplies have high profit margins, which suggests that the business of supplying products or services in the given industry is a worthwhile venture.

- When an organization needs to acquire a needed resource quickly.

Horizontal Integration

Horizontal integration refers to a strategy of seeking ownership of or increased control over a firm's competitors. One of the most significant trends in strategic management today is the increased use of horizontal integration as a growth strategy. Mergers, acquisitions, and takeovers among competitors allow for increased economies of scale and enhanced transfer of resources and competencies. Kenneth Davidson makes the following observation about horizontal integration:

> The trend towards horizontal integration seems to reflect strategists' misgivings about their ability to operate many unrelated businesses. Mergers between direct competitors are more likely to create efficiencies than mergers between unrelated businesses, both because there is a greater potential for eliminating duplicate facilities and because the management of the acquiring firm is more likely to understand the business of the target.[6]

Horizontal integration has become the most favored growth strategy in many industries. For example, explosive growth in e-commerce has telecommunications firms worldwide frantically merging and pursuing horizontal integration to gain competitiveness. Telecommunications mergers occur almost weekly.

Oklahoma City-based Devon Energy recently purchased Calgary, Alberta-based Anderson Exploration to become the largest independent producer of oil and gas in North America. With the acquisition, Devon increased its oil and gas reserves in Canada from 11 percent to 32 percent. The Anderson acquisition came on the heels of Devon's purchase of Woodlands, Texas-based Mitchell Energy & Development. For another horizontal integration example in the energy field, consider Santa Fe International's recent acquisition of Global Marine, which makes it one of the world's largest contract oil drilling firms. The new firm is named GlobalSantaFe Corporation.

In the largest horizontal integration merger ever recorded in the computer industry, Hewlett-Packard (HP) purchased Compaq to become the largest computer company in the world. Previously, HP was number three and Compaq was number two, while Dell was number one. The combined company now holds a 19 percent share of the global personal computer business, leapfrogging leader Dell, which has about 13 percent of the market share.

In one of the most depressed forest products and paper markets in a decade, Westvaco and Mead—two midsize paper companies—recently integrated horizontally to form MeadWestvaco, based in Stamford, Connecticut. The merged company is the nation's second-largest producer of coated papers and one of the largest packaging companies. Westvaco was a large producer of bleached paperboard, which is used in packaging, whereas Mead was a large producer of coated natural kraft, which is used in packaging. The merged company is divesting nonstrategic assets—operations not involved in paper or packaging.

Canadian laser eye-surgery provider TLC Laser Eye Centers recently acquired rival Laser Vision Centers in St. Louis for almost $100 million, creating the largest operator of laser eye-surgery clinics in North America. The deal brings together TLC's strength in urban areas and Laser Vision's strong presence in small towns and rural areas of the United States.

Five guidelines when horizontal integration may be an especially effective strategy are:[7]

- When an organization can gain monopolistic characteristics in a particular area or region without being challenged by the federal government for "tending substantially" to reduce competition.
- When an organization competes in a growing industry.
- When increased economies of scale provide major competitive advantages.
- When an organization has both the capital and human talent needed to successfully manage an expanded organization.
- When competitors are faltering due to a lack of managerial expertise or a need for particular resources that an organization possesses; note that horizontal integration would not be appropriate if competitors are doing poorly, because in that case overall industry sales are declining.

 # INTENSIVE STRATEGIES

Market penetration, market development, and product development are sometimes referred to as *intensive strategies* because they require intensive efforts if a firm's competitive position with existing products is to improve.

Market Penetration

A *market-penetration* strategy seeks to increase market share for present products or services in present markets through greater marketing efforts. This strategy is widely used alone and in combination with other strategies. Market penetration includes increasing the number of salespersons, increasing advertising expenditures, offering extensive sales promotion items, or increasing publicity efforts. Japan's Canon, Inc., has crushed its rival Xerox with an effective market penetration strategy in recent years. Canon established an excellent direct-sales force and a customer service operation; at the same time, it maintains great relations with its dealers. Nearly 75 percent of Canon's business comes from countries other than Japan. Canon has doubled its market share in the fast-growing digital camera industry to about 20 percent of the United States market, thus moving ahead of Kodak.

Five guidelines when market penetration may be an especially effective strategy are:[8]

- When current markets are not saturated with a particular product or service.
- When the usage rate of present customers could be increased significantly.
- When the market shares of major competitors have been declining while total industry sales have been increasing.
- When the correlation between dollar sales and dollar marketing expenditures historically has been high.
- When increased economies of scale provide major competitive advantages.

Market Development

Market development involves introducing present products or services into new geographic areas. The climate for international market development is becoming more favorable. In many industries, such as Internet service providers, it is going to be hard to maintain a competitive edge by staying close to home. For example, AOL is expanding its services aggressively worldwide. In Latin and South America, AOL still trails Terra Lycos and Universo Online, and it is number three or number four in Brazil, Mexico, and Argentina. But AOL is the fastest-growing Internet service provider in Latin and South America, and it expects its operations there to become profitable by 2003. AOL is also expanding into China, even though it is technically illegal today for Chinese individuals to receive foreign satellite programs. AOL now claims to reach more than 10 million mainland households in China through its majority stake in China Entertainment Television Broadcast. AOL is in talks with Beijing to allow the company to set up a separate broadcast channel in the southern Chinese province of Guangdong.

Wal-Mart has used a global-market development strategy to become the largest retailer not only in the United States but also in Canada and Mexico. Wal-Mart's revenues outside the United States now comprise 17 percent of its total, with more than eleven hundred stores in nine countries. Wal-Mart added another 120 stores outside the United States in 2001.

Coca-Cola Company recently launched its new sports-drink, Powerade, into seven European countries, challenging PepsiCo's Gatorade. The number three and four sports drinks in Europe are Aquarius, already produced by Coke, and Lucozade, which is made by Novartis AG's Isostar. Coke believes Europeans age thirteen to twenty-nine, the target market for Powerade, are increasingly making sports a bigger part of their lives. Coke says Powerade increases one's endurance and energy during exercise.

Gap, the large specialty retail store chain, has used a global market development strategy for years, but the company reduced its international store growth to 20 percent in 2001 from 41 percent in 2000. Gap's corporate operating profit margin is about 16 percent, but its margin from international operations is less than 10 percent. According to Forbes, "Gap's failing may be in believing that it can apply uniform merchandising and marketing around the world. In Japan, the tags on Gap clothing are in English. Gap employees cheerfully greet customers with the casual Japanese version of 'hi,' an unaccustomed informality for the mannerly Japanese. Despite all the Americanizing, the Japanese seem to mostly want bargains. Uniqlo, a 480-store Gap rival in Japan, undercuts the Gap on prices by 50 percent."[9]

Six guidelines when market development may be an especially effective strategy are:[10]

- When new channels of distribution are available that are reliable, inexpensive, and of good quality.
- When an organization is very successful at what it does.
- When new untapped or unsaturated markets exist.
- When an organization has the needed capital and human resources to manage expanded operations.
- When an organization has excess production capacity.
- When an organization's basic industry is becoming rapidly global in scope.

Product Development
Product development is a strategy that seeks increased sales by improving or modifying present products or services. Product development usually entails large research and development expenditures.

Microsoft constantly pursues product development. The company recently introduced its Pocket PC 2002 to compete against Palm, Inc., as the leading provider of handheld-device software. Microsoft has several key computer hardware partners, such as Compaq, who are committed to marketing the PC 2002 software on their products.

Catalogs are considered by marketers to be the cheapest way to launch a new retail line of clothes, manage the risk, and test a new market.

Talbots, a retailer of classic women's apparel, recently entered the men's clothing market. Talbots is targeting men in a move that is consistent with its current women's demographic—career-oriented, age 35 and older. If Talbot's new men's line of clothes does well in its 2002 catalogs, then the company plans to open freestanding menswear retail outlets in 2003. Talbots has 762 stores nationwide.

Hampton Inn is pursuing product development by opening 500 small-room, small hotels in small towns, with populations of 10,000 to 30,000. Hampton's 1,100 properties to date are mostly large, with large rooms, and they are located off interstates and in suburban locations. These smaller units will not include restaurants or bellhops, but they will offer swimming pools and business services. Fortunately—or perhaps unfortunately—for Hampton, other competitors have been pursuing the same strategy—including Sleep Inns, La Quinta, Holiday Inn Express, Howard Johnson Express, and Super 8.

Abercrombie & Fitch is employing product development to segment its customers by age. The company finds that high-school-age teenagers have different buying habits than college-age students. For example, college students shun logo-laden clothes, while high-school students love logos. High-school-age students tend to desire more graphics and sparkles on clothes. The two groups do not mix that well in stores either. Thus, Abercrombie recently developed its Hollister stores that cater to the 14-to-18 year olds. By 2003, there will be 80 Hollister stores, each designed to evoke a California-surfing atmosphere. This strategy is designed to allow traditional Abercrombie stores to focus on the older young people.

Five guidelines when product development may be an especially effective strategy to pursue are:[11]

- When an organization has successful products that are in the maturity stage of the product life cycle; the idea here is to attract satisfied customers to try new (improved) products as a result of their positive experience with the organization's present products or services.

- When an organization competes in an industry that is characterized by rapid technological developments.

- When major competitors offer better-quality products at comparable prices.

- When an organization competes in a high-growth industry.

- When an organization has especially strong research and development capabilities.

 DIVERSIFICATION STRATEGIES

There are three general types of *diversification strategies:* concentric, horizontal, and conglomerate. Overall, diversification strategies are becoming less popular as organizations are finding it more difficult to manage diverse business activities. In the 1960s and 1970s, the trend was to diversify so as not to be dependent on any single industry, but the 1980s saw a general reversal of that thinking. Diversification is now on the retreat. Michael Porter of the Harvard Business School says, "Management found [it] couldn't manage the beast." Hence, businesses are selling, or closing, less profitable divisions in order to focus on core businesses.

There are, however, a few companies today that pride themselves on being conglomerates, from small firms such as Pentair Inc. and Blount International to huge companies

NATURAL ENVIRONMENT PERSPECTIVE

Songbirds and Coral Reefs in Trouble

SONGBIRDS

Bluebirds are one of seventy-six songbird species in the United States that have dramatically declined in numbers in the last two decades. Not all birds are considered songbirds, and why birds sing is not clear. Some scientists say they sing when calling for mates or warning of danger, but many scientists now contend that birds sing for sheer pleasure. Songbirds include chickadees, orioles, swallows, mockingbirds, warblers, sparrows, vireos, and the wood thrush. "These birds are telling us there's a problem, something's out of balance in our environment," says Jeff Wells, bird conservation director for the National Audubon Society. Songbirds may be telling us that their air or water is too dirty or that we are destroying too much of their habitat. People collect Picasso paintings and save historic buildings. "Songbirds are part of our natural heritage. Why should we be willing to watch songbirds destroyed anymore than allowing a great work of art be destroyed?" asks Wells. Whatever message songbirds are singing to us today about their natural environment, the message is becoming less and less heard nationwide. Listen when you go outside today. Each of us as individuals, companies, states, and countries should do what we reasonably can to help improve the natural environment for songbirds.

CORAL REEFS

The ocean covers more than 71 percent of the Earth. The destructive effect of commercial fishing on ocean habitats coupled with increasing pollution runoff into the ocean and global warming of the ocean have decimated fisheries, marine life, and coral reefs around the world. The unfortunate consequence of fishing over the last century has been *overfishing*—with the principal reasons being politics and greed. Trawl fishing with nets destroys coral reefs and has been compared to catching squirrels by cutting down forests, since bottom nets scour and destroy vast areas of the ocean. The great proportion of marine life caught in a trawl is "by-catch" juvenile fish and other life that are killed and discarded. Warming of the ocean due to CO_2 emissions also kills thousands of acres of coral reefs annually. The total area of fully protected marine habitats in the United States is only about 50 square miles, compared to some 93 million acres of national wildlife refuges and national parks on the nation's land. Ocean ecosystems and a healthy ocean is vital to the economic and social future of the nation—and, indeed, all countries of the world. Everything we do on land ends up in the ocean, so we all must become better stewards of this last frontier on Earth in order to sustain human survival and the quality of life.

Source: Adapted from Tom Brook, "Declining Numbers Mute Many Birds' Songs," *USA Today* (September 11, 2001): 4A. Also, adapted from John Ogden, "Maintaining Diversity in the Oceans," *Environment* (April 2001): 29–36.

---

such as Textron, Allied Signal, Emerson Electric, General Electric, and Viacom. Viacom's acquisition of CBS for $36 billion turned Viacom into an $80 billion company with diverse assets in broadcast and cable television, movies, radio, theme parks, Internet sites, home video, publishing, and billboards. Similarly, Textron, through numerous diverse acquisitions, now produces and sells Cessna airplanes, Bell helicopters, Jacobsen lawn mowers, golf products, transmissions, consumer loans, and telescopic machinery. Conglomerates prove that focus and diversity are not always mutually exclusive.

Peters and Waterman's advice to firms is to "stick to the knitting" and not to stray too far from the firm's basic areas of competence. However, diversification is still an appropriate and successful strategy sometimes. Hamish Maxwell, Philip Morris's former CEO, says, "We want to become a consumer-products company." Diversification makes sense for Philip Morris because cigarette consumption is declining, product liability suits are a risk, and some investors reject tobacco stocks on principle. In a diversification move, Philip Morris spent $12.9 billion in a hostile takeover of Kraft General Foods, the world's second-largest food producer behind Nestlé.

Concentric Diversification

Adding new, but related, products or services is widely called *concentric diversification*. An example of this strategy is Amazon.com Inc.'s recent move to sell personal computers through its online store. Rather than keeping the computers in its warehouses, however, Amazon will simply transmit orders for computers to wholesaler Ingram Micro, based in Santa Ana, California. Ingram will package and send the computers to customers, so Amazon is minimizing its own risk in this diversification initiative.

The largest African-American-owned business in America, Active Transportation and Automotive Carrier Services (ATACS), based in Louisville, Kentucky, is considering concentric diversification to reverse its falling profitability.[12] The business hauls everything from steel and turbines to heavy trucks, but orders for heavy hauling have lately been down 40 percent, ATACS would like to diversify into hauling lighter cargo.

Six guidelines when concentric diversification may be an effective strategy are provided below.[13]

- When an organization competes in a no-growth or a slow-growth industry.
- When adding new, but related, products would significantly enhance the sales of current products.
- When new, but related, products could be offered at highly competitive prices.
- When new, but related, products have seasonal sales levels that counterbalance an organization's existing peaks and valleys.
- When an organization's products are currently in the declining stage of the product's life cycle.
- When an organization has a strong management team.

Horizontal Diversification

Adding new, unrelated products or services for present customers is called *horizontal diversification*. This strategy is not as risky as conglomerate diversification because a firm already should be familiar with its present customers. For example, consider the increasing number of hospitals that are creating miniature malls by offering banks, bookstores, coffee shops, restaurants, drugstores, and other retail stores within its buildings. Many hospitals previously had only cafeterias, gift shops, and maybe a pharmacy, but the movement into malls and retail stores is aimed at improving the ambiance for patients and their visitors. The new University Pointe Hospital in West Chester, Ohio, has 75,000 square feet of retail space. The CEO says, "Unless we diversify our revenue, we won't be able to fulfill our mission of providing healthcare. We want our hospital to be a place that people want to go to."[14]

Four guidelines when horizontal diversification may be an especially effective strategy are:[15]

- When revenues derived from an organization's current products or services would increase significantly by adding the new, unrelated products.
- When an organization competes in a highly competitive and/or a no-growth industry, as indicated by low industry profit margins and returns.
- When an organization's present channels of distribution can be used to market the new products to current customers.
- When the new products have countercyclical sales patterns compared to an organization's present products.

Conglomerate Diversification

Adding new, unrelated products or services is called *conglomerate diversification*. For example, ESPN is diversifying from sports programming into movies and ministries with the creation of a new division called ESPN Original Entertainment. ESPN's first movie is about basketball coach Bobby Knight called "A Season on the Brink." ESPN is part of the Walt Disney Company. ESPN's ratings dropped 22 percent from 1997 to 2002.[16]

Six guidelines when conglomerate diversification may be an especially effective strategy to pursue are listed below.[17]

- When an organization's basic industry is experiencing declining annual sales and profits
- When an organization has the capital and managerial talent needed to compete successfully in a new industry
- When an organization has the opportunity to purchase an unrelated business that is an attractive investment opportunity
- When there exists financial synergy between the acquired and acquiring firm (note that a key difference between concentric and conglomerate diversification is that the former should be based on some commonality in markets, products, or technology, whereas the latter should be based more on profit considerations)
- When existing markets for an organization's present products are saturated
- When antitrust action could be charged against an organization that historically has concentrated on a single industry

General Electric is a classic firm that is highly diversified. GE makes locomotives, lightbulbs, power plants, and refrigerators; GE manages more credit cards than American Express; GE owns more commercial aircraft than American Airlines.

 ## DEFENSIVE STRATEGIES

In addition to integrative, intensive, and diversification strategies, organizations also could pursue retrenchment, divestiture, or liquidation.

Retrenchment

Retrenchment occurs when an organization regroups through cost and asset reduction to reverse declining sales and profits. Sometimes called a turnaround or reorganizational strategy, retrenchment is designed to fortify an organization's basic distinctive competence. During retrenchment, strategists work with limited resources and face pressure from shareholders, employees, and the media. Retrenchment can entail selling off land and buildings to raise needed cash, pruning product lines, closing marginal businesses, closing obsolete factories, automating processes, reducing the number of employees, and instituting expense control systems.

Michelin North America recently announced that it will cut two thousand jobs—or 7 percent of its workforce—by the end of 2002 due to weak demand for tires. Based in Greenville, South Carolina, Michelin says the job cuts will be made in every location and will involve every job type within the company.

Advanced Micro Devices (AMD) is closing two plants and laying off 2,300 employees—or nearly 15 percent of its workforce—as the chip maker struggles from slowing sales. AMD's major competitor, Intel, is slashing computer chip prices in efforts to keep its market share and to stimulate demand. Gateway in late 2001 switched from AMD to Intel as the primary supplier for its computer chips.

Gateway is undergoing major retrenchment as domestic and worldwide personal computer sales continue to decline. The company recently announced a 25 percent cut in its worldwide staff, and it is closing its operations in Europe, Asia, and Australia. Based in San Diego, Gateway is also closing its manufacturing plant in Salt Lake City and its sales and support centers in California, South Dakota, Utah, and Virginia. CEO Ted Watt says, "We don't have to be a global business to succeed. Outside the United States, we don't have the brand awareness, or the local presence and solutions capability."

The terrorist events of September 11, 2001, and the anthrax scares thereafter resulted in many firms rethinking their efforts to globalize, and many firms are actually pulling back from global operations. For example, Merrill Lynch is scaling back its operations in Japan, using retrenchment, after stumbling in its advertising and marketing efforts there. Toshiba Corp. recently discontinued its manufacturing and marketing of desktop PCs in the United States, focusing instead on Asia and Europe. Toshiba cut 12 percent of its U.S. employees with the announcement.

The office supplies market has slowed to a no-growth situation, and many competing firms are using a retrenchment strategy. Office Depot, for example, is shutting down seventy stores and cutting sixteen hundred jobs, while Office Max is shutting fifty stores and cutting twelve hundred jobs. However, Staples, Inc., at the same time is opening 160 new stores and expanding its catalog and Internet sales. Staples currently has nearly fifteen hundred stores worldwide.

For another retrenchment example, consider that Club Med is closing fifteen of its 120 resorts worldwide. Bookings at Club Med resorts are off from 15 to 50 percent due to the war on terrorism and the reluctance of travelers to travel. Along with the closings, Club Med announced a new $20 million advertising campaign—"Wanna Play"—that emphasizes skiing and sports instead of sensuality.

The U.S. Postal Service expects to close many of its thirty-eight thousand post offices nationwide or reduce hours over the next decade as online transactions for sending and paying bills is expected to reduce first class mail dramatically beginning in 2003.[18] First-class mail volume will peak in 2002 and then decline at an annual rate of 2.5 percent from 2003 to 2008. Advertisers shifting their business to the Internet from bulk mailings also contributes to the Postal Service considering a retrenchment strategy for the future.

In some cases, *bankruptcy* can be an effective type of retrenchment strategy. Bankruptcy can allow a firm to avoid major debt obligations and to void union contracts. There are five major types of bankruptcy: Chapter 7, Chapter 9, Chapter 11, Chapter 12, and Chapter 13.

Chapter 7 bankruptcy is a liquidation procedure used only when a corporation sees no hope of being able to operate successfully or to obtain the necessary creditor agreement. All the organization's assets are sold in parts for their tangible worth.

Chapter 9 bankruptcy applies to municipalities. A municipality successfully declaring bankruptcy is Camden, New Jersey, the state's poorest city and the fifth-poorest city in the United States. A crime-ridden city of eighty-seven thousand, Camden received $62.5 million in state aid and has withdrawn its bankruptcy petition. Between 1980 and 2000, only eighteen U.S. cities declared bankruptcy. Some states do not allow municipalities to declare bankruptcy.

Chapter 11 bankruptcy allows organizations to reorganize and come back after filing a petition for protection. Bankruptcy filings surged 19 percent in 2001 to a record 1.5 million; filings by publicly-traded companies soared 46 percent in 2001 to 257.[19]

Midway Airlines Corporation recently filed for Chapter 11 bankruptcy and fired half of its fourteen hundred employees. With rare exception, Chapter 11 of the U.S. Bankruptcy Code makes no provision for parties other than debtors, creditors, and shareholders. For example, when Enron and Pacific Gas & Electric in California declared bankruptcy in 2001, customers sued for benefits but were denied consideration. Employees and customers of Midway are now in court seeking compensation from Midway.

Also declaring bankruptcy recently was McCrory Corporation, a New York–based discount store operator with 175 stores in the Northeast as well as Arizona, California, New Mexico, Oregon, Texas, and Washington. Founded in 1882, the McCrory retail stores operate under the names Dollar Zone, G.C. Murphy, McCrory, J.J. Newberry, and T.G, & Y.

One of Japan's largest retailers, Mycal Corporation, recently declared bankruptcy after it had amassed 1.55 trillion yen ($13 billion) in debt. Mycal operates hundreds of supermarkets and shopping centers. Historically, Japanese banks have stepped in to aid and save ailing companies, but this trend is changing as banks themselves are struggling to survive, much less prosper.

In the cruise industry, Renaissance Cruises filed for Chapter 11 bankruptcy in late 2001 as the United States officially entered an economic recession. Analysts expect an industrywide shakeout among cruise-line companies. Larger cruise lines, such as Carnival and Royal Caribbean, are launching heavily discounted prices to lure passengers, while smaller cruise companies, such as Disney, Norwegian, and P&O Princess, struggle to compete.

Bethlehem Steel Corporation, the nation's third largest steel company, declared bankruptcy in late 2001. Based in Bethlehem, 50 miles from Philadelphia, the company was once a symbol of American industrial and military might, having produced more than one thousand ships during World War II and girders for the Golden Gate Bridge and Empire State Building.

Polaroid Corporation also declared bankruptcy recently and notified potential acquirers that the company is for sale. Based in Cambridge, Massachusetts, Polaroid had been struggling to turn around its fading instant-photography business and could not meet its debt obligations.

Burlington Industries declared bankruptcy at the end of fiscal 2001 after reporting a loss of $91.1 million. Burlington's CEO George Henderson cited as the primary reason for the company's demise the volume of imported apparel into the United States, which is growing at five times the rate of consumption; he also reported that four out of five garments sold in the United States today are imported. Based in Greensboro, North Carolina, Burlington is a $1.4 billion per year textile maker.

Chiquita Brands International, the banana producer, declared bankruptcy in late 2001 due in part to a worldwide glut in bananas and a drop in prices. The U.S.–European Union eight-year trade battle over EU banana-import quotas ended in late 2001, but it cost Chiquita millions of dollars.

According to the Administrative Office of the U.S. Courts, there were 9,527 Chapter 11 bankruptcies declared for the twelve-month period ending June 30, 2001. During this time period, there were also 206 and 5,422 Chapter 12 and Chapter 13 bankruptcies, respectively. Bankruptcies in 2001 were up almost 30 percent over 2000 according to **bankruptcydata.com**, a Boston-based Web site that tracks such filings.

Chapter 12 bankruptcy was created by the Family Farmer Bankruptcy Act of 1986. This law became effective in 1987 and provides special relief to family farmers with debt equal to or less than $1.5 million.

Chapter 13 bankruptcy is a reorganization plan similar to Chapter 11, but it is available only to small businesses owned by individuals with unsecured debts of less than $100,000 and secured debts of less than $350,000. The Chapter 13 debtor is allowed to operate the business while a plan is being developed to provide for the successful operation of the business in the future.

Five guidelines when retrenchment may be an especially effective strategy to pursue are as follows.[20]

- When an organization has a clearly distinctive competence but has failed to meet its objectives and goals consistently over time
- When an organization is one of the weaker competitors in a given industry
- When an organization is plagued by inefficiency, low profitability, poor employee morale, and pressure from stockholders to improve performance
- When an organization has failed to capitalize on external opportunities, minimize external threats, take advantage of internal strengths, and overcome internal weaknesses over time; that is, when the organization's strategic managers have failed (and possibly will be replaced by more competent individuals)
- When an organization has grown so large so quickly that major internal reorganization is needed

Divestiture

Selling a division or part of an organization is called *divestiture*. Divestiture often is used to raise capital for further strategic acquisitions or investments. Divestiture can be part of an overall retrenchment strategy to rid an organization of businesses that are unprofitable, that require too much capital, or that do not fit well with the firm's other activities. An example company using divestiture as a primary strategy is Lucent Technologies, which is currently trying to divest itself of its Octel division, a manufacturer of equipment and software used for voice-messaging systems. A possible acquirer would be Converse Technology based in Woodbury, New York. Converse controls nearly 60 percent of the $2 billion voice-messaging industry. Octel had sales of about $325 million in 2001.

The nation's largest maker of peanut butter, Procter & Gamble, recently divested itself of its Jif peanut butter and Crisco shortening operations, turning them over to J.M. Smucker, the nation's largest maker of jelly. Smucker nows has a 41 percent market share in jelly, 38 percent in peanut butter, and 24 percent in cooking oils in the United States, making it the leader in all three categories.

Divestiture has become a very popular strategy as firms try to focus on their core strengths, lessening their level of diversification. For example, a few divestitures consummated in 2001 are given in Table 5–3.

Six guidelines when divestiture may be an especially effective strategy to pursue are listed below.[21]

- When an organization has pursued a retrenchment strategy and failed to accomplish needed improvements
- When a division needs more resources to be competitive than the company can provide
- When a division is responsible for an organization's overall poor performance
- When a division is a misfit with the rest of an organization; this can result from radically different markets, customers, managers, employees, values, or needs
- When a large amount of cash is needed quickly and cannot be obtained reasonably from other sources
- When government antitrust action threatens an organization

Liquidation

Selling all of a company's assets, in parts, for their tangible worth is called *liquidation*. Liquidation is a recognition of defeat and consequently can be an emotionally difficult

TABLE 5-3   **Recent Divestitures**

PARENT COMPANY	PART BEING DIVESTED	ACQUIRING COMPANY
Dell Computer	Web-hosting division	FON Group
Citigroup	Citi Capital	GE Capital Fleet Services
Maytag	Blodgett	Middleby Corporation
Westcoast Energy	British Columbia Gas	BC Gas
Westcoast Energy	Union Energy	Epcor Utilities
Westcoast Energy	Westcoast Capital	Epcor Utilities
Credit Suisse	CSFBdirect	Bank of Montreal
Emerson Electric	Chromalox	JPMorgan Partners
General Motors	Hughes Electronics	EchoStar Communications
DuPont	drug division	Bristol-Myers Squibb
Gaylord Entertainment	Word Entertainment	AOL Time Warner

strategy. However, it may be better to cease operating than to continue losing large sums of money.

Thousands of small businesses in the United States liquidate annually without ever making the news. It is tough to start and successfully operate a small business. In China and Russia, thousands of government-owned businesses liquidate annually as those countries try to privatize and consolidate industries.

Two cybercurrency companies, Flooz.com.Inc., in New York, and Beenz Company Ltd., in Britain, recently liquidated. These two companies provided their own currency to customers, who could redeem the "money" as gift certificates at retailers such as Barnes & Noble and J. Crew. Each company cited the worldwide economic recession and credit card fraud as the reasons for the liquidation.

General Motors terminated production of its Chevrolet Camaro and Pontiac Firebird in 2002 and closed the Canadian factory where they were made. Sales of Camaro and Firebird were down 25 percent in 2001, following a decade of slumping market share due largely to competition from imported rivals and sport-utility vehicles.

For the twelve months ended June 30, 2001, there were 21,935 liquidations in the United States according to the Administrative Office of the U.S. Courts, up dramatically from the same period the year before.

Three guidelines when liquidation may be an especially effective strategy to pursue are:[22]

- When an organization has pursued both a retrenchment strategy and a divestiture strategy, and neither has been successful.

- When an organization's only alternative is bankruptcy; liquidation represents an orderly and planned means of obtaining the greatest possible cash for an organization's assets. A company can legally declare bankruptcy first and then liquidate various divisions to raise needed capital.

- When the stockholders of a firm can minimize their losses by selling the organization's assets.

MICHAEL PORTER'S GENERIC STRATEGIES

Probably the three most widely read books on competitive analysis in the 1980s were Michael Porter's (**www.hbs.edu/bios/mporter**) *Competitive Strategy* (Free Press, 1980),

Competitive Advantage (Free Press, 1985), and *Competitive Advantage of Nations* (Free Press, 1989). According to Porter, strategies allow organizations to gain competitive advantage from three different bases: cost leadership, differentiation, and focus. Porter calls these bases *generic strategies*. *Cost leadership* emphasizes producing standardized products at a very low per-unit cost for consumers who are price-sensitive. *Differentiation* is a strategy aimed at producing products and services considered unique industrywide and directed at consumers who are relatively price-insensitive. *Focus* means producing products and services that fulfill the needs of small groups of consumers.

Porter's strategies imply different organizational arrangements, control procedures, and incentive systems. Larger firms with greater access to resources typically compete on a cost leadership and/or differentiation basis, whereas smaller firms often compete on a focus basis.

Porter stresses the need for strategists to perform cost-benefit analyses to evaluate "sharing opportunities" among a firm's existing and potential business units. Sharing activities and resources enhances competitive advantage by lowering costs or raising differentiation. In addition to prompting sharing, Porter stresses the need for firms to "transfer" skills and expertise among autonomous business units effectively in order to gain competitive advantage. Depending upon factors such as type of industry, size of firm, and nature of competition, various strategies could yield advantages in cost leadership, differentiation, and focus.

Cost Leadership Strategies

A primary reason for pursuing forward, backward, and horizontal integration strategies is to gain cost leadership benefits. But cost leadership generally must be pursued in conjunction with differentiation. A number of cost elements affect the relative attractiveness of generic strategies, including economies or diseconomies of scale achieved, learning and experience curve effects, the percentage of capacity utilization achieved, and linkages with suppliers and distributors. Other cost elements to consider in choosing among alternative strategies include the potential for sharing costs and knowledge within the organization, R&D costs associated with new product development or modification of existing products, labor costs, tax rates, energy costs, and shipping costs.

Striving to be the low-cost producer in an industry can be especially effective when the market is composed of many price-sensitive buyers, when there are few ways to achieve product differentiation, when buyers do not care much about differences from brand to brand, or when there are a large number of buyers with significant bargaining power. The basic idea is to underprice competitors and thereby gain market share and sales, driving some competitors out of the market entirely.

A successful cost leadership strategy usually permeates the entire firm, as evidenced by high efficiency, low overhead, limited perks, intolerance of waste, intensive screening of budget requests, wide spans of control, rewards linked to cost containment, and broad employee participation in cost control efforts. Some risks of pursuing cost leadership are that competitors may imitate the strategy, thus driving overall industry profits down; that technological breakthroughs in the industry may make the strategy ineffective; or that buyer interest may swing to other differentiating features besides price. Several example firms that are well known for their low-cost leadership strategies are Wal-Mart, BIC, McDonald's, Black and Decker, Lincoln Electric, and Briggs and Stratton.

Differentiation Strategies

Different strategies offer different degrees of differentiation. Differentiation does not guarantee competitive advantage, especially if standard products sufficiently meet customer needs or if rapid imitation by competitors is possible. Durable products protected by barriers to quick copying by competitors are best. Successful differentiation can mean greater product flexibility, greater compatibility, lower costs, improved service, less maintenance, greater convenience, or more features. Product development is an example of a strategy that offers the advantages of differentiation.

A differentiation strategy should be pursued only after a careful study of buyers' needs and preferences to determine the feasibility of incorporating one or more differentiating features into a unique product that features the desired attributes. A successful differentiation strategy allows a firm to charge a higher price for its product and to gain customer loyalty because consumers may become strongly attached to the differentiation features. Special features that differentiate one's product can include superior service, spare parts availability, engineering design, product performance, useful life, gas mileage, or ease of use.

A risk of pursuing a differentiation strategy is that the unique product may not be valued highly enough by customers to justify the higher price. When this happens, a cost leadership strategy easily will defeat a differentiation strategy. Another risk of pursuing a differentiation strategy is that competitors may develop ways to copy the differentiating features quickly. Firms thus must find durable sources of uniqueness that cannot be imitated quickly or cheaply by rival firms.

Common organizational requirements for a successful differentiation strategy include strong coordination among the R&D and marketing functions and substantial amenities to attract scientists and creative people. Firms pursuing a differentiation strategy include Dr. Pepper, Jenn-Air, The Limited, BMW, Grady-White, Ralph Lauren, Maytag, and Cross.

Focus Strategies

A successful focus strategy depends on an industry segment that is of sufficient size, has good growth potential, and is not crucial to the success of other major competitors. Strategies such as market penetration and market development offer substantial focusing advantages. Midsize and large firms can effectively pursue focus-based strategies only in conjunction with differentiation or cost leadership–based strategies. All firms in essence follow a differentiated strategy. Because only one firm can differentiate itself with the lowest cost, the remaining firms in the industry must find other ways to differentiate their products.

Focus strategies are most effective when consumers have distinctive preferences or requirements and when rival firms are not attempting to specialize in the same target segment. Firms pursuing a focus strategy include San Antonio-based Clear Channel, the nation's largest radio chain, billboard owner, and concert promoter. Clear Channel has used a focus strategy for a decade to achieve $5.3 billion in annual revenues from operations in sixty-three countries, including twelve hundred radio stations, nineteen television stations, and 770,000 outdoor advertising displays. The next largest radio company in the nation is Infinity Broadcasting Corp., which owns only 183 radio stations. Clear Channel owns eight radio stations in each of the following cities: Los Angeles, Houston, Denver, and Washington, D.C.

Bally Total Fitness Holding Corporation, the nation's leader in health clubs, recently acquired Crunch, a large health-club company. Bally is allowing New York-based Crunch to keep its name and to expand from nineteen clubs to forty clubs before 2004. Bally operates about four hundred clubs with four million members. Obviously pursuing a focus strategy, Bally had just purchased the Sports Clubs of Canada.

Another excellent example of a focus strategy is the fact that Germany's Bayerische Motoren Werke AG (BMW) focuses exclusively on premium, luxury cars. The BMW strategy bucks conventional wisdom in the anto industry to produce for the mass market too.

Risks of pursuing a focus strategy include the possibility that numerous competitors will recognize the successful focus strategy and copy it, or that consumer preferences will drift toward the product attributes desired by the market as a whole. An organization using a focus strategy may concentrate on a particular group of customers, geographic markets, or on particular product-line segments in order to serve a well-defined but narrow market better than competitors who serve a broader market.

The Value Chain

According to Porter, the business of a firm can best be described as a *value chain,* in which total revenues minus total costs of all activities undertaken to develop and market a product or service yields value. All firms in a given industry have a similar value chain, which includes activities such as obtaining raw materials, designing products, building manufacturing facilities, developing cooperative agreements, and providing customer service. A firm will be profitable as long as total revenues exceed the total costs incurred in creating and delivering the product or service. Firms should strive to understand not only their own value chain operations, but also their competitors', suppliers', and distributors' value chains.

MEANS FOR ACHIEVING STRATEGIES

Joint Venture/Partnering

Joint venture is a popular strategy that occurs when two or more companies form a temporary partnership or consortium for the purpose of capitalizing on some opportunity. Often, the two or more sponsoring firms form a separate organization and have shared equity ownership in the new entity. Other types of *cooperative arrangements* include research and development partnerships, cross-distribution agreements, cross-licensing agreements, cross-manufacturing agreements, and joint-bidding consortia.

Joint ventures and cooperative arrangements are being used increasingly because they allow companies to improve communications and networking, to globalize operations, and to minimize risk. Kathryn Rudie Harrigan, professor of strategic management at Columbia University, summarizes the trend toward increased joint venturing:

> In today's global business environment of scarce resources, rapid rates of technological change, and rising capital requirements, the important question is no longer "Shall we form a joint venture?" Now the question is "Which joint ventures and cooperative arrangements are most appropriate for our needs and expectations?" followed by "How do we manage these ventures most effectively?"[23]

In a global market tied together by the Internet, joint ventures, partnerships, and alliances are proving to be a more effective way to enhance corporate growth than mergers and acquisitions.[24] Strategic partnering takes many forms, including outsourcing, information sharing, joint marketing, and joint research and development. Many companies such as Eli Lilly even now host partnership training classes for their managers and partners. There are today more than ten thousand joint ventures formed annually, more than all mergers and acquisitions. There are countless examples of successful strategic alliances, such as Kmart's recent $4.5 billion supply-chain alliance with grocery whole-saler Fleming, which is integrating Kmart's buying, inventory control, and logistics with its own high tech system.

A major reason why firms are using partnering as a means to achieve strategies is globalization. Wal-Mart's successful joint venture with Mexico's Cifra is indicative of how a domestic firm can benefit immensely by partnering with a foreign company to gain substantial presence in that new country. Technology also is a major reason behind the need to form strategic alliances, with the Internet linking widely dispersed partners. The Internet paved the way and legitimized the need for alliances to serve as the primary means for corporate growth. IBM in 2001 doubled its strategic software alliances to more than one hundred by year-end.[25]

Evidence is mounting that firms should use partnering as a means for achieving strategies. However, the sad fact is that most American firms in many industries, such as financial services, forest products, and metals and retailing, still operate in a merger or acquire mode to obtain growth. Partnering is not yet taught at most business schools and is often viewed within companies as a financial issue rather than a strategic issue. However, partnering has become a core competency, a strategic issue of such importance that top management involvement initially and throughout the life of an alliance is vital.[26]

Dell Computer, based in Austin, Texas, and its fierce rival, EMC Corporation, based in Hopkinton, Massachusetts, announced a sales and development alliance in late 2001, one in which Dell will resell and cooperate on the development of EMC's Clarion storage systems. It is interesting that just a year earlier, Dell Chairman Michael Dell had joked that the initials of EMC stood for "Excess Margin Corporation" and insisted that Dell would undercut those margins with lower-cost products.[27]

Cingular Wireless and VoiceStream Wireless recently formed a 50–50 joint venture to share their mobile infrastructure in major U.S. markets. These two companies are saving "hundreds of millions of dollars" in capital expenditures and operating expenses by cooperating in this manner. Another benefit of this venture and others like it is that such agreements do not require approval from the Federal Communications Commission; this is in contrast to a merger or acquisition, which would require approval.

General Motors in the early 2000s weaved together a large number of alliances and joint ventures throughout Asia to enhance its operations. GM's share of the Asian market is now about 16 percent, second only to Toyota. GM attributes its success in Asia to its new partnerships and cooperative arrangements. GM has alliances with the bankrupt Korean automaker Daewoo Motor as well as Japan's Suzuki Motor, Isuzu Motor, Fuji Heavy Industries, and many other rival and supplier firms. GM acknowledges that alliances with non-American firms are more difficult to manage, but it insists that the many Asian partnerships benefit the company immensely and "avoid much of the pain, tension, and risk of a merger."[28]

IBM and the German company Lion Bioscience AG in 2001 established an alliance in which the firms will develop and market their computer technologies and data-mining software as a package to major drug makers and to other research laboratories trying to assimilate research data being generated in human gene research. The companies say their alliance will shorten the discovery and development time for new medicines. The market for genomics equipment should double to $43 billion from 2001 to 2003. IBM formed a new life-sciences division in August 2000.

Burger King Corp. and AOL Time Warner recently formed a strategic alliance that allows the number two hamburger chain's twelve million daily customers to obtain AOL software at the restaurants. This is among the first ventures of its kind in the fast-food industry, which to date has not focused on the Internet revolution. AOL in return is marketing Burger King online.

Sprint and AOL in late 2001 formed a new strategic alliance, one in which AOL will promote Sprint's long-distance phone service while AOL members receive a variety of Sprint long-distance plans. Sprint is the third-ranked long-distance business, but it faces increasing competition from regional bells.

Although ventures and partnerships are preferred over mergers as a means for achieving strategies, certainly they are not all successful. The good news is that joint ventures and partnerships are less risky for companies than mergers, but the bad news is that many alliances fail. Forbes recently reported that about 30 percent of all joint ventures and partnership alliances are outright failures, while another 17 percent have limited success and then dissipate due to problems.[29] There are countless examples of failed joint ventures. A few common problems that cause joint ventures to fail are as follows:

1. Managers who must collaborate daily in operating the venture are not involved in forming or shaping the venture.

2. The venture may benefit the partnering companies but may not benefit customers who then complain about poorer service or criticize the companies in other ways.

3. The venture may not be supported equally by both partners. If supported unequally, problems arise.

4. The venture may begin to compete more with one of the partners than the other.[30]

Swedish telecommunications-equipment maker Telefon L. M. Ericson currently has nine joint ventures in China and is one of that country's largest suppliers of telecommunications network equipment and mobile phones. Ericsson plans to increase its investment in China to $5.1 billion by 2005 from $2.4 billion in 2001.

Six guidelines when a joint venture may be an especially effective strategy to purse are:[31]

- When a privately owned organization is forming a joint venture with a publicly owned organization; there are some advantages to being privately held, such as closed ownership; there are some advantages of being publicly held, such as access to stock issuances as a source of capital. Sometimes, the unique advantages of being privately and publicly held can be synergistically combined in a joint venture.

- When a domestic organization is forming a joint venture with a foreign company; a joint venture can provide a domestic company with the opportunity for obtaining local management in a foreign country, thereby reducing risks such as expropriation and harassment by host country officials.

- When the distinct competencies of two or more firms complement each other especially well.

- When some project is potentially very profitable but requires overwhelming resources and risks; the Alaskan pipeline is an example.

- When two or more smaller firms have trouble competing with a large firm.

- When there exists a need to introduce a new technology quickly.

Joint Ventures in Russia

A joint venture strategy offers a possible way to enter the Russian market. Joint ventures create a mechanism to generate hard currency, which is important because of problems valuing the ruble. Russia's joint venture law has been revised to allow foreigners to own up to 99 percent of the venture and to allow a foreigner to serve as chief executive officer.

The following guidelines are appropriate when considering a joint venture in Russia. First, avoid regions with ethnic conflicts and violence. Also, make sure the potential partner has a proper charter that has been amended to permit joint venture participation. Be aware that businesspeople in these lands have little knowledge of marketing, contract law, corporate law, fax machines, voice mail, and other business practices that Westerners take for granted.

Business contracts with Russian firms should address natural-environment issues because Westerners often get the blame for air and water pollution problems and habitat destruction. Work out a clear means of converting rubles to dollars before entering a proposed joint venture, because neither Russian banks nor authorities can be counted on to facilitate foreign firms' getting dollar profits out of a business. Recognize that chronic shortages of raw materials hamper business in Russia, so make sure an adequate supply of competitively priced, good-quality raw materials is reliably available. Finally, make sure the business contract limits the circumstances in which expropriation would be legal. Specify a lump sum in dollars if expropriation should occur unexpectedly, and obtain expropriation insurance before signing the agreement.

MERGER/ACQUISITION

Merger and acquisition are two commonly used ways to pursue strategies. A *merger* occurs when two organizations of about equal size unite to form one enterprise. An *acquisition* occurs when a large organization purchases (acquires) a smaller firm, or vice versa. When a merger or acquisition is not desired by both parties, it can be called a *takeover* or *hostile takeover*. For example, when Clorox recently acquired First Brands, Clorox made it clear from the start that the union was a takeover, not a merger of equals. Clorox excluded First Brands' executives from the conference call announcing the deal and soon thereafter fired 255 employees at First Brands' headquarters. Perhaps because of the unhealthy takeover climate, Clorox has had trouble with First Brands' products ever since the merger, especially the Glad bag product line. For example, Northrup Grumman Corp. in 2002 launched a hostile takeover attempt of TRW Inc. There are numerous and powerful forces driving once-fierce rivals to merge around the world. Some of these forces are deregulation, technological change, excess capacity, inability to boost profits through price increases, a depressed stock market, and the need to gain economies of scale.

In addition, there are bargains available as companies struggle and while stock prices are low. For example, Palm, the leading handheld computer maker, recently purchased software maker Be for $11 million in stock in late 2001, whereas three years earlier Apple Computer sought to acquire Be for about $300 million. In this recession, cash-starved economy, large firms that do have cash are prowling for opportunistic purchases: SBC Communications acquired Prodigy and Cisco Systems acquired ten small firms in 2002.

Not all mergers are effective and successful. Pricewaterhouse Coopers LLP recently researched mergers and found that the average acquirer's stock was 3.7 percent lower than its industry peer group a year later. *Business Week* and *The Wall Street Journal* studied mergers and concluded that about half produced negative returns to shareholders. Warren Buffett once said in a speech that "too-high purchase price for the stock of an excellent company can undo the effects of a subsequent decade of favorable business developments." So a merger between two firms can yield great benefits, but the price and reasoning must be right.

Within three business days following the Hewlett-Packard proposed acquisition of Compaq, the stock price of each company fell nearly 20 percent. The stock decline cut more than $6 billion off the value of the all-stock deal as analysts and consumers were skeptical of the future success of the merged firm. Recent research indicates that 73 percent of all mergers between domestic and foreign companies fail to prosper or deliver value. For companies acquired between 1998 and 2001 in deals of $15 billion or more, the stocks of the acquirers have underperformed the S&P 500 stock index by 14 percent.[32] A reason why companies still merge—even in the face of odds against success—is the fact that investors and shareholders greatly reward increased market share and geographic expansion, yet they also mercilessly punish firms with flat sales. Future growth expectations account for more than 60 percent of an average company's market value today, up from about 40 percent a decade ago.[33]

Among mergers, acquisitions, and takeovers in recent years, same-industry combinations have predominated. A general market consolidation is occurring in many industries, especially banking, insurance, defense, and healthcare, but also in pharmaceuticals, food, airlines, accounting, publishing, computers, retailing, financial services, and biotechnology. For example, United Airlines and US Airways are still interested in merging, but the Department of Justice is concerned that the merger would not be good for competition. Delta and Continental are also talking about a merger just in case the United/US Air merger is approved. On the global front, Japan's top airline, Japan Airlines, recently acquired the country's number three airline, Japan Air System. The new company controls nearly half of Japan's domestic market, followed by All Nippon Airways, and it is also now the number three global carrier behind United Airlines and American Airlines.

Procter & Gamble (P&G) recently acquired Clairol from Bristol-Myers Squibb. The acquisition gave P&G such brands as Herbal Essences, Aussie, and Clairol to go with its other hair-care products, such as Pantene, Head & Shoulders, Pert, Physique, and Vidal Sassoon. The acquisition marks P&G's first entry into the $1.5 billion hair-coloring business, an area that is growing faster than the shampoo market.

Table 5–4 shows some mergers and acquisitions completed in 2001. There are many reasons for mergers and acquisitions, including the following:

- To provide improved capacity utilization
- To make better use of the existing sales force
- To reduce managerial staff
- To gain economies of scale
- To smooth out seasonal trends in sales
- To gain access to new suppliers, distributors, customers, products, and creditors
- To gain new technology
- To reduce tax obligations

TABLE 5-4   **Some Recent Example Mergers**

ACQUIRING FIRM	ACQUIRED FIRM
Hewlett-Packard	Compaq Computer
SouthTrust Corp.	Bank of Tidewater
eBay	HomesDirect
PepsiCo	Quaker Oats
Sara Lee	Earthgrains Company
Amerada Hess	Triton Energy
Westvaco Corporation	Mead Corporation
Devon	Anderson Exploration
Santa Fe International	Global Marine
Dominion Resources	Louis Dreyfus Natural
AMR	TWA
TLC Laser Eye Centers	Laser Vision Centers
Tyco International Ltd.	Paragon Trade Brands, Inc.
Tellabs	Ocular Networks
Philips Petroleum	Conoco
Royal Caribbean Cruises	Princess Cruises
Barrick Gold Corp.	Homestake Mining Co.
Newport Mining Corp.	Normandy Mining Ltd.
BB&T Corp.	Mid-America Bancorp
BB&T Corp.	Area Bancshares
Northrop Grumman	Newport News Shipbuildung
Medtronic Inc.	VidaMed Inc.
Millennium Pharmaceuticals	Cor Therapeutics Inc.

The volume of mergers completed annually worldwide is growing dramatically and exceeds $1 trillion annually. There are more than ten thousand mergers annually in the United States that total more than $700 billion.

The proliferation of mergers is fueled by companies' drive for market share, efficiency, and pricing power as well as by globalization, the need for greater economies of scale, reduced regulation and antitrust concerns, the Internet, and e-commerce.

A *leveraged buyout* (LBO) occurs when a corporation's shareholders are bought (hence *buyout*) by the company's management and other private investors using borrowed funds (hence *leverage*).[34] Besides trying to avoid a hostile takeover, other reasons for initiating an LBO are senior management decisions that particular divisions do not fit into an overall corporate strategy or must be sold to raise cash, or receipt of an attractive offering price. An LBO takes a corporation private.

STRATEGIC MANAGEMENT IN NONPROFIT AND GOVERNMENTAL ORGANIZATIONS

The strategic-management process is being used effectively by countless nonprofit and governmental organizations, such as the Girl Scouts and Boy Scouts, the Red Cross, chambers of commerce, educational institutions, medical institutions, public utilities, libraries, government agencies, and churches. The nonprofit sector, surprisingly, is by far

America's largest employer. Many nonprofit and governmental organizations outperform private firms and corporations on innovativeness, motivation, productivity, and strategic management. For many nonprofit examples of strategic planning in practice, click on Strategic Planning Links found at the **www.strategyclub.com** Web site.

Compared to for-profit firms, nonprofit and governmental organizations often function as a monopoly, produce a product or service that offers little or no measurability of performance, and are totally dependent on outside financing. Especially for these organizations, strategic management provides an excellent vehicle for developing and justifying requests for needed financial support.

Educational Institutions

Educational institutions are using strategic-management techniques and concepts more frequently. Richard Cyert, president of Carnegic-Mellon University, says, "I believe we do a far better job of strategic management than any company I know." Population shifts nationally from the Northeast and Midwest to the Southeast and West are but one factor causing trauma for educational institutions that have not planned for changing enrollments. Ivy League schools in the Northeast are recruiting more heavily in the Southeast and West. This trend represents a significant change in the competitive climate for attracting the best high school graduates each year.

The first all-Internet law school, Concord University School of Law, boasts nearly two hundred students who can access lectures anytime and chat at fixed times with professors. Online college degrees are becoming common and represent a threat to traditional colleges and universities. "You can put the kids to bed and go to law school," says Andrew Rosen, chief operating officer of Kaplan Education Centers, a subsidiary of the Washington Post Company, that owns Concord. Concord is not accredited by the American Bar Association, which prohibits study by correspondence and requires more than one thousand hours of classroom time.

For a list of college strategic plans, click on strategic-planning links found at the **www.strategyclub.com** Web site, and scroll down through the academic sites.

Medical Organizations

The $200 billion American hospital industry is experiencing declining margins, excess capacity, bureaucratic overburdening, poorly planned and executed diversification strategies, soaring healthcare costs, reduced federal support, and high administrator turnover. The seriousness of this problem is accented by a 20 percent annual decline in inpatient use nationwide. Declining occupancy rates, deregulation, and accelerating growth of health maintenance organizations, preferred provider organizations, urgent care centers, outpatient surgery centers, diagnostic centers, specialized clinics, and group practices are other major threats facing hospitals today. Many private and state-supported medical institutions are in financial trouble as a result of traditionally taking a reactive rather than a proactive approach in dealing with their industry.

Hospitals—originally intended to be warehouses for people dying of tuberculosis, smallpox, cancer, pneumonia, and infectious diseases—are creating new strategies today as advances in the diagnosis and treatment of chronic diseases are undercutting that earlier mission. Hospitals are beginning to bring services to the patient as much as bringing the patient to the hospital; health care is more and more being concentrated in the home and in the residential community, not on the hospital campus. Chronic care will require day-treatment facilities, electronic monitoring at home, user-friendly ambulatory services, decentralized service networks, and laboratory testing. A successful hospital

E-COMMERCE PERSPECTIVE

e-Universities, e-Courses, and e-Learning

Although dot-com companies nationwide are in retreat and failing, educational institutions harnessing the Internet are growing dramatically. For example, the University of Maryland's enrollment in Internet courses grew 50 percent in 2001 to sixty-three thousand, and the institution now offers more than seventy degrees and certificates entirely online (**www.umuc.edu**). The largest online for-profit university, the University of Phoenix Online, enjoyed a 76 percent increase in revenues in 2001 (**http://onl.uophx.edu**). Even the U.S. Army has a rapidly growing e-learning program with more than ten thousand soldiers currently taking courses and earning degrees online from twenty-four participating colleges. The eArmyU Program offers a free laptop and printer and 100 percent of its students' tuition and expects enrollment to hit eighty thousand by 2005 (**www.eArmyu.com**). Indeed, more than 4,000 major colleges and universities in the United States now offer courses over the Internet or use the Web to enhance classes on campus.

More than two million students take courses today from institutions of higher learning in the United States, and that number is expected to increase to over five million by 2006. Since about 50 percent of all higher education students today are over age twenty-five and working, the e-learning approach offers the flexibility such students need to advance their careers through education. At Duke's Fuqua School of Business, 65 percent of an MBA student's work is now done over the Internet and just 35 percent is done in class (**www.fuqua.duke.edu**). Revenues from this e-learning approach are allowing Fuqua to double its faculty. The nation's largest online law school, Concord Law School, has eight hundred students, and graduates can take the California bar exam, although Concord is not accredited by the American Bar Association (**www.concordlawschool.com**).

Corporate spending on e-learning is expected to more than quadruple by 2005 to $18 billion. For example, at IBM, more than 200,000 employees receive education or training online annually, and 75 percent of the firm's Basic Blue course for new managers is online. The new Web approach to the Basic Blue course cut IBM's travel expenses by $350 million in 2001 alone.

Perhaps one of the greatest benefits of the e-learning movement is that it is getting more adults to study throughout their working lives. More adults today view education as a lifelong learning experience, and this is good.

Source: Adapted from William Symonds, "Giving It the Old Online Try," *Business Week* (December 3, 2001): 76–80.

---

strategy for the future will require renewed and deepened collaboration with physicians, who are central to hospitals' well-being, and a reallocation of resources from acute to chronic care in home and community settings.

Current strategies being pursued by many hospitals include creating home health services, establishing nursing homes, and forming rehabilitation centers. Backward integration strategies that some hospitals are pursuing include acquiring ambulance services, waste disposal services, and diagnostic services. Millions of persons annually research medical ailments online, which is causing a dramatic shift in the balance of power between doctor, patient, and hospitals.[35] The number of persons using the Internet to obtain medical information is skyrocketing. A motivated patient using the Internet can gain knowledge on a particular subject far beyond his or her doctor's knowledge, because no person can keep up with the results and implications of billions of dollars of medical research reported weekly. Patients today often walk into the doctor's office with a file folder of the latest articles detailing research and treatment options for their ailments. On Web sites such as America's Doctor (**www.americasdoctor.com**), consumers can consult with a physician in an online chat room twenty-four hours a day. Excellent consumer health Web sites are proliferating, boosted by investments from such firms as

Microsoft, AOL, Reader's Digest, and CBS. Drug companies such as Glaxo Wellcome are getting involved, as are hospitals. The whole strategic landscape of healthcare is changing because of the Internet. Intel recently began offering a new secure medical service whereby doctors and patients can conduct sensitive business on the Internet, such as sharing results of medical tests and prescribing medicine. The ten most successful hospital strategies today are providing free-standing outpatient surgery centers, outpatient surgery and diagnostic centers, physical rehabilitation centers, home health services, cardiac rehabilitation centers, preferred provider services, industrial medicine services, women's medicine services, skilled nursing units, and psychiatric services.[36]

Governmental Agencies and Departments

Federal, state, county, and municipal agencies and departments, such as police departments, chambers of commerce, forestry associations, and health departments, are responsible for formulating, implementing, and evaluating strategies that use taxpayers' dollars in the most cost-effective way to provide services and programs. Strategic-management concepts increasingly are being used to enable governmental organizations to be more effective and efficient. For a list of government agency strategic plans, click on strategic-planning links found at the **www.strategyclub.com** Web site, and scroll down through the government sites.

But strategists in governmental organizations operate with less strategic autonomy than their counterparts in private firms. Public enterprises generally cannot diversify into unrelated businesses or merge with other firms. Governmental strategists usually enjoy little freedom in altering the organizations' missions or redirecting objectives. Legislators and politicians often have direct or indirect control over major decisions and resources. Strategic issues get discussed and debated in the media and legislatures. Issues become politicized, resulting in fewer strategic choice alternatives. There is now more predictability in the management of public sector enterprises.

Government agencies and departments are finding that their employees get excited about the opportunity to participate in the strategic-management process and thereby have an effect on the organization's mission, objectives, strategies, and policies. In addition, government agencies are using a strategic-management approach to develop and substantiate formal requests for additional funding.

STRATEGIC MANAGEMENT IN SMALL FIRMS

Strategic management is vital for large firms' success, but what about small firms? The strategic-management process is just as vital for small companies. From their inception, all organizations have a strategy, even if the strategy just evolves from day-to-day operations. Even if conducted informally or by a single owner/entrepreneur, the strategic-management process can significantly enhance small firms' growth and prosperity. Recent data clearly show that an ever-increasing number of men and women in the United States are starting their own businesses. This means that more individuals are becoming strategists. Widespread corporate layoffs have contributed to an explosion in small businesses and new ideas.

Numerous magazine and journal articles have focused on applying strategic-management concepts to small businesses.[37] A major conclusion of these articles is that a lack of strategic-management knowledge is a serious obstacle for many small business owners. Other problems often encountered in applying strategic-management concepts

VISIT THE NET

Gives the Department of Veteran's Affairs strategic plan. www.va.gov/ StrategicPlan98/html/ StratPlan98_1.html

GLOBAL PERSPECTIVE

Mexico's Lure Starting to Wane

As consumer demand falls and global economies falter, the lure of locating or even keeping business operations in Mexico has faded. Scores of companies such as General Electric, SCI Systems, Goodyear, Michelin, and Flextronics are moving their operations from the U.S.-Mexico border to China and Malaysia. What do China and Malaysia have to offer companies over Mexico? The answer: Wages as low as 60 cents an hour, tax incentives, center tariffs, and close proximity to markets that are growing instead of contracting.

Mexico has long suffered from poor schools, rampant corruption, and outmoded infrastructure, but its close proximity to the United States, its low wages, and the passage of NAFTA were appealing to companies. Mexican President Vicente Fox has promised to boost education spending from 5 percent of Gross Domestic Product (GDP) to 8 percent, but many companies feel this is too little, too late. Telephone penetration in Mexico is among the lowest in Latin America, and Mexico's judicial system is prone to corruption. Mexicans average fewer than

seven years of education, compared with about 10 years for Koreans and Poles. Malaysia and Singapore charge no corporate taxes on electronics assembly, while China and Ireland tax rates are about 10 percent. In contrast, Mexico's tax rate is 34 percent. The level of spending on research and development as a percentage of GDP in Mexico is 0.25 percent, compared to 0.75 percent, 0.85 percent and 2.6 percent in China, India, and the United States, respectively.

Mexico indeed is at a crossroads. To compete more effectively with other low-wage-rate countries such as China, Singapore, Malaysia, and Brazil, Mexico must improve its education system and infrastructure, and it must fight against drug trafficking to attract companies in the twenty-first century. Low wages and hard-working employees are no longer sufficient attractors.

Source: Adapted from Geri Smith, "Is the Magic Starting to Fade?" *Business Week* (August 6, 2001): 42–43.

VISIT THE NET

Site provides sixty sample business plans for small businesses. http://www. bplans.com/sp/ index.cfm?a=bc

to small businesses are a lack of both sufficient capital to exploit external opportunities and a day-to-day cognitive frame of reference. Research also indicates that strategic management in small firms is more informal than in large firms, but small firms that engage in strategic management outperform those that do not. The *CheckMATE* strategic planning software at **www.checkmateplan.com** offers a version especially for small businesses.

CONCLUSION

The main appeal of any managerial approach is the expectation that it will enhance organizational performance. This is especially true of strategic management. Through involvement in strategic-management activities, managers and employees achieve a better understanding of an organization's priorities and operations. Strategic management allows organizations to be efficient, but more important, it allows them to be effective. Although strategic management does not guarantee organizational success, the process allows proactive rather than reactive decision making. Strategic management may represent a radical change in philosophy for some organizations, so strategists must be trained to anticipate and constructively respond to questions and issues as they arise. The sixteen strategies discussed in this chapter can represent a new beginning for many firms, especially if managers and employees in the organization understand and support the plan for action.

We invite you to visit the David page on the Prentice Hall Companion Website at **www.prenhall.com/david** for this chapter's World Wide Web exercise.

KEY TERMS AND CONCEPTS

Acquisition (p. 180)

Backward Integration (p. 163)

Bankruptcy (p. 171)

Combination Strategy (p. 160)

Concentric Diversification (p. 169)

Conglomerate Diversification (p. 170)

Cooperative Arrangements (p. 177)

Cost Leadership (p. 175)

Differentiation (p. 175)

Diversification Strategies (p. 167)

Divestiture (p. 173)

Focus (p. 175)

Forward Integration (p. 161)

Franchising (p. xxx)

Generic Strategies (p. 175)

Horizontal Diversification (p. 169)

Horizontal Integration (p. 164)

Hostile Takeover (p. 180)

Integration Strategies (p. 165)

Intensive Strategies (p. 165)

Joint Venture (p. 177)

Leveraged Buyout (p. 182)

Liquidation (p. 173)

Long-Term Objectives (p. 158)

Market Development (p. 165)

Market Penetration (p. 165)

Merger (p. 180)

Outsourcing (p. 163)

Product Development (p. 166)

Retrenchment (p. 170)

Takeover (p. 180)

Vertical Integration (p. 160)

ISSUES FOR REVIEW AND DISCUSSION

1. How does strategy formulation differ for a small versus a large organization? How does it differ for a for-profit versus a nonprofit organization?
2. Give recent examples of market penetration, market development, and product development.
3. Give recent examples of forward integration, backward integration, and horizontal integration.
4. Give recent examples of concentric diversification, horizontal diversification, and conglomerate diversification.
5. Give recent examples of joint venture, retrenchment, divestiture, and liquidation.
6. Do you think hostile takeovers are unethical? Why or why not?
7. What are the major advantages and disadvantages of diversification?
8. What are the major advantages and disadvantages of an integrative strategy?

9. How does strategic management differ in profit and nonprofit organizations?
10. Why is it not advisable to pursue too many strategies at once?
11. Consumers can purchase tennis shoes, food, cars, boats, and insurance on the Internet. Are there any products today than cannot be purchased online? What is the implication for traditional retailers?
12. What are the pros and cons of a firm merging with a rival firm?
13. Does the United States lead in small business start-ups globally?
14. Visit the *CheckMATE* Strategic Planning software Web site at **www.checkmateplan.com**, and discuss the benefits offered.
15. Read one of the suggested current readings at the end of this chapter. Prepare a five-minute oral report on the topic.

NOTES

1. JOHN BYRNE, "Strategic Planning—It's Back," *Business Week* (August 26, 1996): 46.
2. STEVEN C. BRANDT, *Strategic Planning in Emerging Companies* (Reading, MA: Addison-Wesley, 1981). Reprinted with permission of the publisher.

3. ROB WHERRY, "Ice Cream Wars," *Forbes* (May 28, 2001): 160.
4. Adapted from F.R. DAVID, "How Do We Choose Among Alternative Growth Strategies?" *Managerial Planning* 33, no. 4 (January–February 1985): 14–17, 22.

5. Ibid.
6. KENNETH DAVIDSON, "Do Megamergers Make Sense?" *Journal of Business Strategy* 7, no. 3 (Winter 1987): 45.
7. op. cit., DAVID.
8. Ibid.
9. KELLY BARRON, "Culture Gap," *Forbes* (March 19, 2001): 62.
10. op. cit., DAVID.
11. Ibid.
12. THOMAS KELLNER, "A Tough Haul," *Forbes* (March 19, 2001): 186.
13. SHEILA MUTO, "Seeing a Boost, Hospitals Turn to Retail Stores," *Wall Street Journal* (November 7, 2001): B1 & B8.
14. op. cit., DAVID.
15. op. cit., DAVID.
16. BRUCE ORWALL, "ESPN Adds Entertainment Shows To Its Playbook." *Wall Street Journal* (March 6, 2002): B1.
17. Ibid.
18. MIKE SNIDER, "E-mail Use May Force Postal Service Cuts," *USA Today* (October 20, 1999): 1A.
19. CHRISTINE DUGAS, "Bankruptcy filings reach record 1.5 million," *USA Today* (February 20, 2002): 1B.
20. op. cit., DAVID.
21. Ibid.
22. Ibid.
23. KATHRYN RUDIE HARRIGAN, "Joint Ventures: Linking for a Leap Forward," *Planning Review* 14, no. 4 (July–August 1986): 10.
24. MATTHEW SCHIFRIN, "Partner or Perish," *Forbes* (May 21, 2001): 26.
25. Ibid., p. 28.
26. Ibid., p. 28.
27. GARY MCWILLIAMS, "Dell Computer, EMC Plan Sales Alliance," *Wall Street Journal* (September 25, 2001), B4.
28. GREGORY WHITE, "In Asia, GM Pins Hopes on a Delicate Web of Alliances," *Wall Street Journal* (October 23, 2001): A23.
29. NIKHIL HUTHEESING, "Marital Blisters," *Forbes* (May 21, 2001): 32.
30. Ibid., p. 32.
31. STEVEN RATTNER, "Mergers: Windfalls or Pitfalls?" *The Wall Street Journal* (October 11, 1999): A22. Also, NIKHIL DEOGUN, "Merger Wave Spurs More Stock Wipeouts," *The Wall Street Journal* (November 29, 1999): C1.
32. PETER KRASS, "Why Do We Do It," *Across the Board*, (May–June 2001): 23.
33. Ibid., p. 24.
34. ROBERT DAVIS, "Net Empowering Patients," *USA Today* (July 14, 1999): 1A.
35. *Hospital* (May 5, 1991): 16.
36. Some recent articles are KEITH D. BROUTHERS, FLORIS ANDRIESSEN, and IGOR NICOLAES, "Driving Blind: Strategic Decision-Making in Small Companies," *Long Range Planning* 31 (1998): 130–138; KARGAR, JAVAD, "Strategic Planning System Characteristics and Planning Effectiveness in Small Mature Firms," *Mid-Atlantic Journal of Business* 32, no. 1 (1996): 19–35; PEEL, MICHAEL J. and JOHN BRIDGE, "How Planning and Capital Budgeting Improve SME Performance," *Long Range Planning* 31, no. 6 (1998): 848–856; SMELTZER, LARRY R., GAIL L. FANN, and V. NEAL NIKOLAISEN, "Environmental Scanning Practices in Small Business," *Journal of Small Business Management* 26, no. 3 (1988): 55–63; STEINER, MICHAEL P. and OLAF SOLEM, "Factors for Success in Small Manufacturing Firms," *Journal of Small Business Management* 26, no. 1 (1988): 51–57.
37. ANNE CAREY and GRANT JERDING, "Internet's Reach on Campus," *USA Today* (August 26, 1999): A1. Also, BILL MEYERS, "It's a Small-Business World," *USA Today* (July 30, 1999): B1–2.

CURRENT READINGS

ALLEN, SANDY, and ASHOK CHANDRASHEKAR. "Outsourcing Services: The Contract Is Just the Beginning." *Business Horizons* 43, no. 2 (March–April 2000): 25.

BAUM, J. ROBERT, EDWIN A. LOCKE, and KEN G. SMITH. "A Multidimensional Model of Venture Growth." *The Academy of Management Journal* 44, no. 2 (April 2001): 292.

CAPRON, L., W. MITCHELL, and A. SWAMINATHAN. "Asset Divestiture Following Horizontal Acquisitions: A Dynamic View." *Strategic Management Journal* 22, no. 9 (September 2001): 817.

CHURCHILL, NEIL C., and JOHN W. MULLINS. "How Fast Can Your Company Afford to Grow?" *Harvard Business Review* (May 2001): 135.

DELMAS, MAGALI A., and ANN K. TERLAAK. "A Framework for Analyzing Environmental Voluntary Agreements." *California Management Review* 43, no. 3 (Spring 2001): 44.

FROST, T. S. "The Geographic Sources of Foreign Subsidiaries' Innovations." *Strategic Management Journal* 22, no. 2 (February 2001): 101.

GARVIN, DAVID A., and MICHAEL A. ROBERTO. "What You Don't Know About Making Decisions." *Harvard Business Review* (September 2001): 108.

GILLEY, K. MATTHEW, and ABDUL RASHEED. "Making More by Doing Less: An Analysis of Outsourcing and Its Effects on Firm Performance." *Journal of Management* 26, no. 4 (2000): 763.

GUPTA, ANIL K., and VIJAY GOVINDARAJAN. "Managing Global Expansion: A Conceptual Framework." *Business Horizons* 43, no. 2 (March–April 2000): 45.

GUPTA, ANIL K., and VIJAY GOVINDARAJAN. "Converting Global Presence into Global Competitive Advantage." *The Academy of Management Executive* 15, no. 2 (May 2001): 45.

HAMBRICK, D. C., J. LI, K. XIN, and A. S. TSUI. "Compositional Gaps and Downward Spirals in International Joint Venture." *Strategic Management Journal* 22, no. 11 (November 2001): 1033.

HENSMANS, MANUEL, FRANS A. J. VAN DEN BOSH, and HENK W. VOLBERDA. "Clicks vs. Bricks in the Emerging Online Financial Services Industry." *Long Range Planning* 34, no. 2 (April 2001): 231.

HOFFMAN, WERNER H., and ROMAN SCHLOSSER. "Success Factors of Strategic Alliances in Small and Medium-sized Enterprises—An Empirical Survey." *Long Range Planning* 34, no. 3 (June 2001): 357.

INSINGA, RICHARD C., and MICHAEL J. WERLE. "Linking Outsourcing to Business Strategy." *The Academy of Management Executive* 14, no. 4 (November 2000): 58.

JUDGE, WILLIAM Q., and JOEL A. RYMAN. "The Shared Leadership Challenge in Strategic Alliances: Lessons from the US Healthcare Industry." *The Academy of Management Executive* 15, no. 2 (May 2001): 71.

KERNS, CHARLES D. "Strengthen Your Business Partnership: A Framework and Application." *Business Horizons* 43, no. 4 (July–August 2000): 17.

KUEMMERLE, WALTER. "Go Global—or No?" *Harvard Business Review* (June 2001): 37.

LUO, Y. "Product Diversification in International Joint Ventures: Performances Implications in an Emerging Market." *Strategic Management Journal* 23, no. 1 (January 2002): 1.

MARKS, MITCHELL LEE, and PHILIP H. MIRVIS. "Making Mergers and Acquisitions Work: Strategic and Psychological Preparation." *The Academy of Management Executive* 15, no. 2 (May 2001): 80.

MCCARTY, WILLIAM, MARK KASOFF, and DOUG SMITH. "The Importance of International Business at the Local Level." *Business Horizons* 43, no. 3 (May–June 2000): 35.

MONTI, JOSEPH A., and GEORGE S. YIP. "Taking the High Road When Going International." *Business Horizons* 43, no. 4 (July–August 2000): 65.

PARKHE, ARVIND. "Executive Briefing/Global Business Alliances." *Business Horizons* 43, no. 5 (September–October 2000): 2.

RAMASWAMY, K. "Organizational Ownership, Competitive Intensity, and Firm Performance: An Empirical Study of the Indian Manufacturing Sector." *Strategic Management Journal* 22, no. 10 (October 2001): 989.

SCHULZE, W. S., A. MAINKAR, and R. W. COTTERILL. "Ecological Investigation of Firm-Effects in Horizontal Mergers." *Strategic Management Journal* 22, no. 4 (April 2001): 335.

SMITH, KEN G., WALTER J. FERRIER, and CURTIS M. GRIMM. "King of the Hill: Dethroning the Industry Leader." *The Academy of Management Executive* 15, no. 2 (May 2001): 59.

SONG, MICHAEL, and MITZI M. MONTOYA-WEISS. "The Effect of Perceived Technological Uncertainty on Japanese New Product Development." *The Academy of Management Journal* 44, no. 1 (February 2001): 61.

SWINK, MORGAN L., and VINCENT A. MABERT. "Product Development Partnerships: Balancing the Needs of OEMs and Suppliers." *Business Horizons* 43, no. 3 (May–June 2000): 59.

VERMEULEN, FREEK, and HARRY BARKEMA. "Learning Through Acquisitions." *Academy of Management* 44, no. 3 (June 2001): 457.

WOLFINBARGER, MARY, and MARY C. GILLY. "Shopping Online for Freedom, Control, and Fun." *California Management Review* 43, no. 2 (Winter 2001): 34.

WRIGHT, P., M. KROLL, A. LADO, and B. VAN MESS. "The Structure of Ownership and Corporate Acquisition Strategies." *Strategic Management Journal* 23, no. 1 (January 2002): 41.

EXPERIENTIAL EXERCISES

EXPERIENTIAL EXERCISE 5A ▶

What Happened at American Airlines (AMR) in the Year 2002?

PURPOSE

In performing business policy case analysis, you will need to find epilogue information about the respective companies to determine what strategies actually were employed since the time of the case. Comparing *what actually happened* with *what you would have recommended and expected to happen* is an important part of business policy case analysis. Do not recommend what the firm actually did, unless in-depth analysis of the situation at the time reveals those strategies to have been best among all feasible alternatives. This exercise gives you experience conducting library research to determine what strategies airlines pursued in 2002.

INSTRUCTIONS

Step 1   Look up American Airlines, US Air, and United Airlines on the Internet. Find some recent articles about firms in the airline industry. Scan Moody's, Dun & Bradstreet, and Standard & Poor's publications for information. Check the **www.investor.stockpoint.com** Web site.

Step 2   Summarize your findings in a three-page report entitled "Strategies of American Airlines in 2002." Also include your personal reaction to American Airlines strategies in terms of their attractiveness.

EXPERIENTIAL EXERCISE 5B ▶

Examining Strategy Articles

PURPOSE

Strategy articles can be found weekly in journals, magazines, and newspapers. By reading and studying strategy articles, you can gain a better understanding of the strategic-management process. Several of the best journals in which to find corporate strategy articles are *Planning Review, Long Range Planning, Journal of Business Strategy*, and *Strategic Management Journal*. These journals are devoted to reporting the results of empirical research in strategic management. They apply strategic-management concepts to specific organizations and industries. They introduce new strategic-management techniques and provide short case studies on selected firms.

Other good journals in which to find strategic-management articles are *Harvard Business Review, Sloan Management Review, Business Horizons, California Management Review, Academy of Management Review, Academy of Management Journal, Academy of Management Executive, Journal of Management*, and *Journal of Small Business Management*.

In addition to journals, many magazines regularly publish articles that focus on business strategies. Several of the best magazines in which to find applied strategy articles are *Dun's Business Month, Fortune, Forbes, Business Week, Inc.*, and *Industry Week*. Newspapers such as *USA Today, The Wall Street Journal, The New York Times,* and *Barrons* cover strategy events when they occur—for example, a joint venture announcement, a bankruptcy declaration, a new advertising campaign start, acquisition of a company, divestiture of a division, a chief executive officer's hiring or firing, or a hostile takeover attempt.

In combination, journal, magazine, and newspaper articles can make the business policy course more exciting. They allow current strategies of profit and nonprofit organizations to be identified and studied.

INSTRUCTIONS

Step 1   Go to your college library and find a recent journal article that focuses on a strategic-management topic. Select your article from one of the journals listed earlier, not from a magazine. Copy the article and bring it to class.

Step 2   Give a three-minute oral report summarizing the most important information in your article. Include comments giving your personal reaction to the article. Pass your article around in class.

EXPERIENTIAL EXERCISE 5C ▶

Classifying Some Year 2002 Strategies

PURPOSE

This exercise can improve your understanding of various strategies by giving you experience classifying strategies. This skill will help you use the strategy-formulation tools presented later. Consider the following ten year 2002 strategies by various firms:

1. Swedish phone company Telia AB acquired Finland's phone company, Sonera Corp. in 2002. This was the first merger of two national phone companies in Europe.

2. eBay shut down its Internet auction operations in Japan in March 2002, conceding its market share there to Yahoo! and Japan's Softbank Corp.

3. General Electric announced it would sell off its property-and-casualty insurance operations.

4. Japan's top pharmaceutical company, Takeda Chemical Industries, is increasing its outsourcing of drug manufacturing operations from 30 percent in 2002 to 70 percent in 2006.

5. Ford is totally redesigning its Ford Expedition and Lincoln Navigator sport-utility-vehicles (SUVs) to reverse falling sales and profits.

6. Travelocity.com acquired Site59.com, a "last-minute" travel company.

7. Dell Computer signed a $5 billion contract to have Philips Electronics NV supply its computer tubes, monitors, and peripherals.

8. Merck & Co., the large drug company, is selling off its pharmacy-benefits division, Medco.

9. Adolph Coors Co. of Colorado acquired Carling Brewers of the United Kingdom.

10. eBay acquired NeoCom of Taiwan in bid to expand into that country.

INSTRUCTIONS

Step 1   On a separate sheet of paper, number from 1 to 10. These numbers correspond to the strategies described above.

Step 2   What type of strategy best describes the 10 actions cited above? Indicate your answers.

Step 3   Exchange papers with a classmate, and grade each other's paper as your instructor gives the right answers.

EXPERIENTIAL EXERCISE 5D ▶

How Risky Are Various Alternative Strategies?

PURPOSE

This exercise focuses on how risky various alternative strategies are for organizations to pursue. Different degrees of risk are based largely on varying degrees of *externality*, defined as movement away from present business into new markets and products. In general, the greater the degree of externality, the greater the probability of loss resulting from unexpected events. High-risk strategies generally are less attractive than low-risk strategies.

INSTRUCTIONS

Step 1   On a separate sheet of paper, number vertically from 1 to 10. Think of 1 as "most risky," 2 as "next most risky," and so forth to 10, "least risky."

Step 2   Write the following strategies beside the appropriate number to indicate how risky you believe the strategy is to pursue: horizontal integration, horizontal diversification, liquidation, forward integration, backward integration, product development, market development, market penetration, joint venture/partnering, and conglomerate diversification.

Step 3   Grade your paper as your teacher gives you the right answers and supporting rationale. Each correct answer is worth 10 points.

EXPERIENTIAL EXERCISE 5E ▶

Developing Alternative Strategies for My University

PURPOSE

It is important for representatives from all areas of a college or university to identify and discuss alternative strategies that could benefit faculty, students, alumni, staff, and other constituencies. As you complete this exercise, notice the learning and understanding that occurs as people express differences of opinions. Recall that *the process of planning is more important than the document.*

INSTRUCTIONS

Step 1   Recall or locate the external opportunity/threat and internal strength/weakness factors that you identified as part of Experiential Exercise 1D. If you did not do that exercise, discuss now as a class important external and internal factors facing your college or university.

Step 2   Identify and put on the chalkboard alternative strategies that you feel could benefit your college or university. Your proposed actions should allow the institution to capitalize on particular strengths, improve upon certain weaknesses, avoid external threats, and/or take advantage of particular external opportunities. List at least twenty possible strategies on the board. Number the strategies as they are written on the board.

Step 3   On a separate sheet of paper, number from 1 to the total number of strategies listed on the board. Everyone in class individually should rate the strategies identified, using a 1 to 3 scale, where 1 = *I do not support implementation*, 2 = *I am neutral about implementation*, and 3 = *I strongly support implementation*. In rating the strategies, recognize that your institution cannot do everything desired or potentially beneficial.

Step 4   Go to the board and record your ratings in a row beside the respective strategies. Everyone in class should do this, going to the board perhaps by rows in the class.

Step 5   Sum the ratings for each strategy so that a prioritized list of recommended strategies is obtained. This prioritized list reflects the collective wisdom of your class. Strategies with the highest score are deemed best.

Step 6   Discuss how this process could enable organizations to achieve understanding and commitment from individuals.

Step 7   Share your class results with a university administrator, and ask for comments regarding the process and top strategies recommended.

EXPERIENTIAL EXERCISE 5F ▶

Lessons in Doing Business Globally

PURPOSE

The purpose of this exercise is to discover some important lessons learned by local businesses that do businesses internationally.

INSTRUCTIONS

Contact several local business leaders by phone. Find at least three firms that engage in international or export operations. Ask the businessperson to give you several important lessons that his or her firm has learned in doing business globally. Record the lessons on paper, and report your findings to the class.

6

STRATEGY ANALYSIS AND CHOICE

CHAPTER OBJECTIVES

After studying this chapter, you should be able to do the following:

1. Describe a three-stage framework for choosing among alternative strategies.
2. Explain how to develop a TOWS Matrix, SPACE Matrix, BCG Matrix, IE Matrix, and QSPM.
3. Identify important behavioral, political, ethical, and social responsibility considerations in strategy analysis and choice.
4. Discuss the role of intuition in strategic analysis and choice.
5. Discuss the role of organizational culture in strategic analysis and choice.
6. Discuss the role of a board of directors in choosing among alternative strategies.

NOTABLE QUOTES

Strategic management is not a box of tricks or a bundle of techniques. It is analytical thinking and commitment of resources to action. But quantification alone is not planning. Some of the most important issues in strategic management cannot be quantified at all.

PETER DRUCKER

Objectives are not commands; they are commitments. They do not determine the future; they are the means to mobilize resources and energies of an organization for the making of the future.

PETER DRUCKER

Life is full of lousy options.

GENERAL P. X. KELLEY

When a crisis forces choosing among alternatives, most people will choose the worst possible one.

RUDIN'S LAW

Strategy isn't something you can nail together in slapdash fashion by sitting around a conference table.

TERRY HALLER

Planning is often doomed before it ever starts, either because too much is expected of it or because not enough is put into it.

T. J. CARTWRIGHT

To acquire or not to acquire, that is the question.

ROBERT J. TERRY

Corporate boards need to work to stay away from the traps that force every member to go along with the majority. Devil's advocates represent one easy-to-implement solution.

CHARLES SCHWENK

Whether it's broke or not, fix it—make it better. Not just products, but the whole company if necessary.

BILL SAPORITO

Strategy analysis and choice largely involve making subjective decisions based on objective information. This chapter introduces important concepts that can help strategists generate feasible alternatives, evaluate those alternatives, and choose a specific course of action. Behavioral aspects of strategy formulation are described, including politics, culture, ethics, and social responsibility considerations. Modern tools for formulating strategies are described, and the appropriate role of a board of directors is discussed.

THE NATURE OF STRATEGY ANALYSIS AND CHOICE

As indicated by Figure 6–1, this chapter focuses on generating and evaluating alternative strategies, as well as an selecting strategies to pursue. Strategy analysis and choice seeks to determine alternative courses of action that could best enable the firm to achieve its mission and objectives. The firm's present strategies, objectives, and mission, coupled with the external and internal audit information, provide a basis for generating and evaluating feasible alternative strategies.

FIGURE 6–1

A Comprehensive Strategic-Management Model

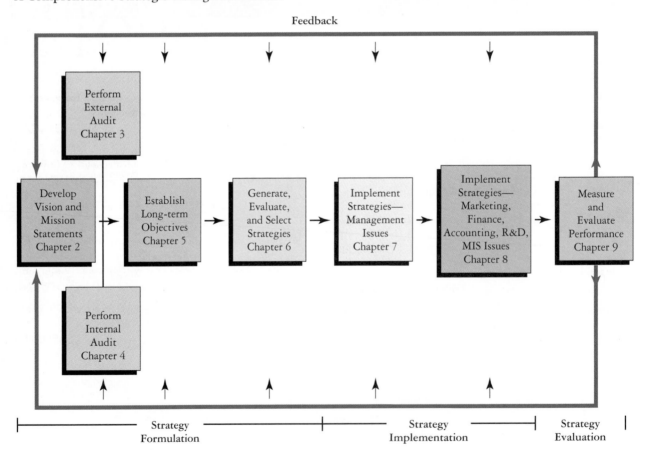

Unless a desperate situation confronts the firm, alternative strategies will likely represent incremental steps that move the firm from its present position to a desired future position. Alternative strategies do not come out of the wild blue yonder, they are derived from the firm's vision, mission, objectives, external audit, and internal audit; they are consistent with, or build on, past strategies that have worked well. Note from the Natural Environment Perspective box that natural environment attitudes of people can be an important factor in deciding among alternative strategies.

The Process of Generating and Selecting Strategies

Strategists never consider all feasible alternatives that could benefit the firm, because there are an infinite number of possible actions and an infinite number of ways to implement those actions. Therefore, a manageable set of the most attractive alternative strategies must be developed. The advantages, disadvantages, trade-offs, costs, and benefits of these strategies should be determined. This section discusses the process that many firms use to determine an appropriate set of alternative strategies.

VISIT THE NET

Cautions that planners must not usurp the responsibility of line managers in strategic planning.
http://www.csuchico.edu/mgmt/strategy/module1/sld050.htm

NATURAL ENVIRONMENT PERSPECTIVE

Formulating Strategies Based on Environmental Attitudes

Americans can be grouped into categories based on their attitudes, actions, and concern toward natural environment deterioration and preservation, Those individuals most concerned about the natural environment tend to be female, have higher household income, and live in the Midwest or Northeast. These individuals especially engage in activities such as not purchasing products from companies that are environmentally irresponsible, avoiding purchasing aerosol products, recycling paper and bottles, using biodegradable products, and contributing money to environmental groups. This information can be helpful to companies in formulating strategies such as market development (where to locate new facilities), product development (manufacturing new equipment or developing green products), and market penetration (whom to focus advertising efforts upon).

Individuals with a high concern rather than a low concern for the natural environment are relatively young, with a mean age of thirty-nine. They also are relatively smart: A full 69 percent have had some college or are college graduates. Individuals with a high concern for the natural environment have household incomes over $50,000, tend to be Internet savvy (62 percent own a personal computer), and tend to be female.

Web sites offering environmentally friendly products are **EthicalShopper.com**, **GreenHome.com**, and **EcoMall.com**, as well as **DolphinBlue.com**, which sells recycled paper and office supplies, and **EcoBaby. com**, which sells environmentally safe baby products. The Internet has made it easier for those who might not normally go out of their way to buy environmentally friendly products to find those products easily. Analysts expect the demand for green products to decline in the short run due to the economy and the fixation on terrorism; but in the long run, this demand should increase as young people grow into positions of power as heads of both households and businesses. Today's young people constitute the first generation to have been taught in school about the consequence of human actions on the earth's health.

Source: Adapted from the Roper Organization, 205 East 42nd Street, New York, NY 10017. Also from Joe Schwartz and Thomas Miller, "The Earth's Best Friends," *American Demographics* (February 1991): 28. Also adapted from Rebecca Gardyn, "Saving the Earth, One Click at a Time," *American Demographics* (January 2001): 30–33.

Identifying and evaluating alternative strategies should involve many of the managers and employees who earlier assembled the organizational vision and mission statements, performed the external audit, and conducted the internal audit. Representatives from each department and division of the firm should be included in this process, as was the case in previous strategy-formulation activities. Recall that involvement provides the best opportunity for managers and employees to gain an understanding of what the firm is doing and why, and to become committed to helping the firm accomplish its objectives.

All participants in the strategy analysis and choice activity should have the firm's external and internal audit information by their sides. This information, coupled with the firm's mission statement, will help participants crystallize in their own minds particular strategies that they believe could benefit the firm most. Creativity should be encouraged in this thought process.

Alternative strategies proposed by participants should be considered and discussed in a meeting or series of meetings. Proposed strategies should be listed in writing. When all feasible strategies identified by participants are given and understood, the strategies should be ranked in order of attractiveness by all participants, with 1 = should not be implemented, 2 = possibly should be implemented, 3 = probably should be implemented, and 4 = definitely should be implemented. This process will result in a prioritized list of best strategies that reflects the collective wisdom of the group.

A COMPREHENSIVE STRATEGY-FORMULATION FRAMEWORK

Important strategy-formulation techniques can be integrated into a three-stage decision-making framework, as shown in Figure 6–2. The tools presented in this framework are applicable to all sizes and types of organizations and can help strategists identify, evaluate, and select strategies.

Stage 1 of the formulation framework consists of the EFE Matrix, the IFE Matrix, and the Competitive Profile Matrix (CPM). Called the *Input Stage,* Stage 1 summarizes the basic input information needed to formulate strategies. Stage 2, called the *Matching*

FIGURE 6–2

The Strategy-Formulation Analytical Framework

STAGE 1: THE INPUT STAGE		
External Factor Evaluation (EFE) Matrix	Competitive Profile Matrix (CPM)	Internal Factor Evaluation (IFE) Matrix

STAGE 2: THE MATCHING STAGE				
Threats-Opportunities-Weaknesses-Strengths (TOWS) Matrix	Strategic Position and Action Evaluation (SPACE) Matrix	Boston Consulting Group (BCG) Matrix	Internal-External (IE) Matrix	Grand Strategy Matrix

STAGE 3: THE DECISION STAGE
Quantitative Strategic Planning Matrix (QSPM)

Stage, focuses upon generating feasible alternative strategies by aligning key external and internal factors. Stage 2 techniques include the Threats-Opportunities-Weaknesses-Strengths (TOWS) Matrix, the Strategic Position and Action Evaluation (SPACE) Matrix, the Boston Consulting Group (BCG) Matrix, the Internal-External (IE) Matrix, and the Grand Strategy Matrix. Stage 3, called the *Decision Stage,* involves a single technique, the Quantitative Strategic Planning Matrix (QSPM). A QSPM uses input information from Stage 1 to objectively evaluate feasible alternative strategies identified in Stage 2. A QSPM reveals the relative attractiveness of alternative strategies and thus provides an objective basis for selecting specific strategies.

All nine techniques included in the *strategy-formulation framework* require the integration of intuition and analysis. Autonomous divisions in an organization commonly use strategy-formulation techniques to develop strategies and objectives. Divisional analyses provide a basis for identifying, evaluating, and selecting among alternative corporate-level strategies.

Strategists themselves, not analytic tools, are always responsible and accountable for strategic decisions. Lenz emphasized that the shift from a words-oriented to a numbers-oriented planning process can give rise to a false sense of certainty; it can reduce dialogue, discussion, and argument as a means for exploring understandings, testing assumptions, and fostering organizational learning.[1] Strategists therefore must be wary of this possibility and use analytical tools to facilitate, rather than to diminish, communication. Without objective information and analysis, personal biases, politics, emotions, personalities, and *halo error* (the tendency to put too much weight on a single factor) unfortunately may play a dominant role in the strategy-formulation process.

THE INPUT STAGE

Procedures for developing an EFE Matrix, an IFE Matrix, and a CPM were presented in the previous two chapters. The information derived from these three matrices provides basic input information for the matching and decision stage matrices described later in this chapter.

The input tools require strategists to quantify subjectivity during early stages of the strategy-formulation process. Making small decisions in the input matrices regarding the relative importance of external and internal factors allows strategists to generate and evaluate alternative strategies more effectively. Good intuitive judgment is always needed in determining appropriate weights and ratings.

THE MATCHING STAGE

Strategy is sometimes defined as the match an organization makes between its internal resources and skills and the opportunities and risks created by its external factors.[2] The matching stage of the strategy-formulation framework consists of five techniques that can be used in any sequence: the TOWS Matrix, the SPACE Matrix, the BCG Matrix, the IE Matrix, and the Grand Strategy Matrix. These tools rely upon information derived from the input stage to match external opportunities and threats with internal strengths and weaknesses. *Matching* external and internal critical success factors is the key to effectively generating feasible alternative strategies. For example, a firm with excess working capital (an internal strength) could take advantage of the cell phone industry's 20 percent annual growth

VISIT THE NET

Gives purpose and characteristics of objectives. http://www.csuchico.edu/mgmt/strategy/module1/sld022.htm

VISIT THE NET

Gives example objectives. http://www.csuchico.edu/mgmt/strategy/module1/sld024.htm

TABLE 6-1   Matching Key External and Internal Factors to Formulate Alternative Strategies

KEY INTERNAL FACTOR		KEY EXTERNAL FACTOR		RESULTANT STRATEGY
Excess working capacity (an internal strength)	+	20% annual growth in the cell phone industry (an external opportunity)	=	Acquire Cellfone, Inc.
Insufficient capacity (an internal weakness)	+	Exit of two major foreign competitors from the industry (an external opportunity)	=	Pursue horizontal integration by buying competitors' facilities
Strong R&D expertise (an internal strength)	+	Decreasing numbers of younger adults (an external threat)	=	Develop new products for older adults
Poor employee morale (an internal weakness)	+	Strong union activity (an external threat)	=	Develop a new employee benefits package

rate (an external opportunity) by acquiring Cellfone, Inc., a firm in the cell phone industry. This example portrays simple one-to-one matching. In most situations, external and internal relationships are more complex, and the matching requires multiple alignments for each strategy generated. The basic concept of matching is illustrated in Table 6–1.

Any organization, whether military, product-oriented, service-oriented, governmental, or even athletic, must develop and execute good strategies to win. A good offense without a good defense, or vice versa, usually leads to defeat. Developing strategies that use strengths to capitalize on opportunities could be considered an offense, whereas strategies designed to improve upon weaknesses while avoiding threats could be termed defensive. Every organization has some external opportunities and threats and internal strengths and weaknesses that can be aligned to formulate feasible alternative strategies.

The Threats-Opportunities-Weaknesses-Strengths (TOWS) Matrix

The *Threats-Opportunities-Weaknesses-Strengths (TOWS) Matrix* is an important matching tool that helps managers develop four types of strategies: SO (strengths-opportunities) Strategies, WO (weaknesses-opportunities) Strategies, ST (strengths-threats) Strategies, and WT (weaknesses-threats) Strategies.[3] Matching key external and internal factors is the most difficult part of developing a TOWS Matrix and requires good judgment—and there is no one best set of matches. Note in Table 6-1 that the first, second, third, and fourth strategies are SO, WO, ST, and WT strategies, respectively.

SO Strategies use a firm's internal strengths to take advantage of external opportunities. All managers would like their organizations to be in a position in which internal strengths can be used to take advantage of external trends and events. Organizations generally will pursue WO, ST, or WT strategies in order to get into a situation in which they can apply SO Strategies. When a firm has major weaknesses, it will strive to overcome them and make them strengths. When an organization faces major threats, it will seek to avoid them in order to concentrate on opportunities.

WO Strategies aim at improving internal weaknesses by taking advantage of external opportunities. Sometimes key external opportunities exist, but a firm has internal weaknesses that prevent it from exploiting those opportunities. For example, there may be a high demand for electronic devices to control the amount and timing of fuel injection in automobile engines (opportunity), but a certain auto parts manufacturer may lack the technology required for producing these devices (weakness). One possible WO Strategy would be to acquire this technology by forming a joint venture with a firm having competency in this area. An alternative WO Strategy would be to hire and train people with the required technical capabilities.

VISIT THE NET

Gives a nice sample strategic plan, including the bases for developing a TOWS Matrix.
http://www.planware.org/strategicsample.htm

ST Strategies use a firm's strengths to avoid or reduce the impact of external threats. This does not mean that a strong organization should always meet threats in the external environment head-on. An example of ST Strategy occurred when Texas Instruments used an excellent legal department (a strength) to collect nearly $700 million in damages and royalties from nine Japanese and Korean firms that infringed on patents for semi-conductor memory chips (threat). Rival firms that copy ideas, innovations, and patented products are a major threat in many industries. This is still a major problem for U.S. firms selling products in China.

WT Strategies are defensive tactics directed at reducing internal weakness and avoiding external threats. An organization faced with numerous external threats and internal weaknesses may indeed be in a precarious position. In fact, such a firm may have to fight for its survival, merge, retrench, declare bankruptcy, or choose liquidation.

A schematic representation of the TOWS Matrix is provided in Figure 6–3. Note that a TOWS Matrix is composed of nine cells. As shown, there are four key factor cells, four strategy cells, and one cell that is always left blank (the upper-left cell). The four strat-

E-COMMERCE PERSPECTIVE

Most U.S. Servicepersons May Soon Carry Pocket Computers

The USS *McFaul,* a U.S. destroyer stationed offshore near Afghanistan, is a designated "test platform" for handheld computers. Tests are proving to be very successful. Sailors on board download their e-mail and access the ship's Plan of the Day by plugging into infrared ports located throughout the ship. In Afghanistan, the handheld computers are being used by commandos on the ground as logistical and tactical weapons to gain a competitive advantage. Programs are available to map enemy locations, track personnel, and conduct heat-stress surveys. The U.S. Army says, "We are trying to provide our soldiers with information dominance." The U.S. Army now uses handheld computers to expedite such tasks as keeping track of equipment and food supplies. In 2001, Palm, Inc., sold between 30,000 and 50,000 Palms to the Navy and 25,000 to 30,000 units to the Army. The devices are mostly being used for data collection and information dissemination, but their uses are being expanded daily.

Soldiers and sailors carry the devices into action because the devices can track enemy and friendly troop and equipment movements. Handheld computers can interact with laser binoculars. Commander Sutherland of the U.S. Atlantic Fleet says, "Handheld computers are a tremendous morale booster among servicepersons." They can send and receive e-mail messages as well as manage military operations more efficiently and effectively with these devices. Companies producing these products today include Palm, Inc.; Symbol Technologies, Inc.; Paravant Computer Systems; and Microsoft. Mobile phones also are increasingly being used in the military. The following table gives worldwide mobile-phone market leaders.

Source: Adapted from Pui-Wing Tam, "U.S. Forces Pack Pocket Computers in Afghanistan," *The Wall Street Journal* (October 23, 2001): B1. Also, adapted from David Pringle, "Motorola Hopes Early Push in 3G Market Yields Gains," *Wall Street Journal* (March 28, 2002): B4.

COMPANY	—SHIPMENTS, IN MILLIONS OF UNITS—			—MARKET SHARE—	
	2001	2000	% CHANGE	2001	2000
Nokia	139.67	126.37	+10.5%	35.0%	30.6%
Motorola	59.09	60.09	− 1.7	14.8	14.6
Siemens	29.75	26.99	+10.2	7.4	6.5
Samsung	28.23	20.64	+36.8	7.1	5.0
Ericsson	26.96	41.47	−35.0	6.7	10.0
Others	115.88	137.17	−15.5	29.0	33.2
Total	399.58	412.73	− 3.2	—	—

FIGURE 6–3

The TOWS Matrix

	STRENGTHS—S	WEAKNESSES—W
Always leave blank	1. 2. 3. 4. 5. 6. 7. 8. 9. 10. List strengths	1. 2. 3. 4. 5. 6. 7. 8. 9. 10. List weaknesses
OPPORTUNITIES—O 1. 2. 3. 4. 5. List opportunities 6. 7. 8. 9. 10.	SO STRATEGIES 1. 2. 3. 4. Use strengths to take 5. advantage of opportunities 6. 7. 8. 9. 10.	WO STRATEGIES 1. 2. 3. 4. Overcome weaknesses by 5. taking advantage of 6. opportunities 7. 8. 9. 10.
THREATS—T 1. 2. 3. 4. List threats 5. 6. 7. 8. 9. 10.	ST STRATEGIES 1. 2. 3. 4. Use strengths to avoid 5. threats 6. 7. 8. 9. 10.	WT STRATEGIES 1. 2. 3. 4. Minimize weaknesses and 5. avoid threats 6. 7. 8. 9. 10.

egy cells, labeled *SO, WO, ST,* and *WT,* are developed after completing four key factor cells, labeled *S, W, O,* and *T.* There are eight steps involved in constructing a TOWS Matrix:

1. List the firm's key external opportunities.
2. List the firm's key external threats.
3. List the firm's key internal strengths.
4. List the firm's key internal weaknesses.
5. Match internal strengths with external opportunities, and record the resultant SO Strategies in the appropriate cell.
6. Match internal weaknesses with external opportunities, and record the resultant WO Strategies.
7. Match internal strengths with external threats, and record the resultant ST Strategies.

FIGURE 6–4

TOWS Matrix for Carnival Cruise Lines in 2002

	STRENGTHS—S	WEAKNESSES—W
	1. Holds 34% market share 2. Largest fleet of ships 3. Six different cruise lines 4. Innovator in cruise travel industry 5. Largest variety of ships 6. Building largest cruise ship 7. High brand recognition 8. Headquartered in Miami 9. Internet friendly with online booking	1. Major loss in affiliated operations 2. Increased debt from building new ships 3. Not serving Asian market
OPPORTUNITIES—O 1. Air travel has decreased (9/11) 2. Asian market not being served 3. Possible acquisition of Princess Cruise Lines 4. New weather forecasting systems available 5. Rising demand for all-inclusive vacation packages 6. Families have increased disposable incomes 7. Marriage rates are up—more honeymoons	**SO STRATEGIES** 1. Increase capacity of ships to obtain travelers from air industry (S6, O1, O3) 2. Display the weather of vacation locations on Web site (S9, O4) 3. Offer Trans-Atlantic cruises (S6, O4) 4. Acquire P & O Princess (S1, O3)	**WO STRATEGIES** 1. Begin serving Japan and Pacific Islands (W3, O2, O3, O4) 2. Use weather forecasting to alert customers of potential storm during their vacation (W1, O4)
THREATS—T 1. Decrease in travel since 9/11 2. Terrorism 3. Competition within industry 4. Competition among other types of vacations 5. Economic recession 6. Chance of natural disasters 7. Increasing fuel prices 8. Changing government regulations	**ST STRATEGIES** 1. Advertising Carnival's ship variety, brand recognition, and safety policies (S3, S7, T1, T2, T5) 2. Advertise alternate vacations that are not affected by hurricane season (S3, T5, T7) 3. Offer discounts on Carnival Web site (S9, T6)	**WT STRATEGIES** 1. Lower prices of cruises during hurricane season (W1, T6) 2. Research viability of entering other foreign markets (W2, W3, T8, T9)

8. Match internal weaknesses with external threats, and record the resultant WT Strategies.

The purpose of each Stage 2 matching tool is to generate feasible alternative strategies, not to select or determine which strategies are best. Not all of the strategies developed in the TOWS Matrix, therefore, will be selected for implementation. A sample TOWS Matrix for Carnival Cruise Lines, is provided in Figure 6–4.

The strategy-formulation guidelines provided in Chapter 5 can enhance the process of matching key external and internal factors. For example, when an organization has both the capital and human resources needed to distribute its own products (internal strength) and distributors are unreliable, costly, or incapable of meeting the firm's needs (external threat), then forward integration can be an attractive ST Strategy. When a firm has excess production capacity (internal weakness) and its basic industry is experiencing declining annual sales and profits (external threat), then concentric diversification can be an effective WT Strategy. It is important to use specific, rather than general, strategy terms when developing a TOWS Matrix. In addition, it is important to include the "S1, O2"-type notation after each strategy in the TOWS Matrix. This notation reveals the rationale for each alternative strategy.

The Strategic Position and Action Evaluation (SPACE) Matrix

The *Strategic Position and Action Evaluation (SPACE) Matrix*, another important Stage 2 matching tool, is illustrated in Figure 6–5. Its four-quadrant framework indicates whether aggressive, conservative, defensive, or competitive strategies are most appropriate for a given organization. The axes of the SPACE Matrix represent two internal dimensions (*financial strength* [FS] and *competitive advantage* [CA]) and two external dimensions (*environmental stability* [ES] and *industry strength* [IS]). These four factors are the most important determinants of an organization's overall strategic position.[4]

Depending upon the type of organization, numerous variables could make up each of the dimensions represented on the taxes of the SPACE Matrix. Factors that were included earlier in the firm's EFE and IFE matrices should be considered in developing a SPACE Matrix. Other variables commonly included are given in Table 6–2 on page 206. For example, return on investment, leverage liquidity, working capital, and cash flow are commonly considered to be determining factors of an organization's financial strength. Like the TOWS Matrix, the SPACE Matrix should both be tailored to the particular organization being studied and based on factual information as much as possible.

The steps required to develop a SPACE Matrix are as follows:

1. Select a set of variables to define financial strength (FS), competitive advantage (CA), environmental stability (ES), and industry strength (IS).

2. Assign a numerical value ranging from +1 (worst) to +6 (best) to each of the variables that make up the FS and IS dimensions. Assign a numerical value ranging from −1 (best) to −6 (worst) to each of the variables that make up the ES and CA dimensions.

3. Compute an average score for FS, CA, IS, and ES by summing the values given to the variables of each dimension and then by dividing by the number of variables included in the respective dimension.

4. Plot the average scores for FS, IS, ES, and CA on the appropriate axis in the SPACE Matrix.

5. Add the two scores on the *x*-axis and plot the resultant point on X. Add the two scores on the *y*-axis and plot the resultant point on Y. Plot the intersection of the new *xy* point.

6. Draw a *directional vector* from the origin of the SPACE Matrix through the new intersection point. This vector reveals the type of strategies recommended for the organization: aggressive, competitive, defensive, or conservative.

Some examples of strategy profiles that can emerge from a SPACE analysis are shown in Figure 6–6 on page 207. The directional vector associated with each profile suggests the type of strategies to pursue: aggressive, conservative, defensive, or competi-

FIGURE 6–5

The SPACE Matrix

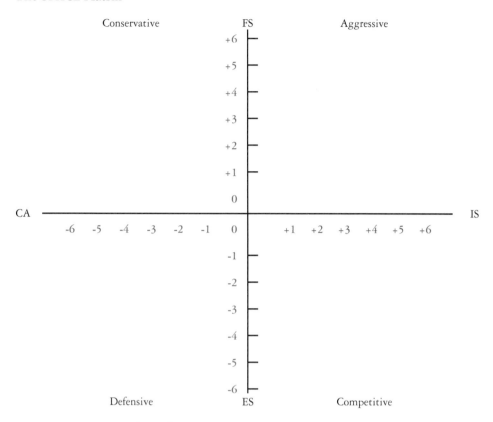

Source: H. Rowe, R. Mason, and K. Dickel, *Strategic Management and Business Policy: A Methodological Approach* (Reading, MA: Addison-Wesley Publishing Co. Inc., © 1982): 155. Reprinted with permission of the publisher.

tive. When a firm's directional vector is located in the *aggressive quadrant* (upper-right quadrant) of the SPACE Matrix, an organization is in an excellent position to use its internal strengths to (1) take advantage of external opportunities, (2) overcome internal weaknesses, and (3) avoid external threats. Therefore, market penetration, market development, product development, backward integration, forward integration, horizontal integration, conglomerate diversification, concentric diversification, horizontal diversification, or a combination strategy all can be feasible, depending on the specific circumstances that face the firm.

The directional vector may appear in the *conservative quadrant* (upper-left quadrant) of the SPACE Matrix, which implies staying close to the firm's basic competencies and not taking excessive risks. Conservative strategies most often include market penetration, market development, product development, and concentric diversification. The directional vector may be located in the lower-left or *defensive quadrant* of the SPACE Matrix, which suggests that the firm should focus on rectifying internal weaknesses and avoiding external threats. Defensive strategies include retrenchment, divestiture, liquidation, and concentric diversification. Finally, the directional vector may be located in the lower-right or *competitive quadrant* of the SPACE Matrix, indicating competitive strategies. Competitive strategies include backward, forward, and horizontal integration; market penetration; market development; product development; and joint ventures.

TABLE 6-2   **Example Factors that Make Up the SPACE Matrix Axes**

INTERNAL STRATEGIC POSITION	EXTERNAL STRATEGIC POSITION
Financial Strength (FS)	*Environmental Stability (ES)*
Return on investment	Technological changes
Leverage	Rate of inflation
Liquidity	Demand variability
Working capital	Price range of competing products
Cash flow	Barriers to entry into market
Ease of exit from market	Competitive pressure
Risk involved in business	Price elasticity of demand
Competitive Advantage (CA)	*Industry Strength (IS)*
Market share	Growth potential
Product quality	Profit potential
Product life cycle	Financial stability
Customer loyalty	Technological know-how
Competition's capacity utilization	Resource utilization
Technological know-how	Capital intensity
Control over suppliers and distributors	Ease of entry into market
	Productivity, capacity utilization

Source: H. Rowe, R. Mason, and K. Dickel, *Strategic Management and Business Policy: A Methodological Approach* (Reading, MA: Addison-Wesley Publishing Co. Inc., © 1982): 155–156. Reprinted with permission of the publisher.

A SPACE Matrix analysis for a bank is provided in Table 6–3 on page 208. Note that the competitive strategies are recommended.

The Boston Consulting Group (BCG) Matrix

Autonomous divisions (or profit centers) of an organization make up what is called a *business portfolio*. When a firm's divisions compete in different industries, a separate strategy often must be developed for each business. The *Boston Consulting Group (BCG) Matrix* and the Internal-External (IE) Matrix are designed specifically to enhance a multidivisional firm's efforts to formulate strategies. (BCG is a private management consulting firm based in Boston. BCG employs about 1,400 consultants worldwide but is cutting its workforce by 12 percent in 2002.)

The BCG Matrix graphically portrays differences among divisions in terms of relative market share position and industry growth rare. The BCG Matrix allows a multidivisional organization to manage its portfolio of businesses by examining the relative market share position and the industry growth rate of each division relative to all other divisions in the organization. *Relative market share position* is defined as the ratio of a division's own market share in a particular industry to the market share held by the largest rival firm in that industry. For example, in Table 6–4 on page 209, the relative market share of the *Wall Street Journal* is 1.78/2.24, which is 79 percent.

Relative market share position is given on the *x*-axis of the BCG Matrix. The midpoint on the *x*-axis usually is set at .50, corresponding to a division that has half the market share of the leading firm in the industry. The *y*-axis represents the industry growth rate in sales, measured in percentage terms. The growth rate percentages on the *y*-axis could range from −20 to +20 percent, with 0.0 being the midpoint. These numerical

FIGURE 6–6

Example Strategy Profiles

Aggressive Profiles

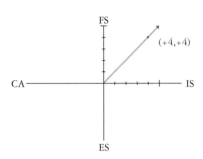

A financially strong firm that has achieved major competitive advantages in a growing and stable industry

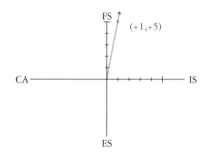

A firm whose financial strength is a dominating factor in the industry

Conservative Profiles

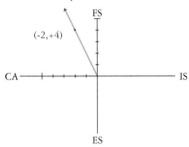

A firm that has achieved financial strength in a stable industry that is not growing; the firm has no major competitive advantages

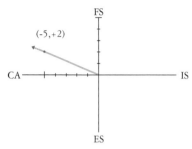

A firm that suffers from major competitive disadvantages in an industry that is technologically stable but declining in sales

Competitive Profiles

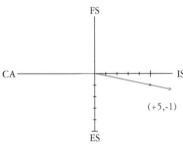

A firm with major competitive advantages in a high-growth industry

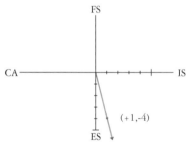

An organization that is competing fairly well in an unstable industry

Defensive Profiles

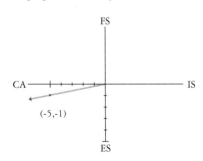

A firm that has a very weak competitive position in a negative growth, stable industry

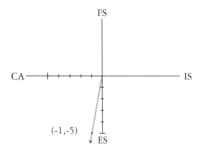

A financially troubled firm in a very unstable industry

Source: H. Rowe, R. Mason, and K. Dickel, *Strategic Management and Business Policy: A Methodological Approach* (Reading, MA: Addison-Wesley Publishing Co. Inc., © 1982): 155. Reprinted with permission of the publisher.

TABLE 6–3   A SPACE Matrix for a Bank

FINANCIAL STRENGTH	RATINGS
The bank's primary capital ratio is 7.23 percent, which is 1.23 percentage points over the generally required ratio of 6 percent.	1.0
The bank's return on assets is negative 0.77, compared to a bank industry average ratio of positive 0.70.	1.0
The bank's net income was $183 million, down 9 percent from a year earlier.	3.0
The bank's revenues increased 7 percent to $3.46 billion.	4.0
	9.0

INDUSTRY STRENGTH	
Deregulation provides geographic and product freedom.	4.0
Deregulation increases competition in the banking industry.	2.0
Pennsylvania's interstate banking law allows the bank to acquire other banks in New Jersey, Ohio, Kentucky, the District of Columbia, and West Virginia.	4.0
	10.0

ENVIRONMENTAL STABILITY	
Less-developed countries are experiencing high inflation and political instability.	−4.0
Headquartered in Pittsburgh, the bank historically has been heavily dependent on the steel, oil, and gas industries. These industries are depressed.	−5.0
Banking deregulation has created instability throughout the industry.	−4.0
	−13.0

COMPETITIVE ADVANTAGE	
The bank provides data processing services for more than 450 institutions in 38 states.	−2.0
Superregional banks, international banks, and nonbanks are becoming increasingly competitive.	−5.0
The bank has a large customer base.	−2.0
	−9.0

CONCLUSION

ES Average is −13.0 ÷ 3 = −4.33 IS Average is + 10.0 ÷ 3 = 3.33
CA Average is −9.0 ÷ 3 = −3.00 FS Average is + 9.0 ÷ 4 = 2.25
Directional Vector Coordinates: x-axis: −3.00 + (+3.33) = +0.33
　　　　　　　　　　　　　　　　y-axis: −4.33 + (+2.25) = −2.08
The bank should pursue Competitive Strategies.

ranges on the x- and y-axes are often used, but other numerical values could be established as deemed appropriate for particular organizations.

An example of a BCG Matrix appears in Figure 6–7 on page 210. Each circle represents a separate division. The size of the circle corresponds to the proportion of corporate revenue generated by that business unit, and the pie slice indicates the proportion of corporate profits generated by that division. Divisions located in Quadrant I of the BCG Matrix are called Question Marks, those located in Quadrant II are called Stars, those located in Quadrant III are called Cash Cows, and those divisions located in Quadrant IV are called Dogs. As indicated in the Global Perspective box on page 211, more Japanese firms are becoming Stars by changing policies that previously discouraged women from becoming managers.

- Question Marks—Divisions in Quadrant I have a low relative market share position, yet they compete in a high-growth industry. Generally these firms' cash needs are high and their cash generation is low. These businesses are called *Question*

TABLE 6-4

A. Market Share of the Ten Largest Banks in Central Europe

COMPANY	MARKET SHARE %
KBC NV of Belgium	11.7
Hypo Vereinsbank AG of Germany	9.9
Unicredito Italiano SpA of Italy	7.7
Societe Generale	7.7
Citibank of the USA	7.6
Erste Bank	7.4
BCI/Intesa	5.4
ING	4.4
RZB	4.0
Commerzbank	3.8
Other Banks	69.6%

B. Sales of the Ten Largest U.S. Newspapers

COMPANY	AVERAGE DAILY CIRCULATION (IN MILLIONS)
USA Today	2.24
The Wall Street Journal	1.78
The New York Times	1.11
The Los Angeles Times	0.97
The Washington Post	0.76
The New York Daily News	0.73
The Chicago Tribune	0.62
Newsday	0.58
Houston Chronicle	0.55
The New York Post	0.53

C. Market Share of the Leading U.S. Rental Car Companies

COMPANY	MARKET SHARE (%)
Hertz	29.1
Avis	22.6
National	15.4
Budget	12.0
Alamo	09.8
Dollar	08.9
Other	02.2

Source: Adapted from Matthew Karnitschnig, "Western Banks Quickly Expand Share of Market in Central and Eastern Europe," *The Wall Street Journal* (September 11, 2001): A21. Also, Matthew Rose and Patricia Callahan, "Can Newspapers Hold On to Postattack Readers?" *The Wall Street Journal* (October 30, 2001): B4. Also, Kortney Stringer, "Reservations Grow Over Rental-Car Industry's Weak Links," *Wall Street Journal* (November 14, 2001): B4.

Marks because the organization must decide whether to strengthen them by pursuing an intensive strategy (market penetration, market development, or product development) or to sell them.

- Stars—Quadrant II businesses (often called *Stars*) represent the organization's best long-run opportunities for growth and profitability. Divisions with a high relative market share and a high industry growth rate should receive substantial investment to maintain or strengthen their dominant positions. Forward, back-

FIGURE 6–7

The BCG Matrix

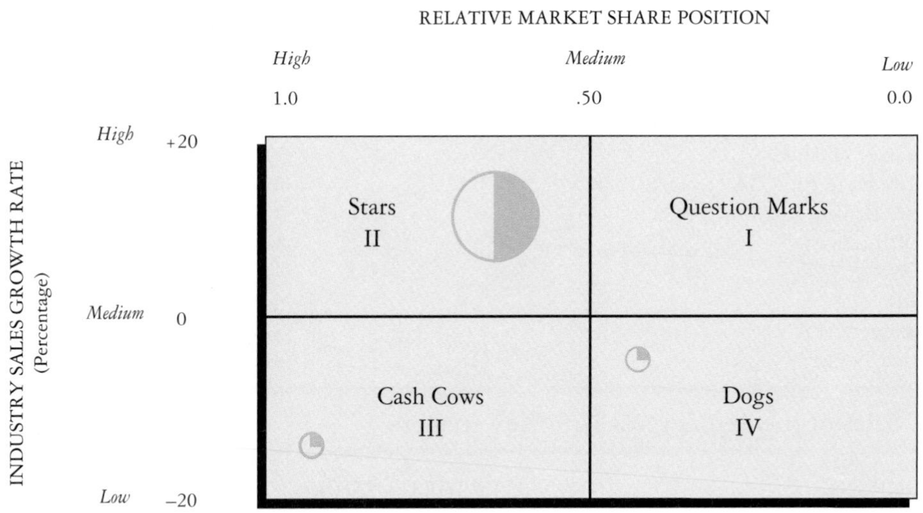

RELATIVE MARKET SHARE POSITION

Source: Adapted from Boston Consulting Group, *Perspectives on Experience* (Boston: The Boston Consulting Group, 1974).

ward, and horizontal integration; market penetration; market development; product development; and joint ventures are appropriate strategies for these divisions to consider.

- Cash Cows—Divisions positioned in Quadrant III have a high relative market share position but compete in a low-growth industry. Called *Cash Cows* because they generate cash in excess of their needs, they are often milked. Many of today's Cash Cows were yesterday's Stars. Cash Cow divisions should be managed to maintain their strong position for as long as possible. Product development or concentric diversification may be attractive strategies for strong Cash Cows. However, as a Cash Cow division becomes weak, retrenchment or divestiture can become more appropriate.

- Dogs—Quadrant IV divisions of the organization have a low relative market share position and compete in a slow- or no-market-growth industry; they are *Dogs* in the firm's portfolio. Because of their weak internal and external position, these businesses are often liquidated, divested, or trimmed down through retrenchment. When a division first becomes a Dog, retrenchment can be the best strategy to pursue because many Dogs have bounced back, after strenuous asset and cost reduction, to become viable, profitable divisions.

The major benefit of the BCG Matrix is that it draws attention to the cash flow, investment characteristics, and needs of an organization's various divisions. The divisions of many firms evolve over time: Dogs become Question Marks, Question Marks become Stars, Stars become Cash Cows, and Cash Cows become Dogs in an ongoing counterclockwise motion. Less frequently, Stars become Question Marks, Question Marks become Dogs, Dogs become Cash Cows, and Cash Cows become Stars (in a clockwise motion). In some organizations, no cyclical motion is apparent. Over time, organizations should strive to achieve a portfolio of divisions that are Stars.

One example of a BCG Matrix is provided in Figure 6–8 on page 212, which illustrates an organization composed of five divisions with annual sales ranging from $5,000 to $60,000. Division 1 has the greatest sales volume, so the circle representing that division is the largest one in the matrix. The circle corresponding to Division 5 is the smallest because its sales volume ($5,000) is least among all the divisions. The pie slices within the circles reveal the percent of corporate profits contributed by each division. As shown, Division 1 contributes the highest profit percentage, 39 percent. Notice in the diagram that Division 1 is considered a Star, Division 2 is a Question Mark, Division 3 is also a Question Mark, Division 4 is a Cash Cow, and Division 5 is a Dog.

The BCG Matrix, like all analytical techniques, has some limitations. For example, viewing every business as either a Star, Cash Cow, Dog, or Question Mark is an oversimplification; many businesses fall right in the middle of the BCG Matrix and thus are not easily classified. Furthermore, the BCG Matrix does not reflect whether or not various divisions or their industries are growing over time; that is, the matrix has no temporal qualities, but rather it is a snapshot of an organization at a given point in time. Finally, other variables besides relative market share position and industry growth rate in sales, such as size of the market and competitive advantages, are important in making strategic decisions about various divisions.

The Internal-External (IE) Matrix

The *Internal-External (IE) Matrix* positions an organization's various divisions in a nine-cell display, illustrated in Figure 6–9 on page 213. The IE Matrix is similar to the BCG Matrix in that both tools involve plotting organization divisions in a schematic diagram; this is why they are both called portfolio matrices. Also, the size of each circle represents the percentage sales contribution of each division, and pie slices reveal the percentage profit contribution of each division in both the BCG and IE Matrix.

GLOBAL PERSPECTIVE

Changing Role of Women in Japan

Japan's population is projected to decline by nearly half by the end of the twenty-first century, while the aging population puts a huge burden on working people. Consequently, the conservative and male-dominated Japanese legislature is reconsidering gender equality. In 1999, the Japanese legislature passed a sweeping "basic law" to promote equal participation in society by men and women. This law covers everything from equal hiring and promotion in business and government to common practices such as listing boys' names ahead of girls' names on class rosters in public schools. Also in 1999, the legislature passed a new law that bans sexual discrimination in the workplace. The law also bans child pornography and sex with minors. Further in 1999, Japan became the last member of the United Nations to approve relatively safe, low-dose birth control pills. These are all legislative victories for Japanese women who now feel more comfortable having children or

joining the workforce if they desire. New Japanese law also encourages men to join in helping women in child rearing and housework. Currently Japanese men do only 6 percent of the housework and 11 percent of the work caring for children or elders.

Any national culture that prohibits or discourages women from working outside the home disadvantages firms in that particular country as they strive to compete with firms in other countries that capitalize on the proven capability of women to perform equally with men in nearly all jobs. Certainly it will take years to change this type of business culture, but Japan got started in 1999. This business culture shift should enhance Japan's business competitiveness worldwide.

Source: Adapted from Steven Butler, "In Japan, Finally the Women Catch a Break," *U.S. News & World Report* (July 5, 1999): 41.

FIGURE 6–8

An Example BCG Matrix

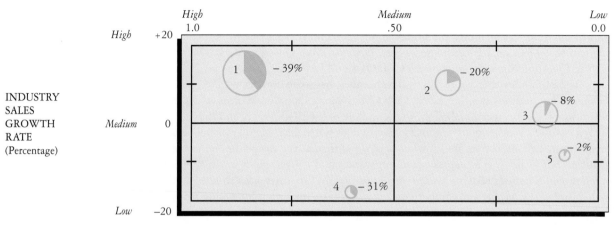

Division	Revenues	Percent Revenues	Profits	Percent Profits	Percent Market Share	Percent Growth Rate
1	$60,000	37	$10,000	39	80	+15
2	40,000	24	5,000	20	40	+10
3	40,000	24	2,000	8	10	1
4	20,000	12	8,000	31	60	−20
5	5,000	3	500	2	5	−10
Total	$165,000	100	$25,500	100		

But there are some important differences between the BCG Matrix and the IE Matrix. First, the axes are different. Also, the IE Matrix requires more information about the divisions than the BCG Matrix. Furthermore, the strategic implications of each matrix are different. For these reasons, strategists in multidivisional firms often develop both the BCG Matrix and the IE Matrix in formulating alternative strategies. A common practice is to develop a BCG Matrix and an IE Matrix for the present and then develop projected matrices to reflect expectations of the future. This before-and-after analysis forecasts the expected effect of strategic decisions on an organization's portfolio of divisions.

The IE Matrix is based on two key dimensions: the IFE total weighted scores on the x-axis and the EFE total weighted scores on the y-axis. Recall that each division of an organization should construct an IFE Matrix and an EFE Matrix for its part of the organization. The total weighted scores derived from the divisions allow construction of the corporate-level IE Matrix. On the x-axis of the IE Matrix, an IFE total weighted score of 1.0 to 1.99 represents a weak internal position; a score of 2.0 to 2.99 is considered average; and a score of 3.0 to 4.0 is strong. Similarly, on the y-axis, an EFE total weighted score of 1.0 to 1.99 is considered low; a score of 2.0 to 2.99 is medium; and a score of 3.0 to 4.0 is high.

The IE Matrix can be divided into three major regions that have different strategy implications. First, the prescription for divisions that fall into cells I, II, or IV can be described as *grow and build*. Intensive (market penetration, market development, and product development) or integrative (backward integration, forward integration, and horizontal integration) strategies can be most appropriate for these divisions. Second, divisions that fall into cells III, V, or VII can be managed best with *hold and maintain* strategies; market penetration and product development are two commonly employed

FIGURE 6–9

The Internal-External (IE) Matrix

THE IFE TOTAL WEIGHTED SCORES

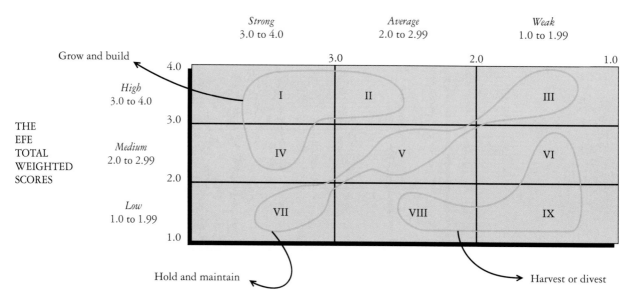

Source: The IE Matrix was developed from the General Electric (GE) Business Screen Matrix. For a description of the GE Matrix see Michael Allen, "Diagramming GE's Planning for What's WATT," in R. Allio and M. Pennington, eds., *Corporate Planning: Techniques and Applications.* (New York: AMACOM, 1979).

strategies for these types of divisions. Third, a common prescription for divisions that fall into cells VI, VIII, or IX is *harvest or divest*. Successful organizations are able to achieve a portfolio of businesses positioned in or around cell I in the IE Matrix.

An example of a completed IE Matrix is given in Figure 6–10 on page 214, which depicts an organization composed of four divisions. As indicated by the positioning of the circles, *grow and build* strategies are appropriate for Division 1, Division 2, and Division 3. Division 4 is a candidate for *harvest or divest*. Division 2 contributes the greatest percentage of company sales and thus is represented by the largest circle. Division 1 contributes the greatest proportion of total profits; it has the largest-percentage pie slice.

The Grand Strategy Matrix

In addition to the TOWS Matrix, SPACE Matrix, BCG Matrix, and IE Matrix, the *Grand Strategy Matrix* has become a popular tool for formulating alternative strategies. All organizations can be positioned in one of the Grand Strategy Matrix's four strategy quadrants. A firm's divisions likewise could be positioned. As illustrated in Figure 6–11 on page 215, the Grand Strategy Matrix is based on two evaluative dimensions: competitive position and market growth. Appropriate strategies for an organization to consider are listed in sequential order of attractiveness in each quadrant of the matrix.

Firms located in Quadrant I of the Grand Strategy Matrix are in an excellent strategic position. For these firms, continued concentration on current markets (market penetration and market development) and products (product development) is an appropriate strategy. It is unwise for a Quadrant I firm to shift notably from its established competitive advantages. When a Quadrant I organization has excessive resources, then

FIGURE 6–10

An Example IE Matrix

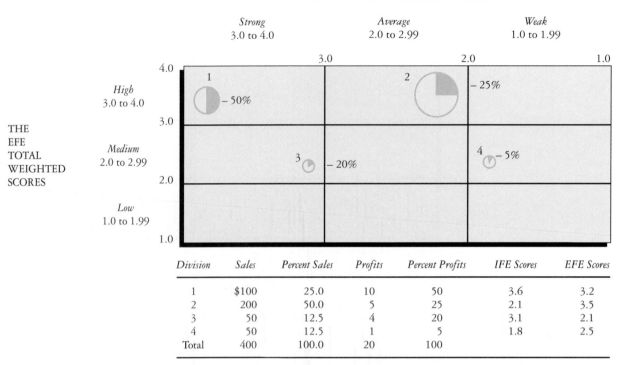

THE IFE TOTAL WEIGHTED SCORES

Division	Sales	Percent Sales	Profits	Percent Profits	IFE Scores	EFE Scores
1	$100	25.0	10	50	3.6	3.2
2	200	50.0	5	25	2.1	3.5
3	50	12.5	4	20	3.1	2.1
4	50	12.5	1	5	1.8	2.5
Total	400	100.0	20	100		

backward, forward, or horizontal integration may be effective strategies. When a Quadrant I firm is too heavily committed to a single product, then concentric diversification may reduce the risks associated with a narrow product line. Quadrant I firms can afford to take advantage of external opportunities in several areas: They can take risks aggressively when necessary.

Firms positioned in Quadrant II need to evaluate their present approach to the marketplace seriously. Although their industry is growing, they are unable to compete effectively, and they need to determine why the firm's current approach is ineffective and how the company can best change to improve its competitiveness. Because Quadrant II firms are in a rapid-market-growth industry, an intensive strategy (as opposed to integrative or diversification) is usually the first option that should be considered. However, if the firm is lacking a distinctive competence or competitive advantage, then horizontal integration is often a desirable alternative. As a last resort, divestiture or liquidation should be considered. Divestiture can provide funds needed to acquire other businesses or buy back shares of stock.

Quadrant III organizations compete in slow-growth industries and have weak competitive positions. These firms must make some drastic changes quickly to avoid further decline and possible liquidation. Extensive cost and asset reduction (retrenchment) should be pursued first. An alternative strategy is to shift resources away from the current business into different areas (diversify). If all else fails, the final options for Quadrant III businesses are divestiture or liquidation.

Finally, Quadrant IV businesses have a strong competitive position but are in a slow-growth industry. These firms have the strength to launch diversified programs into more

FIGURE 6–11

The Grand Strategy Matrix

RAPID MARKET GROWTH

Quadrant II	*Quadrant I*
1. Market development	1. Market development
2. Market penetration	2. Market penetration
3. Product development	3. Product development
4. Horizontal integration	4. Forward integration
5. Divestiture	5. Backward integration
6. Liquidation	6. Horizontal integration
	7. Concentric diversification

WEAK COMPETITIVE POSITION ———————————————— STRONG COMPETITIVE POSITION

Quadrant III	*Quadrant IV*
1. Retrenchment	1. Concentric diversification
2. Concentric diversification	2. Horizontal diversification
3. Horizontal diversification	3. Conglomerate diversification
4. Conglomerate diversification	4. Joint ventures
5. Divestiture	
6. Liquidation	

SLOW MARKET GROWTH

Source: Adapted from Roland Christensen, Norman Berg, and Malcolm Salter, *Policy Formulation and Administration* (Homewood, IL): Richard D. Irwin, 1976): 16–18.

promising growth areas: Quadrant IV firms have characteristically high cash-flow levels and limited internal growth needs and often can pursue concentric, horizontal, or conglomerate diversification successfully. Quadrant IV firms also may pursue joint ventures.

 ## THE DECISION STAGE

Analysis and intuition provide a basis for making strategy-formulation decisions. The matching techniques just discussed reveal feasible alternative strategies. Many of these strategies will likely have been proposed by managers and employees participating in the strategy analysis and choice activity. Any additional strategies resulting from the matching analyses could be discussed and added to the list of feasible alternative options. As indicated earlier in this chapter, participants could rate these strategies on a 1 to 4 scale so that a prioritized list of the best strategies could be achieved.

The Quantitative Strategic Planning Matrix (QSPM)

Other than ranking strategies to achieve the prioritized list, there is only one analytical technique in the literature designed to determine the relative attractiveness of feasible alternative actions. This technique is the *Quantitative Strategic Planning Matrix (QSPM)*, which comprises Stage 3 of the strategy-formulation analytical framework.[5] This technique objectively indicates which alternative strategies are best. The QSPM uses input from Stage 1 analyses and matching results from Stage 2 analyses to decide objectively among alternative strategies. That is, the EFE Matrix, IFE Matrix, and Competitive Profile Matrix that make up Stage 1, coupled with the TOWS Matrix, SPACE Matrix, BCG Matrix, IE Matrix, and Grand Strategy Matrix that make up Stage 2, provide the needed information for setting up the QSPM (Stage 3). The QSPM is a tool that allows strategists to evaluate alternative strategies objectively, based on previously identified external and internal critical success factors. Like other strategy-formulation analytical tools, the QSPM requires good intuitive judgment.

The basic format of the QSPM is illustrated in Table 6–5. Note that the left column of a QSPM consists of key external and internal factors (from Stage 1), and the top row consists of feasible alternative strategies (from Stage 2). Specifically, the left column of a QSPM consists of information obtained directly from the EFE Matrix and IFE Matrix. In a column adjacent to the critical success factors, the respective weights received by each factor in the EFE Matrix and the IFE Matrix are recorded.

The top row of a QSPM consists of alternative strategies derived from the TOWS Matrix, SPACE Matrix, BCG Matrix, IE Matrix, and Grand Strategy Matrix. These matching tools usually generate similar feasible alternatives. However, not every strategy suggested by the matching techniques has to be evaluated in a QSPM. Strategists should use good intuitive judgment in selecting strategies to include in a QSPM.

Conceptually, the QSPM determines the relative attractiveness of various strategies based on the extent to which key external and internal critical success factors are capitalized upon or improved. The relative attractiveness of each strategy within a set of alternatives is computed by determining the cumulative impact of each external and internal critical success factor. Any number of sets of alternative strategies can be included in the QSPM, and any number of strategies can make up a given set, but only strategies within a given set are evaluated relative to each other. For example, one set of strategies may include concentric, horizontal, and conglomerate diversification, whereas another set may include issuing stock and selling a division to raise needed capital. These two sets of strategies are totally different, and the QSPM evaluates strategies only within sets. Note in Table 6–6 that three strategies are included, and they make up just one set.

TABLE 6–5   **The Quantitative Strategic Planning Matrix—QSPM**

		STRATEGIC ALTERNATIVES		
Key Factors	*Weight*	*Strategy 1*	*Strategy 2*	*Strategy 3*
Key External Factors				
Economy				
Political/Legal/Governmental				
Social/Cultural/Demographic/Environmental				
Technological				
Competitive				
Key Internal Factors				
Management				
Marketing				
Finance/Accounting				
Production/Operations				
Research and Development				
Management Information Systems				

TABLE 6-6   A QSPM for Campbell Soup Company

STRATEGIC ALTERNATIVES

Key Factors	Weight	Joint Venture in Europe		Joint Venture in Asia	
		AS	TAS	AS	TAS
Opportunities					
1. One European currency—Euro	.10	4	.40	2	.20
2. Rising health consciousness in selecting foods	.15	4	.60	3	.45
3. Free market economies arising in Asia	.10	2	.20	4	.40
4. Demand for soups increasing 10% annually	.15	3	.45	4	.60
5. NAFTA	.05	—	—	—	—
Threats					
1. Food revenues increasing only 1% annually	.10	3	.30	4	.40
2. ConAgra's Banquet TV Dinners lead market with 27.4 percent share	.05	—	—	—	—
3. Unstable economies in Asia	.10	4	.40	1	.10
4. Tin cans are not biodegradable	.05	—	—	—	—
5. Low value of the dollar	.15	4	.60	2	.30
	1.0				
Strengths					
1. Profits rose 30%	.10	4	.40	2	.20
2. New North American division	.10	—	—	—	—
3. New health-conscious soups are successful	.10	4	.40	2	.20
4. Swanson TV dinners' market share has increased to 25.1%	.05	4	.20	3	.15
5. One-fifth of all managers' bonuses is based on overall corporate performance	.05	—	—	—	—
6. Capacity utilization increased from 60% to 80%	.15	3	.45	4	.60
Weaknesses					
1. Pepperidge Farm sales have declined 7%	.05	—	—	—	—
2. Restructuring cost $302 million	.05	—	—	—	—
3. The company's European operation is losing money	.15	2	.30	4	.60
4. The company is slow in globalizing	.15	4	.60	3	.45
5. Pretax profit margin of 8.4% is only one-half industry average	.05	—	—	—	—
Sum Total Attractiveness Score	1.0		5.30		4.65

AS = Attractiveness Score; TAS = Total Attractiveness Score

Attractiveness Score: 1 = not attractive; 2 = somewhat attractive; 3 = reasonably attractive; 4 = highly attractive.

A QSPM for a food company is provided in Table 6-6. This example illustrates all the components of the QSPM: Strategic Alternatives, Key Factors, Weights, Attractiveness Scores (AS), Total Attractiveness Scores (TAS), and the Sum Total Attractiveness Score. The three new terms just introduced—(1) Attractiveness Scores, (2) Total Attractiveness Scores, and (3) the Sum Total Attractiveness Score—are defined and explained below as the six steps required to develop a QSPM are discussed.

Step 1   **Make a list of the firm's key external opportunities/threats and internal strengths/weaknesses in the left column of the QSPM.** This information should be taken directly from the EFE Matrix and IFE Matrix. A minimum of ten external critical success factors and ten internal critical success factors should be included in the QSPM.

Step 2   **Assign weights to each key external and internal factor.** These weights are identical to those in the EFE Matrix and the IFE Matrix. The weights are presented in a straight column just to the right of the external and internal critical success factors.

Step 3   **Examine the Stage 2 (matching) matrices, and identify alternative strategies that the organization should consider implementing.** Record these strategies in the top row of the QSPM. Group the strategies into mutually exclusive sets if possible.

Step 4   **Determine the Attractiveness Scores (AS)** defined as numerical values that indicate the relative attractiveness of each strategy in a given set of alternatives. *Attractiveness Scores* are determined by examining each key external or internal factor, one at a time, and asking the question, "Does this factor affect the choice of strategies being made?" If the answer to this question is *yes*, then the strategies should be compared relative to that key factor. Specifically, Attractiveness Scores should be assigned to each strategy to indicate the relative attractiveness of one strategy over others, considering the particular factor. The range for Attractiveness Scores is 1 = not attractive, 2 = somewhat attractive, 3 = reasonably attractive, and 4 = highly attractive. If the answer to the above question is *no,* indicating that the respective key factor has no effect upon the specific choice being made, then do not assign Attractiveness Scores to the strategies in that set. Use a dash to indicate that the key factor does not affect the choice being made. Note: If you assign an AS score to one strategy, then assign AS score(s) to the other. In other words, if one strategy receives a dash, then all others must receive a dash in a given row.

Step 5   **Compute the Total Attractiveness Scores.** *Total Attractiveness Scores (TAS)* are defined as the product of multiplying the weights (Step 2) by the Attractiveness Scores (Step 4) in each row. The Total Attractiveness Scores indicate the relative attractiveness of each alternative strategy, considering only the impact of the adjacent external or internal critical success factor. The higher the Total Attractiveness Score, the more attractive the strategic alternative (considering only the adjacent critical success factor).

Step 6   **Compute the Sum Total Attractiveness Score.** Add Total Attractiveness Scores in each strategy column of the QSPM. The *Sum Total Attractiveness Scores (STAS)* reveal which strategy is most attractive in each set of alternatives. Higher scores indicate more attractive strategies, considering all the relevant external and internal factors that could affect the strategic decisions. The magnitude of the difference between the Sum Total Attractiveness Scores in a given set of strategic alternatives indicates the relative desirability of one strategy over another.

In Table 6-6, two alternative strategies—establishing a joint venture in Europe and establishing a joint venture in Asia—are being considered by Campbell Soup.

Note that NAFTA has no impact on the choice being made between the two strategies, so a dash (–) appears several times across that row. Several other factors also have no effect on the choice being made, so dashes are recorded in those rows as well. If a particular factor affects one strategy but not the other, it affects the choice being made, so attractiveness scores should be recorded. The sum total attractiveness score of 5.30 in Table 6-6 indicates that the joint venture in Europe is a more attractive strategy when compared to the joint venture in Asia.

You should have a rationale for each AS score assigned. In Table 6-6, the rationale for the AS scores in the first row is that the unification of Western Europe creates more stable business conditions in Europe than in Asia. The AS score of 4 for the joint venture in Europe and 2 for the joint venture in Asia indicates that the European venture is highly attractive and the Asian venture is somewhat attractive, considering only the first critical success factor. AS scores, therefore, are not mere guesses; they should be rational, defensible, and reasonable. Avoid giving each strategy the same AS score. Note in Table 6-6 that dashes are inserted all the way across the row when used. Also note that double 4s, or double 3s, or double 2s, or double 1s are never in a given row. These are important guidelines to follow in constructing a QSPM.

Positive Features and Limitations of the QSPM

A positive feature of the QSPM is that sets of strategies can be examined sequentially or simultaneously. For example, corporate-level strategies could be evaluated first, followed by division-level strategies, and then function-level strategies. There is no limit to the number of strategies that can be evaluated or the number of sets of strategies that can be examined at once using the QSPM.

Another positive feature of the QSPM is that it requires strategists to integrate pertinent external and internal factors into the decision process. Developing a QSPM makes it less likely that key factors will be overlooked or weighted inappropriately. A QSPM draws attention to important relationships that affect strategy decisions. Although developing a QSPM requires a number of subjective decisions, making small decisions along the way enhances the probability that the final strategic decisions will be best for the organization. A QSPM can be adapted for use by small and large for-profit and nonprofit organizations and can be applied to virtually any type of organization. A QSPM can especially enhance strategic choice in multinational firms because many key factors and strategies can be considered at once. It also has been applied successfully by a number of small businesses.[6]

The QSPM is not without some limitations. First, it always requires intuitive judgments and educated assumptions. The ratings and attractiveness scores require judgmental decisions, even though they should be based on objective information. Discussion among strategists, managers, and employees throughout the strategy-formulation process, including development of a QSPM, is constructive and improves strategic decisions. Constructive discussion during strategy analysis and choice may arise because of genuine differences of interpretation of information and varying opinions. Another limitation of the QSPM is that it can be only as good as the prerequisite information and matching analyses upon which it is based.

CULTURAL ASPECTS OF STRATEGY CHOICE

All organizations have a culture. *Culture* includes the set of shared values, beliefs, attitudes, customs, norms, personalities, heroes, and heroines that describe a firm. Culture is the unique way an organization does business. It is the human dimension that creates solidarity and meaning, and it inspires commitment and productivity in an organization when strategy changes are made. All human beings have a basic need to make sense of the world, to feel in control, and to make meaning. When events threaten meaning, individuals react defensively. Managers and employees may even sabotage new strategies in an effort to recapture the status quo.

It is beneficial to view strategic management from a cultural perspective because success often rests upon the degree of support that strategies receive from a firm's culture. If a firm's strategies are supported by cultural products such as values, beliefs, rites, rituals, ceremonies, stories, symbols, language, heroes, and heroines, then managers often can implement changes swiftly and easily. However, if a supportive culture does not exist and is not cultivated, then strategy changes may be ineffective or even counter-productive. A firm's culture can become antagonistic to new strategies, and the result of that antagonism may be confusion and disarray.

Strategies that require fewer cultural changes may be more attractive because extensive changes can take considerable time and effort. Whenever two firms merge, it becomes especially important to evaluate and consider culture-strategy linkages. For example, Hewlett-Packard (HP) and Compaq completed their merger in May 2002, but their company cultures are quite different. Compaq's culture is top-down oriented, whereas the HP culture, called the HP Way, is based on "management by walking around." Compaq is a marketer that spends only 3.5 percent of revenues on R&D, whereas HP is an inventor that spends 6 percent of its revenues annually on R&D. Compaq focuses on a few major products, whereas HP boasts a wide array of products in many categories. Compaq's management style can be described as outgoing, whereas HP's is introspective and analytical.[7] Compaq's workforce is highly competitive, aggressive, and takes risks, whereas the HP Way is to base decisions more on experience, professionalism, and careful analysis.

Culture provides an explanation for the difficulties a firm encounters when it attempts to shift its strategic direction, as the following statement explains:

> Not only has the "right" corporate culture become the essence and foundation of corporate excellence, but success or failure of needed corporate reforms hinges on management's sagacity and ability to change the firm's driving culture in time and in tune with required changes in strategies.[8]

THE POLITICS OF STRATEGY CHOICE

All organizations are political. Unless managed, political maneuvering consumes valuable time, subverts organizational objectives, diverts human energy, and results in the loss of some valuable employees. Sometimes political biases and personal preferences get unduly embedded in strategy choice decisions. Internal politics affect the choice of strategies in all organizations. The hierarchy of command in an organization, combined with the career aspirations of different people and the need to allocate scarce resources, guarantees the formation of coalitions of individuals who strive to take care of themselves first and the organization second, third, or fourth. Coalitions of individuals often form around key strategy issues that face an enterprise. A major responsibility of strategists is to guide the development of coalitions, to nurture an overall team concept, and to gain the support of key individuals and groups of individuals.

In the absence of objective analyses, strategy decisions too often are based on the politics of the moment. With development of improved strategy-formation tools, political factors become less important in making strategic decisions. In the absence of objectivity, political factors sometimes dictate strategies, and this is unfortunate. Managing political relationships is an integral part of building enthusiasm and esprit de corps in an organization.

A classic study of strategic management in nine large corporations examined the political tactics of successful and unsuccessful strategists.[9] Successful strategists were found to let weakly supported ideas and proposals die through inaction and to establish additional hurdles or tests for strongly supported ideas considered unacceptable but not openly opposed. Successful strategists kept a low political profile on unacceptable proposals and strived to let most negative decisions come from subordinates or a group consensus, thereby reserving their personal vetoes for big issues and crucial moments. Successful strategists did a lot of chatting and informal questioning to stay abreast of how things were progressing and to know when to intervene. They led strategy but did not dictate it. They gave few orders, announced few decisions, depended heavily on informal questioning, and sought to probe and clarify until a consensus emerged.

Successful strategists generously and visibly rewarded key thrusts that succeeded. They assigned responsibility for major new thrusts to *champions*, the individuals most strongly identified with the idea or product and whose futures were linked to its success. They stayed alert to the symbolic impact of their own actions and statements so as not to send false signals that could stimulate movements in unwanted directions.

Successful strategists ensured that all major power bases within an organization were represented in, or had access to, top management. They interjected new faces and new views into considerations of major changes. (This is important because new employees and managers generally have more enthusiasm and drive than employees who have been with the firm a long time. New employees do not see the world the same old way; nor do they act as screens against changes.) Successful strategists minimized their own political exposure on highly controversial issues and in circumstances in which major opposition from key power centers was likely. In combination, these findings provide a basis for managing political relationships in an organization.

Because strategies must be effective in the marketplace and capable of gaining internal commitment, the following tactics used by politicians for centuries can aid strategists:

- *Equifinality:* It is often possible to achieve similar results using different means or paths. Strategists should recognize that achieving a successful outcome is more important than imposing the method of achieving it. It may be possible to generate new alternatives that give equal results but with far greater potential for gaining commitment.

- *Satisfying:* Achieving satisfactory results with an acceptable strategy is far better than failing to achieve optimal results with an unpopular strategy.

- *Generalization:* Shifting focus from specific issues to more general ones may increase strategists' options for gaining organizational commitment.

- *Focus on Higher-Order Issues:* By raising an issue to a higher level, many short-term interests can be postponed in favor of long-term interests. For instance, by focusing on issues of survival, the auto and steel industries were able to persuade unions to make concessions on wage increases.

- *Provide Political Access on Important Issues:* Strategy and policy decisions with significant negative consequences for middle managers will motivate intervention behavior from them. If middle managers do not have an opportunity to take a position on such decisions in appropriate political forums, they are capable of successfully resisting the decisions after they are made. Providing such political access provides strategists with information that otherwise might not be available and that could be useful in managing intervention behavior.[10]

THE ROLE OF A BOARD
OF DIRECTORS

A "director" according to *Webster's Dictionary* is "one of a group of persons entrusted with the overall direction of a corporate enterprise." A *board of directors* is a group of individuals who are elected by the ownership of a corporation to have oversight and guidance over management and who look out for shareholders' interests. The act of oversight and direction is referred to as *governance*. The National Association of Corporate Directors defines governance as "the characteristic of ensuring that long-term strategic objectives and plans are established and that the proper management structure is in place to achieve those objectives, while at the same time making sure that the structure functions to maintain the corporation's integrity, reputation, and responsibility to its various constituencies." This broad scope of responsibility for the board shows how boards are being held accountable for the entire performance of the firm. In the recent Enron Corporation bankruptcy and scandal, the firm's board of directors is being sued by shareholders for mismanaging their interests. New accounting rules in the United States and Europe are being passed to enhance corporate-governance codes and to require much more extensive financial disclosure among publicly held firms. The roles and duties of a board of directors can be divided into four broad categories, as indicated in Table 6–7.

The widespread lack of involvement by boards of directors in the strategic-management process is changing in America, especially since the Enron Corporation failure.[11] Historically, boards of directors mostly have been insiders who would not second-guess top executives on strategic issues. It generally has been understood that strategists are responsible and accountable for implementing strategy, so they, not board members, should formulate strategy. Consequently, chief executive officers usually avoided discussions of overall strategy with directors because the results of those discussions often restricted their freedom of action. The judgments of board members seldom were used on acquisitions, divestitures, large capital investments, and other strategic matters. Often, the board would meet only annually to fulfill its minimum legal requirements; in many organizations, boards served merely a traditional legitimizing role.

Today, boards of directors are composed mostly of outsiders who are becoming more involved in organizations' strategic management. The trend in America is toward much greater board member accountability with smaller boards, now averaging twelve members rather than eighteen as they did a few years ago. Smaller boards can discuss issues more easily; individuals in small groups take responsibility more personally.

Just as directors are beginning to place more emphasis on staying informed about an organization's health and operations, they are also taking a more active role in ensuring that publicly issued documents are accurate representations of a firm's status. It is becoming widely recognized that a board of directors has legal responsibilities to stockholders and society for all company activities, for corporate performance, and for ensuring that a firm has an effective strategy. Failure to accept responsibility for auditing or evaluating a firm's strategy is considered a serious breach of a director's duties. Stockholders, government agencies, and customers are filing legal suits against directors for fraud, omissions, inaccurate disclosures, lack of due diligence, and culpable ignorance about a firm's operations with increasing frequency. Liability insurance for directors has become exceptionally expensive and has caused numerous directors to resign.

Boards of directors in corporate America today are seriously evaluating strategic plans, evaluating the top management team, and assuming responsibility for management succession. TIAA-CREF, the nation's largest pension fund, now regularly evaluates governance practices at more than fifteen hundred companies in which it owns a stake. *Business Week*'s annual board of director's evaluation posited that good boards of directors actively perform the following responsibilities:[12]

Table 6–7   Board of Director Duties and Responsibilities

1. CONTROL AND OVERSIGHT OVER MANAGEMENT
   a. Select the Chief Executive Officer
   b. Sanction the CEO's team
   c. Provide the CEO with a forum
   d. Assure managerial competency
   e. Evaluate management's performance
   f. Set management's salary levels, including fringe benefits
   g. Guarantee managerial integrity through continuous auditing
   h. Chart the corporate course
   i. Devise and revise policies to be implemented by management

2. ADHERENCE TO LEGAL PRESCRIPTIONS
   a. Keep abreast of new laws
   b. Ensure the entire organization fulfills legal prescriptions
   c. Pass bylaws and related resolutions
   d. Select new directors
   e. Approve capital budgets
   f. Authorize borrowing, new stock issues, bonds, and so on

3. CONSIDERATION OF STAKEHOLDERS' INTERESTS
   a. Monitor product quality
   b. Facilitate upward progression in employee quality of work life
   c. Review labor policies and practices
   d. Improve the customer climate
   e. Keep community relations at the highest level
   f. Use influence to better governmental, professional association, and educational contacts
   g. Maintain good public image

4. ADVANCEMENT OF STOCKHOLDERS' RIGHTS
   a. Preserve stockholders' equity
   b. Stimulate corporate growth so that the firm will survive and flourish
   c. Guard against equity dilution
   d. Assure equitable stockholder representation
   e. Inform stockholders through letters, reports, and meetings
   f. Declare proper dividends
   g. Guarantee corporate survival

VISIT THE NET

Elaborates on role of a board of directors.
http://www.csuchico.edu/mgmt/strategy/module1/sld054.htm

- Evaluate the CEO annually.
- Link the CEO's pay to specific goals.
- Evaluate long-range strategy.
- Evaluate board members' performance through a governance committee.
- Compensate board members only in company stock.
- Require each director to own a large amount of company stock.
- Ensure that no more than two board members are insiders (work for the company).
- Require directors to retire at age seventy.
- Place the entire board up for election every year.

- Limit the number of other boards a member can serve on.
- Ban directors who draw consulting fees or other monies from the company.
- Ban interlocking directorships.

Two rulings particularly affected the role of boards of directors in the strategy-formulation process. First, the Supreme Court of Delaware ruled that the directors of the Trans Union Corporation violated the interests of shareholders when they hastily accepted a takeover bid from the Marmon Group; that ruling eroded the so-called business judgment rule, which protects directors from liability as long as their decisions represent a good-faith effort to serve the best interests of the corporation. One clear signal from the Trans Union case is that haste can be costly for board members.

In another landmark ruling that illustrates how boards of directors increasingly are being held responsible for the overall performance of organizations, the Federal Deposit Insurance Corporation forced Continental Illinois to accept the resignations of ten of the troubled bank's outside directors. The impact of increasing legal pressures on board members is that directors are demanding greater and more regular access to financial performance information.

Some boardroom reforms that are lessening the likelihood of lawsuits today include increasing the percentage of outsiders on the board, separating the positions of CEO and chairperson, requiring directors to hold substantial amounts of stock in the firm, and decreasing the board size. Outsiders now outnumber insiders at 90 percent of all American firms' boards, and the average number of outsiders is three times that of insiders.

A direct response of increased pressure on directors to stay informed and execute their responsibilities is that audit committees are becoming commonplace. A board of directors should conduct an annual strategy audit in much the same fashion that it reviews the annual financial audit. In performing such an audit, a board could work jointly with operating management and/or seek outside counsel.

The trend among corporations toward decreased diversification, increased takeover activity, increased legal pressures, multidivisional structures, and multinational operations augments the problem of keeping directors informed. Boards should play a role beyond that of performing a strategic audit. They should provide greater input and advice in the strategy-formulation process to ensure that strategists are providing for the long-term needs of the firm. This is being done through the formation of three particular board committees: nominating committees to propose candidates for the board and senior officers of the firm; compensation committees to evaluate the performance of top executives and determine the terms and conditions of their employment; and public policy committees to give board-level attention to company policies and performance on subjects of concern such as business ethics, consumer affairs, and political activities.

VISIT THE NET

Provides nice details about strategic planning at a church. http://www.apeo.org/guide/

Powerful boards of directors are associated with high organizational performance. Powerful boards participate in corporate decisions more fully, share their experiences with the CEO regarding certain strategies, and are actively involved in industry analysis. Firms can develop more powerful boards by regularly reviewing board committee activities, evaluating board meetings, and involving the board more extensively in strategic issues. More companies are paying board members partly or totally in stock, which gives outside directors more reason to identify with the shareholders they represent rather than with the CEO they oversee.

Church boards have historically been made up of parishioners only, but an increasing number of churches are placing outsiders (nonmembers) on their boards.[13] These outsiders include influential persons in the community who have financial planning, fundraising, trust management, and other desired skills. Churches want to create endowments and capitalize on older members' growing estates.

CONCLUSION

The essence of strategy formulation is an assessment of whether an organization is doing the right things and how it can be more effective in what it does. Every organization should be wary of becoming a prisoner of its own strategy, because even the best strategies become obsolete sooner or later. Regular reappraisal of strategy helps management avoid complacency. Objectives and strategies should be consciously developed and coordinated and should not merely evolve out of day-to-day operating decisions.

An organization with no sense of direction and no coherent strategy precipitates its own demise. When an organization does not know where it wants to go, it usually ends up some place it does not want to be. Every organization needs to consciously establish and communicate clear objectives and strategies.

Modern strategy-formulation tools and concepts are described in this chapter and integrated into a practical three-stage framework. Tools such as the TOWS Matrix, SPACE Matrix, BCG Matrix, IE Matrix, and QSPM can significantly enhance the quality of strategic decisions, but they should never be used to dictate the choice of strategies. Behavioral, cultural, and political aspects of strategy generation and selection are always important to consider and manage. Because of increased legal pressure from outside groups, boards of directors are assuming a more active role in strategy analysis and choice. This is a positive trend for organizations.

> **VISIT THE NET**
>
> *Gives the strategic plans of numerous government agencies.* http://www.financenet.gov/financenet/fed/docs/strat.htm

We invite you to visit the David page on the Prentice Hall Companion Website at **www.prenhall.com/david** for this chapter's World Wide Web exercise.

KEY TERMS AND CONCEPTS

Aggressive Quadrant (p. 205)

Attractiveness Scores (AS) (p. 218)

Boards of Directors (p. 221)

Boston Consulting Group (BCG) Matrix (p. 206)

Business Portfolio (p. 206)

Cash Cows (p. 210)

Champions (p. 221)

Competitive Advantage (CA) (p. 203)

Competitive Quadrant (p. 205)

Conservative Quadrant (p. 205)

Culture (p. 219)

Decision Stage (p. 198)

Defensive Quadrant (p. 205)

Directional Vector (p. 204)

Dogs (p. 210)

Environmental Stability (ES) (p. 203)

Financial Strength (FS) (p. 203)

Governance (p. 222)

Grand Strategy Matrix (p. 213)

Halo Error (p. 198)

Industry Strength (IS) (p. 203)

Input Stage (p. 197)

Internal-External (IE) Matrix (p. 211)

Long-Term Objectives (p. xxx)

Matching (p. 199)

Matching Stage (p. 197)

Quantitative Strategic Planning Matrix (QSPM) (p. 215)

Question Marks (p. 208)

Relative Market Share Position (p. 206)

SO Strategies (p. 200)

ST Strategies (p. 201)

Stars (p. 209)

Strategic Position and Action Evaluation (SPACE) Matrix (p. 203)

Strategy-Formulation Framework (p. 198)

Sum Total Attractiveness Scores (STAS) (p. 218)

Threats-Opportunities-Weaknesses-Strengths (TOWS) Matrix (p. 200)

Total Attractiveness Scores (TAS) (p. 218)

WO Strategies (p. 200)

WT Strategies (p. 201)

ISSUES FOR REVIEW AND DISCUSSION

1. How would application of the strategy-formulation framework differ from a small to a large organization?

2. What types of strategies would you recommend for an organization that achieves total weighted scores of 3.6 on the IFE and 1.2 on the EFE Matrix?

3. Given the following information, develop a SPACE Matrix for the XYZ Corporation:
   FS = +2; ES = −6; CA = −2; IS = +4.

4. Given the information in the table below, develop a BCG Matrix and an IE Matrix:

Divisions	1	2	3
Profits	$10	$15	$25
Sales	$100	$50	$100
Relative Market Share	0.2	0.5	0.8
Industry Growth Rate	+.20	+.10	−.10
IFE Total Weighted Scores	1.6	3.1	2.2
EFE Total Weighted Scores	2.5	1.8	3.3

5. Explain the steps involved in developing a QSPM.

6. How would you develop a set of objectives for your school or business?

7. What do you think is the appropriate role of a board of directors in strategic management? Why?

8. Discuss the limitations of various strategy-formulation analytical techniques.

9. Explain why cultural factors should be an important consideration in analyzing and choosing among alternative strategies.

10. How are the TOWS Matrix, SPACE Matrix, BCG Matrix, IE Matrix, and Grand Strategy Matrix similar? How are they different?

11. How would for-profit and nonprofit organizations differ in their applications of the strategy-formulation framework?

12. Select an article from the suggested readings at the end of this chapter, and prepare a report on that article for your class.

13. Calculate the Relative Market Share Position of the Budget rental car company based on section C of Table 6-4 data.

NOTES

1. R. T. LENZ, "Managing the Evolution of the Strategic Planning Process," *Business Horizons* 30, no. 1 (January–February 1987): 37.

2. ROBERT GRANT, "The Resource-Based Theory of Competitive Advantage: Implications for Strategy Formulation," *California Management Review* (Spring 1991): 114.

3. HEINZ WEIHRICH, "The TOWS Matrix: A Tool for Situational Analysis," *Long Range Planning* 15, no. 2 (April 1982): 61.

4. H. ROWE, R. MASON, and K. DICKEL, *Strategic Management and Business Policy: A Methodological Approach* (Reading, MA: Addison-Wesley Publishing Co. Inc., 1982): 155–156. Reprinted with permission of the publisher.

5. FRED DAVID, "The Strategic Planning Matrix—A Quantitative Approach," *Long Range Planning* 19, no. 5 (October 1986): 102. ANDRE GIB and ROBERT MARGULIES, "Making Competitive Intelligence Relevant to the User," *Planning Review* 19, no. 3 (May–June 1991): 21.

6. FRED DAVID, "Computer-Assisted Strategic Planning in Small Businesses," *Journal of Systems Management* 36, no. 7 (July 1985): 24–34.

7. JON SWARTZ, "How Will Compaq, H-P Fit Together?" *USA Today* (September 6, 2001): 3B.

8. Y. ALLARIE and M. FIRSIROTU, "How to Implement Radical Strategies in Large Organizations," *Sloan Management Review* 26, no. 3 (Spring 1985): 19. Another excellent article is P. Shrivastava, "Integrating Strategy Formulation with Organizational Culture," *Journal of Business Strategy* 5, no. 3 (Winter 1985): 103–111.

9. JAMES BRIAN QUINN, *Strategies for Change: Logical Incrementalism* (Homewood, IL: Richard D. Irwin, 1980): 128–145. These political tactics are listed in A. Thompson and A. Strickland, *Strategic Management: Concepts and Cases* (Plano, TX: Business Publications, 1984): 261.

10. WILLIAM GUTH and IAN MACMILLAN, "Strategy Implementation Versus Middle Management Self-Interest," *Strategic Management Journal* 7, no. 4 (July–August 1986): 321.

11. CAROL HYMOWITZ, "Serving on a Board Now Means Less Talk, More Accountability," *Wall Street Journal* (January 29, 2002): p. B1.

12. "Best and Worst Corporate Boards of Directors," *Business Week* (November 25, 1996): 82–98.

13. LISA MILLER, "Seeking Cash and Connections, Churches Revamp Boards," *The Wall Street Journal* (September 23, 1999): B1.

CURRENT READINGS

BROWN, ROGER. "How We Built a Strong Company in a Weak Industry." *Harvard Business Review* (February 2001): 51.

CARPENTER, MASON A., and JAMES D. WESTPHAL. "The Strategic Context of External Network Ties: Examining the Impact of Director Appointments on Board Involvement in Strategic Decision Making." *The Academy of Management Journal* 44, no. 4 (August 2001): 639.

CLAPHAM, MARIA. "Employee Creativity: The Role of Leadership." *The Academy of Management Executive* 14, no. 3 (August 2000): 138.

COLES, JERILYN W., VICTORIA B. WILLIAMS, and NILANJAN SEN. "An Examination of the Relationship of Governance Mechanisms to Performance." *Journal of Management* 27, no. 1 (January–February 2001): 23.

DAVENPORT, THOMAS H., JEANNE G. HARIS, DAVID W. DE LONG, and ALVIN L. JACOBSON. "Data to Knowledge to Results: Building an Analytic Capability." *California Management Review* 43, no. 2 (Winter 2001): 117.

DEHAENE, ALEXANDER, VEERLE DE VUYST, and HUBERT OOGHE. "Corporate Performance and Board Structure in Belgian Companies." *Long Range Planning* 34, no. 3 (June 2001): 383.

EISENHARDT, KATHLEEN M., and DONALD N. SULL. "Strategy as Simple Rules." *Harvard Business Review* (January 2001): 106.

FERNANDO, MARIO. "Are Popular Management Techniques a Waste of Time?" *The Academy of Management Executive* 15, no. 3 (August 2001): 138.

FLORIDA, RICHARD, and DEREK DAVIDSON. "Gaining from Green Management: Environmental Management Systems Inside and Outside the Factory." *California Management Review* 43, no. 3 (Spring 2001): 64.

JUDGE, WILLIAM Q., and JOEL A. RYMAN. "The Shared Leadership Challenge in Strategic Alliances: Lessons from the U.S. Healthcare Industry." *The Academy of Management Executive* 15, no. 2 (May 2001): 71.

RANFT, ANNETTE L., and HUGH M. O'NEILL. "Board Composition and High-Flying Founders: Hints of Trouble to Come?" *The Academy of Management Executive* 15, no. 1 (February 2001): 126.

RIGBY, DARRELL. "Management Tools and Techniques: A Survey." *California Management Review* 43, no. 2 (Winter 2001): 139.

SIDERS, MARK A., GERARD GEORGE, and RAVI DHARWADKAR. "The Relationship of Internal and External Commitment Foci to Objective Job Performance Measures." *The Academy of Management Journal* 44, no. 3 (June 2001): 570.

UNSWORTH, KERRIE. "Unpacking Creativity." *The Academy of Management Review* 26, no. 2 (April 2001): 289.

ZAHRA, SHAKER A., DONALD NEUBAUM, and MORTEN HUSE. "Entrepreneurship in Medium-Sized Companies: Exploring the Effects of Ownership and Governance Systems." *Journal of Management* 26, no. 5 (September–October 2000): 947.

EXPERIENTIAL EXERCISES

PURPOSE

The most widely used strategy-formulation technique among American firms is the TOWS Matrix. This exercise requires the development of a TOWS Matrix for American Airlines (AMR). Matching key external and internal factors in a TOWS Matrix requires good intuitive and conceptual skills. You will improve with practice in developing a TOWS Matrix.

INSTRUCTIONS

Recall from Experiential Exercise 1A that you already may have determined AMR's external opportunities/threats and internal strengths/weaknesses. This information could be used to complete this exercise. Follow the steps outlined below:

Step 1   On a separate sheet of paper, construct a large nine-cell diagram that will represent your TOWS Matrix. Label the cells appropriately.

Step 2   Record AMR's opportunities/threats and strengths/weaknesses appropriately in your diagram.

Step 3   Match external and internal factors to generate feasible alternative strategies for AMR. Record SO, WO, ST, and WT strategies in the appropriate cells of the TOWS Matrix. Use the proper notation to indicate the rationale for the strategies. You do not necessarily have to have strategies in all four strategy cells.

Step 4   Compare your TOWS Matrix to another student's TOWS Matrix. Discuss any major differences.

PURPOSE

Should AMR pursue aggressive, conservative, competitive, or defensive strategies? Develop a SPACE Matrix for AMR to answer this question. Elaborate on the strategic implications of your directional vector. Be specific in terms of strategies that could benefit AMR.

INSTRUCTIONS

Step 1   Join with two other people in class, and develop a joint SPACE Matrix for AMR.

Step 2   Diagram your SPACE Matrix on the board. Compare your matrix with other team's matrices.

Step 3   Discuss the implications of your SPACE Matrix.

PURPOSE

Portfolio matrices are widely used by multidivisional organizations to help identify and select strategies to pursue. A BCG analysis identifies particular divisions that should receive fewer resources than others. It may identify some divisions that need to be divested. This exercise can give you practice developing a BCG Matrix.

INSTRUCTIONS

Step 1   Place the following five column headings at the top of a separate sheet of paper: Divisions, Revenues, Profits, Relative Market Share Position, Industry Growth Rate.

Step 2   Complete a BCG Matrix for AMR.

Step 3   Compare your BCG Matrix to other students' matrices. Discuss any major differences.

EXPERIENTIAL EXERCISE 6D ▶

Developing a QSPM for American Airlines (AMR)

PURPOSE

This exercise can give you practice developing a Quantitative Strategic Planning Matrix to determine the relative attractiveness of various strategic alternatives.

INSTRUCTIONS

Step 1   Join with two other students in class to develop a joint QSPM for AMR.

Step 2   Go to the blackboard and record your strategies and their Sum Total Attractiveness Score. Compare your team's strategies and sum total attractiveness score to those of other teams. Be sure not to assign the same AS score in a given row. Recall that dashes should be inserted all the way across a given row when used.

Step 3   Discuss any major differences.

EXPERIENTIAL EXERCISE 6E ▶

Formulating Individual Strategies

PURPOSE

Individuals and organizations are alike in many ways. Each has competitors and each should plan for the future. Every individual and organization faces some external opportunities and threats and has some internal strengths and weaknesses. Both individuals and organizations establish objectives and allocate resources. These and other similarities make it possible for individuals to use many strategic-management concepts and tools. This exercise is designed to demonstrate how the TOWS Matrix can be used by individuals to plan their futures. As one nears completion of a college degree and begins interviewing for jobs, planning can be particularly important.

INSTRUCTIONS

On a separate sheet of paper, construct a TOWS Matrix. Include what you consider to be your major external opportunities, your major external threats, your major strengths, and your major weaknesses. An internal weakness may be a low grade point average. An external opportunity may be that your university offers a graduate program that interests you. Match key external and internal factors by recording in the appropriate cell of the matrix alternative strategies or actions that would allow you to capitalize upon your strengths, overcome your weaknesses, take advantage of your external opportunities, and minimize the impact of external threats. Be sure to use the appropriate matching notation in the strategy cells of the matrix. Because every individual (and organization) is unique, there is no one right answer to this exercise.

EXPERIENTIAL EXERCISE 6F ▶

The Mach Test

PURPOSE

The purpose of this exercise is to enhance your understanding and awareness of the impact that behavioral and political factors can have on strategy analysis and choice.

INSTRUCTIONS

Step 1   On a separate sheet of paper, number from 1 to 10. For each of the ten statements given below, record a *1, 2, 3, 4,* or *5* to indicate your attitude, where

1 = I disagree a lot.
2 = I disagree a little.
3 = My attitude is neutral.
4 = I agree a little.
5 = I agree a lot.

1. The best way to handle people is to tell them what they want to hear.
2. When you ask someone to do something for you, it is best to give the real reason for wanting it, rather than a reason that might carry more weight.
3. Anyone who completely trusts anyone else is asking for trouble.
4. It is hard to get ahead without cutting corners here and there.
5. It is safest to assume that all people have a vicious streak, and it will come out when they are given a chance.
6. One should take action only when it is morally right.
7. Most people are basically good and kind.
8. There is no excuse for lying to someone else.
9. Most people forget more easily the death of their father than the loss of their property.
10. Generally speaking, people won't work hard unless they're forced to do so.

Step 2   Add up the numbers you recorded beside statements 1, 3, 4, 5, 9, and 10. This sum is Subtotal One. For the other four statements, reverse the numbers you recorded, so a 5 becomes a *1,* 4 becomes *2,* 2 becomes *4,* 1 becomes *5,* and *3* remains *3.* Then add those four numbers to get Subtotal Two. Finally, add Subtotal One and Subtotal Two to get your Final Score.

YOUR FINAL SCORE

Your Final Score is your Machiavellian Score. Machiavellian principles are defined in a dictionary as "manipulative, dishonest, deceiving, and favoring political expediency over morality." These tactics are not desirable, are not ethical, and are not recommended in the strategic-management process! You may, however, encounter some highly Machiavellian individuals in your career, so beware. It is important for strategists not to manipulate others in the pursuit of organizational objectives. Individuals today recognize and resent manipulative tactics more than ever before. J. R. Ewing (on a television show in the 1980s, *Dallas*) was a good example of someone who was a high Mach (score over 30). The National Opinion Research Center used this short quiz in a random sample of American adults and found the national average Final Score to be 25.[1] The higher your score, the more Machiavellian (manipulative) you rend to be. The following scale is descriptive of individual scores on this test:

- Below 16:   Never uses manipulation as a tool.
- 16 to 20:   Rarely uses manipulation as a tool.
- 21 to 25:   Sometimes uses manipulation as a tool.
- 26 to 30:   Often uses manipulation as a tool.
- Over 30:   Always uses manipulation as a tool.

TEST DEVELOPMENT

The Mach (Machiavellian) test was developed by Dr. Richard Christie, whose research suggests the following tendencies:

1. Men generally are more Machiavellian than women.
2. There is no significant difference between high Machs and low Machs on measures of intelligence or ability.
3. Although high Machs are detached from others, they are detached in a pathological sense.
4. Machiavellian Scores are not statistically related to authoritarian values.
5. High Machs tend to be in professions that emphasize the control and manipulation of individuals—for example, law, psychiatry, and behavioral science.
6. Machiavellianism is not significantly related to major demographic characteristics such as educational level or marital status.
7. High Machs tend to come from a city or have urban backgrounds.
8. Older adults tend to have lower Mach scores than younger adults.[2]

A classic book on power relationships, *The Prince*, was written by Niccolo Machiavelli. Several excerpts from *The Prince* are given below.

> Men must either be cajoled or crushed, for they will revenge themselves for slight wrongs, while for grave ones they cannot. The injury therefore that you do to a man should be such that you need not fear his revenge.
>
> We must bear in mind . . . that there is nothing more difficult and dangerous, or more doubtful of success, than an attempt to introduce a new order of things in any state. The innovator has for enemies all those who derived advantages from the old order of things, while those who expect to be benefitted by the new institution will be but lukewarm defenders.
>
> A wise prince, therefore, will steadily pursue such a course that the citizens of his state will always and under all circumstances feel the need for his authority, and will therefore always prove faithful to him.
>
> A prince should seem to be merciful, faithful, humane, religious, and upright, and should even be so in reality, but he should have his mind so trained that, when occasion requires it, he may know how to change to the opposite.[3]

NOTES

1. RICHARD CHRISTIE and FLORENCE GEIS, *Studies in Machiavellianism* (Orlando, FL: Academic Press, 1970). Material in this exercise adapted with permission of the authors and the Academic Press.
2. Ibid., 82–83.
3. NICCOLO MACHIAVELLI, *The Prince* (New York: The Washington Press, 1963).

EXPERIENTIAL EXERCISE 6G ▶

Developing a BCG Matrix for My University

PURPOSE

Developing a BCG Matrix for many nonprofit organizations, including colleges and universities, is a useful exercise. Of course, there are no profits for each division or department—and in some cases no revenues. However, you can be creative in performing a BCG Matrix. For example, the pie slice in the circles can represent the number of majors receiving jobs upon graduation, or the number of faculty teaching in that area, or some other variable that you believe is important to consider. The size of the circles can represent the number of students majoring in particular departments or areas.

INSTRUCTIONS

Step 1   On a separate sheet of paper, develop a BCG Matrix for your university. Include all academic schools, departments, or colleges.

Step 2   Diagram your BCG Matrix on the blackboard.

Step 3   Discuss differences among the BCG Matrices on the board.

EXPERIENTIAL EXERCISE 6H ▶

The Role of Boards of Directors

PURPOSE

This exercise will give you a better understanding of the role of boards of directors in formulating, implementing, and evaluating strategies.

INSTRUCTIONS

Identify a person in your community who serves on a board of directors. Make an appointment to interview that person, and seek answers to the questions given below. Summarize your findings in a five-minute oral report to the class.

On what board are you a member?

How often does the board meet?

How long have you served on the board?

What role does the board play in this company?

How has the role of the board changed in recent years?

What changes would you like to see in the role of the board?

To what extent do you prepare for the board meeting?

To what extent are you involved in strategic management of the firm?

EXPERIENTIAL EXERCISE 6I ▶

Locating Companies in a Grand Strategy Matrix

PURPOSE

The Grand Strategy Matrix is a popular tool for formulating alternative strategies. All organizations can be positioned in one of the Grand Strategy Matrix's four strategy quadrants. The divisions of a firm likewise could be positioned. The Grand Strategy Matrix is based on two evaluative dimensions: competitive position and market growth. Appropriate strategies for an organization to consider are listed in sequential order of attractiveness in each quadrant of the matrix. This exercise gives you experience using a Grand Strategy Matrix.

INSTRUCTIONS

Using the year-end 2001 financial information provided, prepare a Grand Strategy Matrix on a separate sheet of paper. Write the respective company names in the appropriate quadrant of the matrix. Based on this analysis, what strategies are recommended for each company?

COMPANY	COMPANY SALES/PROFIT GROWTH (%)	INDUSTRY	INDUSTRY SALES/PROFITS GROWTH (%)
Apple Computer	−14/−47	Computers	−1/−77
PeopleSoft	+19/+31	Computers	−1/−77
Kroger	+7/+42	Food	+5/+10
Supervalue	−6/−68	Food	+5/+10
MBNA	+27/+29	Banks	−8/−15
Bank of America	−9/−10	Banks	−8/−15
General Motors	−4/−87	Automotive	−6/0
Eaton Corporation	−12/−53	Automotive	−6/0

Business Week (Spring 2002): 87–114.

PART 3

Strategy Implementation

7 IMPLEMENTING STRATEGIES: MANAGEMENT ISSUES

CHAPTER OUTLINE

- The Nature of Strategy Implementation
- Annual Objectives
- Policies
- Resource Allocation
- Managing Conflict
- Matching Structure with Strategy
- Restructuring, Reengineering, and E-Engineering
- Linking Performance and Pay to Strategies
- Managing Resistance to Change
- Managing the Natural Environment
- Creating a Strategy-Supportive Culture
- Production/Operations Concerns When Implementing Strategies
- Human Resource Concerns When Implementing Strategies

EXPERIENTIAL EXERCISE 7A
Revising American Airline's (AMR's) Organizational Chart

EXPERIENTIAL EXERCISE 7B
Do Organizations Really Establish Objectives?

EXPERIENTIAL EXERCISE 7C
Understanding My University's Culture

CHAPTER OBJECTIVES

After studying this chapter, you should be able to do the following:

1. Explain why strategy implementation is more difficult than strategy formulation.
2. Discuss the importance of annual objectives and policies in achieving organizational commitment for strategies to be implemented.
3. Explain why organizational structure is so important in strategy implementation.
4. Compare and contrast restructuring and reengineering.
5. Describe the relationships between production/operations and strategy implementation.
6. Explain how a firm can effectively link performance and pay to strategies.
7. Discuss employee stock ownership plans (ESOPs) as a strategic-management concept.
8. Describe how to modify an organizational culture to support new strategies.
9. Discuss the culture in Mexico, Russia, and Japan.
10. Describe the glass ceiling in the United States.

NOTABLE QUOTES

You want your people to run the business as if it were their own.

WILLIAM FULMER

The ideal organizational structure is a place where ideas filter up as well as down, where the merit of ideas carries more weight than their source, and where participation and shared objectives are valued more than executive orders.

EDSON SPENCER

A management truism says structure follows strategy. However, this truism is often ignored. Too many organizations attempt to carry out a new strategy with an old structure.

DALE McCONKEY

Poor Ike; when he was a general, he gave an order and it was carried out. Now, he's going to sit in that office and give an order and not a damn thing is going to happen.

HARRY TRUMAN

Changing your pay plan is a big risk, but not changing it could be a bigger one.

NANCY PERRY

Objectives can be compared to a compass bearing by which a ship navigates. A compass bearing is firm, but in actual navigation, a ship may veer off its course for many miles. Without a compass bearing, a ship would neither find its port nor be able to estimate the time required to get there.

PETER DRUCKER

The best game plan in the world never blocked or tackled anybody.

VINCE LOMBARDI

In most organizations, the top performers are paid too little and the worst performers too much.

CASS BETTINGER

Pretend that every single person you meet has a sign around his or her neck that says, "Make me feel important."

MARY KAY ASH, CEO OF MARY KAY, INC.

The best executive has . . . sense enough to pick good men, and the self-restraint enough to keep from meddling.

THEODORE ROOSEVELT

The strategic-management process does not end when the firm decides what strategy or strategies to pursue. There must be a translation of strategic thought into strategic action. This translation is much easier if managers and employees of the firm understand the business, feel a part of the company, and through involvement in strategy-formulation activities have become committed to helping the organization succeed. Without understanding and commitment, strategy-implementation efforts face major problems.

Implementing strategy affects an organization from top to bottom; it affects all the functional and divisional areas of a business. It is beyond the purpose and scope of this text to examine all of the business administration concepts and tools important in strategy implementation. This chapter focuses on management issues most central to implementing strategies in the year 2003, and Chapter 8 focuses on marketing, finance/accounting, R&D, and management information systems issues.

VISIT THE NET

Gives a good definition of strategy implementation.
http://www.csuchico.edu/mgmt/strategy/module1/sld044.htm

Even the most technically perfect strategic plan will serve little purpose if it is not implemented. Many organizations tend to spend an inordinate amount of time, money, and effort on developing the strategic plan, treating the means and circumstances under which it will be implemented as afterthoughts! Change comes through implementation and evaluation, not through the plan. A technically imperfect plan that is implemented well will achieve more than the perfect plan that never gets off the paper on which it is typed.[1]

THE NATURE OF STRATEGY IMPLEMENTATION

The strategy-implementation stage of strategic management is revealed in Figure 7–1. Successful strategy formulation does not guarantee successful strategy implementation. It is always more difficult to do something (strategy implementation) than to say you are going to do it (strategy formulation)! Although inextricably linked, strategy implementation is fundamentally different from strategy formulation. Strategy formulation and implementation can be contrasted in the following ways:

- Strategy formulation is positioning forces before the action.
- Strategy implementation is managing forces during the action.
- Strategy formulation focuses on effectiveness.
- Strategy implementation focuses on efficiency.
- Strategy formulation is primarily an intellectual process.
- Strategy implementation is primarily an operational process.
- Strategy formulation requires good intuitive and analytical skills.
- Strategy implementation requires special motivation and leadership skills.
- Strategy formulation requires coordination among a few individuals.
- Strategy implementation requires coordination among many individuals.

Strategy-formulation concepts and tools do not differ greatly for small, large, for-profit, or nonprofit organizations. However, strategy implementation varies substantially among different types and sizes of organizations. Implementing strategies requires such actions as altering sales territories, adding new departments, closing facilities, hiring new employees, changing an organization's pricing strategy, developing financial budgets, developing new employee benefits, establishing cost-control procedures,

FIGURE 7–1

A Comprehensive Strategic-Management Model

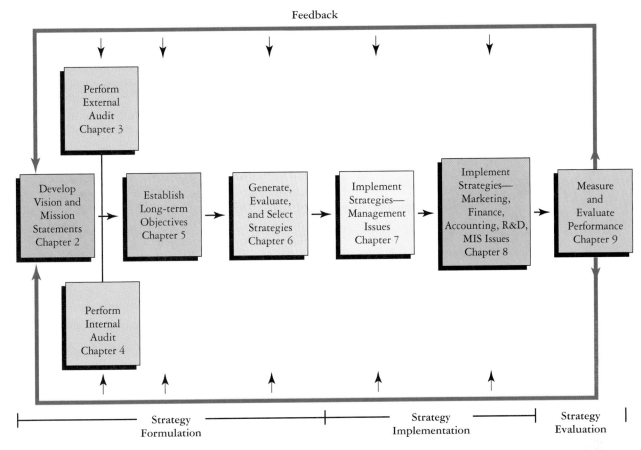

changing advertising strategies, building new facilities, training new employees, transferring managers among divisions, and building a better management information system. These types of activities obviously differ greatly between manufacturing, service, and governmental organizations.

Management Perspectives

In all but the smallest organizations, the transition from strategy formulation to strategy implementation requires a shift in responsibility from strategists to divisional and functional managers. Implementation problems can arise because of this shift in responsibility, especially if strategy-formulation decisions come as a surprise to middle- and lower-level managers. Managers and employees are motivated more by perceived self-interests than by organizational interests, unless the two coincide. Therefore, it is essential that divisional and functional managers be involved as much as possible in strategy-formulation activities. Of equal importance, strategists should be involved as much as possible in strategy-implementation activities.

Management issues central to strategy implementation include establishing annual objectives, devising policies, allocating resources, altering an existing organizational structure, restructuring and reengineering, revising reward and incentive plans, minimizing resistance to change, matching managers with strategy, developing a strategy-supportive culture, adapting production/operations processes, developing an effective human resource function and, if necessary, downsizing. Management changes are necessarily more extensive when strategies to be implemented move a firm in a major new direction.

Managers and employees throughout an organization should participate early and directly in strategy-implementation decisions. Their role in strategy implementation should build upon prior involvement in strategy-formulation activities. Strategists' genuine personal commitment to implementation is a necessary and powerful motivational force for managers and employees. Too often, strategists are too busy to actively support strategy-implementation efforts, and their lack of interest can be detrimental to organizational success. The rationale for objectives and strategies should be understood and clearly communicated throughout an organization. Major competitors' accomplishments, products, plans, actions, and performance should be apparent to all organizational members. Major external opportunities and threats should be clear, and managers' and employees' questions should be answered. Top-down flow of communication is essential for developing bottom-up support.

Firms need to develop a competitor focus at all hierarchical levels by gathering and widely distributing competitive intelligence; every employee should be able to benchmark her or his efforts against best-in-class competitors so that the challenge becomes personal. This is a challenge for strategists of the firm. Firms should provide training for both managers and employees to ensure that they have and maintain the skills necessary to be world-class performers.

 ## ANNUAL OBJECTIVES

Establishing annual objectives is a decentralized activity that directly involves all managers in an organization. Active participation in establishing annual objectives can lead to acceptance and commitment. *Annual objectives* are essential for strategy implementation because they (1) represent the basis for allocating resources; (2) are a primary mechanism for evaluating managers; (3) are the major instrument for monitoring progress toward achieving long-term objectives; and (4) establish organizational, divisional, and departmental priorities. Considerable time and effort should be devoted to ensuring that annual objectives are well conceived, consistent with long-term objectives, and supportive of strategies to be implemented. Approving, revising, or rejecting annual objectives is much more than a rubber-stamp activity. The purpose of annual objectives can be summarized as follows:

> Annual objectives serve as guidelines for action, directing and channeling efforts and activities of organization members. They provide a source of legitimacy in an enterprise by justifying activities to stakeholders. They serve as standards of performance. They serve as an important source of employee motivation and identification. They give incentives for managers and employees to perform. They provide a basis for organizational design.[2]

Clearly stated and communicated objectives are critical to success in all types and sizes of firms. Annual objectives, stated in terms of profitability, growth, and market share by business segment, geographic area, customer groups, and product are common

FIGURE 7–2

The Stamus Company's Hierarchy of Aims

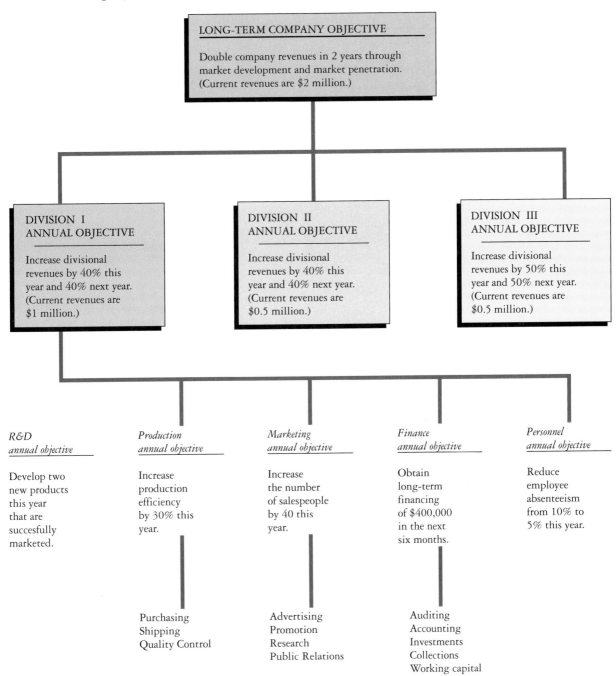

in organizations. Figure 7–2 illustrates how the Stamus Company could establish annual objectives based on long-term objectives. Table 7–1 reveals associated revenue figures that correspond to the objectives outlined in Figure 7–2. Note that, according to plan, the Stamus Company will slightly exceed its long-term objective of doubling company revenues between 2003 and the year 2005.

TABLE 7-1   The Stamus Company's Revenue Expectations
(in millions of dollars)

	2003	2004	2005
Division I Revenues	1.0	1.400	1.960
Division II Revenues	0.5	0.700	0.980
Division III Revenues	0.5	0.750	1.125
Total Company Revenues	2.0	2.850	4.065

Figure 7–2 also reflects how a hierarchy of annual objectives can be established based on an organization's structure. Objectives should be consistent across hierarchical levels and form a network of supportive aims. *Horizontal consistency of objectives* is as important as *vertical consistency of objectives*. For instance, it would not be effective for manufacturing to achieve more than its annual objective of units produced if marketing could not sell the additional units.

Annual objectives should be measurable, consistent, reasonable, challenging, clear, communicated throughout the organization, characterized by an appropriate time dimension, and accompanied by commensurate rewards and sanctions. Too often, objectives are stated in generalities, with little operational usefulness. Annual objectives such as "to improve communication" or "to improve performance" are not clear, specific, or measurable. Objectives should state quantity, quality, cost, and time—and also be verifiable. Terms and phrases such as *maximize, minimize, as soon as possible,* and *adequate* should be avoided.

Annual objectives should be compatible with employees' and managers' values and should be supported by clearly stated policies. More of something is not always better! Improved quality or reduced cost may, for example, be more important than quantity. It is important to tie rewards and sanctions to annual objectives so that employees and managers understand that achieving objectives is critical to successful strategy implementation. Clear annual objectives do not guarantee successful strategy implementation, but they do increase the likelihood that personal and organizational aims can be accomplished. Overemphasis on achieving objectives can result in undesirable conduct, such as faking the numbers, distorting the records, and letting objectives become ends in themselves. Managers must be alert to these potential problems.

POLICIES

Changes in a firm's strategic direction do not occur automatically. On a day-to-day basis, policies are needed to make a strategy work. Policies facilitate solving recurring problems and guide the implementation of strategy. Broadly defined, *policy* refers to specific guidelines, methods, procedures, rules, forms, and administrative practices established to support and encourage work toward stated goals. Policies are instruments for strategy implementation. Policies set boundaries, constraints, and limits on the kinds of administrative actions that can be taken to reward and sanction behavior; they clarify what can and cannot be done in pursuit of an organization's objectives. For example, Carnival's *Paradise* ship has a no-smoking policy anywhere, anytime aboard ship. It is the first cruise ship to comprehensively ban smoking. Another example of corporate policy relates to surfing the Web while at work. About 40 percent of companies today do not have a formal policy preventing employees from surfing the Internet, but software is being marketed now that allows firms to monitor how, when, where, and how long various employees use the Internet at work.

Policies let both employees and managers know what is expected of them, thereby increasing the likelihood that strategies will be implemented successfully. They provide a basis for management control, allow coordination across organizational units, and reduce the amount of time managers spend making decisions. Policies also clarify what work is to be done and by whom. They promote delegation of decision making to appropriate managerial levels where various problems usually arise. Many organizations have a policy manual that serves to guide and direct behavior.

Policies can apply to all divisions and departments (for example, "We are an equal opportunity employer"). Some policies apply to a single department ("Employees in this department must take at least one training and development course each year"). Whatever their scope and form, policies serve as a mechanism for implementing strategies and obtaining objectives. Policies should be stated in writing whenever possible. They represent the means for carrying out strategic decisions. Examples of policies that support a company strategy, a divisional objective, and a departmental objective are given in Table 7–2 on page 242.

Some example issues that may require a management policy are as follows:

- To offer extensive or limited management development workshops and seminars
- To centralize or decentralize employee-training activities
- To recruit through employment agencies, college campuses, and/or newspapers
- To promote from within or to hire from the outside
- To promote on the basis of merit or on the basis of seniority
- To tie executive compensation to long-term and/or annual objectives
- To offer numerous or few employee benefits
- To negotiate directly or indirectly with labor unions
- To delegate authority for large expenditures or to retain this authority centrally
- To allow much, some, or no overtime work
- To establish a high- or low-safety stock of inventory
- To use one or more suppliers
- To buy, lease, or rent new production equipment
- To stress quality control greatly or not
- To establish many or only a few production standards
- To operate one, two, or three shifts
- To discourage using insider information for personal gain
- To discourage sexual harassment
- To discourage smoking at work
- To discourage insider trading
- To discourage moonlighting

 ## RESOURCE ALLOCATION

Resource allocation is a central management activity that allows for strategy execution. In organizations that do not use a strategic-management approach to decision making, resource allocation is often based on political or personal factors. Strategic management enables resources to be allocated according to priorities established by annual objectives.

TABLE 7–2   **A Hierarchy of Policies**

Company Strategy: Acquire a chain of retail stores to meet our sales growth and profitability objectives.
Supporting policies:

1. "All stores will be open from 8 A.M. to 8 P.M.. Monday through Saturday." (This policy could increase retail sales if stores currently are open only 40 hours a week.)

2. "All stores must submit a Monthly Control Data Report." (This policy could reduce expense-to-sales ratios.)

3. "All stores must support company advertising by contributing 5 percent of their total monthly revenues for this purpose." (This policy could allow the company to establish a national reputation.)

4. "All stores must adhere to the uniform pricing guidelines set forth in the Company Handbook." (This policy could help assure customers that the company offers a consistent product in terms of price and quality in all its stores.)

Divisional Objective: Increase the division's revenues from $10 million in 2002 to $15 million in 2004.
Supporting policies:

1. "Beginning in January 2003 each one of this division's salespersons must file a weekly activity report that includes the number of calls made, the number of miles traveled, the number of units sold, the dollar volume sold, and the number of new accounts opened." (This policy could ensure that salespersons do not place too great an emphasis in certain areas.)

2. "Beginning in January 2003, this division will return to its employees 5 percent of its gross revenues in the form of a Christmas bonus." (This policy could increase employee productivity.)

3. "Beginning in January 2003, inventory levels carried in warehouses will be decreased by 30 percent in accordance with a Just-in-Time (JIT) manufacturing approach." (This policy could reduce production expenses and thus free funds for increased marketing efforts.)

Production Department Objective: Increase production from 20,000 units in 2002 to 30,000 units in 2004.
Supporting policies:

1. "Beginning in January 2003, employees will have the option of working up to 20 hours of overtime per week." (This policy could minimize the need to hire additional employees.)

2. "Beginning in January 2003, perfect attendance awards in the amount of $100 will be given to all employees who do not miss a workday in a given year." (This policy could decrease absenteeism and increase productivity.)

3. "Beginning in January 2003, new equipment must be leased rather than purchased." (This policy could reduce tax liabilities and thus allow more funds to be invested in modernizing production processes.)

Nothing could be more detrimental to strategic management and to organizational success than for resources to be allocated in ways not consistent with priorities indicated by approved annual objectives.

All organizations have at least four types of resources that can be used to achieve desired objectives: financial resources, physical resources, human resources, and technological resources. Allocating resources to particular divisions and departments does not mean that strategies will be successfully implemented. A number of factors commonly prohibit effective resource allocation, including an overprotection of resources, too great an emphasis on short-run financial criteria, organizational politics, vague strategy targets, a reluctance to take risks, and a lack of sufficient knowledge.

Below the corporate level, there often exists an absence of systematic thinking about resources allocated and strategies of the firm. Yavitz and Newman explained why:

> Managers normally have many more tasks than they can do. Managers must
> allocate time and resources among these tasks. Pressure builds up. Expenses are

too high. The CEO wants a good financial report for the third quarter. Strategy formulation and implementation activities often get deferred. Today's problems soak up available energies and resources. Scrambled accounts and budgets fail to reveal the shift in allocation away from strategic needs to currently squeaking wheels.[3]

The real value of any resource allocation program lies in the resulting accomplishment of an organization's objectives. Effective resource allocation does not guarantee successful strategy implementation because programs, personnel, controls, and commitment must breathe life into the resources provided. Strategic management itself is sometimes referred to as a "resource allocation process."

MANAGING CONFLICT

Interdependency of objectives and competition for limited resources often leads to conflict. *Conflict* can be defined as a disagreement between two or more parties on one or more issues. Establishing annual objectives can lead to conflict because individuals have different expectations and perceptions, schedules create pressure, personalities are incompatible, and misunderstandings between line managers (such as production supervisors) and staff managers (such as human resource specialists) occur. For example, a collection manager's objective of reducing bad debts by 50 percent in a given year may conflict with a divisional objective to increase sales by 20 percent.

Establishing objectives can lead to conflict because managers and strategists must make trade-offs, such as whether to emphasize short-term profits or long-term growth, profit margin or market share, market penetration or market development, growth or stability, high risk or low risk, and social responsiveness or profit maximization. Conflict is unavoidable in organizations, so it is important that conflict be managed and resolved before dysfunctional consequences affect organizational performance. Conflict is not always bad. An absence of conflict can signal indifference and apathy. Conflict can serve to energize opposing groups into action and may help managers identify problems.

Various approaches for managing and resolving conflict can be classified into three categories: avoidance, defusion, and confrontation. *Avoidance* includes such actions as ignoring the problem in hopes that the conflict will resolve itself or physically separating the conflicting individuals (or groups). *Defusion* can include playing down differences between conflicting parties while accentuating similarities and common interests, compromising so that there is neither a clear winner not loser, resorting to majority rule, appealing to a higher authority, or redesigning present positions. *Confrontation* is exemplified by exchanging members of conflicting parties so that each can gain an appreciation of the other's point of view, or holding a meeting at which conflicting parties present their views and work through their differences.

MATCHING STRUCTURE
WITH STRATEGY

Changes in strategy often require changes in the way an organization is structured for two major reasons. First, structure largely dictates how objectives and policies will be established. For example, objectives and policies established under a geographic organizational structure are couched in geographic terms. Objectives and policies are stated largely in terms of products in an organization whose structure is based on product groups. The structural format for developing objectives and policies can significantly impact all other strategy-implementation activities.

The second major reason why changes in strategy often require changes in structure is that structure dictates how resources will be allocated. If an organization's structure is based on customer groups, then resources will be allocated in that manner. Similarly, if an organization's structure is set up along functional business lines, then resources are allocated by functional areas. Unless new or revised strategies place emphasis in the same areas as old strategies, structural reorientation commonly becomes a part of strategy implementation.

Changes in strategy lead to changes in organizational structure. Structure should be designed to facilitate the strategic pursuit of a firm and, therefore, follows strategy. Without a strategy or reasons for being (mission), companies find it difficult to design an effective structure. Chandler found a particular structure sequence to be often repeated as organizations grow and change strategy over time; this sequence is depicted in Figure 7–3.

There is no one optimal organizational design or structure for a given strategy or type of organization. What is appropriate for one organization may not be appropriate for a similar firm, although successful firms in a given industry do tend to organize themselves in a similar way. For example, consumer goods companies tend to emulate the divisional structure-by-product form of organization. Small firms tend to be functionally structured (centralized). Medium-size firms tend to be divisionally structured (decentralized). Large firms tend to use an SBU (strategic business unit) or matrix structure. As organizations grow, their structures generally change from simple to complex as a result of concatenation, or the linking together of several basic strategies.

Numerous external and internal forces affect an organization; no firm could change its structure in response to every one of these forces, because to do so would lead to chaos. However, when a firm changes its strategy, the existing organizational structure may become ineffective. Symptoms of an ineffective organizational structure include too many levels of management, too many meetings attended by too many people, too much attention being directed toward solving interdepartmental conflicts, too large a span of

VISIT THE NET

Provides software to draw organizational charts easily.

www.smartdraw.com
You may download the SmartDraw software and use it free for thirty days.

FIGURE 7–3

Chandler's Strategy-Structure Relationship

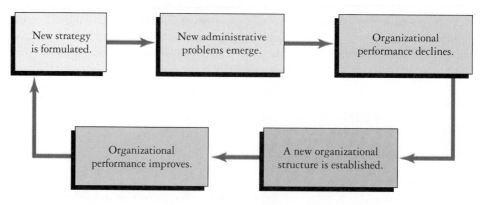

Source: Adapted from Alfred Chandler, *Strategy and Structure* (Cambridge, MA: MIT Press, 1962).

control, and too many unachieved objectives. Changes in structure can facilitate strategy-implementation efforts, but changes in structure should not be expected to make a bad strategy good, to make bad managers good, or to make bad products sell.

Structure undeniably can and does influence strategy. Strategies formulated must be workable, so if a certain new strategy required massive structural changes it would not be an attractive choice. In this way, structure can shape the choice of strategies. But a more important concern is determining what types of structural changes are needed to implement new strategies and how these changes can best be accomplished. We examine this issue by focusing on seven basic types of organizational structure: functional, divisional by geographic area, divisional by product, divisional by customer, divisional process, strategic business unit (SBU), and matrix.

VISIT THE NET

Lists some items that strategy implementation must include.

http://www.csuchico.edu/ mgmt/strategy/module1/ sld045.htm

The Functional Structure

The most widely used structure is the functional or centralized type because this structure is the simplest and least expensive of the seven alternatives. A *functional structure* groups tasks and activities by business function, such as production/operations, marketing, finance/accounting, research and development, and management information systems. A university may structure its activities by major functions that include academic affairs, student services, alumni relations, athletics, maintenance, and accounting. Besides being simple and inexpensive, a functional structure also promotes specialization of labor, encourages efficiency, minimizes the need for an elaborate control system, and allows rapid decision making. Some disadvantages of a functional structure are that it forces accountability to the top, minimizes career development opportunities, and is sometimes times characterized by low employee morale, line/staff conflicts, poor delegation of authority, and inadequate planning for products and markets. Most large companies abandoned the functional structure in favor of decentralization and improved accountability.

The Divisional Structure

The *divisional* or *decentralized structure* is the second-most common type used by American businesses. As a small organization grows, it has more difficulty managing different products and services in different markets. Some form of divisional structure generally becomes necessary to motivate employees, control operations, and compete successfully in diverse locations. The divisional structure can be organized in one of four ways: by geographic area, by product or service, by customer, or by process. With a divisional structure, functional activities are performed both centrally and in each separate division.

Cisco Systems recently discarded its divisional structure by customer and reorganized into a functional structure. CEO John Chambers replaced the three-customer structure based on big businesses, small business, and telecoms, and now the company has centralized its engineering and marketing units so that they focus on technologies such as wireless networks. Chambers says the goal was to eliminate duplication, but the change should not be viewed as a shift in strategy. Chambers' span of control in the new structure is reduced to 12 managers reporting directly to him from 15. He continues to operate Cisco without a chief operating officer or a number 2 executive.

Kodak recently reduced its number of business units from seven by-customer divisions to five by-product divisions. As consumption patterns become increasingly similar worldwide, a by-product structure is becoming more effective than a by-customer or a by-geographic type divisional structure. In the restructuring, Kodak eliminated its global operations division and distributed those responsibilities across the new by-product divisions.

A divisional structure has some clear advantages. First and perhaps foremost, accountability is clear. That is, divisional managers can be held responsible for sales and profit levels. Because a divisional structure is based on extensive delegation of authority, managers and employees can easily see the results of their good or bad performances. As a result, employee morale is generally higher in a divisional structure than it is in centralized structure. Other advantages of the divisional design are that it creates career development opportunities for managers, allows local control of local situations, leads to a competitive climate within an organization, and allows new businesses and products to be added easily.

Bank One recently created a new division named Wingspan, a new bank that is accessible only on the Internet at **wingspanbank.com**. Wingspan competes directly with Bank One and all other banks, offers higher certificate of deposit interest rates than Bank One, and thus is a break from Bank One's traditional strategy of offering the same products through numerous divisions. Bank One CEO John McCoy says, "All of the sudden now, there are ways you can go and get customers without having the full brick and mortar. I'm not about . . . to sit here and let somebody else take my business."[4]

Visa USA Inc., the largest credit card association in the United States, recently formed a separate Internet division named e-Visa. This new division employs thirty-five people and is headed by Michael Beindoff. BellSouth Corporation is reorganizing into five divisions in order to flatten its organizational structure. The new divisions are customer markets, network services, wireless services, international, and advertising and publishing.

The world's largest restaurant company, McDonald's, reorganized its operations in 2001, going from thirty-seven geographic regions in the United States to twenty-one divisions. This streamlining eliminated seven hundred managerial jobs.

The divisional design is not without some limitations, however. Perhaps the most important limitation is that a divisional structure is costly, for a number of reasons. First, each division requires functional specialists who must be paid. Second, there exists some duplication of staff services, facilities, and personnel; for instance, functional specialists are also needed centrally (at headquarters) to coordinate divisional activities. Third, managers must be well qualified because the divisional design forces delegation of authority; better-qualified individuals require higher salaries. A divisional structure can also be costly because it requires an elaborate, headquarters-driven control system. Finally, certain regions, products, or customers may sometimes receive special treatment, and it may be difficult to maintain consistent, companywide practices. Nonetheless, for most large organizations and many small firms, the advantages of a divisional structure more than offset the potential limitations.

A *divisional structure by geographic area* is appropriate for organizations whose strategies need to be tailored to fit the particular needs and characteristics of customers in different geographic areas. This type of structure can be most appropriate for organizations that have similar branch facilities located in widely dispersed areas. A divisional structure by geographic area allows local participation in decision making and improved coordination within a region.

The *divisional structure by product (or services)* is most effective for implementing strategies when specific products or services need special emphasis. Also, this type of structure is widely used when an organization offers only a few products or services, or when an organization's products or services differ substantially. The divisional structure allows strict control over and attention to product lines, but it may also require a more skilled management force and reduced top management control. General Motors, DuPont, and Procter & Gamble use a divisional structure by product to implement strategies. Huffy, the largest bicycle company in the world, is another firm that is highly decentralized based on a divisional-by-product structure. Based in Ohio, Huffy's divisions are the Bicycle division, the Gerry Baby Products division, the Huffy Sports division, YLC Enterprises, and Washington Inventory Service. Harry Shaw, Huffy's chairman, believes decentralization is one of the keys to Huffy's success.

When a few major customers are of paramount importance and many different services are provided to these customers, then a *divisional structure by customer* can be the most effective way to implement strategies. This structure allows an organization to cater effectively to the requirements of clearly defined customer groups. For example, book publishing companies often organize their activities around customer groups such as colleges, secondary schools, and private commercial schools. Some airline companies have two major customer divisions: passengers and freight or cargo services. Merrill Lynch is organized into separate divisions that cater to different groups of customers, including wealthy individuals, institutional investors, and small corporations.

A *divisional structure by process* is similar to a functional structure, because activities are organized according to the way work is actually performed. However, a key difference between these two designs is that functional departments are not accountable for profits or revenues, whereas divisional process departments are evaluated on these criteria. An example of a divisional structure by process is a manufacturing business organized into six divisions: electrical work, glass cutting, welding, grinding, painting, and foundry work. In this case, all operations related to these specific processes would be grouped under the separate divisions. Each process (division) would be responsible for generating revenues and profits. The divisional structure by process can be particularly effective in achieving objectives when distinct production processes represent the thrust of competitiveness in an industry.

The Strategic Business Unit (SBU) Structure

As the number, size, and diversity of divisions in an organization increase, controlling and evaluating divisional operations become increasingly difficult for strategists. Increases in sales often are not accompanied by similar increases in profitability. The span of control becomes too large at top levels of the firm. For example, in a large conglomerate organization composed of 90 divisions, the chief executive officer could have difficulty even remembering the first names of divisional presidents. In multidivisional organizations, an SBU structure can greatly facilitate strategy-implementation efforts.

The *SBU structure* groups similar divisions into strategic business units and delegates authority and responsibility for each unit to a senior executive who reports directly to the chief executive officer. This change in structure can facilitate strategy implementation by improving coordination between similar divisions and channeling accountability to distinct business units. In the ninety-division conglomerate just mentioned, the ninety divisions could perhaps be regrouped into ten SBUs according to certain common characteristics, such as competing in the same industry, being located in the same area, or having the same customers.

Two disadvantages of an SBU structure are that it requires an additional layer of management, which increases salary expenses, and the role of the group vice president is often ambiguous. However, these limitations often do not outweigh the advantages of improved coordination and accountability. Atlantic Richfield and Fairchild Industries are examples of firms that successfully use an SBU-type structure.

The Matrix Structure

A *matrix structure* is the most complex of all designs because it depends upon both vertical and horizontal flows of authority and communication (hence the term *matrix*). In contrast, functional and divisional structures depend primarily on vertical flows of authority and communication. A matrix structure can result in higher overhead because it creates more management positions. Other characteristics of a matrix structure that contribute to overall complexity include dual lines of budget authority (a violation of the unity-of-command principle), dual sources of reward and punishment, shared authority, dual reporting channels, and a need for an extensive and effective communication system.

Despite its complexity, the matrix structure is widely used in many industries, including construction, healthcare, research, and defense. Some advantages of a matrix structure are that project objectives are clear, there are many channels of communication, workers can see the visible results of their work, and shutting down a project can be accomplished relatively easily.

In order for a matrix structure to be effective, organizations need participative planning, training, clear mutual understanding of roles and responsibilities, excellent internal communication, and mutual trust and confidence. The matrix structure is being used more frequently by American businesses because firms are pursuing strategies that add new products, customer groups, and technology to their range of activities. Out of these changes are coming product managers, functional managers, and geographic-area managers, all of whom have important strategic responsibilities. When several variables, such as product, customer, technology, geography, functional area, and line of business, have roughly equal strategic priorities, a matrix organization can be an effective structural form.

RESTRUCTURING, REENGINEERING AND E-ENGINEERING

VISIT THE NET

Provides a PowerPoint presentation on downsizing (restructuring).
http://www.cl.uh.edu/bpa/ hadm/HADM_5731/ ppt_presentations/7down/ index.htm

Restructuring and reengineering are becoming commonplace on the corporate landscape across the United States and Europe. *Restructuring*—also called *downsizing, rightsizing,* or *delayering*—involves reducing the size of the firm in terms of number of employees, number of divisions or units, and number of hierarchical levels in the firm's organizational structure. This reduction in size is intended to improve both efficiency and effectiveness. Restructuring is concerned primarily with shareholder well-being rather than employee well-being.

Recessionary economic conditions are forcing many European companies to downsize, laying off managers and employees. This was almost unheard of prior to the mid-1990s because European labor unions and laws required lengthy negotiations or huge severance checks before workers could be terminated. In contrast to the United States, labor union executives sit on most boards of directors of large European firms.

Job security in European companies is slowly moving toward a U.S. scenario, in which firms lay off almost at will. From banks in Milan to factories in Mannheim, European employers are starting to show people the door in an effort to streamline operations, increase efficiency, and compete against already slim and trim U.S. firms. Massive U.S.-style layoffs are still rare in Europe, but unemployment rates throughout the continent are rising quite rapidly. European firms still prefer to downsize by attrition and retirement rather than by blanket layoffs because of culture, laws, and unions. As indicated in the Global Perspective box, at first Nissan and now hundreds of other Japanese companies are restructured in a manner untraditional to accepted business practices in that nation.

VISIT THE NET

Provides a PowerPoint presentation on reengineering.
http://www.cl.uh.edu/bpa/ hadm/HADM_5731/ ppt_presentations/ 6reengin/index.htm

In contrast, *reengineering* is concerned more with employee and customer well-being than shareholder well-being. Reengineering—also called process management, process innovation, or process redesign—involves reconfiguring or redesigning work, jobs, and processes for the purpose of improving cost, quality, service, and speed.

Reengineering does not usually affect the organizational structure or chart, nor does it imply job lost or employee layoffs. Whereas restructuring is concerned with eliminating or establishing, shrinking or enlarging, and moving organizational departments and divisions, the focus of reengineering is changing the way work is actually carried out.

Reengineering is characterized by many tactical (short-term, business-function–specific) decisions, whereas restructuring is characterized by strategic (long-term, affecting all business functions) decisions.

The Internet is ushering in a new wave of business transformation. No longer is it enough for companies to put up simple Web sites for customers and employees. To take full advantage of the Internet, companies need to change the way they distribute goods, deal with suppliers, attract customers, and serve customers. The Internet eliminates the geographic protection/monopoly of local businesses. Basically, companies need to reinvent the way they do business to take full advantage of the Internet. This whole process

 # GLOBAL PERSPECTIVE

Restructuring at Nissan and Economic Recession Have Changed a Country

Japan Nikkei 225 Stock Index fell another 25 percent in 2001 to new seventeen-year lows as the country's economy shrank another 3.2 percent. Japan's unemployment rate has climbed above 5 percent, and demand for consumer goods has fallen to recession levels. Greater reluctance to downsize and restructure is one reason Japanese companies on average make 5 percent on assets; in contrast, their U.S. counterparts average a 15 percent return on assets.

Nissan is using American-style restructuring to reverse four years of dismal performance. Nissan recently closed five plants, laid off 14 percent of the company workforce, eliminated 21,500 jobs, reduced debt from 1.4 trillion yen to less than half that amount, reduced the number of suppliers from 1,145 to 600, and reduced manufacturing capacity from 2.4 million cars to 1.65 million annually. Called the Nissan Revival Plan, this strategy runs fully against many long-time Japanese business traditions—as noted below. Following Nissan, many other Japanese companies now employ restructuring to become more competitive.

- By laying off thousands of workers, the Nissan Revival Plan disregards the "lifetime employment practice" for which Japanese firms are well-known.

- The Nissan Revival Plan violates *keiretsu*, the Japanese business custom that links manufacturers to suppliers through shareholdings, exchanges of key managers, and long-term relationships.

- The Nissan Revival Plan changes the pay and promotion of managers from seniority to performance. This ends the widespread Japanese custom at Nissan whereby managers are promoted up the corporate ladder merely by stricking around.

- The Nissan Revival Plan dissolves the company's shareholding stake in most of its 1,394 affiliated companies. This Japanese system marries business interests when divorce might be healthier.

- The Nissan Revival Plan calls for a single worldwide advertising agency to keep the company message consistent worldwide.

Following Nissan's lead, hundreds of Japanese companies have recently laid off thousands of employees. Toshiba recently announced twenty thousand job cuts, almost half in Japan. Hitachi closed operations in Singapore and Malaysia, laying off forty-five hundred employees recently. Hitachi has recently axed 10,200 jobs in Japan. Mitsubishi Motors has laid off hundreds of workers. Fujitsu is laying off 16,400 employees. Most young Japanese have now abandoned the hope of landing lifetime jobs.

Source: Adapted from Norihiko Shirouzu, "Nissan Ambitious Restructuring Plan Delivers a Blow to Japan's Longstanding System of Corporate Families," *The Wall Street Journal* (October 20, 1999): A4. James Healey, "Retooling Nissan," *USA Today* (October 19, 1999): 2B.

is being called e-engineering.[5] Dow Corning Corporation and many others have recently appointed an e-commerce top executive.

Restructuring

Firms often employ restructuring when various ratios appear out of line with competitors as determined through benchmarking exercises. *Benchmarking* simply involves comparing a firm against the best firms in the industry on a wide variety of performance-related criteria. Some benchmarking ratios commonly used in rationalizing the need for restructuring are headcount-to-sales-volume, or corporate-staff-to-operating-employees, or span-of-control figures.

The primary benefit sought from restructuring is cost reduction. For some highly bureaucratic firms, restructuring can actually rescue the firm from global competition and demise. But the downside of restructuring can be reduced employee commitment, creativity, and innovation that accompanies the uncertainty and trauma associated with pending and actual employee layoffs.

Another downside of restructuring is that many people today do not aspire to become managers, and many present-day managers are trying to get off the management track.[6] Sentiment against joining management ranks is higher today than ever. About 80 percent of employees say they want nothing to do with management, a major shift from just a decade ago when 60 to 70 percent hoped to become managers. Managing others historically led to enhanced career mobility, financial rewards, and executive perks; but in today's global, more competitive, restructured arena, managerial jobs demand more hours and headaches with fewer financial rewards. Managers today manage more people spread over different locations, travel more, manage diverse functions, and are change agents even when they have nothing to do with the creation of the plan or even disagree with its approach. Employers today are looking for people who can do things, not for people who make other people do things. Restructuring in many firms has made a manager's job an invisible, thankless role. More workers today are self-managed, entrepreneurs, interpreneurs, or team-managed. Managers today need to be counselors, motivators, financial advisors, and psychologists. They also run the risk of becoming technologically behind in their areas of expertise. "Dilbert" cartoons commonly portray managers as enemies or as morons.

Massive restructuring among companies during the economic downturn of 2001–2003 resulted in huge layoffs. An upside to restructuring, however, is that when there are layoffs, those left behind have more opportunity to advance upwards in the firm. Layoff survivors also have more opportunity to gain experience in varied areas of the firm and may be given more responsibilities.[7]

Eastman Chemical in late 2001 established a new by-product divisional organizational structure. The company's two new divisions, Eastman Company and Voridian Company, focus on chemicals and polymers, respectively. The Eastman division focuses on coatings, adhesives, inks, and plastics, whereas the Voridian division focuses on fibers, polyethylene, and other polymers.

America's oldest department store retailer, Sears, Roebuck & Company is restructuring in 2002–2004. The company is abandoning its position as a moderate-priced department store and becoming much more like a mass discount retailer with central checkouts similar to Target and Kohl's. Sears is restructuring to become neither a department store nor a discounter; it is setting itself up to be positioned exactly between the two. The Sears restructuring includes layoffs of thirty-six thousand salaried employees and thirteen hundred additional employees at its Hoffman Estates, Illinois, headquarters. Apparel, the most troubled part of Sears' business, will become more classic, casual, and moderately priced. More national brands will be on the shelf, and footwear will become self-service. Sears will strive to develop a prominent Sears line of apparel similar to its Craftsman tools and Kenmore appliances.

It is interesting to note that in France, laying off employees is almost impossible due to labor laws that require lengthy negotiations and expensive severance packages for any individuals who are laid off. French CEOs in late 2001 sent a letter to Prime Minister Lionel Jospin warning that the strict layoff policies are crippling France's economy and companies. This is true because other European countries such as Germany have recently made it much easier for companies to lay off employees in order to stay competitive—and indeed to survive. Moulinex is an example of a French company that recently tried to lay off 670 employees but was denied this option, so the firm fell into bankruptcy and possible liquidation.

Reengineering

The argument for a firm engaging in reengineering usually goes as follows: Many companies historically have been organized vertically by business function. This arrangement has led over time to managers' and employees' mindsets being defined by their particular functions rather than by overall customer service, product quality, or corporate performance. The logic is that all firms tend to bureaucratize over time. As routines become entrenched, turf becomes delineated and defended, and politics takes precedence over performance. Walls that exist in the physical workplace can be reflections of "mental" walls.

In reengineering, a firm uses information technology to break down functional barriers and create a work system based on business processes, products, or outputs rather than on functions or inputs. Cornerstones of reengineering are decentralization, reciprocal interdependence, and information sharing. A firm that exemplifies complete information sharing is Springfield Remanufacturing Corporation, which provides to all employees a weekly income statement of the firm, as well as extensive information on other companies' performances.

The *Wall Street Journal* recently noted that reengineering today must go beyond knocking down internal walls that keep parts of a company from cooperating effectively; it must also knock down the external walls that prohibit or discourage cooperation with other firms—even rival firms.[8] A maker of disposable diapers echoes this need differently when it says that to be successful "cooperation at the firm must stretch from stump to rump."

Hewlett-Packard is a good example of a company that has knocked down the external barriers to cooperation and practices modern reengineering. The HP of today shares its forecasts with all of its supply-chain partners and shares other critical information with its distributors and other stakeholders. HP does all the buying of resin for its many manufacturers, giving it a volume discount of up to 5 percent. HP has established many alliances and cooperative agreements of the kind discussed in Chapter 5.

A benefit of reengineering is that it offers employees the opportunity to see more clearly how their particular jobs affect the final product or service being marketed by the firm. However, reengineering can also raise manager and employee anxiety, which, unless calmed, can lead to corporate trauma.

LINKING PERFORMANCE AND PAY TO STRATEGIES

Most companies today are practicing some form of pay-for-performance for employees and managers other than top executives. The average employee performance bonus is 6.8 percent of pay for individual performance, 5.5 percent of pay for group productivity, and 6.4 percent of pay for companywide profitability.

Staff control of pay systems often prevents line managers from using financial compensation as a strategic tool. Flexibility regarding managerial and employee compensation is needed to allow short-term shifts in compensation that can stimulate efforts to achieve long-term objectives.

How can an organization's reward system be more closely linked to strategic performance? How can decisions on salary increases, promotions, merit pay, and bonuses be more closely aligned to support the long-term strategic objectives of the organization? There are no widely accepted answers to these questions, but a dual bonus system based on both annual objectives and long-term objectives is becoming common. The percentage of a manager's annual bonus attributable to short-term versus long-term results should vary by hierarchical level in the organization. A chief executive officer's annual bonus could, for example, be determined on a 75 percent short-term and 25 percent long-term basis. It is important that bonuses not be based solely on short-term results because such a system ignores long-term company strategies and objectives.

DuPont Canada has a 16 percent return-on-equity objective. If this objective is met, the company's four thousand employees receive a "performance sharing cash award" equal to 4 percent of pay. If return-on-equity falls below 11 percent, employees get nothing. If return-on-equity exceeds 28 percent, workers receive a 10 percent bonus.

In an effort to cut costs and increase productivity, more and more Japanese companies are switching from seniority-based pay to performance-based approaches. Toyota Motor has switched to a full merit system for twenty thousand of its seventy thousand white-collar workers. Fujitsu, Sony, Matsushita Electric Industrial, and Kao also have switched to merit pay systems. Nearly 30 percent of all Japanese companies have switched to merit pay from seniority pay.[9] This switching is hurting morale at some Japanese companies, which have trained workers for decades to cooperate rather than to compete and to work in groups rather than individually.

Richard Brown, the new CEO of Electronic Data Systems, recently removed the bottom 20 percent of EDS's sales force and said,

> You have to start with an appraisal system that gives genuine feedback and differentiates performance. Some call it ranking people. That seems a little harsh. But you can't have a manager checking a box that says you're either stupendous, magnificent, very good, good, or average. Concise, constructive feedback is the fuel workers use to get better. A company that doesn't differentiate performance risks losing its best people.[10]

Profit sharing is another widely used form of incentive compensation. More than 30 percent of American companies have profit sharing plans, but critics emphasize that too many factors affect profits for this to be a good criterion. Taxes, pricing, or an acquisition would wipe out profits, for example. Also, firms try to minimize profits in a sense to reduce taxes.

Still another criterion widely used to link performance and pay to strategies is gain sharing. *Gain sharing* requires employees or departments to establish performance targets; if actual results exceed objectives, all members get bonuses. More than 26 percent of American companies use some form of gain sharing; about 75 percent of gain sharing plans have been adopted since 1980. Carrier, a subsidiary of United Technologies, has had excellent success with gain sharing in its six plants in Syracuse, New York; Firestone's tire plant in Wilson, North Carolina, has experienced similar success with gain sharing.

Criteria such as sales, profit, production efficiency, quality, and safety could also serve as bases for an effective *bonus system*. If an organization meets certain understood, agreed-upon profit objectives, every member of the enterprise should share in the harvest. A bonus system can be an effective tool for motivating individuals to support strategy-implementation efforts. BankAmerica, for example, recently overhauled its incentive system to link pay to sales of the bank's most profitable products and services. Branch managers receive a base salary plus a bonus based both on the number of new customers and on sales of bank products. Every employee in each branch is also eligible for a bonus if the branch exceeds its goals. Thomas Peterson, a top BankAmerica executive, says, "We want to make people responsible for meeting their goals, so we pay incentives on sales, not on controlling costs or on being sure the parking lot is a swept."

Five tests are often used to determine whether a performance-pay plan will benefit an organization:

1. *Does the plan capture attention?* Are people talking more about their activities and taking pride in early successes under the plan?

2. *Do employees understand the plan?* Can participants explain how it works and what they need to do to earn the incentive?

3. *Is the plan improving communication?* Do employees know more than they used to about the company's mission, plans, and objectives?

4. *Does the plan pay out when it should?* Are incentives being paid for desired results—and being withheld when objectives are not met?

5. *Is the company or unit performing better?* Are profits up? Has market share grown? Have gains resulted in part from the incentives?[11]

In addition to a dual bonus system, a combination of reward strategy incentives such as salary raises, stock options, fringe benefits, promotions, praise, recognition, criticism, fear, increased job autonomy, and awards can be used to encourage managers and employees to push hard for successful strategic implementation. The range of options for getting people, departments, and divisions to actively support strategy-implementation activities in a particular organization is almost limitless. Merck, for example, recently gave each of its thirty-seven thousand employees a ten-year option to buy one hundred shares of Merck stock at a set price of $127. Steven Darien, Merck's vice president of human resources, says, "We needed to find ways to get everyone in the workforce on board in terms of our goals and objectives. Company executives will begin meeting with all Merck workers to explore ways in which employees can contribute more."

Increasing criticism aimed at chief executive officers for their high pay has resulted in executive compensation being linked to performance of their firms more closely than ever before. Although the linkage between CEO pay and corporate performance is getting closer, CEO pay in the United States still can be astronomical.

For 2001, the median total shareholder return among the 350 largest U.S. firms was 3.6 percent while the CEO's total direct compensation declined 0.9 percent.[12] CEO's of the best performing companies generally were rewarded much better than CEO's of poor performing firms.

MANAGING RESISTANCE TO CHANGE

No organization or individual can escape change. But the thought of change raises anxieties because people fear economic loss, inconvenience, uncertainty, and a break in normal social patterns. Almost any change in structure, technology, people, or strategies has the potential to disrupt comfortable interaction patterns. For this reason, people resist change. The strategic-management process itself can impose major changes on individuals and processes. Reorienting an organization to get people to think and act strategically is not an easy task.

Resistance to change can be considered the single greatest threat to successful strategy implementation. Resistance in the form of sabotaging production machines, absenteeism, filing unfounded grievances, and an unwillingness to cooperate regularly occurs in organizations. People often resist strategy implementation because they do not understand what is happening or why changes are taking place. In that case, employees may simply need accurate information. Successful strategy implementation hinges upon managers' ability to develop an organizational climate conducive to change. Change must be viewed as an opportunity rather than as a threat by managers and employees.

Resistance to change can emerge at any stage or level of the strategy-implementation process. Although there are various approaches for implementing changes, three commonly used strategies are a force change strategy, an educative change strategy, and a rational or self-interest change strategy. A *force change strategy* involves giving orders and enforcing those orders; this strategy has the advantage of being fast, but it is plagued by low commitment and high resistance. The *educative change strategy* is one that presents information to convince people of the need for change; the disadvantage of an educative change strategy is that implementation becomes slow and difficult. However, this type of strategy evokes greater commitment and less resistance than does the force change strategy. Finally, a *rational* or *self-interest change strategy* is one that attempts to convince individuals that the change is to their personal advantage. When this appeal is successful, strategy implementation can be relatively easy. However, implementation changes are seldom to everyone's advantage.

The rational change strategy is the most desirable, so this approach is examined a bit further. Managers can improve the likelihood of successfully implementing change by carefully designing change efforts. Jack Duncan described a rational or self-interest change strategy as consisting of four steps. First, employees are invited to participate in the process of change and in the details of transition; participation allows everyone to give opinions, to feel a part of the change process, and to identify their own self-interests regarding the recommended change. Second, some motivation or incentive to change is required; self-interest can be the most important motivator. Third, communication is needed so that people can understand the purpose for the changes. Giving and receiving feedback is the fourth step; everyone enjoys knowing how things are going and how much progress is being made.[13]

Igor Ansoff summarized the need for strategists to manage resistance to change as follows:

> Observation of the historical transitions from one orientation to another shows that, if left unmanaged, the process becomes conflict-laden, prolonged, and costly in both human and financial terms. Management of resistance involves anticipating the focus of resistance and its intensity. Second, it involves eliminating unnecessary resistance caused by misperceptions and insecurities. Third, it involves mustering the power base necessary to assure support for the change. Fourth, it involves planning the process of change. Finally, it involves monitoring and controlling resistance during the process of change . . . [14]

Because of diverse external and internal forces, change is a fact of life in organizations. The rate, speed, magnitude, and direction of changes vary over time by industry and organization. Strategists should strive to create a work environment in which change is recognized as necessary and beneficial so that individuals can adapt to change more easily. Adopting a strategic-management approach to decision making can itself require major changes in the philosophy and operations of a firm.

VISIT THE NET

Provides a PowerPoint presentation on organizational change and managing resistance to change.
http://www.cl.uh.edu/bpa/hadm/HADM_5731/ppt_presentations/5orgchg/index.htm

Strategists can take a number of positive actions to minimize managers' and employees' resistance to change. For example, individuals who will be affected by a change should be involved in the decision to make the change and in decisions about how to implement the change. Strategists should anticipate changes and develop and offer training and development workshops so that managers and employees can adapt to those changes. They also need to communicate the need for changes effectively. The strategic-management process can be described as a process of managing change. Robert Waterman describes how successful organizations involve individuals to facilitate change:

> Implementation starts with, not after, the decision. When Ford Motor Company embarked on the program to build the highly successful Taurus, management gave up the usual, sequential design process. Instead [it] showed the tentative design to the workforce and asked [its] help in devising a car that would be easy to build. Team Taurus came up with no less than 1,401 items suggested by Ford employees. What a contrast from the secrecy that characterized the industry before. When people are treated as the main engine rather than interchangeable parts, motivation, creativity, quality, and commitment to implementation go up.[15]

Organizational change should be viewed today as a continuous process rather than as a project or event. The most successful organizations today continuously adapt to changes in the competitive environment, which themselves continue to change at an accelerating rate. It is not sufficient today to simply react to change. Managers need to anticipate change and ideally be the creator of change. Viewing change as a continuous process is in stark contrast to an old management doctrine regarding change, which was to unfreeze behavior, change the behavior, and then refreeze the new behavior. The new "continuous organizational change" philosophy should mirror the popular "continuous quality improvement philosophy."

VISIT THE NET

Gives good information about why employees may resist change.
http://www.mindtools.com/plreschn.html

MANAGING THE NATURAL ENVIRONMENT

All business functions are affected by natural environment considerations or by striving to make a profit. However, both employees and consumers are especially resentful of firms that take from more than give to the natural environment; likewise, people today are especially appreciative of firms that conduct operations in a way that mends rather than harms the environment.

The U.S. Justice Department recently issued new guidelines for companies to uncover environmental wrongdoing among their managers and employees without exposing themselves to potential criminal liability. The new guidelines give nine hypothetical examples to illustrate the new legal requirements. The examples include Company A, which regularly conducts a comprehensive environmental audit, goes straight to the government as soon as something wrong is turned up, disciplines the responsible people in the company, and gives their names as well as all relevant documentation to the government. The Justice Department will prosecute but be lenient in this case. The extreme example is Company K, which tries to cover up an environmental violation and does not cooperate with the government or provide names. Its audit is narrow, and its compliance program is "no more than a collection of paper." No leniency is likely for this firm.

Monsanto, a large U.S. chemical company, is an excellent example of a firm that protects the natural environment. Monsanto's motto is "Zero Spills, Zero Releases, Zero Incidents, and Zero Excuses."

The 1990s may well be remembered as the decade of the environment. Earth itself has become a stakeholder for all business firms. Consumer interests in businesses' preserving nature's ecological balance and fostering a clean, healthy environment is high. As indicated in the Natural Environment Perspective, an increasing number of businesses today are purchasing their own independent, nonpolluting power source. This strategy is in contrast to continuing to purchase electricity from large, polluting, coal-burning utilities.

The ecological challenge facing all organizations requires managers to formulate strategies that preserve and conserve natural resources and control pollution. Special natural environmental issues include ozone depletion, global warming, depletion of rain forests, destruction of animal habitats, protecting endangered species, developing biodegradable products and packages, waste management, clean air, clean water, erosion, destruction of natural resources, and pollution control. Firms increasingly are developing green product lines that are biodegradable and/or are made from recycled products. Green products sell well.

The Environmental Protection Agency recently reported that U.S. citizens and organizations spend more than about $200 billion annually on pollution abatement. Environmental concerns touch all aspects of a business's operations, including workplace risk exposures, packaging, waste reduction, energy use, alternative fuels, environmental cost accounting, and recycling practices.

Managing as if the earth matters requires an understanding of how international trade, competitiveness, and global resources are connected. Managing environmental affairs can no longer be simply a technical function performed by specialists in a firm; more emphasis must be placed on developing an environmental perspective among all employees and managers of the firm. Many companies are moving environmental affairs from the staff side of the organization to the line side, thus making the corporate environmental group report directly to the chief operating officer.

Societies have been plagued by environmental disasters to such an extent recently that firms failing to recognize the importance of environmental issues and challenges could suffer severe consequences. Managing environmental affairs can no longer be an incidental or secondary function of company operations. Product design, manufacturing, and ultimate disposal should not merely reflect environmental considerations, but also be driven by them. Firms that manage environmental affairs will enhance relations with consumers, regulators, vendors, and other industry players—substantially improving their prospects of success.

Firms should formulate and implement strategies from an environmental perspective. Environmental strategies could include developing or acquiring green businesses, divesting or altering environment-damaging businesses, striving to become a low-cost producer through waste minimization and energy conservation, and pursuing a differentiation strategy through green-product features. In addition to creating strategies, firms could include an environmental representative on the board of directors, conduct regular environmental audits, implement bonuses for favorable environmental results, become involved in environmental issues and programs, incorporate environmental values in mission statements, establish environmentally oriented objectives, acquire environmental skills, and provide environmental training programs for company employees and managers.

California reimburses companies that buy natural gas trucks rather than cheaper diesel ones because diesel exhaust from big trucks and buses account up to 70 percent of the soot in U.S. air.[16] Diesel trucks can emit 100 times more soot than cars. Researchers have found that diesel fumes pose a higher cancer risk than all other air pollution combined.

VISIT THE NET

Gives the strategic plan for a community police consortium, including a section on strategy implementation.
http://www.
communitypolicing.org/
outline.html

NATURAL ENVIRONMENT PERSPECTIVE

Does Your Business Generate Its Own Electricity?

If no, perhaps it should. A new era is upon us: Power production generators are rapidly selling into homes and businesses. Personal power is poised to explode into everyday life just like personal computers did in 1984—and cellular phones more recently. Even the New York City Central Park police station has pulled the plug on its public utility. Companies such as Plug Power LLC of Latham, New York, are selling dishwasher-sized fuel cells for the home for less than four thousand dollars. These new systems, which run on propane or natural gas, not diesel, are exceptionally efficient and nonpolluting. In a fossil fuel plant, only 29 percent of the original energy in the coal or oil remains when it arrives at a home or business. "The era of big central power plants is certainly over," says Chuck Linderman of Edison Electric Institute. Some businesses, such as First National Bank in Omaha, have purchased a personal power system because "being down for one hour would cost the bank about $6 million." Because of storms, big power plants often cut off power to homes and businesses, which is so costly to some businesses; as a result, personal power systems are in great demand. Some large companies leading the way in using personal power systems include McDonald's, Rogan Corporation, Heinemann Bakeries, and Citigroup. Some manufac-

turers of personal power plants include Caterpillar Inc., Ingersoll-Rand Company, and General Electric.

More than one hundred companies have already entered the personal power business, which goes by the name "distributed generation." All public utilities are worried about exponential growth in personal power. Some large utilities in the United States try to make it impossible for homes to switch to personal power, but this is a losing battle. If personal power becomes the standard business practice by 2010 as expected, then the United States can meet the stringent reductions in carbon dioxide emissions agreed to in the international global warming treaty. However, the U.S. did not sign the Kyoto Accords which aimed to reduce global warming by reducing CO_2 omissions. Global warming isn't just a fear, it's a fact—and carbon dioxide from large power plants is a major culprit. CO_2 is the most common air pollutant worldwide, and the United States emits over six million tons of it annually—by far, the most among all countries.

Source: Adapted from: Ann Keeton, "Future Generations—Small Businesses May Soon Be Producing Much of Their Own Power On-site," *The Wall Street Journal* (September 13, 1999): R8. Also, Seth Borenstein, "New Devices May Let Homes Generate Own Electricity," *Wilmington Morning Star* (July 7, 1999): 1A.

Northeast Utilities recently agreed to pay a record $10 million in penalties and to plead guilty to twenty-five felony counts for polluting water near Waterford, Connecticut, and for discharging chlorine into Long Island Sound while concealing those actions. This company previously had discharged hydrazine, a highly toxic chemical used to clean out industrial piping, into area waters without a permit.

CREATING A STRATEGY-SUPPORTIVE CULTURE

Strategists should strive to preserve, emphasize, and build upon aspects of an existing *culture* that support proposed new strategies. Aspects of an existing culture that are antagonistic to a proposed strategy should be identified and changed. Substantial research indicates that new strategies are often market-driven and dictated by competitive forces. For this reason, changing a firm's culture to fit a new strategy is usually more effective than changing a strategy to fit an existing culture. Numerous techniques are available to alter an organization's culture, including recruitment, training, transfer, promotion, restructure of an organization's design, role modeling, and positive reinforcement.

Jack Duncan described *triangulation* as an effective, multimethod technique for studying and altering a firm's culture.[17] Triangulation includes the combined use of obtrusive observation, self-administered questionnaires, and personal interviews to determine the nature of a firm's culture. The process of triangulation reveals changes that need to be made to a firm's culture in order to benefit strategy.

Schein indicated that the following elements are most useful in linking culture to strategy:

1. Formal statements of organizational philosophy, charters, creeds, materials used for recruitment and selection, and socialization
2. Designing of physical spaces, facades, buildings
3. Deliberate role modeling, teaching, and coaching by leaders
4. Explicit reward and status system, promotion criteria
5. Stories, legends, myths, and parables about key people and events
6. What leaders pay attention to, measure, and control
7. Leader reactions to critical incidents and organizational crises
8. How the organization is designed and structured
9. Organizational systems and procedures
10. Criteria used for recruitment, selection, promotion, leveling off, retirement, and "excommunication" of people[18]

In the personal and religious side of life, the impact of loss and change is easy to see.[19] Memories of loss and change often haunt individuals and organizations for years. Ibsen wrote, "Rob the average man of his life illusion and you rob him of his happiness at the same stroke."[20] When attachments to a culture are severed in an organization's attempt to change direction, employees and managers often experience deep feelings of grief. This phenomenon commonly occurs when external conditions dictate the need for a new strategy. Managers and employees often struggle to find meaning in a situation that changed many years before. Some people find comfort in memories; others find solace in the present. Weak linkages between strategic management and organizational culture can jeopardize performance and success. Deal and Kennedy emphasized that making strategic changes in an organization always threatens a culture:

> . . . people form strong attachments to heroes, legends, the rituals of daily life, the hoopla of extravaganza and ceremonies, and all the symbols of the workplace. Change strips relationships and leaves employees confused, insecure, and often angry. Unless something can be done to provide support for transitions from old to new, the force of a culture can neutralize and emasculate strategy changes.[21]

VISIT THE NET

Provides nice information on "What Is Culture" and also provides additional excellent hot links to other culture sites.
http://www.mapnp.org/library/org_thry/culture/culture.htm

The Mexican Culture

Mexico always has been and still is an authoritarian society in terms of schools, churches, businesses, and families. Employers seek workers who are agreeable, respectful, and obedient, rather than innovative, creative, and independent. Mexican workers tend to be activity-oriented rather than problem solvers. When visitors walk into a Mexican business, they are impressed by the cordial, friendly atmosphere. This is almost always true because Mexicans desire harmony rather than conflict; desire for harmony is part of the social fabric in worker-manager relations. There is a much lower tolerance for adversarial relations or friction at work in Mexico as compared to the United States.

Mexican employers are paternalistic, providing workers with more than a paycheck, but in return, they expect allegiance. Weekly food baskets, free meals, free bus service, and free daycare are often a part of compensation. The ideal working conditions for a Mexican worker is the family model, with people all working together, doing their share, according to their designated roles. Mexican workers do not expect or desire a work environment in which self-expression and initiative are encouraged. Whereas U.S. business embodies individualism, achievement, competition, curiosity, pragmatism, informality, spontaneity, and doing more than expected on the job, Mexican businesses stress collectivism, continuity, cooperation, belongingness, formality, and doing exactly what you're told.

In Mexico, business associates rarely entertain at their homes, places reserved exclusively for close friends and family. Business meetings and entertaining are nearly always done at a restaurant. Preserving one's honor, saving face, and looking important is also exceptionally important in Mexico. This is why Mexicans do not accept criticism and change easily; many find it humiliating to acknowledge having made a mistake. A meeting among employees and managers in a business located in Mexico is a forum for giving orders and directions rather than for discussing problems or participating in decision making. Mexican workers want to be closely supervised, cared for, and corrected in a civil manner. Opinions expressed by employees are often regarded as back talk in Mexico. Mexican supervisors are viewed as weak if they explain the rationale for their orders to workers.

Mexicans do not feel compelled to follow rules that are not associated with a particular person in authority they know well or work for. Thus, signs to wear earplugs or safety glasses, or attendance or seniority policies, and even one-way street signs are often ignored. Whereas Americans follow the rules, Mexicans often do not.

Life is slower in Mexico than in the United States. People do not wear watches. The first priority is often assigned to the last request, rather than to the first. Telephone systems break down. Banks may suddenly not have pesos. Phone repair can take months. Electricity for an entire plant or town can be down for hours or even days. Business and government offices open and close at different hours. Buses and taxis may be hours off schedule. Meeting times for appointments are not rigid. Tardiness is common everywhere. Doing business effectively in Mexico requires knowledge of the Mexican way of life, culture, beliefs, and customs.

The Russian Culture

In America, unsuccessful business entrepreneurs are viewed negatively as failures, whereas successful small business owners enjoy high esteem and respect. In Russia, however, there is substantial social pressure against becoming a successful entrepreneur. Being a winner in Russia makes you the object of envy and resentment, a member of the elite rather than of the masses. Although this is slowly changing, personal ambition and success in Russia are often met with vindictiveness and derision. Initiative is met with indifference at best and punishment at worst. In the face of public ridicule and organized crime, however, thousands of Russians, particularly young persons, are opening all kinds of businesses. Public scorn and their own guilt from violating the values they were raised with do not deter many. Because Russian society scorns success, publicizing achievements, material possessions, awards, or privileges earned by Russian workers is not an effective motivational tool for those workers.

The Russian people are best known for their drive, boundless energy, tenacity, hard work, and perseverance in spite of immense obstacles. This is as true today as ever. The notion that the average Russian is stupid or lazy is nonsense; Russians on average are more educated than their American counterparts and bounce up more readily from failure.

In the United States, business ethics and personal ethics are essentially the same. Deception is deception and a lie is a lie whether in business or personal affairs in America. However, in Russia, business and personal ethics are separate. To deceive someone, bribe someone, or lie to someone to promote a business transaction is ethical in Russia, but to deceive a friend or trusted colleague is unethical. There are countless examples of foreign firms being cheated by Russian business partners. The implication of this fact for American businesses is to forge strong personal relationships with their Russian business partners whenever possible; spend time with the Russians, eating, relaxing, and exercising; and in the absence of a personal relationship, be exceptionally cautious with agreements, partnerships, payments, and when granting credit.

The Russian people have great faith and confidence in as well as respect for American products and services. Russians generally have low self-confidence. American ideas, technology, and production practices are viewed by Russians as a panacea that can save them from a gloomy existence. For example, their squeaky telephone system and lack of fax machines make them feel deprived. This mindset presents great opportunity in Russia for American products of all kinds.

Russia has historically been an autocratic state. This cultural factor is evident in business; Russian managers generally exercise power without ever being challenged by subordinates. Delegation of authority and responsibility is difficult and often nonexistent in Russian businesses. The American participative management style is not well received in Russia.

A crackdown on religion is underway in Russia. The government recognizes only Russian Orthodoxy, Judaism, Islam, and Buddhism as indigenous religions. All other faiths and churches, including all other Christian denominations, have to apply each year for permission to practice in Russia. Permission may not be granted. President Putin opposes the anti-religion movement. The lower house of Russia's parliament, the State Duma, is dominated by Communists who favor antireligion and resist further economic reforms.

The Russian republic of Ingushetia recently passed a decree legalizing the practice of polygymy that allows men to have multiple wives, even a harem. The new law is a direct challenge to the Russian government, which has jurisdiction over eighty-nine republics. The Russian Constitution prohibits polygamy, but the criminal code does not provide for any penalty. Ingushetian men take more than one wife, especially when the first wife does not have a son, despite the scientific discovery in 1959 that the father's contribution alone in procreation determines a child's sex.

The Japanese Culture

The Japanese place great importance upon group loyalty and consensus, a concept called *Wa*. Nearly all corporate activities in Japan encourage *Wa* among managers and employees. *Wa* requires that all members of a group agree and cooperate; this results in constant discussion and compromise. Japanese managers evaluate the potential attractiveness of alternative business decisions in terms of the long-term effect on the group's *Wa*. This is why silence, used for pondering alternatives, can be a plus in a formal Japanese meeting. Discussions potentially disruptive to *Wa* are generally conducted in very informal settings, such as at a bar, so as to minimize harm to the group's *Wa*. Entertaining is an important business activity in Japan because it strengthens *Wa*. Formal meetings are often conducted in informal settings. When confronted with disturbing questions or opinions, Japanese managers tend to remain silent, whereas Americans tend to respond directly, defending themselves through explanation and argument.

Most Japanese managers are reserved, quiet, distant, introspective, and other-oriented, whereas most U.S. managers are talkative, insensitive, impulsive, direct, and individual-oriented. Americans often perceive Japanese managers as wasting time and carrying on pointless conversations, whereas U.S. managers often use blunt criticism, ask prying questions, and make quick decisions. These kinds of cultural differences have disrupted many potentially productive Japanese-American business endeavors. Viewing the Japanese communication style as a prototype for all Asian cultures is a stereotype that must be avoided.

Americans have more freedom in the United States to control their own fates than do the Japanese. Life in the United States and life in Japan are very different; the United States offers more upward mobility to its people. This is a great strength of the United States. Sherman explained:

> America is not like Japan and can never be. America's strength is the opposite: It opens its doors and brings the world's disorder in. It tolerates social change that would tear most other societies apart. This openness encourages Americans to adapt as individuals rather than as a group. Americans go west to California to get a new start; they move east to Manhattan to try to make the big time; they move to Vermont or to a farm to get close to the soil. They break away from their parents' religions or values or class; they rediscover their ethnicity. They go to night school; they change their names.[22]

PRODUCTION/OPERATIONS CONCERNS WHEN IMPLEMENTING STRATEGIES

Production/operations capabilities, limitations, and policies can significantly enhance or inhibit the attainment of objectives. Production processes typically constitute more than 70 percent of a firm's total assets. A major part of the strategy-implementation process takes place at the production site. Production-related decisions on plant size, plant location, product design, choice of equipment, kind of tooling, size of inventory, inventory control, quality control, cost control, use of standards, job specialization, employee training, equipment and resource utilization, shipping and packaging, and technological innovation can have a dramatic impact on the success or failure of strategy-implementation efforts.

Examples of adjustments in production systems that could be required to implement various strategies are provided in Table 7–3 for both for-profit and nonprofit organizations. For instance, note that when a bank formulates and selects a strategy to add

TABLE 7-3   **Production Management and Strategy Implementation**

TYPE OF ORGANIZATION	STRATEGY BEING IMPLEMENTED	PRODUCTION SYSTEM ADJUSTMENTS
Hospital	Adding a cancer center (Product Development)	Purchase specialized equipment and add specialized people.
Bank	Adding ten new branches (Market Development)	Perform site location analysis.
Beer brewery	Purchasing a barley farm operation (Backward Integration)	Revise the inventory control system.
Steel manufacturer	Acquiring a fast-food chain (Conglomerate Diversification)	Improve the quality control system.
Computer company	Purchasing a retail distribution chain (Forward Integration)	Alter the shipping, packaging, and transportation systems.

ten new branches, a production-related implementation concern is site location. The largest bicycle company in the United States, Huffy, recently ended its own production of bikes and now contracts out those services to Asian and Mexican manufacturers. Huffy focuses instead on the design, marketing, and distribution of bikes, but it no longer produces bikes itself. The Dayton, Ohio, company closed its plants in Ohio, Missouri, and Mississippi.

Just-in-Time (JIT) production approaches have withstood the test of time. JIT significantly reduces the costs of implementing strategies. With JIT, parts and materials are delivered to a production site just as they are needed, rather than being stockpiled as a hedge against later deliveries. Harley-Davidson reports that at one plant alone, JIT freed $22 million previously tied up in inventory and greatly reduced reorder lead time.

Factors that should be studied before locating production facilities include the availability of major resources, the prevailing wage rates in the area, transportation costs related to shipping and receiving, the location of major markets, political risks in the area or country, and the availability of trainable employees.

For high-technology companies, production costs may not be as important as production flexibility because major product changes can be needed often. Industries such as biogenetics and plastics rely on production systems that must be flexible enough to allow frequent changes and the rapid introduction of new products. An article in *Harvard Business Review* explained why some organizations get into trouble:

> They too slowly realize that a change in product strategy alters the tasks of a production system. These tasks, which can be stated in terms of requirements for cost, product flexibility, volume flexibility, product performance, and product consistency, determine which manufacturing policies are appropriate. As strategies shift over time, so must production policies covering the location and scale of manufacturing facilities, the choice of manufacturing process, the degree of vertical integration of each manufacturing facility, the use of R&D units, the control of the production system, and the licensing of technology.[23]

A common management practice, cross-training of employees, can facilitate strategy implementation and can yield many benefits. Employees gain a better understanding of the whole business and can contribute better ideas in planning sessions. Production/operations managers need to realize, however, that cross-training employees can create problems related to the following issues:

1. It can thrust managers into roles that emphasize counseling and coaching over directing and enforcing.
2. It can necessitate substantial investments in training and incentives.
3. It can be very time-consuming.
4. Skilled workers may resent unskilled workers who learn their jobs.
5. Older employees may not want to learn new skills.

HUMAN RESOURCE CONCERNS WHEN IMPLEMENTING STRATEGIES

The job of human resource manager is changing rapidly as companies continue to downsize and reorganize. Strategic responsibilities of the human resource manager include assessing the staffing needs and costs for alternative strategies proposed during strategy formulation and developing a staffing plan for effectively implementing strategies. This plan must consider how best to manage spiraling healthcare insurance costs. Employers' health coverage expenses consume an average 26 percent of firms' net profits, even though most companies now require employees to pay part of their health insurance premiums. The plan must also include how to motivate employees and managers during a time when layoffs are common and workloads are high.

The human resource department must develop performance incentives that clearly link performance and pay to strategies. The process of empowering managers and employees through their involvement in strategic-management activities yields the greatest benefits when all organizational members understand clearly how they will benefit personally if the firm does well. Linking company and personal benefits is a major new strategic responsibility of human resource managers. Other new responsibilities for human resource managers may include establishing and administering an *employee stock ownership plan (ESOP)*, instituting an effective childcare policy, and providing leadership for managers and employees in a way that allows them to balance work and family.

A well-designed strategic-management system can fail if insufficient attention is given to the human resource dimension. Human resource problems that arise when businesses implement strategies can usually be traced to one of three causes: (1) disruption of social and political structures, (2) failure to match individuals' aptitudes with implementation tasks, and (3) inadequate top management support for implementation activities.[24]

Strategy implementation poses a threat to many managers and employees in an organization. New power and status relationships are anticipated and realized. New formal and informal groups' values, beliefs, and priorities may be largely unknown. Managers and employees may become engaged in resistance behavior as their roles, prerogatives, and power in the firm change. Disruption of social and political structures that accompany strategy execution must be anticipated and considered during strategy formulation and managed during strategy implementation.

A concern in matching managers with strategy is that jobs have specific and relatively static responsibilities, although people are dynamic in their personal development. Commonly used methods that match managers with strategies to be implemented include transferring managers, developing leadership workshops, offering career development activities, promotions, job enlargement, and job enrichment.

A number of other guidelines can help ensure that human relationships facilitate rather than disrupt strategy-implementation efforts. Specifically, managers should do a lot of chatting and informal questioning to stay abreast of how things are progressing and to know when to intervene. Managers can build support for strategy-implementation efforts by giving few orders, announcing few decisions, depending heavily on informal questioning, and seeking to probe and clarify until a consensus emerges. Key thrusts that succeed should be rewarded generously and visibly.

It is surprising that so often during strategy formulation, individual values, skills, and abilities needed for successful strategy implementation are not considered. It is rare that a firm selecting new strategies or significantly altering existing strategies possesses the right line and staff personnel in the right positions for successful strategy implementation. The need to match individual aptitudes with strategy-implementation tasks should be considered in strategy choice.

Inadequate support from strategists for implementation activities often undermines organizational success. Chief executive officers, small business owners, and government agency heads must be personally committed to strategy implementation and express this commitment in highly visible ways. Strategists' formal statements about the importance of strategic management must be consistent with actual support and rewards given for activities completed and objectives reached. Otherwise, stress created by inconsistency can cause uncertainty among managers and employees at all levels.

Perhaps the best method for preventing and overcoming human resource problems in strategic management is to actively involve as many managers and employees as possible in the process. Although time-consuming, this approach builds understanding, trust, commitment, and ownership and reduces resentment and hostility. The true potential of strategy formulation and implementation resides in people.

Employee Stock Ownership Plans (ESOPs)

An *ESOP* is a tax-qualified, defined-contribution, employee-benefit plan whereby employees purchase stock of the company through borrowed money or cash contributions. ESOPs empower employees to work as owners; this is a primary reason why the number of ESOPs grew dramatically throughout the 1980s and 1990s to more than ten thousand plans covering more than fifteen million employees. ESOPs now control more than $80 billion in corporate stock in the United States.

Besides reducing worker alienation and stimulating productivity, ESOPs allow firms other benefits, such as substantial tax savings. Principal, interest, and dividend payments on ESOP-funded debt are tax-deductible. Banks lend money to ESOPs at interest rates below prime. This money can be repaid in pretax dollars, lowering the debt service as much as 30 percent in some cases.

If an ESOP owns more than 50 percent of the firm, those who lend money to the ESOP are taxed on only 50 percent of the income received on the loans. ESOPs are not for every firm, however, because the initial legal, accounting, actuarial, and appraisal fees to set up an ESOP are about $50,000 for a small or midsized firm, with annual administration expenses of about $15,000. Analysts say ESOPs also do not work well in firms that have fluctuating payrolls and profits. Human resource managers in many firms conduct preliminary research to determine the desirability of an ESOP, and then they facilitate its establishment and administration if benefits outweigh the costs.

To establish an ESOP, a firm sets up a trust fund and purchases shares of its stock, which are allocated to individual employee accounts. All full-time employees over the age of twenty-one usually participate in the plan. Allocations of stock to the trust are made on the basis of relative pay, seniority, or some other formula. When an ESOP borrows money to purchase stock, the debt is guaranteed by the company and thus appears on the firm's balance sheet. On average, ESOP employees get $1,300 worth of stock per year, but they cannot take physical possession of the shares until they quit, retire, or die. The median level of employee ownership in ESOP plans is 30 to 40 percent, although the range is from about 10 to 100 percent.

Research confirms that ESOPs can have a dramatic positive effect on employee motivation and corporate performance, especially if ownership is coupled with expanded employee participation and involvement in decision making. Market surveys indicate that customers prefer to do business with firms that are employee-owned.

Many companies are following the lead of Polaroid, which established an ESOP as a tactic for preventing a hostile takeover. Polaroid's CEO MacAllister Booth says, "Twenty years from now we'll find that employees have a sizable stake in every major American corporation." (It is interesting to note here that Polaroid is chartered in the state of Delaware, which requires corporate suitors to acquire 85 percent of a target company's shares to complete a merger; over 50 percent of all American corporations are incorporated in Delaware for this reason.) Wyatt Cafeterias, a southwestern U.S. operator of 120 cafeterias, also adopted the ESOP concept to prevent a hostile takeover. Employee productivity at Wyatt greatly increased since the ESOP began, as illustrated in the following quote:

The key employee in our entire organization is the person serving the customer on the cafeteria line. In the past, because of high employee turnover and entry-level wages for many line jobs, these employees received far less attention and recognition than managers. We now tell the tea cart server, "You own the place. Don't wait for the manager to tell you how to do your job better or how to provide better service. You take care of it." Sure, we're looking for productivity increases, but since we began pushing decisions down to the level of people who deal directly with customers, we've discovered an awesome side effect—suddenly the work crews have this "happy to be here" attitude that the customers really love.[25]

Companies such as Avis, Procter & Gamble, BellSouth, ITT, Xerox, Delta, Austin Industries, Health Trust, the Parsons Corporation, Dyncorp, and Charter Medical have established ESOPs to assist strategists in divesting divisions, going private, and consummating leveraged buyours. ESOPs can be found today in all kinds of firms, from small retailers to large manufacturers. Nearly all ESOPs are established in healthy firms, not failing firms.

Balancing Work Life and Home Life

Work/family strategies have become so popular among companies today that the strategies now represent a competitive advantage for those firms that offer such benefits as elder care assistance, flexible scheduling, job sharing, adoption benefits, an on-site summer camp, employee help lines, pet care, and even lawn service referrals. New corporate titles such as Work/Life Coordinator and Director of Diversity are becoming common.

Working Mother magazine in late 2001 published its listing of "The 100 Best Companies for Working Mothers" (**http://workingmother.com/oct_2001/100best. shtml**). Three especially important variables used in the ranking were availability of flextime, advancement opportunities, and equitable distribution of benefits among companies. *Working Mother's* top ten best companies for working women in 2001 are listed here:

1. Bristol-Myers Squibb Company
2. Citigroup
3. Fannie Mae
4. IBM Corporation
5. Marriott International
6. Morgan Stanley
7. PricewaterhouseCoopers
8. Procter & Gamble Company
9. Prudential
10. Texas Instruments

Human resource managers need to foster a more effective balancing of professional and private lives because nearly sixty million people in the United States are now part of two-career families. A corporate objective to become more lean and mean must today include consideration for the fact that a good home life contributes immensely to a good work life.

The work/family issue is no longer just a women's issue. Some specific measures that firms are taking to address this issue are providing spouse relocation assistance as an employee benefit, providing company resources for family recreational and educational use, establishing employee country clubs such as those at IBM and Bethlehem Steel, and creating family/work interaction opportunities. A study by Joseph Pleck of Wheaton

VISIT THE NET

To see how a large company, Johnson & Johnson, is balancing "Work and Family Issues," visit the Web site www.jnj.com/who_is_jnj/ framework_index.html.

College found that in companies that do not offer paternity leave for fathers as a benefit, most men take short informal paternity leaves anyway by combining vacation time and sick days.

Some organizations have developed family days, when family members are invited into the workplace, taken on plant or office tours, dined by management, and given a chance to see exactly what other family members do each day. Family days are inexpensive and increase the employee's pride in working for the organization. Flexible working hours during the week are another human resource response to the need for individuals to balance work life and home life. The work/family topic is being made part of the agenda at meetings and thus is being discussed in many organizations.

Research indicates that employees who are dissatisfied with childcare arrangements are most likely to be absent or unproductive.[26] Lack of adequate childcare in a community can be a deterrent in recruiting and retaining good managers and employees. Some benefits of on-site childcare facilities are improved employee relations, reduced absenteeism and turnover, increased productivity, enhanced recruitment, and improved community relations.

A recent survey of women managers revealed that one-third would leave their present employer for another employer offering childcare assistance. The Conference Board recently reported that more than five hundred firms in the United States had created on-site or near-site childcare centers for their employees, including Merck, Campbell Soup, Hoffman-LaRoche, Stride-Rite, Johnson Wax, CIGNA, Champion International, Walt Disney World, and Playboy Resorts.

Other common childcare service arrangements include employer-sponsored daycare, childcare information, and referral services. IBM, Steelcase, Honeywell, Citibank, 3M, and Southland have established contracts with third-party childcare information and referral services.

Most of the sixty-four million women in the U.S. labor force are employed in what the Department of Labor calls "nontraditional occupations"—areas of employment in which women now comprise 25 percent or less of the workforce. This list includes pilots, truck drivers, funeral directors, dentists, architects, bellhops, barbers, meter readers, and construction workers. Women in the United States now head one in every four households with children under age eighteen. Women must and should therefore get their fair share of these jobs for our society to progress. More women in the United States are employed as teachers, secretaries, and cashiers than work in any other jobs. Among the jobs in which less than 5 percent of those employed are women include fishermen (4.6 percent), pest control (4.1 percent), airplane pilots and navigators (4.1 percent), firefighting and fire prevention (2.5 percent), construction (2.0 percent), and tool and die makers (0.2 percent).[27]

It is encouraging to note that more and more talented women in business are being promoted to top-level managerial positions in the United States. Carleton Fiorina is CEO of Hewlett-Packard and Andrea Jung is CEO of Avon—by far the largest companies ever run by women. Thirteen percent of Texas Instruments' top executives are women, up from only 2 percent in 1994. Fiorina is only the third woman CEO of a Fortune 500 company; the others include Barad at Mattel and Sandler at Golden West Financial. Among the Fortune 1000 companies, there are only seven female CEOs, so the *glass ceiling* in America still exists and needs to be broken. Only 11.1 percent of all company executives are female among Fortune 500 companies. In the automobile industry, only 8 percent of executives at Ford, DaimlerChrysler, and General Motors are female. However, women buy more than half the vehicles sold in the United States and take part in more than 80 percent of all purchases.[28]

Benefits of a Diverse Workforce

When Toyota was threatened with a boycott by African Americans in late 2001, the company committed almost $8 billion oven ten years to diversify its workforce and to use more minority suppliers. Hundreds of other firms, such as Ford Motor Company and Coca-Cola, are also striving to become more diversified in their workforce. TJX Companies, the parent of fifteen-hundred T.J. Maxx and Marshalls stores, has experienced great benefits of being an exemplary company in terms of diversity. A recent *Wall Street Journal* article listed, in rank order of importance, the following major benefits of having a diverse workforce:[29]

1. Improves corporate culture
2. Improves employee morale
3. Leads to a higher retention of employees
4. Leads to an easier recruitment of new employees
5. Decreases complaints and litigation
6. Increases creativity
7. Decreases interpersonal conflict between employees
8. Enables the organization to move into emerging markets
9. Improves client relations
10. Increases productivity
11. Improves the bottom line
12. Maximizes brand identity
13. Reduces training costs

An organization can perhaps be most effective when its workforce mirrors the diversity of its customers. For global companies, this goal can be optimistic, but it is a worthwhile goal. According to the 2001 census figures, African Americans comprise 13 percent of the U.S. population, followed by Hispanics at 12.5 percent, and Asian Americans at 3.6 percent. Women account for about 46.6 percent of the American workforce. Minorities and women are still scarce in top management positions in America; this problem needs immediate attention.

CONCLUSION

Successful strategy formulation does not at all guarantee successful strategy implementation. Although inextricably interdependent, strategy formulation and strategy implementation are characteristically different. In a single word, strategy implementation means *change*. It is widely agreed that "the real work begins after strategies are formulated." Successful strategy implementation requires the support of as well as discipline and hard work from motivated managers and employees. It is sometimes frightening to think that a single individual can sabotage strategy-implementation efforts irreparably.

Formulating the right strategies is not enough, because managers and employees must be motivated to implement those strategies. Management issues considered central to strategy implementation include matching organizational structure with strategy, linking performance and pay to strategies, creating an organizational climate conducive to change, managing political relationships, creating a strategy-supportive culture, adapting production/operations processes, and managing human resources. Establishing annual objectives, devising policies, and allocating resources are central strategy-implementation activities common to all organizations. Depending on the size and type of the organization, other management issues could be equally important to successful strategy implementation.

 We invite you to visit the David page on the Prentice Hall Companion Website at **www.prenhall.com/david** for this chapter's World Wide Web exercises.

KEY TERMS AND CONCEPTS

Annual Objectives (p. 238)

Avoidance (p. 243)

Benchmarking (p. 250)

Bonus System (p. 252)

Conflict (p. 243)

Confrontation (p. 243)

Culture (p. 257)

Defusion (p. 243)

Delayering (p. 248)

Decentralized Structure (p. 245)

Divisional Structure by Geographic Area, Product, Customer, or Process (pp. 245–246)

Downsizing (p. 248)

Educative Change Strategy (p. 254)

Employee Stock Ownership Plans (ESOP) (p. 264)

Establishing Annual Objectives (p. 238)

Force Change Strategy (p. 254)

Functional Structure (p. 245)

Gain Sharing (p. 252)

Glass Ceiling (p. 266)

Horizontal Consistency of Objectives (p. 240)

Just in Time (JIT) (p. 262)

Matrix Structure (p. 248)

Policy (p. 240)

Profit Sharing (p. 252)

Rational Change Strategy (p. 254)

Reengineering (p. 249)

Resistance to Change (p. 254)

Resource Allocation (p. 241)

Restructuring (p. 248)

Rightsizing (p. 248)

Self-Interest Change Strategy (p. 254)

Strategic Business Unit (SBU) Structure (p. 247)

Triangulation (p. 258)

Vertical Consistency of Objectives (p. 240)

ISSUES FOR REVIEW AND DISCUSSION

1. Allocating resources can be a political and an ad hoc activity in firms that do not use strategic management. Why is this true? Does adopting strategic management ensure easy resource allocation? Why?

2. Compare strategy formulation with strategy implementation in terms of each being an art or a science.

3. Describe the relationship between annual objectives and policies.

4. Identify a long-term objective and two supporting annual objectives for a familiar organization.

5. Identify and discuss three policies that apply to your present business policy class.

6. Explain the following statement: Horizontal consistency of goals is as important as vertical consistency.

7. Describe several reasons why conflict may occur during objective-setting activities.

8. In your opinion, what approaches to conflict resolution would be best for resolving a disagreement between a personnel manager and a sales manager over the firing of a particular salesperson? Why?

9. Describe the organizational culture of your college or university.

10. Explain why organizational structure is so important in strategy implementation.

11. In your opinion, how many separate divisions could an organization reasonably have without using an SBU-type organizational structure? Why?

12. Would you recommend a divisional structure by geographic area, product, customer, or process for a medium-sized bank in your local area? Why?

13. What are the advantages and disadvantages of decentralizing the wage and salary functions of an organization? How could this be accomplished?

14. Consider a college organization with which you are familiar. How did management issues affect strategy implementation in that organization?

15. As production manager of a local newspaper, what problems would you anticipate in implementing a strategy to increase the average number of pages in the paper by 40 percent?

16. Read an article from the suggested readings at the end of this chapter and give a summary report to the class revealing your thoughts on the topic.

17. Do you believe expenditures for childcare or fitness facilities are warranted from a cost/benefit perspective? Why or why not?

18. Explain why successful strategy implementation often hinges on whether the strategy-formulation process empowers managers and employees.

19. Compare and contrast the cultures in Mexico, Russia, and Japan.

20. Discuss the glass ceiling in the United States, giving your ideas and suggestions.

NOTES

1. DALE MCCONKEY, "Planning in a Changing Environment," *Business Horizons* (September–October 1988): 66.

2. A. G. BEDEIAN and W. F. GLUECK, *Management*, 3rd ed. (Chicago: The Dryden Press, 1983): 212.

3. BORIS YAVITZ and WILLIAM NEWMAN, *Strategy in Action: The Execution, Politics, and Payoff of Business Planning* (New York: The Free Press, 1982): 195.

4. RICK BROOKS, "Bank One's Strategy As Competition Grows: New, Online Institution," *USA Today* (August 25, 1999): A1.

5. STEVE HAMM and MARCIA STEPANEK, "From Reengineering to E-engineering," *Business Week* (March 22, 1999): EB 15.

6. "Want to Be a Manager? Many People Say No, Calling Job Miserable," *The Wall Street Journal* (April 4, 1997): 1. Also, STEPHANIE ARMOUR, "Management Loses Its Allure," *USA Today* (October 10, 1997): 1B.

7. STEPHANIE ARMOUR, "Layoff Survivors Climb Ladder Faster," *USA Today* (September 10, 2001), B1.

8. PAUL CARROLL, "No More Business as Usual, Please. Time to Try Something Different," *The Wall Street Journal* (October 23, 2001): A24.

9. JULIE SCHMIT, "Japan Shifts to Merit Pay," *USA Today* (July 23, 1999): 5B.

10. RICHARD BROWN, "Outsider CEO: Inspiring Change With Force and Grace," *USA Today* (July 19, 1999): 3B.

11. YAVITZ and NEWMAN, 58.

12. JOHN JONES, "Winners and Losers," *Wall Street Journal,* (April 11, 2002): B10.

13. JACK DUNCAN, *Management* (New York: Random House, 1983): 381–390.

14. H. IGOR ANSOFF, "Strategic Management of Technology," *Journal of Business Strategy* 7, no. 3 (Winter 1987): 38.

15. ROBERT WATERMAN, JR., "How the Best Get Better," *Business Week* (September 14, 1987): 104.

16. TRACI WATSON, "Pollution From Trucks Targeted," *USA Today* (July 7, 1999): 4A.

17. JACK DUNCAN, "Organizational Culture: Getting a Fix on an Elusive Concept," *Academy of Management Executive* 3, no. 3 (August 1989): 229.

18. E. H. SCHEIN, "The Role of the Founder in Creating Organizational Culture," *Organizational Dynamics* (Summer 1983): 13–28.

19. T. DEAL and A. KENNEDY, "Culture: A New Look Through Old Lenses," *Journal of Applied Behavioral Science* 19, no. 4 (1983): 498–504.

20. H. IBSEN, "The Wild Duck," in O. G. Brochett and L. Brochett (eds.), *Plays for the Theater* (New York: Holt, Rinehart & Winston, 1967). Also, R. Pascale, "The Paradox of 'Corporate Culture': Reconciling Ourselves to Socialization," *California Management Review* 28, 2 (1985): 26, 37–40.

21. T. DEAL and A. KENNEDY, *Corporate Cultures: The Rites and Rituals of Corporate Life* (Reading, MA: Addison-Wesley, 1982): 256.

22. STRATFORD SHERMAN, "How to Beat the Japanese," *Fortune* (April 10, 1989): 145.
23. ROBERT STOBAUGH and PIERO TELESIO, "Match Manufacturing Policies and Product Strategy," *Harvard Business Review* 61, no. 2 (March–April 1983): 113.
24. R. T. LENZ and MARJORIE LYLES, "Managing Human Resource Problems in Strategy Planning Systems," *Journal of Business Strategy* 60, no. 4 (Spring 1986): 58.
25. J. WARREN HENRY, "ESOPs with Productivity Payoffs," *Journal of Business Strategy* (July–August 1989): 33.
26. RICHARD LEVINE, "Childcare: Inching up the Corporate Agenda," *Management Review* 78, no. 1 (January 1989): 43.
27. DEWAYNE WICKHAM, "Women Still Fighting for Job Equality," *USA Today* (August 31, 1999): 15A.
28. MICHELINE MAYNARD, "Practically Alone at the Top," *USA Today* (September 7, 1999): B1.
29. JULIE BENNETT, "Corporate Downsizing Doesn't Deter Search for Diversity," *The Wall Street Journal* (October 23, 2001): B18.

CURRENT READINGS

ARTHUR, JEFFREY B., and LYNDA AIMAN-SMITH. "Gain Sharing and Organizational Learning: An Analysis of Employee Suggestions over Time." *The Academy of Management Journal* 44, no. 4 (August 2001): 737.

BARUCH, YEHUDA. "No Such Thing as a Global Manager." *Business Horizons* 45, no. 1 (January–February 2002): 36.

BEGLEY, THOMAS M., and DAVID P. BOYD. "Articulating Corporate Values Through Human Resource Policies." *Business Horizons* 43, no. 4 (July–August 2000): 8.

BLOOM, MATT, and JOHN G. MICHAEL. "The Relationships among Organizational Context, Pay Dispersion, and Managerial Turnover." *The Academy of Management Journal* 45, no. 1 (February 2002): 33.

BOYD, B. K., and A. SALAMIN. "Strategic Reward Systems: A Contingency Model of Pay System Design." *Strategic Management Journal* 22, no. 8 (August 2001): 777.

CANNELLA, JR., ALBERT A., and WEI SHEN. "So Close and Yet So Far: Promotion Versus Exit for CEO Heirs Apparent." *Academy of Management* 44, no. 2 (April 2001): 271.

CARPENTER, M. A., and W. G. SANDERS. "Top Management Team Compensation: The Missing Link Between CEO Pay and Firm Performance?" *Strategic Management Journal* 23, no. 4 (April 2002): 367.

CASE, JOHN. "When Salaries Aren't Secret." *Harvard Business Review* (May 2001): 37.

CHILTON, KENNETH W. "Reengineering U.S. Environmental Protection." *Business Horizons* 43, no. 2 (March–April 2000): 7.

DENIS, JEAN-LOUIS, LISE LAMOTHE, and ANN LANGLEY. "The Dynamics of Collective Leadership and Strategic Change in Pluralistic Organizations." *The Academy of Management Journal* 44, no. 4 (August 2001): 809.

FIOL, C. MARLENE, EDWARD J. O'CONNOR, and HERMAN AGUINIS. "All for One and One for All? The Development and Transfer of Power Across Organizational Levels." *The Academy of Management Review* 26, no. 2 (April 2001): 224.

GELETKANYCZ, M. A., B. K. BOYD, and S. FINKELSTEIN. "The Strategic Value of CEO External Directorate Networks: Implications for CEO Compensation." *Strategic Management Journal* 22, no. 9 (September 2001): 889.

GOOLD, MICHAEL, and ANDREW CAMPBELL. "Do You Have a Well-Designed Organization?" *Harvard Business Review* (March 2002): 117.

HENDERSON, DAVID A., GABRIEL G. RAMIREZ, ROBERT J. HOUSE, and PHANISH PURANAM. "Does Leadership Matter? CEO Leadership Attributes and Profitability Under Conditions of Perceived Environmental Uncertainty." *The Academy of Management Journal* 44, no. 1 (February 2001): 96.

HEWLETT, SYLVIA ANN. "Executive Women and the Myth of Having It All." *Harvard Business Review* (April 2002): 66.

HUDSON, KATHERINE M. "Transforming a Conservative Company—One Laugh at a Time." *Harvard Business Review* (July–August 2001): 45.

JEHN, KAREN A., and ELIZABETH A. MANNIX. "The Dynamic Nature of Conflict: A Longitudinal Study of Intragroup Conflict and Group Performance." *The Academy of Management Journal* 44, no. 2 (April 2001): 238.

KELLER, ROBERT T. "Cross-Functional Project Groups in Research and New Product Development: Diversity, Communications, Job Stress, and Outcomes." *The Academy of Management Journal* 44, no. 3 (June 2001): 547.

KING, ADELAIDE WILCOX, SALLY W. FOWLER, and CARL P. ZEITHAML. "Managing Organizational Competencies for Competitive Advantage: The Middle-Management Edge." *The Academy of Management Executive* 15, no. 2 (May 2001): 95.

KNIGHT, DON, CATHY C. DURHAM, and EDWIN A. LOCKE. "The Relationship of Team Goals, Incentives, and Efficacy to Strategic Risk, Tactical Implementation, and Performance." *The Academy of Management Journal* 44, no. 2 (April 2001): 326.

MARKS, MICHAEL LEE, and PHILIP H. MIRVIS. "Making Mergers and Acquisitions Work: Strategic and Psychological Preparation." *The Academy of Management Executive* 15, no. 2 (May 2001): 80.

MEZIAS, JOHN, PETER GRINYER, and WILLIAM D. GUTH. "Changing Collective Cognition: A Process Model for Strategic Change." *Long Range Planning* 34, no. 1 (February 2001): 71.

NAIR, A., and S. KOTHA. "Does Group Membership Matter? Evidence from the Japanese Steel Industry." *Strategic Management Journal* 22, no. 3 (March 2001): 221.

NELSON, DEBRA L., and RONALD J. BURKE. "Women Executives: Health, Stress, and Success." *The Academy of Management Executive* 14, no. 2 (May 2000): 107.

RAMUS, CATHERINE A. "Organizational Support for Employees: Encouraging Creative Ideas for Environmental Sustainability." *California Management Review* 43, no. 3 (Spring 2001): 85.

RAYNOR, MICHAEL E., and JOSEPH L. BOWER. "Lead from the Center: How to Manage Divisions Dynamically." *Harvard Business Review* (May 2001): 92.

SHAW, J. D., N. GUPTA, and J. E. DELERY. "Congruence Between Technology and Compensation Systems: Implications for Strategy Implementations." *Strategic Management Journal* 22, no. 4 (April 2001): 379.

TULGAN, BRUCE. "Real Pay for Performance." *Journal of Business Strategy* 22, no. 3 (May/June 2001): 19.

WOLF, J., and W. G. EGELHOFF. "A Reexamination and Extension of International Strategy-Structure Theory." *Strategic Management Journal* 23, no. 2 (February 2002): 181.

WRZESNIEWSKI, AMY, and JANE E. DUTTON. "Crafting a Job: Revisioning Employees as Active Crafters of Their Work." *The Academy of Management Review* 26, no. 2 (April 2001): 179.

EXPERIENTIAL EXERCISES

**EXPERIENTIAL
EXERCISE 7A** ▶

Revising American Airline's (AMR's) Organizational Chart

PURPOSE

Developing and altering organizational charts is an important skill for strategists to possess. This exercise can improve your skill in altering an organization's hierarchical structure in response to new strategies being formulated.

INSTRUCTIONS

Step 1   Turn back to the American Airlines (AMR) Cohesion Case (p. 32). On a separate sheet of paper, diagram an organizational chart that you believe would best suit AMR's needs if the company decided to form a divisional structure by-product.

Step 2   Provide as much detail in your chart as possible, including the names of individuals and the titles of positions.

**EXPERIENTIAL
EXERCISE 7B** ▶

Do Organizations Really Establish Objectives?

PURPOSE

Objectives provide direction, allow synergy, aid in evaluation, establish priorities, reduce uncertainty, minimize conflicts, stimulate exertion, and aid in both the allocation of resources and the design of jobs. This exercise will enhance your understanding of how organizations use or misuse objectives.

INSTRUCTIONS

Step 1   Join with one other person in class to form a two-person team.

Step 2   Contact by telephone the owner or manager of an organization in your city or town. Request a thirty-minute personal interview or meeting with that person for the purpose of discussing "business objectives." During your meeting, seek answers to the following questions:

1.   Do you believe it is important for a business to establish and clearly communicate long-term and annual objectives? Why or why not?

2.   Does your organization establish objectives? If yes, what type and how many? How are the objectives communicated to individuals? Are your firm's objectives in written form or simply communicated orally?

3.   To what extent are managers and employees involved in the process of establishing objectives?

4.   How often are your business objectives revised and by what process?

Step 3   Take good notes during the interview. Let one person be the note taker and one person do most of the talking. Have your notes typed up and ready to turn in to your professor.

Step 4   Prepare a five-minute oral presentation for the class, reporting the results of your interview. Turn in your typed report.

**EXPERIENTIAL
EXERCISE 7C** ▶

Understanding My University's Culture

PURPOSE

It is something of an art to uncover the basic values and beliefs that are buried deeply in an organization's rich collection of stories, language, heroes, heroines, and rituals, yet culture can be the most important factor in implementing strategies.

INSTRUCTIONS

Step 1   On a separate sheet of paper, list the following terms: hero/heroine, belief, metaphor, language, value, symbol, story, legend, saga, folktale, myth, ceremonial, rite, and ritual.

Step 2   For your college or university, give examples of each term. If necessary, speak with faculty, staff, alumni, administration, or fellow students of the institution to identify examples of each term.

Step 3   Report your findings to the class. Tell the class how you feel regarding cultural products being consciously used to help implement strategies.

8 IMPLEMENTING STRATEGIES: MARKETING, FINANCE/ACCOUNTING, R&D, AND MIS ISSUES

CHAPTER OUTLINE

- The Nature of Strategy Implementation
- Marketing Issues
- Finance/Accounting Issues
- Research and Development (R&D) Issues
- Management Information Systems (MIS) Issues

EXPERIENTIAL EXERCISE 8A
Developing a Product-Positioning Map for American Airlines (AMR)

EXPERIENTIAL EXERCISE 8B
Performing an EPS/EBIT Analysis for American Airlines (AMR)

EXPERIENTIAL EXERCISE 8C
Preparing Pro Forma Financial Statements for American Airlines (AMR)

EXPERIENTIAL EXERCISE 8D
Determining the Cash Value of American Airlines (AMR)

EXPERIENTIAL EXERCISE 8E
Developing a Product-Positioning Map for My University

EXPERIENTIAL EXERCISE 8F
Do Banks Require Pro Forma Statements?

CHAPTER OBJECTIVES

After studying this chapter, you should be able to do the following:

1. Explain market segmentation and product positioning as strategy-implementation tools.

2. Discuss procedures for determining the worth of a business.

3. Explain why pro forma financial analysis is a central strategy-implementation tool.

4. Explain how to evaluate the attractiveness of debt versus stock as a source of capital to implement strategies.

5. Discuss the nature and role of research and development in strategy implementation.

6. Explain how management information systems can determine the success of strategy-implementation efforts.

NOTABLE QUOTES

The greatest strategy is doomed if it's implemented badly.
                              BERNARD REIMANN

There is no "perfect" strategic decision. One always has to pay a price. One always has to balance conflicting objectives, conflicting opinions, and conflicting priorities. The best strategic decision is only an approximation—and a risk.
                              PETER DRUCKER

The real question isn't how well you're doing today against your own history, but how you're doing against your competitors.

                              DONALD KRESS

As market windows open and close more quickly, it is important that R&D be tied more closely to corporate strategy.
                              WILLIAM SPENSER

Most of the time, strategists should not be formulating strategy at all; they should be getting on with implementing strategies they already have.

                              HENRY MINTZBERG

Strategies have no chance of being implemented successfully in organizations that do not market goods and services well, in firms that cannot raise needed working capital, in firms that produce technologically inferior products, or in firms that have a weak information system. This chapter examines marketing, finance/accounting, R&D, and management information systems (MIS) issues that are central to effective strategy implementation. Special topics include market segmentation, market positioning, evaluating the worth of a business, determining to what extent debt and/or stock should be used as a source of capital, developing pro forma financial statements, contracting R&D outside the firm, and creating an information support system. Manager and employee involvement and participation are essential for success in marketing, finance/accounting, R&D, and MIS activities.

THE NATURE OF STRATEGY IMPLEMENTATION

The quarterback can call the best play possible in the huddle, but that does not mean the play will go for a touchdown. The team may even lose yardage unless the play is executed (implemented) well. Less than 10 percent of strategies formulated are successfully implemented! There are many reasons for this low success rate, including failing to segment markets appropriately, paying too much for a new acquisition, and falling behind competitors in R&D.

Strategy implementation directly affects the lives of plant managers, division managers, department managers, sales managers, product managers, project managers, personnel managers, staff managers, supervisors, and all employees. In some situations, individuals may not have participated in the strategy-formulation process at all and may not appreciate, understand, or even accept the work and thought that went into strategy formulation. There may even be foot dragging or resistance on their part. Managers and employees who do not understand the business and are not committed to the business may attempt to sabotage strategy-implementation efforts in hopes that the organization will return to its old ways. The strategy-implementation stage of the strategic-management process is emphasized in Figure 8–1.

MARKETING ISSUES

VISIT THE NET

An excellent PowerPoint presentation on marketing issues related to strategic management.
http://www.cl.uh.edu/bpa/hadm/HADM_5731/ppt_presentations/3mktpln/index.htm

Countless marketing variables affect the success or failure of strategy implementation, and the scope of this text does not allow us to address all those issues. Some examples of marketing decisions that may require policies are as follows:

1. To use exclusive dealerships or multiple channels of distribution
2. To use heavy, light, or no TV advertising
3. To limit (or not) the share of business done with a single customer
4. To be a price leader or a price follower
5. To offer a complete or limited warranty
6. To reward salespeople based on straight salary, straight commission, or a combination salary/commission
7. To advertise online or not

FIGURE 8–1

A Comprehensive Strategic-Management Model

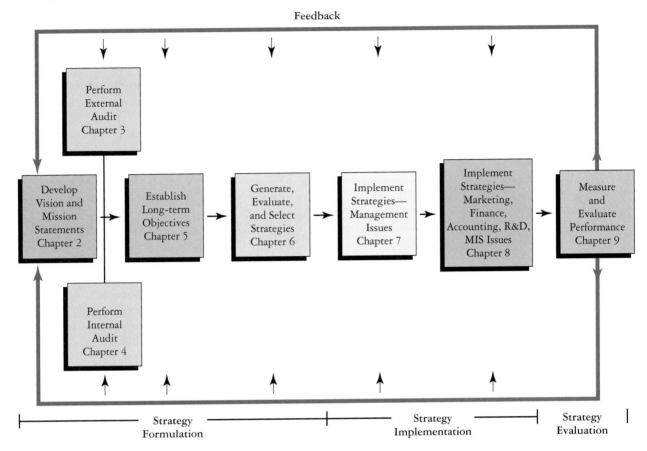

A marketing issue of increasing concern to consumers today is the extent to which companies can track individuals' movements on the Internet—and even be able to identify an individual by name and e-mail address. Individuals' wanderings on the Internet are no longer anonymous, as many persons believe. Marketing companies such as Doubleclick, Flycast, AdKnowledge, AdForce, and Real Media have sophisticated methods to identify who you are and your particular interests.[1] If you are especially concerned about being tracked, visit the **www.networkadvertising.org** Web site that gives details about how marketers today are identifying you and your buying habits.

Recently completed research reveals that Web advertising dollars spent by businesses was 27 percent of total advertising expenditures in 2002, up from 17 percent in 1999. Web advertising's market share increase will come at the expense of all other media. Newspapers, radio, magazines, television, and the Yellow Pages have long worried about online rivals siphoning off advertising dollars. This worry now totals about $600 billion in business advertising expenditures annually being diverted to online media.

Two variables are of central importance to strategy implementation: *market segmentation* and *product positioning*. Market segmentation and product positioning rank as marketing's most important contributions to strategic management.

Market Segmentation

Market segmentation is widely used in implementing strategies, especially for small and specialized firms. Market segmentation can be defined as the subdividing of a market into distinct subsets of customers according to needs and buying habits.

Market segmentation is an important variable in strategy implementation for at least three major reasons. First, strategies such as market development, product development, market penetration, and diversification require increased sales through new markets and products. To implement these strategies successfully, new or improved market-segmentation approaches are required. Second, market segmentation allows a firm to operate with limited resources because mass production, mass distribution, and mass advertising are not required. Market segmentation enables a small firm to compete successfully with a large firm by maximizing per-unit profits and per-segment sales. Finally, market segmentation decisions directly affect *marketing mix variables:* product, place, promotion, and price, as indicated in Table 8–1. For example, SnackWells, a pioneer in reduced-fat snacks, has shifted its advertising emphasis from low-fat to great taste as part of its new market-segmentation strategy.

Perhaps the most dramatic new market-segmentation strategy is the targeting of regional tastes. Firms from McDonald's to General Motors are increasingly modifying their products to meet different regional preferences within the United States. Campbell's has a spicier version of its nacho cheese soup for the Southwest, and Burger King offers breakfast burritos in New Mexico but not in South Carolina. Geographic and demographic bases for segmenting markets are the most commonly employed, as illustrated in Table 8–2. Note that gender is a popular demographic segmentation variable, and is discussed further in the E-Commerce Perspective box.

Evaluating potential market segments requires strategists to determine the characteristics and needs of consumers, to analyze consumer similarities and differences, and to develop consumer group profiles. Segmenting consumer markets is generally much simpler and easier than segmenting industrial markets, because industrial products, such as electronic circuits and forklifts, have multiple applications and appeal to diverse customer groups. Note in Figure 8–2 that customer age is used to segment automobile car purchases. Note that older buyers especially like Cadillacs and Buicks.

Segmentation is a key to matching supply and demand, which is one of the thorniest problems in customer service. Segmentation often reveals that large, random fluctuations in demand actually consist of several small, predictable, and manageable patterns.

VISIT THE NET

Provides CheckMATE, the industry leader in strategic planning software worldwide. This is easy-to-use software that is Windows-based. Twenty-three different industry versions are available.
www.checkmateplan.com

VISIT THE NET

Gives the strategic plan for the Medical University of South Carolina, including a section on strategy implementation. http://www.musc.edu/plan

TABLE 8–1   The Marketing Mix Component Variables

PRODUCT	PLACE	PROMOTION	PRICE
Quality	Distribution channels	Advertising	Level
Features and options	Distribution coverage	Personal selling	Discounts and
Style	Outlet location	Sales promotion	allowances
Brand name	Sales territories	Publicity	Payment terms
Packaging	Inventory levels		
Product line	and locations		
Warranty	Transportation carriers		
Service level			
Other services			

Source: E. Jerome McCarthy, *Basic Marketing: A Managerial Approach*, 9th ed. (Homewood, IL: Richard D. Irwin, Inc., 1987): 37–44.

TABLE 8-2   **Alternative Bases for Market Segmentation**

VARIABLE	TYPICAL BREAKDOWNS
GEOGRAPHIC	
Region	Pacific, Mountain, West North Central, West South Central, East North Cental, East South Central, South Atlantic, Middle Atlantic, New England
County Size	A,B,C,D
City Size	Under 5,000; 5,000–20,000; 20,000–50,000; 50,000–100,000; 100,000–250,000; 250,000–500,000; 500,000–1,000,000; 1,000,000–4,000,000; 4,000,000 or over
Density	Urban, suburban, rural
Climate	Northern, southern
DEMOGRAPHIC	
Age	Under 6, 6–11, 12–19, 20–34, 35–49, 50–64, 65+
Gender	Male, female
Family Size	1–2, 3–4, 5+
Family Life Cycle	Young, single; young, married, no children; young, married, youngest child under 6; young, married, youngest child 6 or over; older, married, with children; older, married, no children under 18; older, single; other
Income	Under $10,000; $10,001–$15,000; $15,001–$20,000; $20,001–$30,000; $30,001–$50,000; $50,001–$70,000; $70,001–$100,000; over $100,000
Occupation	Professional and technical; managers, officials, and proprietors; clerical, sales; craftsmen, foremen; operatives; farmers; retired; students; housewives; unemployed
Education	Grade school or less; some high school; high school graduate; some college; college graduate
Religion	Catholic, Protestant, Jewish, Islamic, other
Race	White, Asian, Hispanic, African American
Nationality	American, British, French, German, Scandinavian, Italian, Latin American, Middle Eastern, Japanese
PSYCHOGRAPHIC	
Social Class	Lower lowers, upper lowers, lower middles, upper middles, lower uppers, upper uppers
Personality	Compulsive, gregarious, authoritarian, ambitious
BEHAVIORAL	
Use Occasion	Regular occasion, special occasion
Benefits Sought	Quality, service, economy
User Status	Nonuser, ex-user, potential user, first-time user, regular user
Usage Rate	Light user, medium user, heavy user
Loyalty Status	None, medium, strong, absolute
Readiness Stage	Unaware, aware, informed, interested, desirous, intending to buy
Attitude Toward Product	Enthusiastic, positive, indifferent, negative, hostile

Source: Adapted from Philip Kotler, *Marketing Management: Analysis, Planning and Control,* © 1984: 256. Adapted by permission of Prentice-Hall, Inc., Englewood Cliffs, New Jersey.

Matching supply and demand allows factories to produce desirable levels without extra shifts, overtime, and subcontracting. Matching supply and demand also minimizes the number and severity of stock-outs. The demand for hotel rooms, for example, can be dependent on foreign tourists, businesspersons, and vacationers. Focusing on these three market segments separately, however, can allow hotel firms to predict overall supply and demand more effectively.

FIGURE 8–2

Average Age of Automobile Buyers, by brand

Plymouth	38	Pontiac	42	Infiniti	45
Mitsubishi	38	Acura	42	Subaru	45
Volkswagen	38	Hyundai	42	Oldsmobile	46
Honda	41	Suzuki	42	Saturn	46
Isuzu	41	Audi	42	Chrysler	47
Kia	41	Daewoo	43	Lexus	47
Land Rover	41	Chevrolet	43	Jaguar	49
Mazda	41	Porsche	43	Mercury	50
Nissan	41	Saab	43	Lincoln	51
BMW	42	GMC	44	Cadillac	53
Dodge	42	Toyota	44	Buick	57
Jeep	42	Volvo	44		
Ford	42	Mercedes-Benz	45		

Source: Adapted from Norihiko Shirouzu, "This Is Not Your Father's Toyota," *Wall Street Journal* (March 26, 2002): B1.

Banks now are segmenting markets to increase effectiveness. "You're dead in the water if you aren't segmenting the market," says Anne Moore, president of a bank consulting firm in Atlanta. As indicated in the E-Commerce Perspective box, the Internet makes market segmentation easier today because consumers naturally form "communities" on the Web.

E-COMMERCE PERSPECTIVE

Male versus Female Internet Usage Globally

Note from the table below that the U.S. and Canada are the only countries in the would where female Internet usage is higher than male usage. Note that in many countries, including Germany, Italy, and India, male usage exceeds female usage by more than 20 percent.

COUNTRY	FEMALE	MALE	COUNTRY	FEMALE	MALE
Argentina	45.4%	54.6%	Japan	42.3%	57.7%
Australia	46.9	53.1	Mexico	40.6	59.4
Austria	42.8	57.2	Netherlands	43.1	57.0
Belgium	40.5	59.5	New Zealand	49.6	50.4
Brazil	43.1	56.9	Norway	43.4	56.6
Canada	51.9	48.1	Singapore	45.0	55.0
Denmark	44.8	55.2	South Africa	43.1	56.9
Finland	47.0	53.0	South Korea	45.9	54.1
France	39.8	60.2	Spain	41.1	58.9
Germany	39.0	61.0	Sweden	44.9	55.1
Hong Kong	43.9	56.1	Switzerland	41.4	58.6
India	33.9	66.1	Taiwan	45.0	55.0
Ireland	45.2	64.8	United Kingdom	44.5	55.5
Israel	42.6	57.4	United States	51.4	48.6
Italy	36.4	63.6			

Source: Adapted from Brad Reagan, "The Great Divide," *Wall Street Journal* (April 15, 2002): R4.

Does the Internet Make Market Segmentation Easier?

Yes. The segments of people that marketers want to reach online are much more precisely defined than the segments of people reached through traditional forms of media, such as television, radio, and magazines. For example, **Quepasa.com** is widely visited by Hispanics. Marketers aiming to reach college students, who are notoriously difficult to reach via traditional media, focus on sites such as **collegeclub.com** and **studentadvantage.com**. The gay and lesbian population, which is estimated to comprise about 5 percent of the U.S. population, has always been difficult to reach via traditional media but now can be focused on sites such as **gay.com**. Marketers can reach persons interested in specific topics, such as travel or fishing, by placing banners on related Web sites.

People all over the world are congregating into virtual communities on the Web by becoming members/customers/visitors of Web sites that focus on an endless range of topics. People in essence segment themselves by nature of the Web sites that comprise their "favorite places," and many of these Web sites sell information regarding their "visitors." Businesses and groups of individuals all over the world pool their purchasing power in Web sites to get volume discounts.

Product Positioning

After markets have been segmented so that the firm can target particular customer groups, the next step is to find out what customers want and expect. This takes analysis and research. A severe mistake is to assume the firm knows what customers want and expect. Countless research studies reveal large differences between how customers define service and rank the importance of different service activities and how producers view services. Many firms have become successful by filling the gap between what customers and producers see as good service. What the customer believes is good service is paramount, not what the producer believes service should be.

Identifying target customers upon whom to focus marketing efforts sets the stage for deciding how to meet the needs and wants of particular consumer groups. Product positioning is widely used for this purpose. Positioning entails developing schematic representations that reflect how your products or services compare to competitors' on dimensions most important to success in the industry. The following steps are required in product positioning:

1. Select key criteria that effectively differentiate products or services in the industry.
2. Diagram a two-dimensional product-positioning map with specified criteria on each axis.
3. Plot major competitors' products or services in the resultant four-quadrant matrix.
4. Identify areas in the positioning map where the company's products or services could be most competitive in the given target market. Look for vacant areas (niches).
5. Develop a marketing plan to position the company's products or services appropriately.

Because just two criteria can be examined on a single product-positioning map, multiple maps are often developed to assess various approaches to strategy implementation. Multidimensional scaling could be used to examine three or more criteria simultaneously, but this technique requires computer assistance and is beyond the scope of this text. Some examples of product-positioning maps are illustrated in Figure 8–3.

FIGURE 8–3

Examples of Product-Positioning Maps

A. A PRODUCT-POSITIONING MAP
    FOR BANKS

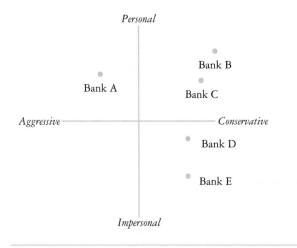

B. A PRODUCT-POSITIONING MAP
    FOR PERSONAL COMPUTERS

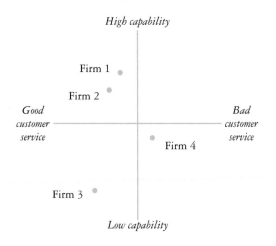

C. A PRODUCT-POSITIONING MAP FOR
    MENSWEAR RETAIL STORES

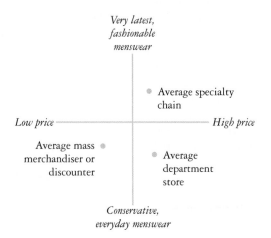

D. A PRODUCT-POSITIONING MAP
    FOR THE RENTAL CAR MARKET

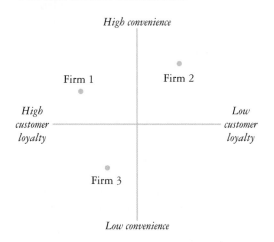

VISIT THE NET

*Provides the 2000
Strategic Plan of the
National Archives and
Records Administration,
including "What Must We
Do to Get There?"
(implementation) issues.*
www.archives.gov/about_us/
strategic_planning_and_
reporting/strategic_
planning_and_reporting.html

Some rules for using product positioning as a strategy-implementation tool are the following:

1. Look for the hole or *vacant niche*. The best strategic opportunity might be an unserved segment.

2. Don't squat between segments. Any advantage from squatting (such as a larger target market) is offset by a failure to satisfy one segment. In decision-theory terms, the intent here is to avoid suboptimization by trying to serve more than one objective function.

3. Don't serve two segments with the same strategy. Usually, a strategy successful with one segment cannot be directly transferred to another segment.

4. Don't position yourself in the middle of the map. The middle usually means a strategy that is not clearly perceived to have any distinguishing characteristics. This rule can vary with the number of competitors. For example, when there are only two competitors, as in U.S. presidential elections, the middle becomes the preferred strategic position.[2]

An effective product-positioning strategy meets two criteria: (1) it uniquely distinguishes a company from the competition, and (2) it leads customers to expect slightly less service than a company can deliver. Firms should not create expectations that exceed the service the firm can or will deliver. Network Equipment Technology is an example of a company that keeps customer expectations slightly below perceived performance. This is a constant challenge for marketers. Firms need to inform customers about what to expect and then exceed the promise. Underpromise and then overdeliver!

 ## FINANCE/ACCOUNTING ISSUES

In this section, we examine several finance/accounting concepts considered to be central to strategy implementation: acquiring needed capital, developing pro forma financial statements, preparing financial budgets, and evaluating the worth of a business. Some examples of decisions that may require finance/accounting policies are:

1. To raise capital with short-term debt, long-term debt, preferred stock, or common stock.
2. To lease or buy fixed assets.
3. To determine an appropriate dividend payout ratio.
4. To use LIFO (Last-in, First-out), FIFO (First-in, First-out), or a market-value accounting approach.
5. To extend the time of accounts receivable.
6. To establish a certain percentage discount on accounts within a specified period of time.
7. To determine the amount of cash that should be kept on hand.

Acquiring Capital to Implement Strategies

Successful strategy implementation often requires additional capital. Besides net profit from operations and the sale of assets, two basic sources of capital for an organization are debt and equity. Determining an appropriate mix of debt and equity in a firm's capital structure can be vital to successful strategy implementation. An *Earnings Per Share/Earnings Before Interest and Taxes (EPS/EBIT) analysis* is the most widely used technique for determining whether debt, stock, or a combination of debt and stock is the best alternative for raising capital to implement strategies. This technique involves an examination of the impact that debt versus stock financing has on earnings per share under various assumptions as to EBIT.

Theoretically, an enterprise should have enough debt in its capital structure to boost its return on investment by applying debt to products and projects earning more than the cost of the debt. In low earning periods, too much debt in the capital structure of an organization can endanger stockholders' return and jeopardize company survival. Fixed debt obligations generally must be met, regardless of circumstances. This does not mean that stock issuances are always better than debt for raising capital. Some special concerns with stock issuances are dilution of ownership, effect on stock price, and the need to share future earnings with all new shareholders.

Without going into detail on other institutional and legal issues related to the debt versus stock decision, EPS/EBIT may be best explained by working through an example. Let's say the Brown Company needs to raise $1 million to finance implementation of a market-development strategy. The company's common stock currently sells for $50 per share, and 100,000 shares are outstanding. The prime interest rate is 10 percent, and the company's tax rate is 50 percent. The company's earnings before interest and taxes next year are expected to be $2 million if a recession occurs, $4 million if the economy stays as is, and $8 million if the economy significantly improves. EPS/EBIT analysis can be used to determine if all stock, all debt, or some combination of stock and debt is the best capital financing alternative. The EPS/EBIT analysis for this example is provided as shown in Table 8–3.

As indicated by the EPS values of 9.5, 19.50, and 39.50 in Table 8–3, debt is the best financing alternative for the Brown Company if a recession, boom, or normal year is expected. An EPS/EBIT chart can be constructed to determine the breakeven point, where one financing alternative becomes more attractive than another. Figure 8–4 indicates that issuing common stock is the least attractive financing alternative for the Brown Company.

EPS/EBIT analysis is a valuable tool for making the capital financing decisions needed to implement strategies, but several considerations should be made whenever using this technique. First, profit levels may be higher for stock or debt alternatives when EPS levels are lower. For example, looking only at the earnings after taxes (EAT) values in Table 8–3, you can see that the common stock option is the best alternative, regardless of economic conditions. If the Brown Company's mission includes strict profit maximization, as opposed to the maximization of stockholders' wealth or some other criterion, then stock rather than debt is the best choice of financing.

Another consideration when using EPS/EBIT analysis is flexibility. As an organization's capital structure changes, so does its flexibility for considering future capital needs. Using all debt or all stock to raise capital in the present may impose fixed obligations, restrictive covenants, or other constraints that could severely reduce a firm's ability to raise additional capital in the future. Control is also a concern. When additional

TABLE 8-3   **EPS/EBIT Analysis for the Brown Company (in millions)**

	COMMON STOCK FINANCING			DEBT FINANCING			COMBINATION FINANCING		
	Recession	*Normal*	*Boom*	*Recession*	*Normal*	*Boom*	*Recession*	*Normal*	*Boom*
EBIT	$2.0	$ 4.0	$ 8.0	$2.0	$ 4.0	$ 8.0	$2.0	$ 4.0	$ 8.0
Interest[a]	0	0	0	.10	.10	.10	.05	.05	.05
EBT	2.0	4.0	8.0	1.9	3.9	7.9	1.95	3.95	7.95
Taxes	1.0	2.0	4.0	.95	1.95	3.95	.975	1.975	3.975
EAT	1.0	2.0	4.0	.95	1.95	3.95	.975	1.975	3.975
#Shares[b]	.12	.12	.12	.10	.10	.10	.11	.11	.11
EPS[c]	8.33	16.66	33.33	9.5	19.50	39.50	8.86	17.95	36.14

[a]The annual interest charge on $1 million at 10% is $100,000 and on $0.5 million is $50,000. This row is in $, not %.
[b]To raise all of the needed $1 million with stock, 20,000 new shares must be issued, raising the total to 120,000 shares outstanding. To raise one-half of the needed $1 million with stock, 10,000 new shares must be issued, raising the total to 110,000 shares outstanding.
[c]EPS = Earnings After Taxes (EAT) divided by shares (number of shares outstanding).

FIGURE 8–4

An EPS/EBIT Chart for the Brown Company

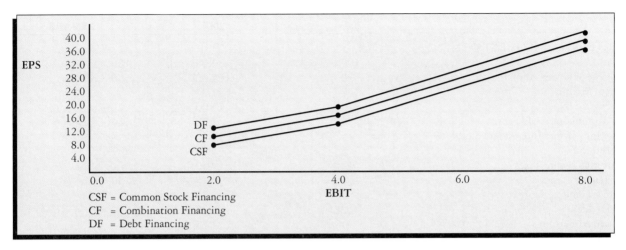

CSF = Common Stock Financing
CF = Combination Financing
DF = Debt Financing

stock is issued to finance strategy implementation, ownership and control of the enterprise are diluted. This can be a serious concern in today's business environment of hostile takeovers, mergers, and acquisitions.

Dilution of ownership can be an overriding concern in closely held corporations in which stock issuances affect the decision-making power of majority stockholders. For example, the Smucker family owns 30 percent of the stock in Smucker's, a well-known jam and jelly company. When Smucker's acquired Dickson Family, Inc., the company used mostly debt rather than stock in order not to dilute the family ownership.

When using EPS/EBIT analysis, timing in relation to movements of stock prices, interest rates, and bond prices becomes important. In times of depressed stock prices, debt may prove to be the most suitable alternative from both a cost and a demand standpoint. However, when cost of capital (interest rates) is high, stock issuances become more attractive.

Pro Forma Financial Statements

Pro forma (projected) financial statement analysis is a central strategy-implementation technique because it allows an organization to examine the expected results of various actions and approaches. This type of analysis can be used to forecast the impact of various implementation decisions (for example, to increase promotion expenditures by 50 percent to support a market-development strategy, to increase salaries by 25 percent to support a market-penetration strategy, to increase research and development expenditures by 70 percent to support product development, or to sell $1 million of common stock to raise capital for diversification). Nearly all financial institutions require at least three years of projected financial statements whenever a business seeks capital. A pro forma income statement and balance sheet allow an organization to compute projected financial ratios under various strategy-implementation scenarios. When compared to prior years and to industry averages, financial ratios provide valuable insights into the feasibility of various strategy-implementation approaches.

Primarily as a result of the Enron collapse and accounting scandal, companies today are being much more diligent in preparing pro forma financial statements to "reasonably rather than too optimistically" project future expenses and earnings. There is much more care not to mislead shareholders and other constituencies.[3]

TABLE 8-4   **A Pro Forma Income Statement and Balance Sheet for the Litten Company (in millions)**

	PRIOR YEAR 2003	PROJECTED YEAR 2004	REMARKS
PRO FORMA INCOME STATEMENT			
Sales	100	150.00	50% increase
Cost of Goods Sold	70	105.00	70% of sales
Gross Margin	30	45.00	
Selling Expense	10	15.00	10% of sales
Administrative Expense	5	7.50	5% of sales
Earnings Before Interest and Taxes	15	22.50	
Interest	3	3.00	
Earnings Before Taxes	12	19.50	
Taxes	6	9.75	50% rate
Net Income	6	9.75	
Dividends	2	5.00	
Retained Earnings	4	4.75	
PRO FORMA BALANCE SHEET			
Assets			
Cash	5	7.75	Plug figure
Accounts Receivable	2	4.00	Incr. 100%
Inventory	20	45.00	
Total Current Assets	27	56.75	
Land	15	15.00	
Plant and Equipment	50	80.00	Add 3 new plants at $10 million each
Less Depreciation	10	20.00	
Net Plant and Equipment	40	60.00	
Total Fixed Assets	55	75.00	
Total Assets	82	131.75	
Liabilities			
Accounts Payable	10	10.00	
Notes Payable	10	10.00	
Total Current Liabilities	20	20.00	
Long-term Debt	40	70.00	Borrowed $30 million
Additional Paid-in-Capital	20	35.00	Issued 100,000 shares at $150 each
Retained Earnings	2	6.75	2 + 4.75
Total Liabilities and Net Worth	82	131.75	

A 2004 pro forma income statement and balance sheet for the Litten Company are provided in Table 8–4. The pro forma statements for Litten are based on five assumptions: (1) The company needs to raise $45 million to finance expansion into foreign markets; (2) $30 million of this total will be raised through increased debt and $15 million through common stock; (3) sales are expected to increase 50 percent; (4) three new facilities, costing a total of $30 million, will be constructed in foreign markets; and (5) land for the new facilities is already owned by the company. Note in Table 8–4 that Litten's strategies and its implementation are expected to result in a sales increase from $100 million to $150 million and in a net increase in income from $6 million to $9.75 million in the forecasted year.

There are six steps in performing pro forma financial analysis:

1. Prepare the pro forma income statement before the balance sheet. Start by forecasting sales as accurately as possible.

2. Use the percentage-of-sales method to project cost of goods sold (CGS) and the expense items in the income statement. For example, if CGS is 70 percent of sales in the prior year (as it is in Table 8–4), then use that same percentage to calculate CGS in the future year—unless there is a reason to use a different percentage. Items such as interest, dividends, and taxes must be treated independently and cannot be forecasted using the percentage-of-sales method.

3. Calculate the projected net income.

4. Subtract from the net income any dividends to be paid and add the remaining net income to Retained Earnings. Reflect the Retained Earnings total on both the income statement and balance sheet because this item is the key link between the two projected statements.

5. Project the balance sheet items, beginning with retained earnings and then forecasting stockholders' equity, long-term liabilities, current liabilities, total liabilities, total assets, fixed assets, and current assets (in that order). Use the cash account as the plug figure—that is, use the cash account to make the assets total the liabilities and net worth. Then make appropriate adjustments. For example, if the cash needed to balance the statements is too small (or too large), make appropriate changes to borrow more (or less) money than planned.

6. List comments (remarks) on the projected statements. Any time a significant change is made in an item from a prior year to the projected year, an explanation (remark) should be provided. Remarks are essential because otherwise pro formas are meaningless.

The U.S. Securities and Exchange Commission (SEC) warned in late 2001 that it will launch fraud investigations if pro forma numbers are misleading or if they omit information that's important to investors.[4] Pro forma statements must conform with generally accepted accounting principles (GAAP) and must not be designed to hide poor expected results.

Financial Budgets

A *financial budget* is a document that details how funds will be obtained and spent for a specified period of time. Annual budgets are most common, although the period of time for a budget can range from one day to more than ten years. Fundamentally, financial budgeting is a method for specifying what must be done to complete strategy implementation successfully. Financial budgeting should not be thought of as a tool for limiting expenditures but rather as a method for obtaining the most productive and profitable use of an organization's resources. Financial budgets can be viewed as the planned allocation of a firm's resources based on forecasts of the future.

There are almost as many different types of financial budgets as there are types of organizations. Some common types of budgets include cash budgets, operating budgets, sales budgets, profit budgets, factory budgets, capital budgets, expense budgets, divisional budgets, variable budgets, flexible budgets, and fixed budgets. When an organization is experiencing financial difficulties, budgets are especially important in guiding strategy implementation.

Perhaps the most common type of financial budget is the *cash budget*. The Financial Accounting Standards Board (FASB) has mandated that every publicly held company in the United States must issue an annual cash-flow statement in addition to the usual financial reports. The statement includes all receipts and disbursements of cash in operations, investments, and financing. It supplements the Statement on Changes in Financial

TABLE 8-5   A Six-Month Cash Budget for the Toddler Toy Company in 2004

CASH BUDGET (IN THOUSANDS)	JULY	AUG.	SEPT.	OCT.	NOV.	DEC.	JAN.
Receipts							
Collections	$12,000	$21,000	$31,000	$35,000	$22,000	$18,000	$11,000
Payments							
Purchases	14,000	21,000	28,000	14,000	14,000	7,000	
Wages and Salaries	1,500	2,000	2,500	1,500	1,500	1,000	
Rent	500	500	500	500	500	500	
Other Expenses	200	300	400	200	—	100	
Taxes	—	8,000	—	—	—	—	
Payment on Machine	—	—	10,000	—	—	—	
Total Payments	$16,200	$31,800	$41,400	$16,200	$16,000	$8,600	
Net Cash Gain (Loss) During Month	−4,200	−10,800	−10,400	18,800	6,000	9,400	
Cash at Start of Month If No Borrowing Is Done	6,000	1,800	−9,000	−19,400	−600	5,400	
Cumulative Cash (Cash at start plus gains or minus losses)	1,800	−9,000	−19,400	−600	5,400	14,800	
Less Desired Level of Cash	−5,000	−5,000	−5,000	−5,000	−5,000	−5,000	
Total Loans Outstanding to Maintain $5,000 Cash Balance	$3,200	$14,000	$24,400	$5,600	—	—	
Surplus Cash	—	—	—	—	400	9,800	

Position formerly included in the annual reports of all publicly held companies. A cash budget for the year 2004 for the Toddler Toy Company is provided in Table 8–5. Note that Toddler is not expecting to have surplus cash until November 2004.

The severe economic downturn of 2001–2002 led many companies to deplete their cash positions. Ford Motor's cash position, for example, fell from $18 billion at the end of 2000 to less than $11 billion at the end of 2001. Thousands of "good" companies, such as Disney and Campbell Soup, have seen their debt ratings downgraded, thus raising the cost of borrowing. More than one hundred twenty U.S. companies defaulted on $74 billion of debt (bonds) in the first nine months of 2001, a domestic record.[5]

Financial budgets have some limitations. First, budgetary programs can become so detailed that they are cumbersome and overly expensive. Overbudgeting or underbudgeting can cause problems. Second, financial budgets can become a substitute for objectives. A budget is a tool and not an end in itself. Third, budgets can hide inefficiencies if based solely on precedent rather than on periodic evaluation of circumstances and standards. Finally, budgets are sometimes used as instruments of tyranny that result in frustration, resentment, absenteeism, and high turnover. To minimize the effect of this last concern, managers should increase the participation of subordinates in preparing budgets.

Evaluating the Worth of a Business

Evaluating the worth of a business is central to strategy implementation because integrative, intensive, and diversification strategies are often implemented by acquiring other firms. Other strategies, such as retrenchment and divestiture, may result in the sale of a division of an organization or of the firm itself. Thousands of transactions occur each year in which businesses are bought or sold in the United States. In all these cases, it is necessary to establish the financial worth or cash value of a business to successfully implement strategies.

All the various methods for determining a business's worth can be grouped into three main approaches: what a firm owns, what a firm earns, or what a firm will bring in the market. But it is important to realize that valuation is not an exact science. The valuation of a firm's worth is based on financial facts, but common sense and intuitive judgment must enter into the process. It is difficult to assign a monetary value to some factors—such as a loyal customer base, a history of growth, legal suits pending, dedicated employees, a favorable lease, a bad credit rating, or good patents—that may not be reflected in a firm's financial statements. Also, different valuation methods will yield different totals for a firm's worth, and no prescribed approach is best for a certain situation. Evaluating the worth of a business truly requires both qualitative and quantitative skills.

The first approach in evaluating the worth of a business is determining its net worth or stockholders' equity. Net worth represents the sum of common stock, additional paid-in capital, and retained earnings. After calculating net worth, add or subtract an appropriate amount for goodwill and overvalued or undervalued assets. This total provides a reasonable estimate of a firm's monetary value. If a firm has goodwill, it will be listed on the balance sheet, perhaps as "intangibles."

The second approach to measuring the value of a firm grows out of the belief that the worth of any business should be based largely on the future benefits its owners may derive through net profits. A conservative rule of thumb is to establish a business's worth as five times the firm's current annual profit. A five-year average profit level could also be used. When using the approach, remember that firms normally suppress earnings in their financial statements to minimize taxes.

The third approach, letting the market determine a business's worth, involves three methods. First, base the firm's worth on the selling price of a similar company. A potential problem, however, is that sometimes comparable figures are not easy to locate, even though substantial information on firms that buy or sell to other firms is available in major libraries. The second approach is called the *price-earnings ratio method*. To use this method, divide the market price of the firm's common stock by the annual earnings per share and multiply this number by the firm's average net income for the past five years. The third approach can be called the *outstanding shares method*. To use this method, simply multiply the number of shares outstanding by the market price per share and add a premium. The premium is simply a per-share dollar amount that a person or firm is willing to pay to control (acquire) the other company. As indicated in the Global Perspective, European firms aggressively are acquiring American firms, using these and perhaps other methods for evaluating the worth of their target companies.

Business evaluations are becoming routine in many situations. Businesses have many strategy-implementation reasons for determining their worth in addition to preparing to be sold or to buy other companies. Employee plans, taxes, retirement packages, mergers, acquisitions, expansion plans, banking relationships, death of a principal, divorce, partnership agreements, and IRS audits are other reasons for a periodic valuation. It is just good business to have a reasonable understanding of what your firm is worth. This knowledge protects the interests of all parties involved.

Deciding Whether to Go Public

Going public means selling off a percentage of your company to others in order to raise capital; consequently, it dilutes the owners' control of the firm. Going public is not recommended for companies with less than $10 million in sales because the initial costs can be too high for the firm to generate sufficient cash flow to make going public worthwhile. One dollar in four is the average total cost paid to lawyers, accountants, and underwriters when an initial stock issuance is under $1 million; one dollar in twenty will go to cover these costs for issuances over $20 million.

In addition to initial costs involved with a stock offering, there are costs and obligations associated with reporting and management in a publicly held firm. For firms with more than $10 million in sales, going public can provide major advantages: It can allow

GLOBAL PERSPECTIVE

September 11, 2001, Events Usher in Corporate Retreat from Global Operations

Cutbacks in foreign direct investment had begun prior to the terrorists attacks on September 11, 2001, but following that event, companies have accelerated their retreat from globalization. For example, Gateway withdrew from Asia and Europe, AT&T dissolved its joint venture with British Telecommunications, Merrill Lynch closed many offices in Asia, and Ford Motor reduced its operations in Europe. U.S. telecom and energy companies have withdrawn from expansion in South America. Where globalization used to mean openness and new opportunity, now for many companies it means more vulnerability, more government involvement, and higher security risks and costs.

Ralph Shrader, CEO of consulting firm Booze-Allen & Hamilton, recently said, "I do not know of any companies that aren't carefully reevaluating their global strategies in light of the recession and September 11." Evidence of the globalization pull-back is that between 2001 and 2000 cross-border mergers declined 50 percent, and flows of direct foreign investment around the world dropped 40 percent. The decline in globalization has reduced American exports and imports dramatically, which further hampers the domestic economy.

There are major risks when firms reduce their enthusiasm for and interest in globalization. First,

these firms forfeit their ability to build a wider customer base and make it possible for foreign competitors to strengthen their own competitive hand. Former General Electric CEO Jack Welch says, "The biggest competitive threat on the horizon are those companies whose names we can't spell or pronounce." Still, 95 percent of the world's population lives outside the United States, and that group is growing much faster than the American population. Second, U.S. corporate investment abroad is vital to giving poorer nations the chance to develop and become viable members of the world economy rather than breeding grounds for terrorism and despair. Winning the war on terrorism may hinge more on the efforts of U.S. companies than on the U.S. military in the global economic sphere.

China is a notable exception to overall foreign investment curtailment as U.S. investment in that country continues to increase. For example, Motorola is investing $6.6 billion on production in China from 2002–2006, and it is the largest foreign investor in China. Motorola intends to be the leader in wireless, Internet, and broadband in China, where it already has $5 billion in annual sales and more than thirteen thousand employees.

Source: Adapted from Jeffrey Garten, "The Wrong Time for Companies to Beat a Global Retreat," *Business Week* (December 17, 2001): 22.

the firm to raise capital to develop new products, build plants, expand, grow, and market products and services more effectively.

RESEARCH AND DEVELOPMENT (R&D) ISSUES

Research and development (R&D) personnel can play an integral part in strategy implementation. These individuals are generally charged with developing new products and improving old products in a way that will allow effective strategy implementation. R&D employees and managers perform tasks that include transferring complex technology, adjusting processes to local raw materials, adapting processes to local markets, and altering products to particular tastes and specifications. Strategies such as product development, market penetration, and concentric diversification require that new products be successfully developed and that old products be significantly improved. But the level of management support for R&D is often constrained by resource availability.

Technological improvements that affect consumer and industrial products and services shorten product life cycles. Companies in virtually every industry are relying on the development of new products and services to fuel profitability and growth. However, in 2002 U.S. companies plan to boost R&D spending by only 2.2 percent, compared to increases of 5.4 percent in 2001 and 10.8 percent in 2000.[6] Some firms, such as 3M, plan to keep their R&D expenditures at 6 percent of sales despite a weak economy and lower earnings.

Surveys suggest that the most successful organizations use an R&D strategy that ties external opportunities to internal strengths and is linked with objectives. Well-formulated R&D policies match market opportunities with internal capabilities. R&D policies can enhance strategy implementation efforts to:

1. Emphasize product or process improvements.
2. Stress basic or applied research.
3. Be leaders or followers in R&D.
4. Develop robotics or manual-type processes.
5. Spend a high, average, or low amount of money on R&D.
6. Perform R&D within the firm or to contract R&D to outside firms.
7. Use university researchers or private sector researchers.

There must be effective interactions between R&D departments and other functional departments in implementing different types of generic business strategies. Conflicts between marketing, finance/accounting, R&D, and information systems departments can be minimized with clear policies and objectives. Table 8–6 gives some examples of R&D activities that could be required for successful implementation of various strategies. Many American utility, energy, and automotive companies are employing their research and development departments to determine how the firm can effectively reduce its gas emissions.

Many firms wrestle with the decision to acquire R&D expertise from external firms or to develop R&D expertise internally. The following guidelines can be used to help make this decision:

1. If the rate of technical progress is slow, the rate of market growth is moderate, and there are significant barriers to possible new entrants, then in-house R&D is the preferred solution. The reason is that R&D, if successful, will result in a temporary product or process monopoly that the company can exploit.

TABLE 8–6   Research and Development Involvement in Selected Strategy-Implementation Situations

TYPE OF ORGANIZATION	STRATEGY BEING IMPLEMENTED	R&D ACTIVITY
Pharmaceutical company	Product development	Test the effects of a new drug on different subgroups.
Boat manufacturer	Concentric diversification	Test the performance of various keel designs under various conditions.
Plastic container manufacturer	Market penetration	Develop a biodegradable container.
Electronics company	Market development	Develop a telecommunications system in a foreign country.

2. If technology is changing rapidly and the market is growing slowly, then a major effort in R&D may be very risky, because it may lead to the development of an ultimately obsolete technology or one for which there is no market.

3. If technology is changing slowly but the market is growing quickly, there generally is not enough time for in-house development. The prescribed approach is to obtain R&D expertise on an exclusive or nonexclusive basis from an outside firm.

4. If both technical progress and market growth are fast, R&D expertise should be obtained through acquisition of a well-established firm in the industry.[7]

There are at least three major R&D approaches for implementing strategies. The first strategy is to be the first firm to market new technological products. This is a glamorous and exciting strategy but also a dangerous one. Firms such as 3M and General Electric have been successful with this approach, but many other pioneering firms have fallen, with rival firms seizing the initiative.

A second R&D approach is to be an innovative imitator of successful products, thus minimizing the risks and costs of start-up. This approach entails allowing a pioneer firm to develop the first version of the new product and to demonstrate that a market exists. Then, laggard firms develop a similar product. This strategy requires excellent R&D personnel and an excellent marketing department.

A third R&D strategy is to be a low-cost producer by mass-producing products similar to but less expensive than products recently introduced. As a new product is accepted by customers, price becomes increasingly important in the buying decision. Also, mass marketing replaces personal selling as the dominant selling strategy. This R&D strategy requires substantial investment in plant and equipment, but fewer expenditures in R&D than the two approaches described earlier.

R&D activities among American firms need to be more closely aligned to business objectives. There needs to be expanded communication between R&D managers and strategists. Corporations are experimenting with various methods to achieve this improved communication climate, including different roles and reporting arrangements for managers and new methods to reduce the time it takes research ideas to become reality.

Perhaps the most current trend in R&D management has been lifting the veil of secrecy whereby firms, even major competitors, are joining forces to develop new products. Collaboration is on the rise due to new competitive pressures, rising research costs, increasing regulatory issues, and accelerated product development schedules. Companies not only are working more closely with each other on R&D, but they are also turning to consortia at universities for their R&D needs. More than 600 research consortia are now in operation in the United States. Lifting of R&D secrecy among many firms through collaboration has allowed the marketing of new technologies and products even before they are available for sale.

MANAGEMENT INFORMATION SYSTEMS (MIS) ISSUES

Firms that gather, assimilate, and evaluate external and internal information most effectively are gaining competitive advantages over other firms. Recognizing the importance of having an effective *management information system (MIS)* will not be an option in the future; it will be a requirement. Information is the basis for understanding in a firm. In many industries, information is becoming the most important factor differentiating successful

NATURAL ENVIRONMENT PERSPECTIVE

The Natural Environment Cost/Benefit Analysis

Carol Browner is former head of the Environmental Protection Agency (EPA) under President Clinton. She recently said, "If we find ourselves subjecting the health protections of our children and our most vulnerable citizens to the outcome of cost/benefit analysis, literally putting a price on their heads, we will have dishonored our past and devalued our future." Do you agree with Browner? Yes or no?

At what point do the costs of preserving the natural environment exceed the benefits? People make trade-off decisions every day that affect their health and billfold. For example, if you buy a large car instead of a small one, you will be protected better from a collision, but you may have less money for a mammogram. Similarly, more costly environmental regulations may harm people just by making them less able to afford regular doctor visits, safe cars, and good insurance. The EPA estimates that full compliance with its new smog and soot standards will cost companies and individuals almost $50 billion a year.

Can we afford these new regulations given that our weak economy has severely reduced individuals' disposable income for taking care of their own health and other needs?

After debating for a year with local city officials in Houston, Texas, the EPA signed an agreement in late 2001 which requires that city to reduce its air pollution 75 percent by 2007. Houston currently is one of the nation's most polluted cities.

All of life is full of trade-off decisions. Smog on balance is detrimental to health, but smog also blocks out ultraviolet radiation. The new EPA smog standards will make air easier to breathe, but it will also cause several thousand more cases of skin cancer and cataracts annually. We must not ignore the trade-off benefits/costs in policing pollution and caring for the natural environment.

Source: Adapted from Ira Carnahan, "Where Money Is No Object," *Forbes* (March 5, 2001): 78.

and unsuccessful firms. The process of strategic management is facilitated immensely in firms that have an effective information system. Many companies are establishing a new approach to information systems, one that blends the technical knowledge of the computer experts with the vision of senior management.

Information collection, retrieval, and storage can be used to create competitive advantages in ways such as cross-selling to customers, monitoring suppliers, keeping managers and employees informed, coordinating activities among divisions, and managing funds. Like inventory and human resources, information is now recognized as a valuable organizational asset that can be controlled and managed. Firms that implement strategies using the best information will reap competitive advantages in the twenty-first century.

A good information system can allow a firm to reduce costs. For example, online orders from salespersons to production facilities can shorten materials ordering time and reduce inventory costs. Direct communications between suppliers, manufacturers, marketers, and customers can link elements of the value chain together as though they were one organization. Improved quality and service often result from an improved information system.

Firms must increasingly be concerned about computer hackers and take specific measures to secure and safeguard corporate communications, files, orders, and business conducted over the Internet. Gap, Playboy Enterprises, Hitachi America, PeopleSoft, and Twentieth Century Fox average over thirty computer intrusion attempts daily. Thousands of companies today are plagued by computer hackers who include disgruntled employees, competitors, bored teens, sociopaths, thieves, spies, and hired agents. Computer vulnerability is a giant, expensive headache.

Dun & Bradstreet is an example of a company that has an excellent information system. Every D&B customer and client in the world has a separate nine-digit number. The database of information associated with each number has become so widely used that it is like a business social security number. D&B reaps great competitive advantages from its information system.

In many firms, information technology is doing away with the workplace and allowing employees to work at home or anywhere, anytime. The mobile concept of work allows employees to work the traditional 9-5 workday across any of the twenty-four time zones around the globe. Affordable desktop videoconferencing software developed by AT&T, Lotus, or Vivo Software allows employees to "beam in" whenever needed. Any manager or employee who travels a lot away from the office is a good candidate for working at home rather than in an office provided by the firm. Salespersons or consultants are good examples, but any person whose job largely involves talking to others or handling information could easily operate at home with the proper computer system and software. The accounting firm Ernst & Young has reduced its office space requirements by 2 million square feet over the past three years by allowing employees to work at home.

Many people see the officeless office trend as leading to a resurgence of family togetherness in American society. Even the design of homes may change from having large open areas to having more private small areas conducive to getting work done.[8]

CONCLUSION

Successful strategy implementation depends on cooperation among all functional and divisional managers in an organization. Marketing departments are commonly charged with implementing strategies that require significant increases in sales revenues in new areas and with new or improved products. Finance and accounting managers must devise effective strategy-implementation approaches at low cost and minimum risk to that firm. R&D managers have to transfer complex technologies or develop new technologies to successfully implement strategies. Information systems managers are being called upon more and more to provide leadership and training for all individuals in the firm. The nature and role of marketing, finance/accounting, R&D, and management information systems activities, coupled with the management activities described in Chapter 7, largely determine organizational success.

We invite you to visit the David page on the Prentice Hall Companion Website at **www.prenhall.com/david** for this chapter's World Wide Web exercises.

KEY TERMS AND CONCEPTS

Cash Budget (p. 287)
EPS/EBIT Analysis (p. 283)
Financial Budget (p. 287)
Management Information Systems (MIS) (p. 292)

Market Segmentation (p. 277)
Marketing Mix Variables (p. 278)
Outstanding Shares Method (p. 289)
Price-Earnings Ratio Method (p. 289)
Product Positioning (p. 277)

Pro Forma (Projected) Financial Statement Analysis (p. 285)
Research and Development (R&D) (p. 290)
Vacant Niche (p. 282)

ISSUES FOR REVIEW AND DISCUSSION

1. Suppose your company has just acquired a firm that produces battery-operated lawn mowers, and strategists want to implement a market-penetration strategy. How would you segment the market for this product? Justify your answer.

2. Explain how you would estimate the total worth of a business.

3. Diagram and label clearly a product-positioning map that includes six fast-food restaurant chains.

4. Explain why EPS/EBIT analysis is a central strategy-implementation technique.

5. How would the R&D role in strategy implementation differ in small versus large organizations?

6. Discuss the limitations of EPS/EBIT analysis.

7. Explain how marketing, finance/accounting, R&D, and management information systems managers' involvement in strategy formulation can enhance strategy implementation.

8. Consider the following statement: "Retained earnings on the balance sheet are not monies available to finance strategy implementation." Is it true or false? Explain.

9. Explain why pro forma financial statement analysis is considered both a strategy-formulation and a strategy-implementation tool.

10. Describe some marketing, finance/accounting, R&D, and management information systems activities that a small restaurant chain might undertake to expand into a neighboring state.

11. Select one of the suggested readings at the end of this chapter, find that article in your college library, and summarize it in a five-minute oral report for the class.

12. Discuss the management information system at your college or university.

13. What effect is e-commerce having on firms' efforts to segment markets?

NOTES

1. LESLIE MILLER and ELIZABETH WEISE, "E-Privacy—FTC Studies 'Profiling' by Web Sites," *USA Today* (November 8, 1999): 1A, 2A.

2. RALPH BIGGADIKE, "The Contributions of Marketing to Strategic Management," *Academy of Management Review* 6, no. 4 (October 1981): 627.

3. PHYLLIS PLITCH, "Companies in Many Sectors Give Earnings a Pro Forma Makeover, Survey Finds," *Wall Street Journal* (January 22, 2002): A4.

4. MONICA ROMAN, "When Pro Forma Is Bad Form," *Business Week* (December 17, 2001): 50.

5. MATT KRANTZ, "Debt Weighs More as Firms Gobble Cash," *USA Today* (October 10, 2001): B1.

6. AMY MERRICK, "U.S. Research Spending to Rise Only 3.2 Percent," *Wall Street Journal* (December 28, 2001): A2.

7. PIER ABETTI, "Technology: A Key Strategic Resource," *Management Review* 78, no. 2 (February 1989): 38.

8. Adapted from EDWARD BAIG, "Welcome to the Officeless Office," *Business Week* (June 26, 1995).

CURRENT READINGS

DUTTON, JANE E., SUSAN J. ASHFORD, REGINA M. O'NEILL, and KATHERINE A. LAWRENCE. "Moves That Matter: Issue Selling and Organizational Change." *The Academy of Management Journal* 44, no. 4 (August 2001): 716.

HERREMANS, IRENE M., JOHN K. RYANS, JR., and RAJ AGGARWAL. "Linking Advertising and Brand Value." *Business Horizons* 43, no. 3 (May–June 2000): 19.

MEDCOF, J. W. "Resource-Based Strategy and Managerial Power in Networks of Internationally Dispersed Technology Units." *Strategic Management Journal* 22, no. 11 (November 2001): 999.

PAGELL, MARK, STEVE MELNYK, and ROBERT HANDFIELD. "Do Trade-offs Exist in Operations Strategy? Insights from the Stamping Die Industry." *Business Horizons* 43, no. 3 (May–June 2000): 69.

POLONSKY, MICHAEL JAY, and PHILIP J. ROSENBERGER III. "Reevaluating Green Marketing: A Strategic Approach." *Business Horizons* 44, no. 5 (September–October 2001): 21.

SCHROEDER, R. G., K. A. BATES, and M. A. JUNTTILA. "A Resource-Based View of Manufacturing Strategy and the Relationship to Manufacturing Processes." *Strategic Management Journal* 23, no. 2 (February 2002): 105.

SLATER, S. F., and E. M. OLSON. "Marketing's Contribution to the Implementation of Business Strategy: An Empirical Analysis." *Strategic Management Journal* 22, no. 11 (November 2001): 1055.

SMITH, H. JEFF. "Information Privacy and Marketing: What the U.S. Should (and Shouldn't) Learn from Europe." *California Management Review* 43, no. 2 (Winter 2001): 8.

SEYBOLD, PATRICIA B. "Get Inside the Lives of Your Customers." *Harvard Business Review* (May 2001): 80.

EXPERIENTIAL EXERCISES

EXPERIENTIAL EXERCISE 8A ▶

Developing a Product-Positioning Map for American Airlines (AMR)

PURPOSE

Organizations continually monitor how their products and services are positioned relative to competitors. This information is especially useful for marketing managers, but is also used by other managers and strategists.

INSTRUCTIONS

Step 1   On a separate sheet of paper, develop a product-positioning map for American Airlines (AMR).

Step 2   Go to the blackboard and diagram your product-positioning map.

Step 3   Compare your product-positioning map with those diagrammed by other students. Discuss any major differences.

EXPERIENTIAL EXERCISE 8B ▶

Performing an EPS/EBIT Analysis For American Airlines (AMR)

PURPOSE

An EPS/EBIT analysis is one of the most widely used techniques for determining the extent that debt and/or stock should be used to finance strategies to be implemented. This exercise can give you practice performing EPS/EBIT analysis.

INSTRUCTIONS

Let's say AMR needs to raise $2 billion to begin flying to twenty new countries around the world in 2001. Determine whether AMR should have used all debt, all stock, or a 50-50 combination of debt and stock to finance this market-development strategy. Assume a 50 percent tax rate, 10 percent interest rate, AMR stock price of $70 per share, and an annual dividend of $2.00 per share of common stock. The EBIT range for 2001 is between $1 billion and $1.5 billion. A total of 90 million shares of common stock are outstanding. Develop an EPS/EBIT chart to reflect your analysis.

EXPERIENTIAL EXERCISE 8C ▶

Preparing Pro Forma Financial Statements for American Airlines (AMR)

PURPOSE

This exercise is designed to give you experience preparing pro forma financial statements. Pro forma analysis is a central strategy-implementation technique because it allows managers to anticipate and evaluate the expected results of various strategy-implementation approaches.

INSTRUCTIONS

Step 1   Work with a classmate. Develop a 2003 pro forma income statement and balance sheet for AMR. Assume that AMR plans to raise $900 million in 2002 to begin flights to ten AMR new countries and plans to obtain 50 percent financing from a bank and 50 percent financing from a stock issuance. Make other assumptions as needed, and state them clearly in written form.

Step 2   Compute AMR's current ratio, debt-to-equity ratio, and return-on-investment ratio for 1999, 2000, and 2001. How do your 2002 projected ratios compare to the 2000 and 2001 ratios? Why is it important to make this comparison?

Step 3   Bring your pro forma statements to class, and discuss any problems or questions you encountered.

Step 4 Compare your pro forma statements to the statements of other students. What major differences exist between your analysis and the work of other students?

EXPERIENTIAL EXERCISE 8D ▶

Determining the Cash Value of American Airlines (AMR)

PURPOSE

It is simply good business practice to periodically determine the financial worth or cash value of your company. This exercise gives you practice determining the total worth of a company using several methods. Use 2001 as the sample year.

INSTRUCTIONS

Step 1 Calculate the financial worth of AMR based on three methods: (1) the net worth or stockholders' equity, (2) the future value of AMR earnings, and (3) the price-earnings ratio.

Step 2 In a dollar amount, how much is AMR worth?

Step 3 Compare your analyses and conclusions with those of other students.

EXPERIENTIAL EXERCISE 8E ▶

Developing a Product-Positioning Map for My University

PURPOSE

The purpose of this exercise is to give you practice developing product-positioning maps. Nonprofit organizations, such as universities, are increasingly using product-positioning maps to determine effective ways to implement strategies.

INSTRUCTIONS

Step 1 Join with two other people in class to form a group of three.

Step 2 Jointly prepare a product-positioning map that includes your institution and four other colleges or universities in your state.

Step 3 Go to the blackboard and diagram your product-positioning map.

Step 4 Discuss differences among the maps diagrammed on the board.

EXPERIENTIAL EXERCISE 8F ▶

Do Banks Require Pro Forma Statements?

PURPOSE

The purpose of this exercise is to explore the practical importance and use of projected financial statements in the banking business.

INSTRUCTIONS

Contact two local bankers by phone and seek answers to the questions listed below. Record the answers you receive, and report your findings to the class.

1. Does your bank require projected financial statements as part of a business loan application?
2. How does your bank use projected financial statements when they are part of a business loan application?
3. What special advice do you give potential business borrowers in preparing projected financial statements?

PART 4
Strategy Evaluation

9

STRATEGY REVIEW, EVALUATION, AND CONTROL

CHAPTER OUTLINE

- The Nature of Strategy Evaluation
- A Strategy-Evaluation Framework
- Published Sources of Strategy-Evaluation Information
- Characteristics of an Effective Evaluation System
- Contingency Planning
- Auditing
- Using Computers to Evaluate Strategies

EXPERIENTIAL EXERCISE 9A
Preparing a Strategy-Evaluation Report for American Airlines (AMR)

EXPERIENTIAL EXERCISE 9B
Evaluating My University's Strategies

EXPERIENTIAL EXERCISE 9C
Who Prepares an Environmental Audit?

CHAPTER OBJECTIVES

After studying this chapter, you should be able to do the following:

1. Describe a practical framework for evaluating strategies.
2. Explain why strategy evaluation is complex, sensitive, and yet essential for organizational success.
3. Discuss the importance of contingency planning in strategy evaluation.
4. Discuss the role of auditing in strategy evaluation.
5. Explain how computers can aid in evaluating strategies.

NOTABLE QUOTES

Complicated controls do not work. They confuse. They misdirect attention from what is to be controlled to the mechanics and methodology of the control.

SEYMOUR TILLES

Although Plan A may be selected as the most realistic . . . the other major alternatives should not be forgotten. They may well serve as contingency plans.

DALE McCONKEY

Organizations are most vulnerable when they are at the peak of their success.

R. T. LENZ

Strategy evaluation must make it as easy as possible for managers to revise their plans and reach quick agreement on the changes.

DALE McCONKEY

While strategy is a word that is usually associated with the future, its link to the past is no less central. Life is lived forward but understood backward. Managers may live strategy in the future, but they understand it through the past.

HENRY MINTZBERG

Unless strategy evaluation is performed seriously and systematically, and unless strategists are willing to act on the results, energy will be used up defending yesterday. No one will have the time, resources, or will to work on exploiting today, let alone to work on making tomorrow.

PETER DRUCKER

The best-formulated and best-implemented strategies become obsolete as a firm's external and internal environments change. It is essential, therefore, that strategists systematically review, evaluate, and control the execution of strategies. This chapter presents a framework that can guide managers' efforts to evaluate strategic-management activities, to make sure they are working, and to make timely changes. Management information systems being used to evaluate strategies are discussed. Guidelines are presented for formulating, implementing, and evaluating strategies.

THE NATURE OF STRATEGY EVALUATION

The strategic-management process results in decision that can have significant, long-lasting consequences. Erroneous strategic decisions can inflict severe penalties and can be exceedingly difficult, if not impossible, to reverse. Most strategists agree, therefore, that strategy evaluation is vital to an organization's well-being; timely evaluations can alert management to problems or potential problems before a situation becomes critical. Strategy evaluation includes three basic activities: (1) examining the underlying bases of a firm's strategy, (2) comparing expected results with actual results, and (3) taking corrective actions to ensure that performance conforms to plans. The strategy-evaluation stage of the strategic-management process is illustrated in Figure 9–1.

Adequate and timely feedback is the cornerstone of effective strategy evaluation. Strategy evaluation can be no better than the information on which it operates. Too much pressure from top managers may result in lower managers contriving numbers they think will be satisfactory.

Strategy evaluation can be a complex and sensitive undertaking. Too much emphasis on evaluating strategies may be expensive and counterproductive. No one likes to be evaluated too closely! The more managers attempt to evaluate the behavior of others, the less control they have. Yet too little or no evaluation can create even worse problems. Strategy evaluation is essential to ensure that stated objectives are being achieved.

In many organizations, strategy evaluation is simply an appraisal of how well an organization has performed. Have the firm's assets increased? Has there been an increase in profitability? Have sales increased? Have productivity levels increased? Have profit margin, return on investment, and earnings-per-share ratios increased? Some firms argue that their strategy must have been correct if the answers to these types of questions are affirmative. Well, the strategy or strategies may have been correct, but this type of reasoning can be misleading, because strategy evaluation must have both a long-run and short-run focus. Strategies often do not affect short-term operating results until it is too late to make needed changes.

It is impossible to demonstrate conclusively that a particular strategy is optimal or even to guarantee that it will work. One can, however, evaluate it for critical flaws. Richard Rumelt offered four criteria that could be used to evaluate a strategy: consistency, consonance, feasibility, and advantage. Described in Table 9–1, *consonance* and *advantage* are mostly based on a firm's external assessment, whereas *consistency* and *feasibility* are largely based on an internal assessment.

Strategy evaluation is important because organizations face dynamic environments in which key external and internal factors often change quickly and dramatically. Success today is no guarantee of success tomorrow! An organization should never be lulled into complacency with success. Countless firms have thrived one year only to struggle for survival the following year. Organizational trouble can come swiftly, as further evidenced by the examples described in Table 9–2.

VISIT THE NET

Gives excellent additional information about evaluating strategies, including some analytical tools. http://www.mindtools.com/plevplan.html

VISIT THE NET

Describes the how and why of strategy evaluation. http://www.csuchico.edu/mgmt/strategy/module1/sld046.htm

FIGURE 9–1

A Comprehensive Strategic-Management Model

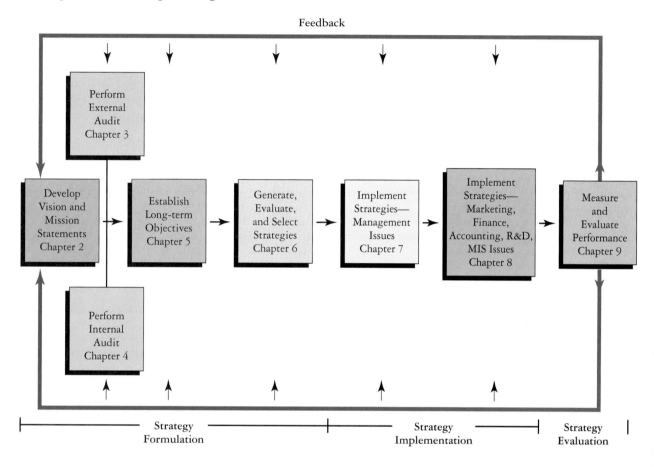

Strategy evaluation is becoming increasingly difficult with the passage of time, for many reasons. Domestic and world economies were more stable in years past, product life cycles were longer, product development cycles were longer, technological advancement was slower, change occurred less frequently, there were fewer competitors, foreign companies were weak, and there were more regulated industries. Other reasons why strategy evaluation is more difficult today include the following trends:

1. A dramatic increase in the environment's complexity
2. The increasing difficulty of predicting the future with accuracy
3. The increasing number of variables
4. The rapid rate of obsolescence of even the best plans
5. The increase in the number of both domestic and world events affecting organizations
6. The decreasing time span for which planning can be done with any degree of certainty[1]

A fundamental problem facing managers today is how to effectively control employees in light of modern organizational demands for greater flexibility, innovation,

TABLE 9-1   Rumelt's Criteria for Evaluating Strategies

CONSISTENCY

A strategy should not present inconsistent goals and policies. Organizational conflict and interdepartmental bickering are often symptoms of managerial disorder, but these problems may also be a sign of strategic inconsistency. There are three guidelines to help determine if organizational problems are due to inconsistencies in strategy:

- If managerial problems continue despite changes in personnel and if they tend to be issue-based rather than people-based, then strategies may be inconsistent.
- If success for one organizational department means, or is interpreted to mean, failure for another department, then strategies may be inconsistent.
- If policy problems and issues continue to be brought to the top for resolution, then strategies may be inconsistent.

CONSONANCE

Consonance refers to the need for strategists to examine *sets of trends* as well as individual trends in evaluating strategies. A strategy must represent an adaptive response to the external environment and to the critical changes occurring within it. One difficulty in matching a firm's key internal and external factors in the formulation of strategy is that most trends are the result of interactions among other trends. For example, the daycare explosion came about as a combined result of many trends that included a rise in the average level of education, increased inflation, and an increase in women in the workforce. Although single economic or demographic trends might appear steady for many years, there are waves of change going on at the interaction level.

FEASIBILITY

A strategy must neither overtax available resources nor create unsolvable subproblems. The final broad test of strategy is its feasibility; that is, can the strategy be attempted within the physical, human, and financial resources of the enterprise? The financial resources of a business are the easiest to quantify and are normally the first limitation against which strategy is evaluated. It is sometimes forgotten, however, that innovative approaches to financing are often possible. Devices such as captive subsidiaries, sale-leaseback arrangements, and tying plant mortgages to long-term contracts have all been used effectively to help win key positions in suddenly expanding industries. A less quantifiable, but actually more rigid, limitation on strategic choice is that imposed by individual and organizational capabilities. In evaluating a strategy, it is important to examine whether an organization has demonstrated in the past that it possesses the abilities, competencies, skills, and talents needed to carry out a given strategy.

ADVANTAGE

A strategy must provide for the creation and/or maintenance of a competitive advantage in a selected area of activity. Competitive advantages normally are the result of superiority in one of three areas: (1) resources, (2) skills, or (3) position. The idea that the positioning of one's resources can enhance their combined effectiveness is familiar to military theorists, chess players, and diplomats. Position can also play a crucial role in an organization's strategy. Once gained, a good position is defensible—meaning that it is so costly to capture that rivals are deterred from full-scale attacks. Positional advantage tends to be self-sustaining as long as the key internal and environmental factors that underlie it remain stable. This is why entrenched firms can be almost impossible to unseat, even if their raw skill levels are only average. Although not all positional advantages are associated with size, it is true that larger organizations tend to operate in markets and use procedures that turn their size into advantage, while smaller firms seek product/marker positions that exploit other types of advantage. The principal characteristic of good position is that it permits the firm to obtain advantage from policies that would not similarly benefit rivals without the same position. Therefore, in evaluating strategy, organizations should examine the nature of positional advantages associated with a given strategy.

Source: Adapted from Richard Rumelt, "The Evaluation of Business Strategy," in W. F. Glueck, ed., *Business Policy and Strategic Management* (New York: McGraw-Hill, 1980): 359–367.

TABLE 9-2   **Examples of Organizational Trouble**

A. Large Companies That Experienced More Than A 38% Decline in Revenues in 2001

	PERCENT DECREASE
KINDER MORGAN	−61%
MICRON TECHNOLOGY	−58
CONEXANT SYSTEMS	−56
PMC-SIERRA	−54
TERADYNE	−53
VITESSE SEMICONDUCTOR	−50
ADC TELECOMMUNICATIONS	−46
COMPUTER ASSOCIATES INTL.	−45
APPLIED MATERIALS	−41
ALTERA	−39

B. Large Companies That Experienced More Than an 85% Decline in Return on Equity

	PERCENT
JDS UNIPHASE	−747.6%
NORTEL NETWORKS	−503.9
PMC-SIERRA	−234.8
APPLIED MICRO CIRCUITS	−203.7
LUCENT TECHNOLOGIES	−105.0
CORNING	−101.4
CIENA	−92.7
CONEXANT SYSTEMS	−91.8
SPRINT PCS GROUP	−87.8
BROADCOM	−85.5

Source: "The Best Performers," *Business Week* (Spring 2002): 37–38.

creativity, and initiative from employees.[2] How can managers today ensure that empowered employees acting in an entrepreneurial manner do not put the well-being of the business at risk? Recall that Kidder, Peabody & Company lost $350 million when one of its traders allegedly booked fictitious profits; Sears, Roebuck and Company took a $60 million charge against earnings after admitting that its automobile service businesses were performing unnecessary repairs. The costs to companies such as these in terms of damaged reputations, fines, missed opportunities, and diversion of management's attention are enormous.

When empowered employees are held accountable for and pressured to achieve specific goals and are given wide latitude in their actions to achieve them, there can be dysfunctional behavior. For example, Nordstrom, the upscale fashion retailer known for outstanding customer service, was subjected to lawsuits and fines when employees underreported hours worked in order to increase their sales per hour—the company's primary performance criterion. Nordstrom's customer service and earnings were enhanced until the misconduct was reported, at which time severe penalties were levied against the firm.

The Process of Evaluating Strategies

Strategy evaluation is necessary for all sizes and kinds of organizations. Strategy evaluation should initiate managerial questioning of expectations and assumptions, should trigger a review of objectives and values, and should stimulate creativity in generating

VISIT THE NET

Elaborates on the "taking corrective actions" phase of strategy evaluation.
http://www.csuchico.edu/ mgmt/strategy/module1/ sld047.htm

alternatives and formulating criteria of evaluation.[3] Regardless of the size of the organization, a certain amount of *management by wandering around* at all levels is essential to effective strategy evaluation. Strategy-evaluation activities should be performed on a continuing basis, rather than at the end of specified periods of time or just after problems occur. Waiting until the end of the year, for example, could result in a firm closing the barn door after the horses have already escaped.

Evaluating strategies on a continuous rather than on a periodic basis allows benchmarks of progress to be established and more effectively monitored. Some strategies take years to implement; consequently, associated results may not become apparent for years. Successful strategists combine patience with a willingness to take corrective actions promptly when necessary. There always comes a time when corrective actions are needed in an organization! Centuries ago, a writer (perhaps Solomon) made the following observations about change:

> There is a time for everything,
> A time to be born and a time to die,
> A time to plant and a time to uproot,
> A time to kill and a time to heal,
> A time to tear down and a time to build,
> A time to weep and a time to laugh,
> A time to mourn and a time to dance,
> A time to scatter stones and a time to gather them,
> A time to embrace and a time to refrain,
> A time to search and a time to give up,
> A time to keep and a time to throw away,
> A time to tear and a time to mend,
> A time to be silent and a time to speak,
> A time to love and a time to hate,
> A time for war and a time for peace.[4]

Managers and employees of the firm should be continually aware of progress being made toward achieving the firm's objectives. As critical success factors change, organizational members should be involved in determining appropriate corrective actions. If assumptions and expectations deviate significantly from forecasts, then the firm should renew strategy-formulation activities, perhaps sooner than planned. In strategy evaluation, like strategy formulation and strategy implementation, people make the difference. Through involvement in the process of evaluating strategies, managers and employees become committed to keeping the firm moving steadily toward achieving objectives.

A STRATEGY-EVALUATION FRAMEWORK

Table 9–3 summarizes strategy-evaluation activities in terms of key questions that should be addressed, alternative answers to those questions, and appropriate actions for an organization to take. Notice that corrective actions are almost always needed except when (1) external and internal factors have not significantly changed and (2) the firm is progressing satisfactorily toward achieving stated objectives. Relationships among strategy-evaluation activities are illustrated in Figure 9–2.

TABLE 9-3   A Strategy-Evaluation Assessment Matrix

HAVE MAJOR CHANGES OCCURRED IN THE FIRM'S INTERNAL STRATEGIC POSITION?	HAVE MAJOR CHANGES OCCURRED IN THE FIRM'S EXTERNAL STRATEGIC POSITION?	HAS THE FIRM PROGRESSED SATISFACTORILY TOWARD ACHIEVING ITS STATED OBJECTIVES?	RESULT
No	No	No	Take corrective actions
Yes	Yes	Yes	Take corrective actions
Yes	Yes	No	Take corrective actions
Yes	No	Yes	Take corrective actions
Yes	No	No	Take corrective actions
No	Yes	Yes	Take corrective actions
No	Yes	No	Take corrective actions
No	No	Yes	Continue present strategic course

Reviewing Bases of Strategy

As shown in Figure 9–2, *reviewing the underlying bases of an organization's strategy* could be approached by developing a revised EFE Matrix and IFE Matrix. A *revised IFE Matrix* should focus on changes in the organization's management, marketing, finance/accounting, production/operations, R&D, and management information systems strengths and weaknesses. A *revised EFE Matrix* should indicate how effective a firm's strategies have been in response to key opportunities and threats. This analysis could also address such questions as the following:

1. How have competitors reacted to our strategies?
2. How have competitors' strategies changed?
3. Have major competitors' strengths and weaknesses changed?
4. Why are competitors making certain strategic changes?
5. Why are some competitors' strategies more successful than others?
6. How satisfied are our competitors with their present market positions and profitability?
7. How far can our major competitors be pushed before retaliating?
8. How could we more effectively cooperate with our competitors?

Numerous external and internal factors can prohibit firms from achieving long-term and annual objectives. Externally, actions by competitors, changes in demand, changes in technology, economic changes, demographic shifts, and governmental actions may prohibit objectives from being accomplished. Internally, ineffective strategies may have been chosen or implementation activities may have been poor. Objectives may have been too optimistic. Thus, failure to achieve objectives may not be the result of unsatisfactory work by managers and employees. All organizational members need to know this to encourage their support for strategy-evaluation activities. Organizations desperately need to know as soon as possible when their strategies are not effective. Sometimes managers and employees on the front lines discover this well before strategists.

External opportunities and threats and internal strengths and weaknesses that represent the bases of current strategies should continually be monitored for change. It is not really a question of whether these factors will change, but rather when they will change and in what ways. Some key questions to address in evaluating strategies are given here.

VISIT THE NET

The Small Business Administration Web site provides a forty-page Business Plan Outline.
http://www.sba.gov/ starting/businessplan.html

FIGURE 9–2

A Strategy-Evaluation Framework

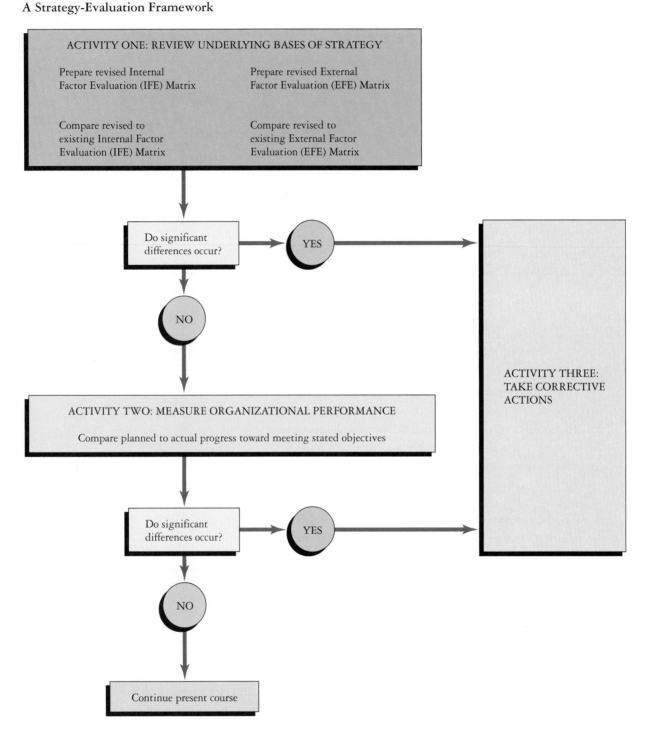

1. Are our internal strengths still strengths?
2. Have we added other internal strengths? If so, what are they?
3. Are our internal weaknesses still weaknesses?
4. Do we now have other internal weaknesses? If so, what are they?
5. Are our external opportunities still opportunities?
6. Are there now other external opportunities? If so, what are they?
7. Are our external threats still threats?
8. Are there now other external threats? If so, what are they?
9. Are we vulnerable to a hostile takeover?

Measuring Organizational Performance

Another important strategy-evaluation activity is *measuring organizational performance*. This activity includes comparing expected results to actual results, investigating deviations from plans, evaluating individual performance, and examining progress being made toward meeting stated objectives. Both long-term and annual objectives are commonly used in this process. Criteria for evaluating strategies should be measurable and easily verifiable. Criteria that predict results may be more important than those that reveal what already has happened. For example, rather than simply being informed that sales in the last quarter were 20 percent under what was expected, strategists need to know that sales in the next quarter may be 20 percent below standard unless some action is taken to counter the trend. Really effective control requires accurate forecasting.

Failure to make satisfactory progress toward accomplishing long-term or annual objectives signals a need for corrective actions. Many factors, such as unreasonable policies, unexpected turns in the economy, unreliable suppliers or distributors, or ineffective strategies, can result in unsatisfactory progress toward meeting objectives. Problems can result from ineffectiveness (not doing the right things) or inefficiency (doing the right things poorly).

Determining which objectives are most important in the evaluation of strategies can be difficult. Strategy evaluation is based on both quantitative and qualitative criteria. Selecting the exact set of criteria for evaluating strategies depends on a particular organization's size, industry, strategies, and management philosophy. An organization pursuing a retrenchment strategy, for example, could have an entirely different set of evaluative criteria from an organization pursuing a market-development strategy. Quantitative criteria commonly used to evaluate strategies are financial ratios, which strategists use to make three critical comparisons: (1) comparing the firm's performance over different time periods, (2) comparing the firm's performance to competitors', and (3) comparing the firm's performance to industry averages. Some key financial ratios that are particularly useful as criteria for strategy evaluation are as follows:

1. Return on investment (ROI)
2. Return on equity (ROE)
3. Profit margin
4. Market share
5. Debt to equity
6. Earnings per share
7. Sales growth
8. Asset growth

VISIT THE NET

Provides strategic management handbooks with detailed instructions for planning in certain U.S. states. http://www.opm. state.ct.us/mgmt/busguide/ 50states/guides.htm

But there are some potential problems associated with using quantitative criteria for evaluating strategies. First, most quantitative criteria are geared to annual objectives rather than long-term objectives. Also, different accounting methods can provide different results on many quantitative criteria. Third, intuitive judgments are almost always involved in deriving quantitative criteria. For these and other reasons, qualitative criteria are also important in evaluating strategies. Human factors such as high absenteeism and turnover rates, poor production quality and quantity rates, or low employee satisfaction can be underlying causes of declining performance. Marketing, finance/accounting, R&D, or management information systems factors can also cause financial problems. Seymour Tilles identified six qualitative questions that are useful in evaluating strategies:

1. Is the strategy internally consistent?
2. Is the strategy consistent with the environment?
3. Is the strategy appropriate in view of available resources?
4. Does the strategy involve an acceptable degree of risk?
5. Does the strategy have an appropriate time framework?
6. Is the strategy workable?[5]

Some additional key questions that reveal the need for qualitative or intuitive judgments in strategy evaluation are as follows:

1. How good is the firm's balance of investments between high-risk and low-risk projects?
2. How good is the firm's balance of investments between long-term and short-term projects?
3. How good is the firm's balance of investments between slow-growing markets and fast-growing markets?
4. How good is the firm's balance of investments among different divisions?
5. To what extent are the firm's alternative strategies socially responsible?
6. What are the relationships among the firm's key internal and external strategic factors?
7. How are major competitors likely to respond to particular strategies?

Taking Corrective Actions

The final strategy-evaluation activity, *taking corrective actions,* requires making changes to reposition a firm competitively for the future. Examples of changes that may be needed are altering an organization's structure, replacing one or more key individuals, selling a division, or revising a business mission. Other changes could include establishing or revising objectives, devising new policies, issuing stock to raise capital, adding additional salespersons, allocating resources differently, or developing new performance incentives. Taking corrective actions does not necessarily mean that existing strategies will be abandoned or even that new strategies must be formulated.

> The probabilities and possibilities for incorrect or inappropriate actions increase geometrically with an arithmetic increase in personnel. Any person directing an overall undertaking must check on the actions of the participants as well as the results that they have achieved. If either the actions or results do not comply with preconceived or planned achievements, then corrective actions are needed.[6]

No organization can survive as an island; no organization can escape change. Taking corrective actions is necessary to keep an organization on track toward achieving scared objectives. In his thought-provoking books, *Future Shock* and *The Third Wave,*

VISIT THE NET

*Provides the U.S. Customs'
Strategic Plan.* www.
customs.treas.gov/about/
strat/index.htm

Alvin Toffler argued that business environments are becoming so dynamic and complex that they threaten people and organizations with *future shock,* which occurs when the nature, types, and speed of changes overpower an individual's or organization's ability and capacity to adapt. Strategy evaluation enhances an organization's ability to adapt successfully to changing circumstances. Brown and Agnew referred to this notion as *corporate agility.*[7]

Taking corrective actions raises employees' and managers' anxieties. Research suggests that participation in strategy-evaluation activities is one of the best ways to overcome individuals' resistance to change. According to Erez and Kanfer, individuals accept change best when they have a cognitive understanding of the changes, a sense of control over the situation, and an awareness that necessary actions are going to be taken to implement the changes.[8]

Strategy evaluation can lead to strategy-formulation changes, strategy-implementation changes, both formulation and implementation changes, or no changes at all. Strategists cannot escape having to revise strategies and implementation approaches sooner or later. Hussey and Langham offered the following insight on taking corrective actions:

> Resistance to change is often emotionally based and not easily overcome by rational argument. Resistance may be based on such feelings as loss of status, implied criticism of present competence, fear of failure in the new situation, annoyance at not being consulted, lack of understanding of the need for change, or insecurity in changing from well-known and fixed methods. It is necessary, therefore, to overcome such resistance by creating situations of participation and [a] full explanation when changes are envisaged.[9]

Corrective actions should place an organization in a better position to capitalize upon internal strengths; to take advantage of key external opportunities; to avoid, reduce, or mitigate external threats; and to improve internal weaknesses. Corrective actions should have a proper time horizon and an appropriate amount of risk. They should be internally consistent and socially responsible. Perhaps most important, corrective actions strengthen an organization's competitive position in its basic industry. Continuous strategy evaluation keeps strategists close to the pulse of an organization and provides information needed for an effective strategic-management system. Carter Bayles described the benefits of strategy evaluation as follows:

> Evaluation activities may renew confidence in the current business strategy or point to the need for actions to correct some weaknesses, such as erosion of product superiority or technological edge. In many cases, the benefits of strategy evaluation are much more far-reaching, for the outcome of the process may be a fundamentally new strategy that will lead, even in a business that is already turning a respectable profit, to substantially increased earnings. It is this possibility that justifies strategy evaluation, for the payoff can be very large.[10]

PUBLISHED SOURCES OF STRATEGY-EVALUATION INFORMATION

A number of publications are helpful in evaluating a firm's strategies. For example, *Fortune* annually identifies and evaluates the Fortune 1,000 (the largest manufacturers) and the Fortune 50 (the largest retailers, transportation companies, utilities, banks, insurance companies, and diversified financial corporations in the United States). *Fortune* ranks the best and worst performers on various factors such as return on investment, sales volume, and profitability. In its March issue each year, *Fortune* publishes its strategy evaluation research

NATURAL ENVIRONMENT PERSPECTIVE

How Much Carbon Dioxide Is Your Firm Emitting?

To the dismay of Europeans and indeed many Americans, the U.S. federal government withdrew from the Kyoto Protocol, an international treaty to reduce the output of CO_2 emissions and five other greenhouse gases. President Bush says the treaty will hurt the nation's economy. However, recognizing the importance of this issue, numerous states within the United States are tackling the issue with passion. Seven states in particular have recently instituted effective CO_2 monitoring programs, including New Jersey, Massachusetts, New York, New Hampshire, North Carolina, Florida, and Illinois. Perhaps New Jersey best leads this effort: Fifty-six of that state's

colleges and community colleges also have joined the state's environmental program, agreeing to measure and curb their own emissions.

Global warming isn't just a fear. It's a fact. Carbon dioxide is the major culprit and the most common air pollutant. Plants, of course, breathe in carbon dioxide, which is the reason why widespread cutting of trees and rain forests and the clearing of land and harvesting kelp in the oceans are so detrimental to the natural environment. The following statistics reveal annual carbon-dioxide emissions for various countries worldwide. Note that the United States is guiltiest.

	Total Tons (Millions)	*Tons per Capita*
United States	5,475	20.52
China	3,196	2.68
Russia	1,820	12.26
Japan	1,126	9.03
India	910	0.90
Germany	833	10.24
United Kingdom	539	9.29
Ukraine	437	8.48
Canada	433	14.83
Italy	411	7.19
South Korea	370	8.33
Mexico	359	3.93

Continents and countries relative share of harmful CO_2 emissions is given below:

Eastern Europe and former Soviet Union	27%
United States	22%
Western Europe	17%
Other Asian countries	13%
China	11%
Latin America	4%
Africa	3%

Source: Adapted from "Clear Skies Are Goal as Pollution Is Turning into a Commodity," *The Wall Street Journal* (October 3, 1997): A4. Also, "States Are Stepping in to Reduce Levels of Carbon Dioxide," *The Wall Street Journal* (September 11, 2001): A28.

in an article entitled "America's Most Admired Companies." Nine key attributes serve as evaluative criteria: quality of management; innovativeness; quality of products or services; long-term investment value; financial soundness; community and environmental responsibility; ability to attract, develop, and keep talented people; use of corporate assets; and international acumen. In October of each year, *Fortune* publishes additional strategy evaluation research in an article entitled "The World's Most Admired Companies."[11] The Global Perspective box reveals the best managed companies in Britain, France, Germany, and elsewhere in Europe. *Fortune*'s 2001 evaluation in Table 9–4 reveals the firms ranked as the top ten most admired (best managed).

Another excellent evaluation of corporations in America, "The Annual Report on American Industry," is published annually in the January issue of *Forbes*. It provides a detailed and comprehensive evaluation of hundreds of American companies in many different industries. *Business Week, Industry Week,* and *Dun's Business Month* also periodically publish detailed evaluations of American businesses and industries. Although published

TABLE 9-4   **Top Ten**

RANK	COMPANY
1	General Electric
2	Southwest Airlines
3	Wal-Mart Stores
4	Microsoft
5	Berkshire Hathaway
6	Home Depot
7	Johnson & Johnson
8	FedEx
9	Citigroup
10	Intel

Source: **http://www.fortune.com/lists/mostadmired/index.html** (from the Mar. 4, 2002 issue of *Fortune*)

sources of strategy-evaluation information focus primarily on large, publicly held businesses, the comparative ratios and related information are widely used to evaluate small businesses and privately owned firms as well.

 ## CHARACTERISTICS OF AN EFFECTIVE EVALUATION SYSTEM

Strategy evaluation must meet several basic requirements to be effective. First, strategy-evaluation activities must be economical; too much information can be just as bad as too little information; and too many controls can do more harm than good. Strategy-evaluation activities also should be meaningful; they should specifically relate to a firm's objectives. They should provide managers with useful information about tasks over which they have control and influence. Strategy-evaluation activities should provide timely information; on occasion and in some areas, managers may need information daily. For example, when a firm has diversified by acquiring another firm, evaluative information may be needed frequently. However, in an R&D department, daily or even weekly evaluative information could be dysfunctional. Approximate information that is timely is generally more desirable as a basis for strategy evaluation than accurate information that does not depict the present. Frequent measurement and rapid reporting may frustrate control rather than give better control. The time dimension of control must coincide with the time span of the event being measured.

Strategy evaluation should be designed to provide a true picture of what is happening. For example, in a severe economic downturn, productivity and profitability ratios may drop alarmingly, although employees and managers are actually working harder. Strategy evaluations should portray this type of situation fairly. Information derived from the strategy-evaluation process should facilitate action and should be directed to those individuals in the organization who need to take action based on it. Managers commonly ignore evaluative reports that are provided for informational purposes only; not all managers need to receive all reports. Controls need to be action-oriented rather than information-oriented.

GLOBAL PERSPECTIVE

What Are the Best Companies in Britain, France, Germany, and Switzerland?

Fortune annually evaluates companies within particular countries. The evaluative criteria are management, products/services, innovativeness, long-term investment value, financial soundness, getting/keeping talent, social/environmental responsibility/wise use of assets, and international acumen. In 2001, the best companies in Britain, France, Germany, and Switzerland were ranked on these criteria and are listed below in rank order:

Company	Industry	Company	Industry
Britain		*Germany*	
Royal Dutch/Shell Group	Petroleum refining	BMW	Motor vehicles
BP	Petroleum refining	Volkswagen	Motor vehicles
Tesco	Food and drugstores	BASF	Chemicals
HSBC Holdings	Banks	Siemens	Electronics
J. Sainsbury	Food and drugstores	Bayer	Chemicals
France		*Switzerland*	
L'Oréal	Soaps, cosmetics	Nestlé	Food
Vivendi Universal	Entertainment	ABB	Electronics
Total Fina Elf	Petroleum refining	UBS	Banks
Christian Dior (LVMH)	Soaps, cosmetics	Novartis Group	Pharmaceuticals
Vinci	Engineering, Construction	Swiss Re	Insurance P&C (stock)

Source: http://www.fortune.com/lists/globaladmired/country_list.html (from the March 4, 2002 issue of *Fortune*)

The strategy-evaluation process should not dominate decisions; it should foster mutual understanding, trust, and common sense. No department should fail to cooperate with another in evaluating strategies. Strategy evaluations should be simple, not too cumbersome, and not too restrictive. Complex strategy-evaluation systems often confuse people and accomplish little. The test of an effective evaluation system is its usefulness, not its complexity.

Large organizations require a more elaborate and detailed strategy-evaluation system because it is more difficult to coordinate efforts among different divisions and functional areas. Managers in small companies often communicate with each other and their employees daily and do not need extensive evaluative reporting systems. Familiarity with local environments usually makes gathering and evaluating information much easier for small organizations than for large businesses. But the key to an effective strategy-evaluation system may be the ability to convince participants that failure to accomplish certain objectives within a prescribed time is not necessarily a reflection of their performance.

There is no one ideal strategy-evaluation system. The unique characteristics of an organization, including its size, management style, purpose, problems, and strengths, can determine a strategy-evaluation and control system's final design. Robert Waterman offered the following observation about successful organizations' strategy-evaluation and control systems:

> Successful companies treat facts as friends and controls as liberating. Morgan Guaranty and Wells Fargo not only survive but thrive in the troubled waters of bank deregulation, because their strategy evaluation and control systems are sound, their risk is contained, and they know themselves and the competitive situation so well. Successful companies have a voracious hunger for facts. They see information where others see only data. They love comparisons, rankings, anything that removes decision making from the realm of mere opinion. Successful companies maintain tight, accurate financial controls. Their people don't regard controls as an imposition of autocracy but as the benign checks and balances that allow them to be creative and free.[12]

 ## CONTINGENCY PLANNING

A basic premise of good strategic management is that firms plan ways to deal with unfavorable and favorable events before they occur. Too many organizations prepare contingency plans just for unfavorable events; this is a mistake, because both minimizing threats and capitalizing on opportunities can improve a firm's competitive position.

Regardless of how carefully strategies are formulated, implemented, and evaluated, unforeseen events such as strikes, boycotts, natural disasters, arrival of foreign competitors, and government actions can make a strategy obsolete. To minimize the impact of potential threats, organizations should develop contingency plans as part of their strategy-evaluation process. *Contingency plans* can be defined as alternative plans that can be put into effect if certain key events do not occur as expected. Only high-priority areas require the insurance of contingency plans. Strategists cannot and should not try to cover all bases by planning for all possible contingencies. But in any case, contingency plans should be as simple as possible.

Some contingency plans commonly established by firms include the following:

1. If a major competitor withdraws from particular markets as intelligence reports indicate, what actions should our firm take?
2. If our sales objectives are not reached, what actions should our firm take to avoid profit losses?
3. If demand for our new product exceeds plans, what actions should our firm take to meet the higher demand?
4. If certain disasters occur—such as loss of computer capabilities; a hostile takeover attempt; loss of patent protection; or destruction of manufacturing facilities because of earthquakes, tornados, or hurricanes—what actions should our firm take?
5. If a new technological advancement makes our new product obsolete sooner than expected, what actions should our firm take?

Too many organizations discard alternative strategies not selected for implementation although the work devoted to analyzing these options would render valuable information.

Alternative strategies not selected for implementation can serve as contingency plans in case the strategy or strategies selected do not work.

When strategy-evaluation activities reveal the need for a major change quickly, an appropriate contingency plan can be executed in a timely way. Contingency plans can promote a strategist's ability to respond quickly to key changes in the internal and external bases of an organization's current strategy. For example, if underlying assumptions about the economy turn out to be wrong and contingency plans are ready, then managers can make appropriate changes promptly.

In some cases, external or internal conditions present unexpected opportunities. When such opportunities occur, contingency plans could allow an organization to capitalize on them quickly. Linneman and Chandran reported that contingency planning gave users such as DuPont, Dow Chemical, Consolidated Foods, and Emerson Electric three major benefits: (1) It permitted quick response to change, (2) it prevented panic in crisis situations, and (3) it made managers more adaptable by encouraging them to appreciate just how variable the future can be. They suggested that effective contingency planning involves a seven-step process:

1. Identify both beneficial and unfavorable events that could possibly derail the strategy or strategies.
2. Specify trigger points. Calculate about when contingent events are likely to occur.
3. Assess the impact of each contingent event. Estimate the potential benefit or harm of each contingent event.
4. Develop contingency plans. Be sure that contingency plans are compatible with current strategy and are economically feasible.
5. Assess the counter impact of each contingency plan. That is, estimate how much each contingency plan will capitalize on or cancel out its associated contingent event. Doing this will quantify the potential value of each contingency plan.
6. Determine early warning signals for key contingent events. Monitor the early warning signals.
7. For contingent events with reliable early warning signals, develop advance action plans to take advantage of the available lead time.[13]

 ## AUDITING

A frequently used tool in strategy evaluation is the audit. *Auditing* is defined by the American Accounting Association (AAA) as "a systematic process of objectively obtaining and evaluating evidence regarding assertions about economic actions and events to ascertain the degree of correspondence between those assertions and established criteria, and communicating the results to interested users."[14] Since the Enron, Worldcom, and Johnson & Johnson scandals in 2002, auditing has taken on greater emphasis and care in companies. Independent auditors basically are certified public accountants (CPAs) who provide their services to organizations for a fee; they examine the financial statements of an organization to determine whether they have been prepared according to generally accepted accounting principles (GAAP) and whether they fairly represent the activities of the firm. Independent auditors use a set of standards called generally accepted audit-

TABLE 9-5   **Key Strategy-Evaluation Questions**

1. Do you feel that the strategic-management system exists to provide service to you in your day-to-day work? How has it helped you in this respect?
2. Has the strategic-management system provided the service that you feel was promised at the start of its design and implementation? In which areas has it failed and succeeded, in your opinion?
3. Do you consider that the strategic-management system has been implemented with due regard to costs and benefits? Are there any areas in which you consider the costs to be excessive?
4. Do you feel comfortable using the system? Could more attention have been paid to matching the output of the system to your needs and, if so, in what areas?
5. Is the system flexible enough in your opinion? If not, where should changes be made?
6. Do you still keep a personal store of information in a notebook or elsewhere? If so, will you share that information with the system? Do you see any benefits in so doing?
7. Is the strategic-management system still evolving? Can you influence this evolution and, if not, why not?
8. Does the system provide timely, relevant, and accurate information? Are there any areas of deficiency?
9. Do you think that the strategic-management system makes too much use of complex procedures and models? Can you suggest areas in which less complicated techniques might be used to advantage?
10. Do you consider that there has been sufficient attention paid to the confidentiality and security of the information in the system? Can you suggest areas for improvement of these aspects of its operation?

Source: Adapted from K. J. Radford, *Information Systems for Strategic Decisions,* © 1978: 220–221. Adapted by permission of Prentice-Hall, Inc., Englewood Cliffs, New Jersey. Also, Lloyd Byars, *Strategic Management* (New York: Harper & Row, 1984): 237.

ing standards (GAAS). Public accounting firms often have a consulting arm that provides strategy-evaluation services. The Arthur Andersen public accounting firm in 2001 experienced serious troubles in auditing the accounting practices of Enron Corporation.

Two government agencies—the General Accounting Office (GAO) and the Internal Revenue Service (IRS)—employ government auditors responsible for making sure that organizations comply with federal laws, statutes, and policies. GAO and IRS auditors can audit any public or private organization. The third group of auditors consists of employees within an organization who are responsible for safeguarding company assets, for assessing the efficiency of company operations, and for ensuring that generally accepted business procedures are practiced. To evaluate the effectiveness of an organization's strategic-management system, internal auditors often seek answers to the questions posed in Table 9–5.

The Environmental Audit

For an increasing number of firms, overseeing environmental affairs is no longer a technical function performed by specialists; rather, it has become an important strategic-management concern. Product design, manufacturing, transportation, customer use, packaging, product disposal, and corporate rewards and sanctions should reflect environmental considerations. Firms that effectively manage environmental affairs are benefiting from constructive relations with employees, consumers, suppliers, and distributors.

Shimell emphasized the need for organizations to conduct environmental audits of their operations and to develop a Corporate Environmental Policy (CEP).[15] Shimell contended that an environmental audit should be as rigorous as a financial audit and should include training workshops in which staff can help design and implement the policy. The CEP should be budgeted, and requisite funds should be allocated to ensure that it is not a public relations facade. A Statement of Environmental Policy should be published periodically to inform shareholders and the public of environmental actions taken by the firm.

Instituting an environmental audit can include moving environmental affairs from the staff side of the organization to the line side. Some firms are also introducing environmental criteria and objectives in their performance appraisal instruments and systems. Conoco, for example, ties compensation of all its top managers to environmental action plans. Occidental Chemical includes environmental responsibilities in all its job descriptions for positions.

USING COMPUTERS TO EVALUATE STRATEGIES

When properly designed, installed, and operated, a computer network can efficiently acquire information promptly and accurately. Networks can allow diverse strategy-evaluation reports to be generated for—and responded to by—different levels and types of managers. For example, strategists will want reports concerned with whether the mission, objectives, and strategies of the enterprise are being achieved. Middle managers could require strategy-implementation information, such as whether construction of a new facility is on schedule or a product's development is proceeding as expected. Lower-level managers could need evaluation reports that focus on operational concerns, such as absenteeism and turnover rates, productivity rates, and the number and nature of grievances.

Business today has become so competitive that strategists are being forced to extend planning horizons and to make decisions under greater degrees of uncertainty. As a result, more information has to be obtained and assimilated to formulate, implement, and evaluate strategic decisions. In any competitive situation, the side with the best intelligence (information) usually wins; computers enable managers to evaluate vast amounts of information quickly and accurately. Use of the Internet, World Wide Web, e-mail, and search engines can make the difference today between a firm that is up-to-date or out-of-date in the currentness of information the firm uses to make strategic decisions.

A limitation of management-based systems when it comes to evaluating and monitoring strategy execution is that personal values, attitudes, morals, preferences, politics, personalities, and emotions are not programmable. This limitation accents the need to view computers as tools, rather than as actual decision-making devices. Computers can significantly enhance the process of effectively integrating intuition and analysis in strategy evaluation. The General Accounting Office of the U.S. government offered the following conclusions regarding the appropriate role of computers in strategy evaluation:

> The aim is to enhance and extend judgment. Computers should be looked upon
> not as a provider of solutions, but rather as a framework which permits science

and judgment to be brought together and made explicit. It is the explicitness of this structure, the decision-maker's ability to probe, modify, and examine "What if?" alternatives, that is of value in extending judgment.[16]

CONCLUSION

This chapter presents a strategy-evaluation framework that can facilitate accomplishment of annual and long-term objectives. Effective strategy evaluation allows an organization to capitalize on internal strengths as they develop, to exploit external opportunities as they emerge, to recognize and defend against threats, and to mitigate internal weaknesses before they become detrimental.

Strategists in successful organizations take the time to formulate, implement, and then evaluate strategies deliberately and systematically. Good strategists move their organization forward with purpose and direction, continually evaluating and improving the firm's external and internal strategic position. Strategy evaluation allows an organization to shape its own future rather than allowing it to be constantly shaped by remote forces that have little or no vested interest in the well-being of the enterprise.

Although not a guarantee for success, strategic management allows organizations to make effective long-term decisions, to execute those decisions efficiently, and to take corrective actions as needed to ensure success. Computer networks and the Internet help to coordinate strategic-management activities and to ensure that decisions are based on good information. A key to effective strategy evaluation and to successful strategic management is an integration of intuition and analysis:

> A potentially fatal problem is the tendency for analytical and intuitive issues to polarize. This polarization leads to strategy evaluation that is dominated by either analysis or intuition, or to strategy evaluation that is discontinuous, with a lack of coordination among analytical and intuitive issues.[17]

Strategists in successful organizations realize that strategic management is first and foremost a people process. It is an excellent vehicle for fostering organizational communication. People are what make the difference in organizations.

> The real key to effective strategic management is to accept the premise that the planning process is more important than the written plan, that the manager is continuously planning and does not stop planning when the written plan is finished. The written plan is only a snapshot as of the moment it is approved. If the manager is not planning on a continuous basis—planning, measuring, and revising—the written plan can become obsolete the day it is finished. This obsolescence becomes more of a certainty as the increasingly rapid rate of change makes the business environment more uncertain.[18]

We invite you to visit the David page on the Prentice Hall Companion Website at **www.prenhall.com/david** for this chapter's World Wide Web exercises.

KEY TERMS AND CONCEPTS

Advantage (p. 300)
Auditing (p. 314)
Consistency (p. 300)
Consonance (p. 300)
Contingency Plans (p. 313)
Corporate Agility (p. 309)
Feasibility (p. 300)

Future Shock (p. 309)
Management by Wandering Around
(p. 304)
Measuring Organizational
Performance (p. 307)

Reviewing the Underlying Bases of
an Organization's Strategy
(p. 305)
Revised EFE Matrix (p. 305)
Revised IFE Matrix (p. 305)
Taking Corrective Actions (p. 308)

ISSUES FOR REVIEW AND DISCUSSION

1. Why has strategy evaluation become so important in business today?
2. BellSouth Services is considering putting divisional EFE and IFE matrices online for continual updating. How would this affect strategy evaluation?
3. What types of quantitative and qualitative criteria do you think David Glass, CEO of Wal-Mart, uses to evaluate the company's strategy?
4. As owner of a local, independent supermarket, explain how you would evaluate the firm's strategy.
5. Under what conditions are corrective actions not required in the strategy-evaluation process?
6. Identify types of organizations that may need to evaluate strategy more frequently than others. Justify your choices.
7. As executive director of the state forestry commission, in what way and how frequently would you evaluate the organization's strategies?
8. Identify some key financial ratios that would be important in evaluating a bank's strategy.
9. As owner of a chain of hardware stores, describe how you would approach contingency planning.
10. Strategy evaluation allows an organization to take a proactive stance toward shaping its own future. Discuss the meaning of this statement.

NOTES

1. DALE MCCONKEY, "Planning in a Changing Environment," *Business Horizons* (September–October 1988): 64.
2. ROBERT SIMONS, "Control in an Age of Empowerment," *Harvard Business Review* (March–April 1995): 80.
3. DALE ZAND, "Reviewing the Policy Process," *California Management Review* 21, no. 1 (Fall 1978): 37.
4. ECCLES. 3: 1–8.
5. SEYMOUR TILLES, "How to Evaluate Corporate Strategy," *Harvard Business Review* 41 (July–August 1963): 111–121.
6. CLAUDE GEORGE, JR., *The History of Management Thought* (Englewood Cliffs, New Jersey: Prentice-Hall, 1968), 165–166.
7. JOHN BROWN and NEIL AGNEW, "Corporate Agility," *Business Horizons* 25, no. 2 (March–April 1982): 29.
8. M. EREZ and F. KANFER, "The Role of Goal Acceptance in Goal Setting and Task Performance," *Academy of Management Review* 8, no. 3 (July 1983): 457.
9. D. HUSSEY and M. LANGHAM, *Corporate Planning: The Human Factor* (Oxford, England: Pergamon Press, 1979): 138.
10. CARTER BAYLES, "Strategic Control: The President's Paradox," *Business Horizons* 20, no. 4 (August 1977): 18.
11. See the March 4, 2002 issue of *Fortune.*
12. ROBERT WATERMAN, JR., "How the Best Get Better," *Business Week* (September 14, 1987): 105.
13. ROBERT LINNEMAN and RAJAN CHANDRAN, "Contingency Planning: A Key to Swift Managerial Action in the Uncertain Tomorrow," *Managerial Planning* 29, no. 4 (January–February 1981): 23–27.
14. American Accounting Association, *Report of Committee on Basic Auditing Concepts* (1971): 15–74.
15. PAMELA SHIMELL, "Corporate Environmental Policy in Practice," *Long Range Planning* 24, no. 3 (June 1991): 10.
16. GAO *Report* PAD—80–21, 17.
17. MICHAEL MCGINNIS, "The Key to Strategic Planning: Integrating Analysis and Intuition," *Sloan Management Review* 26, no. 1 (Fall 1984): 49.
18. MCCONKEY, 72.

CURRENT READINGS

BLOUNT, SALLY, and GREGORY A. JANICIK. "When Plans Change: Examining How People Evaluate Timing Canges in Work Organizations." *The Academy of Management Review*, 26, no. 4 (October 2001): 566.

GELETKANYCZ, MARTA A., and SYLVIA SLOAN BLACK. "Bound by the Past? Experience-Based Effects on Commitment to the Strategic Status Quo." *Journal of Management* 27, no. 1 (2001): 3.

HITT, MICHAEL A., LEONARD BIERMAN, KATSUHIKO SHIMIZU, and RAHUL KOCHHAR. "Direct and Moderating Effects of Human Capital on Strategy and Performance in Professional Service Firms: A Resource-Based Perspective." *The Academy of Management Journal* 44, no. 1 (February 2001): 13.

HUY, QUY NGUYEN. "Time, Temporal Capability, and Planned Change." *The Academy of Management Review* 26, no. 4 (October 2001): 601.

PEIPERL, MAURY A. "Getting 360-Degree Feedback Right." *Harvard Business Review* (January 2001): 142.

SCHULZ, MARTIN. "The Uncertain Relevance of Newness: Organizational Learning and Knowledge Flows." *The Academy of Management Journal* 44, no. 4 (August 2001): 661.

EXPERIENTIAL EXERCISES

EXPERIENTIAL EXERCISE 9A ▶

Preparing a Strategy-Evaluation Report for American Airlines (AMR)

PURPOSE

This exercise can give you experience locating strategy-evaluation information. Use of the Internet coupled with published sources of information can significantly enhance the strategy-evaluation process. Performance information on competitors, for example, can help put into perspective a firm's own performance.

INSTRUCTIONS

Step 1   Visit **www.invester.stockpoint.com** to locate strategy-evaluation information on AMR's competitors. Read five to ten articles written in the last six months that discuss the airline industry.

Step 2   Summarize your research findings by preparing a strategy-evaluation report for your instructor. Include in your report a summary of AMR's strategies and performance in 2001 and a summary of your conclusions regarding the effectiveness of AMR's strategies.

Step 3   Based on your analysis, do you feel that AMR is pursuing effective strategies? What recommendations would you offer to AMR's chief executive officer?

EXPERIENTIAL EXERCISE 9B ▶

Evaluating My University's Strategies

PURPOSE

An important part of evaluating strategies is determining the nature and extent of changes in an organization's external opportunities/threats and internal strengths/weaknesses. Changes in these underlying critical success factors can indicate a need to change or modify the firm's strategies.

INSTRUCTIONS

As a class, discuss positive and negative changes in your university's external and internal factors during your college career. Begin by listing on the board new or emerging opportunities and threats. Then identify strengths and weaknesses that have changed significantly during your college career. In light of the external and internal changes that were identified, discuss whether your university's strategies need modifying. Are there any new strategies that you would recommend? Make a list to recommend to your department chair, dean, or chancellor.

EXPERIENTIAL EXERCISE 9C ▶

Who Prepares on Environmental Audit?

PURPOSE

The purpose of this activity is to determine the nature and prevalence of environmental audits among companies in your state.

INSTRUCTIONS

Contact by phone at least five different plant managers or owners of large businesses in your area. Seek answers to the questions listed below. Present your findings in a written report to your instructor.

1.   Does your company conduct an environmental audit? If yes, please describe the nature and scope of the audit.

2. Are environmental criteria included in the performance evaluation of managers? If yes, please specify the criteria.

3. Are environmental affairs more a technical function or a management function in your company?

4. Does your firm offer any environmental workshops for employees? If yes, please describe them.

Name Index

Note: Page numbers followed by *f* indicate figures; page numbers followed by *t* indicate tables; page numbers followed by *n* indicate notes.

SUBJECT INDEX

Note: Page numbers followed by *f* indicate figures; page numbers followed by *t* indicate tables.

A

Accounting. *See also* Financial ratio analysis; Strategy implementation
audit checklist, 142–143
case study, 39–42
functions, 138
in strategy implementation process (*see under* Strategy implementation)
Acquisitions, 180–182, 182*t*
Action stage. *See* Strategy implementation
Activity ratios, 140, 141*t*
Advantage, in strategy evaluation, 300, 302*t*
Advertising, 134
Aggressive quadrant, 205, 205*f*, 207*f*
Aging, of U.S. population, 84–86
Air pollution, 86, 87, 88. *See also* Environmental issues
Almanac of Business & Industrial Financial Ratios, 139
Americans for Tax Reform, 89
Annual objectives, 12–13, 238–240. *See also* Strategy implementation
Annual Statement Studies, 139
Antiterrorism and Effective Death Penalty Act, 22
Argentina
AOL in, 166
Internet use in, 280
The Art of War (Tzu), 25, 26*t*
Assumptions, in planning, 105–106
Attractiveness Scores, 217*t*, 218–219
Auditing, 314–316, 315*t*. *See also* External audits; Internal audits
Australia, Internet use in, 280
Austria, Internet use in, 280
Avoidance, 243

B

Backward integration, 161*t*, 163–164
Bankruptcy, 171–172
Bargaining power, 101
BCG Matrix. *See* Boston Consulting Group (BCG) Matrix
Belgium
culture in, 126
Internet use in, 280
Benchmarking, 250
Birds, declining number of, 168
Boards of directors, 221–224, 223*t*
Body language, 126*t*, 127

Bonuses, 158, 252–253
Boston Consulting Group (BCG) Matrix, 206, 208–212
company listings by industry type, 209*t*
examples of, 210*f*, 212*f*
Brazil
AOL in, 166
Internet use in, 280
natural resources in, 106
Budgets. *See* Capital budgeting; Financial budgets
Building Leaders (Conger), 8
Business ethics, 20. *See also* Ethics
Business portfolio, 206

C

CA (competitive advantage), 93, 204, 206*t*, 208*t*
Canada
carbon dioxide emissions in, 310
Internet use in, 280
Wal-Mart in, 166
Capital budgeting, 138. *See also* Financial budgets
Cash budgets, 287–288, 288*t*
Cash cows, 210–211, 210*f*
CEP (Corporate Environmental Policy), 316
CERES principles, 38
Champions, in strategy choice, 221
Change, adapting to, 7–8, 253–255
Chapter 7 bankruptcy, 171
Chapter 9 bankruptcy, 171
Chapter 11 bankruptcy, 171–172
Chapter 12 bankruptcy, 172
Chapter 13 bankruptcy, 172
Chief information officers (CIOs), 93
Chief technology officers (CTOs), 93
Childcare, companies assisting with, 266
China
airline industry in, 47
AOL in, 166
carbon dioxide emissions in, 310
culture in, 125, 126, 128
economy of, 108–110, 109*f*
industry in, 86
Kodak success in, 107
liquidations in, 174
Motorola production in, 290
U.S. operations in, 186
U.S. trade with, 84
Churches, 85, 224, 260

CI (competitive intelligence), 94–97
CIOs (chief information officers), 93
Code of business ethics, 20. *See also* Ethics
Combination strategies, 160
Communication. *See also* Management information systems (MISs)
cultural differences in, 125, 126*t*
internal audits providing, 121–122
in motivating employees, 131–132
retreats providing, 14
in strategy implementation, 238
Competitive advantage (CA), 93, 204, 206*t*, 208*t*
Competitive Advantage of Nations (Porter), 175
Competitive Advantage (Porter), 175
Competitive analysis, 98–101, 99*f*, 99*t*
Competitive forces, 94–98, 95*t*, 96*t*
Competitive intelligence (CI), 94–97
Competitive Profile Matrix (CPM), 112, 112*t*
Competitive quadrant, 205, 205*f*, 207*f*
Competitive Strategy (Porter), 174
Computers, in strategy evaluation, 316–317. *See also* Internet; Technological forces
Computer viruses, 97
Concentric diversification, 161*t*, 169
Concern for employees, 69, 71*t*, 72*t*. *See also* Employees
Concern for public image, 69, 70*t*, 72*t*
Concern for survival, growth, and profitability, 69, 70*t*, 72*t*
Conflict, managing, 243
Confrontation, 243
Conglomerate diversification, 170
Conservative quadrant, 205, 205*f*, 207*f*
Consistency, in strategy evaluation, 300, 302*t*
Consonance, in strategy evaluation, 300, 302*t*
Contingency plans, 313–314
Controlling, as management function, 129*t*, 132–133
Cooperative arrangements, 177
Coral reefs, 168
Corporate agility, 309
Corporate Environmental Policy (CEP), 316
Corrective actions, 308–309
Cost/benefit analysis, 137
Cost leadership strategies, 175
Cost reduction, 250
CPM (Competitive Profile Matrix), 112, 112*t*
Creed statements, 59. *See also* Mission statements
CTOs (chief technology officers), 93

Company Index

Note: Page numbers followed by *n* indicate notes. Page numbers followed by *t* indicate tables.